U.S. PHILANTHROPIC FOUNDATIONS

U.S. Philanthropic

THEIR HISTORY, STRUCTURE,

BY

WARREN WEAVER

HARPER & ROW, PUBLISHERS

Foundations

MANAGEMENT, AND RECORD

With contributions by
GEORGE M. BEADLE, ARNE TISELIUS,
LEE A. DUBRIDGE, JOSEPH C. HINSEY, GEORGE J. STIGLER,
ERWIN N. GRISWOLD, WHITNEY J. OATES,
BROOKS ATKINSON, ANATOLE CHUJOY, DONALD L. ENGLE,
RICHARD MCLANATHAN, BROCK CHISHOLM, LORD BOYD-ORR,
FREDERICK OSBORN, PHILIP E. MOSELY, GEORGE M. BECKMANN,
FRED M. HECHINGER, FLORA M. RHIND
AND BARRY BINGHAM

NEW YORK, EVANSTON, AND LONDON

I-R

CONTENTS

v

INTRODUCTION

Philanthropy expresses certain postulates of American life, notably decentralized responsibility and voluntary action. American society has established a diversified pattern of separate educational systems, resting for financial support upon governmental and private sources. The variety of sources ensures diversity and distribution of control and responsibility. Philanthropy through its role in the private sector is indispensable for the maintenance of the variety of financial sources.

Federal tax exemption for *bona fide* philanthropic contributions and expenditures in support of education reflects national support for the educational pattern. Looking through the intricacies of revenue codes and tax administration, one discerns the nature of the choice to be made. Private funds earned and owned by private citizens are subject to taxation. The educational system requires financial support. The American people through Congress may use federal taxation to encourage citizens to apply part of their private funds to the support of education, thus helping to make such support as broadly based as possible. In the alternative, the American people may use federal taxation to absorb such funds into the federal treasury and funnel them through the federal treasury to the support of education, thus intensifying a current prospect that education may become increasingly dependent upon the federal government. It is the former choice, evidenced by the provisions for federal tax exemption, which the American people have made and to which they have adhered. By the choice, they have reaffirmed their commitment to voluntary action and widespread responsibility.

Parallel choices have arisen and have been similarly made in relation to the scientific, religious, and charitable sectors of philanthropic activity.

A citizen of the United States who wants to contribute funds for philanthropic uses may do so along either of two broad lines. He may make direct gifts to schools, universities, churches, hospitals, museums, orphanages, or settlement houses. If the sums which he desires to give are large, and especially if he wishes to organize his contributions systematically over a period of years throughout the nation or the world, he may donate his funds to a general philanthropic foundation established to make grants for educational, scientific, religious, or charitable purposes. Along either line, as a private citizen he gives his own private money, devoting it exclusively to public purposes through recipient institutions committed to serve only public needs. In so doing, he vindicates another postulate of American life, corollary to the traditions of voluntary organization and pluralistic responsibility. In American society, "public purposes" and "public service" are broader in scope than "government purposes" and "government service."

While government is of course one of the highest forms of public service, it is by no means the only form. In many situations, a public function may be performed within either a governmental or a private framework. Public need of higher education is met by Harvard University and the Massachusetts Institute of Technology, privately organized nonprofit institutions located in Massachusetts, as well as by the University of Massachusetts, an instrumentality of the state government; by the privately organized nonprofit University of Chicago as well as by the state University of Illinois. The Museum of Modern Art in New York City, a privately organized nonprofit corporation, serves the same public purpose as the Metropolitan Museum of Art, supported by funds of the City of New York together with contributions from private donors. "Public hospitals" may be established and operated either as instrumentalities of state or city governments or as nonprofit private organizations governed by boards of trustees serving without compensation. They are sharply distinguished from hospitals which are private in the sense that they are proprietary and earn profit for the owners. Fellowships to promising students of science given by "private" philanthropic foundations represent no less public a service than fellowships granted by the National Science Foundation. Neither the public nature nor the public usefulness of a service is necessarily determined by whether the source of financial support is "private" or "governmental."

If an institution devotes all its resources exclusively to educational, scientific, religious, charitable, or other public purposes and applies none of its resources to the pecuniary advantage of any person (other than regular compensation for services rendered), it is a public institution. If it is nongovernmental and derives its resources from gifts by private donors (or income from the investment of such gifts), it is a privately organized public institution. A general philanthropic foundation is such a privately organized public institution.

The general philanthropic foundation in America as a distinctive institution is barely a century old. Its characteristic attributes have evolved largely within the past fifty years, and it is primarily within the last three decades that it has multiplied in numbers and grown diverse in type. The increasing number and variety have generated an expanding public interest. They have also provoked public concern and not a little confusion.

Some philanthropic foundations are large organizations and their size may cause anxiety. The anxiety is understandable in view of the traditional American attitude toward concentrations of power. But the size of individual philanthropic foundations must be appraised with regard to the economic, social, and political environment. A philanthropic foundation which appears large when observed apart looks smaller when examined in relation to contemporary corporations engaged in manufacturing, finance, insurance, communications, electric power, or mass distribution, or in relation to modern labor unions. The resources of even the largest philanthropic foundation are very small indeed in comparison with those of the national government.

The federal government provides much financial assistance to education, research, health, and the relief and reduction of poverty. The federal assistance is indispensable, but as it mounts in relation to other sources of support, unintended risks may arise for the pluralistic and diversified American institutional pattern. There is a need for general philanthropic foundations large enough to offer realistic alternative sources of financial assistance to meet particular needs of universities, schools, hospitals, churches, museums, orphanages, or settlement houses. Even with such alternative sources available, our universities and other nonprofit educational, scientific, or charitable organizations may not find it easy to maintain their basic independence in accepting aid from the national government. Without such alternatives, they would find it harder despite the best of intentions.

The newness of the general philanthropic foundation as an institution, the variety of its forms, its blend of public and private characteristics, and the importance and subtlety of its functions make it hard to understand. The difficulty is compounded by the fact that it is still evolving. It is not only the general public that finds it hard to understand. The difficulty is shared by many trustees and officers of philanthropic foundations.

For more than a decade, the American Academy of Arts and Sciences has sought to foster scholarly inquiry into the nature and functions of philanthropic foundations. Almost three years ago, the Academy was gratified to learn that Dr. Warren Weaver proposed to devote his insight and experience to an examination and evaluation of philanthropic foundations in American life.

From the time when the Rockefeller Foundation first extended its support beyond medicine and public health to the natural sciences, giving priority to the sciences concerned with life, Dr. Weaver guided the foundation's work in the natural sciences. During the same period of more than a quarter of a century and thereafter, he served as a trustee of the Sloan-Kettering Institute, a member of the National Science Board of the National Science Foundation, a trustee and vice president of the Alfred P. Sloan Foundation, a trustee of the Academy of Religion and Mental Health, a director of the Council on Library Resources, and president of the American Association for the Advancement of Science. In an address on "The Imperfections of Science" before the American Philosophical Society in 1960, Dr. Weaver warned his listeners that "I am going to be speaking of imperfections; but . . . I will also be speaking of something which I love." Apostrophizing science as his "Dark Lady of the Laboratories," he delineated her imperfections but called Shakespeare to witness that:

> And yet, by heaven, I think my love as rare
> As any she belied with false compare.

The Academy accepted an invitation to serve as sponsor of Dr. Weaver's study and designated an advisory committee of three of its members to represent it: Dr. James R. Killian, Jr., chairman of the corporation of Massachusetts Institute of Technology; President Nils Y. Wessell of Tufts University; and Professor Milton Katz, director, International Legal Studies, Harvard Law School, chairman. As sponsor, the Academy confined its role to an effort to facilitate Dr. Weaver's work. The substance and form of the book which has resulted are wholly his own.

As chairman of the advisory committee of the American Academy of Arts and Sciences, I welcome the opportunity to help introduce Dr. Weaver's book to the public.

MILTON KATZ

Cambridge, Massachusetts
September 15, 1966

PREFACE

This volume has resulted from an extensive series of discussions with foundation officials and scholars, culminating in a decision by the American Academy of Arts and Sciences to sponsor the production of a book on modern philanthropy as practiced by private foundations.

The American Academy of Arts and Sciences was established by the Council and House of Representatives in General Court of the Province of Massachusetts Bay in 1780. The statute which created the academy listed various high purposes, and concluded with the summary pronouncement that the stated end and design of the institution of the said academy was ". . . in fine, to cultivate every art and science which may tend to advance the interest, honor, dignity, and happiness of a free, independent, and virtuous people."

The membership of the academy falls into four sections: the mathematical and physical sciences, the biological sciences (including medicine), the social arts and sciences (including law, administration, and affairs), and the humanities (including philosophy, theology, history, archeology, philology, criticism, literature, and the fine arts). The membership of approximately two thousand is made up mainly of fellows, and also includes over three hundred foreign honorary members and fellows emeriti.

The subject treated in this book is one of long-standing interest to the academy, a meeting having been devoted to it some time ago.

Foundations have over recent years been under fire. There have been official investigations, and there has been some criticism in news media, in articles, and in books. The official investigations, and some of the private inquiries, have turned up some instances of practices which, whether or not narrowly legal, are obviously and in a very few cases outrageously bad.

However few and exceptional are the cases of unsocial and unethical practice, they are the ones which attract public attention, especially when they are emphasized and distorted by individuals who can personally profit from the role of protector of the taxpayer.

When a fake doctor is discovered and unmasked, the public is interested; but it does not conclude that the medical profession is a grand fraud. The public knows from direct experience how valuable, and how essential to our society are the services of our doctors. The public concludes from the exceedingly rare bad instance that we must be sure that the laws and the supervision of medical services are such as to minimize the risk of such bad cases; but the public also clearly realizes that this must not be done in a way which would handicap the beneficial services of the vast majority of doctors.

Not only has there been deserved criticism of a very few instances of bad foundation practice, but there have also been misleading and at times gross inaccuracies in statements made about foundations, including some of the most prominent ones. This has led to some public question as to whether the "privileges enjoyed by tax-free foundations" should be continued.

This is a fair, timely, and important question. It can properly be answered only in the light of information concerning the benefits which society does, or does not, obtain from the whole body of activity of philanthropic foundations.

The word "foundation" means more than one thing, and groups called that have done—and not done—very widely different things.

Indeed the range and variety are so vast that it would require a number of books to examine the whole field. This book does not pretend to cover the waterfront. It gives only minor attention to community foundations, at least partly because these are community efforts which are largely local in their impact, which are to a great extent community controlled, and whose purposes therefore are not likely to be misunderstood.

This book will also not attempt to review the detailed record of corporation-, or company-sponsored, foundations. Only rather incidentally will the record of personal or family foundations be considered. For all of these mentioned types, however, there will be discussion of the significant rules and procedures (public accountability for example) which should be followed by foundations of these, as well as all other, types.

Except for very incidental mention, this book will not deal with foundations outside our own country. The great modern philanthropic foundation is, in spite of its ancient origins, primarily an American invention. This invention has spread to other parts of the world, notably Europe. The story of this spreading development is an important and fascinating one, which would itself require a volume.

This book does attempt to consider the issues of principles and procedures for all types of philanthropic foundations. Several chapters, for example, review all of the types of criticism of foundations of which the author is aware.

As far as record of accomplishment is concerned, the emphasis is primarily on the larger foundations of the sort called "research or general purpose foundations." This concentration of emphasis arises almost automatically. For example, in the eighteen contributions which form the second part of the book, the collaborating authors were not in the least told to restrict themselves to certain foundations or types of foundations. They were simply asked: Tell what you know about the value, or lack of value, of foundation activities in your field. That there is frequent mention of the larger foundations is inevitable; but the reader will also find in these contributed chapters the names of a considerable number of smaller foundations, some of them "family" in character, some "special purpose" rather than general purpose.

The central purpose of the book is to bring dependable information to bear on the question: Does the positive record of the American philanthropic foundations justify the continuing existence of these tax-free institutions? It seems important to spread out some characteristic parts of the record in a form which will be generally understandable and interesting. For a social instrument will in the long run be continued and supported only provided people—a very large number of all sorts of people—understand the instrument and approve of its results.

The detailed labor of writing all of the book other than the contributed Chapters 15 through 32 was assigned to myself. In addition to twenty-eight years of experience as an officer of the Rockefeller Foundation followed by seven years as vice president and as a special consultant of the Alfred P. Sloan Foundation, I have had, concurrently, more than twenty-five years' experience in eight other foundations and federal granting agencies such as the National Science Foundation and the National Institutes of Health.

The book obviously owes a great deal to the essential help of all of the considerable number of collaborators whose views are quoted or summarized. Much generous and able assistance came from F. Emerson Andrews of the Foundation Library Center, as well as from colleagues and friends in a number of foundations, especially President J. G. Harrar of the Rockefeller Foundation and President Everett N. Case of the Alfred P. Sloan Foundation. Dr. Ronald Shilen served as research assistant to the author, and he contributed importantly to the collection and organization of the record. I am also indebted to Mrs. John A. Willis for checking the final manuscript for errors. The advisory committee of the American Academy of Arts and Sciences has been most helpful. A special, and specially pleasant, debt should be acknowledged to my son Warren Weaver, Jr., who has given detailed criticism to all portions of the text written by me.

All of this generously offered help is deeply appreciated, but all the responsibility for the book (apart, of course, from Chapters 15 through 32, which were written by the indicated authors) clearly rests on me.

WARREN WEAVER

New Milford, Connecticut
Spring, 1966

A voluntary deed by a man impressed with a sense of responsibility and brotherhood of man is infinitely more precious to our national ideals and national spirit than a thousandfold poured from the treasury of the government under the compulsion of law.

—HERBERT HOOVER

PART I

The Historical Origins and the
Dimensions of Modern Philanthropy

CHAPTER 1

Pre-Christian Philanthropy

Philanthropy is not a modern invention. Concern for one's fellow men extends back to ancient times. A wide range of incentives leads individuals to altruistic action. The human family has presumably always contained a few prideful persons who would use almost any method to perpetuate their power and fame, but also many who aid their fellow men for religious reasons based partly on unselfish motives and partly on concern for their own salvation.

The acts through which philanthropic motivation is expressed have changed greatly since older times, reflecting alterations in social structures, in ways of thinking, and in the practical opportunities available for helping others.

Communication and transport in the modern world, for example, have profoundly influenced the range of concern of both individuals and states. No one could worry many years ago about the illness and hunger of people in a distant part of the world of which he had never heard. Centuries ago, men who asked Cain's question "Am I my brother's keeper?" necessarily thought only of close relatives and near neighbors. They could not have been disturbed about the condition of men in equatorial Africa or in Southeast Asia, for they were unaware of their existence and their needs. Even if they had known, they would have been powerless to act.

Not only recent scientific and technological advances, but other major changes in man's political, intellectual, and social life have altered the concepts and practices of philanthropy. The rise in power of the medieval church, the Reformation, the Industrial Revolution, the development of the free enterprise system in our

3

own country, the creation of great personal fortunes—movements such as these have greatly influenced both the concepts of philanthropy and the ways in which these concepts are realized.

Unselfishness is not wholly a human invention. An article in a recent scientific journal on "The Evolution of Altruism" reported that some seventy million years ago, as is known from fossil records of Miocene times, there existed organized societies of termites and ants. Within such insect societies—bees, wasps, ants, and others —there were then, and still are, groups whose activities can in some broad sense be labeled as altruistic, with members of these groups performing specialized functions for the good of the larger society, often at individual sacrifice. For example, insects that are specialized servants of the larger group are themselves usually sexless.

There are "great difficulties in explaining, by the classical theory of natural selection, any case of behavior by which an animal promotes the advantages of other members of the species, not its direct descendants, at the expense of his own."[1] * In circumstances where the gain to the group is more than double the loss to the individual, such behavior can, however, be explained.

More recently a biologist, studying the chain of life in the sea, found "support for a community theory of evolution according to which short-term advantages to individual species are sacrificed for long-term benefits for an entire living community."[2]

"Many people would be surprised to learn the extent to which animals help their own kind. Even the popular view of the wild animals of Africa as ferocious beasts, 'red in tooth and claw,' is at least partially mistaken. Throughout the animal world there is much behavior which is peaceful, cooperative and even 'altruistic.' "[3]

Such creatures as wolves, so fierce in all legends, turn out to have been greatly maligned. The great arctic explorer V. Stefansson tried for many years to run down on this continent, in Russia, and elsewhere, an authentic case in which packs of wolves had attacked one or more humans. He found not one reliable incident.[4] Indeed recent experience has indicated that wolves, if met with understanding and kindness, respond fully as affectionately as do domesticated dogs.[5]

* Notes begin on p. 459

It is thus interesting to observe that altruistic behavior is an invention of nature herself; that the earliest philanthropic activity occurred many millions of years before *Homo sapiens* appeared; and that nature must value such behavior, since she has seen fit to continue it over vast periods of time.

Sir Arthur Keith, in his *New Theory of Human Evolution,* has said:

> Altruism is both inborn and instinctive. The explanation of the origin of altruism which I would offer is very similar to that given by Darwin. Altruism is a vast expansion of family sympathy. Family sympathy has a diffusive and exuberant quality; it becomes wider and wider in its influence, until it includes all members of the primal group; it again expands when groups are fused into tribes and again when tribes are combined to form nations. The peoples that have survived to form the large nations of modern times are those which are gifted with a full endowment of generous sympathy, a quality nearly akin to altruism.[6]

Some cultures, especially those operating on slender survival margins, adopt harsh measures in their treatment of the infirm aged, the handicapped, and the seriously ill. But the charitable urge to help those in need is of ancient origin. At the time of the Five Rulers in China, more than two thousand years before Christ, it was recorded by Li Ki that oriental families recognized the needs of the fatherless, of the old man with no wife or sons, and of the elderly woman with no husband; and regular allowances were provided for them.

Tithing, or the giving of one-tenth of income, was not limited to the Hebrews. It was a form of taxation for general purposes in many lands; but among the Hebraic peoples it was "a religiously sanctioned gift to God and the poor." Indeed, the ancient Hebrews left much evidence of their commitment to the "blessed obligation" of *hesed,* translated in the Old Testament as "mercy," with the corresponding word in the New Testament translated as "charity."

However, the very phrase "blessed obligation" at least in part implies that those who are charitable will be rewarded. And the wish to propitiate the gods played an important role in many of the earliest efforts to establish procedures by means of which an individual could set aside a part of his wealth and could provide that, after his death and theoretically forever, these funds would be used to preserve his memory and ensure the peace of his soul.

Thus Harkhuf, an Egyptian nobleman who lived some twenty-three hundred years before Christ, saw to it that his charities were recorded on his tomb, the hieroglyphs stating that he had given these gifts because "I desired that it might be well with me in the great god's presence."

This and comparable acts of the Pharaohs "are the earliest known efforts at projecting private will beyond life . . . they constitute the most rudimentary form of the foundation."[7]

These methods to control after death the use of wealth were available to rulers, but the ordinary man of the ancient world was more restricted in his opportunities. In our modern sense, the right to make a will and testament of the total property of a man did not exist until about 500 B.C. Although there were many more ancient exceptions in connection with mortuary and temple service, there were nevertheless strong traditions of family inheritance. Not only then, but to some extent even now, both custom and law affect the rights of a spouse and those of the first-born heir.

F. Emerson Andrews, the president of the Foundation Library Center and a man who has for many years been a wise and dedicated student of foundation procedures, has emphasized the distinction between the concept of giving that resulted from Judeo-Christian influences and, on the other hand, the concept that seems to have found its first important expression with the Greeks and the early Romans.[8]

The former of these is best characterized by the word "charity." This kindly word, which, in its early Latin form *caritas* and its Greek form *charis,* meant in the first instance a high price—dearness—came to signify grace and gratitude. It was not used, in either Latin or Greek, in connection with affectionate relations between members of a family; but always referred to the good-will relation of an individual to those outside his own family. Thus in the Judeo-Christian tradition charity is a merciful giving, sanctified by the Church, and chiefly directed toward the immediate needs of the hungry, the sick, the suffering. This is the kind of unselfish direct assistance that we associate with the Good Samaritan.

Among the Greeks and Romans, however, the object of the giving was not really individual needy people, but rather the public at large. The intent was not so much to relieve suffering as to enrich life. This broader Greek concept of giving is more closely related to that of the modern philanthropic foundation than is the Judeo-Christian concept of charitable giving. Indeed most modern foundations, and almost all the large ones, exclude gifts for personal relief. The modern foundation almost never entirely eliminates the wholly natural desire of the founder, traceable back to the earliest examples, that his donations bring esteem to him while alive and honor to his memory after he dies. But the modern foundation adds new depth and power to the Greek philosophy of giving.

One of the most notable and familiar expressions of the Greek concept of philanthropy was Plato's Academy. Founded in Athens about 387 B.C., it was largely devoted to theories of ideas, to cosmogony, and to general theories of knowledge and perception. Education, in the utopian society Plato sponsored, involved heavy emphasis on music and gymnastics. Plato considered that the aim of culture was to produce gentlemen, using this word in a sense that Jefferson would have understood and approved.

Plato left this academy, along with an endowment of productive land, to a nephew, with the stipulation that it was to be administered for the benefit of Plato's student-followers. The nephew, in turn, left the foundation—for it was in effect that—to Xenocrates for use by personnel of the school. In the absence of means for setting up a permanent legal entity which could assure continuance, the plan was for each owner-director, during his life, to turn over the property to a living legal heir who could hopefully be trusted to carry on.

It is interesting to note that in Plato's great pupil Aristotle there was, as Bertrand Russell has observed ". . . an almost complete absence of what may be called benevolence or philanthropy. The sufferings of mankind, in so far as he is aware of them, do not move him emotionally; he holds them, intellectually, to be an evil, but there is no evidence that they cause him unhappiness except when the sufferers happen to be his friends."[9]

In the Greek tradition of broad gifts for the populace as a whole, the Athenian citizen Herodes Atticus gave a water supply to the city of Troas, a theatre to Corinth, a stadium to Delphi, aqueducts for Canusium in Italy, baths for Thermopylae. Many if not most of the other benefactions of that period were similar to his. These community-wide gifts were not "charity" in the Judeo-Christian sense. They were more closely related to what we today call philanthropy.

Pre-Christian Rome largely followed the Greek pattern of bene-factions for the populace. Later, however, the Judeo-Christian type of charity did appear in many Roman municipalities, which had organizations to aid in the feeding, clothing, and educating of needy children. The division between the two concepts of giving was never absolute nor permanent.

During the closing years of the pre-Christian era, important developments in Roman custom and law liberalized the rules governing inheritance and began to furnish a dependable continuity for philanthropic activities.

In 150 B.C. Roman law further broadened the legal heir concept by declaring charitable organizations to be both "sentient reasonable beings" and also "immutable undying persons. . . . This interpretation gave foundations immutability plus all the advantages of natural heirs save the right to receive bequests."[10] However paradoxical that ruling, it was undoubtedly important to the birth of the permanent foundation idea and, indeed, to the legal concept of a corporation.

Following these advantages gained about 150 B.C., "founda-tion-like" organizations—guilds, societies, and *collegia,* which were somewhat like modern fraternal organizations—grew in number and activities. Along with their financial strength, their political power increased. And because of just such political involvements, the Roman Senate, in 65 B.C., restrained the philan-thropic associations. In A.D. 96, however, with the beginning of the reign of the "five good emperors," the early "foundations" recovered their good standing and their privilege of permanence. Nerva accorded the cities the right to accept and administer bequests of funds; Trajan extended this privilege to towns and Hadrian to villages; and, important indeed from our point of view, Marcus Aurelius permitted even private groups to receive bequests.

The foundation idea had been born.

CHAPTER 2

A Thousand Years of Ecclesiastical Foundations

From the first, Christianity established church funds. Charity was not only sponsored as a moral duty, but its administration was closely knit into the eccelesiastical organizations. In addition to the charitable obligations of the living, the Church taught that a dying man should, before it was too late, make practical atonement for his sins. With the Church's representative always present as death drew near, one can easily see why the religious authorities became the chief recipient of such funds and accordingly the chief administrators of charity. "The teachings of Jesus set up a new and lofty personal ethic for givers," as Andrews has pointed out, "which became the most important single influence on the philanthropy of the Western World."[1]

In the early centuries of the Christian era, however, substantial philanthropic funds continued under political rather than religious control. Between A.D. 192 and 324, for example, a struggle for political power led the then reigning Roman military emperors to "borrow" foundation funds which had been entrusted to municipal treasuries. Shortly thereafter Constantine I realized that the state would have to face the problem of replacing these vanished monies intended for relief of the poor, and issued an edict reaffirming the legal rights of the Church to receive legacies and to administer them in accordance with the wishes of the donors and assuring the Church of unrestricted and indeed protected use of its property and income. From that time on, Constantine used the Church, rather than any instrument of the state, to handle the problem of distributing public monies to the needy.

With this assurance of retention and control, the Church endowments multiplied in number and increased in size. Having at the same time an effective monopoly of the exercise of charity, the Church accumulated prodigious resources.

Certain bishops and abbots were unable to resist the temptations which accompanied this power, and they diverted to other purposes some funds intended for the succor of the poor and afflicted. In A.D. 453 the Emperor Valentinian put a stop to these improper practices, and during a subsequent century of relatively good behavior the Church remained the chief almoner both in the Roman Empire and wherever else Christianity was the dominant religion.

During the first half of the fifth century A.D., the Emperor Justinian I set up three successive commissions within which the eminent jurist Tribonian played a leading role. These commissions were charged with the task of disentangling the mass of older laws, senate decrees, and judicial interpretations. They simplified and refined these confused records, laying the basis for that famous reformulation of Roman law which was to go down in history as the Justinian Code. It had a profound effect on philanthropy, for the previous laws governing the ecclesiastical foundations were at least partially contradictory and generally ineffective. They failed to furnish adequate legal guides for those who managed relief programs, and failed to protect charitable funds from greed and corruption.

Then, near the mid-point of the fifth century, the legal basis of the ecclesiastical foundations was further improved. The laws of *Piae Causae*, the Roman Empire's early regulations of the obligations and privileges of those who managed endowments for "pious," i.e., charitable purposes, were brought into closer conformity with existing social conditions.

Among the long list of legal principles affecting foundations is one developed by the Romans before the Christian era, and later known as *"cy pres."* It has continued to be important up to the present time.[2] The expression *"cy pres"* is an abbreviation of a Norman French phrase for "as near as possible." This legal doctrine recognizes that donors who make a gift in perpetuity sometimes lay down conditions which later operate in a manner inconsistent with the original intention; while in other cases, circumstances may render the original stipulations inappropriate or impossible of fulfillment.

In terms more clear to the nonlawyer than is much other legal language, the doctrine of *cy pres* has been defined as ". . . the principle that equity will . . . when an original specific intent becomes impossible or impracticable of fulfillment, substitute another plan of administration which is believed to approach the original scheme as closely as possible. It is the theory that equity has the power to mold the charitable trust to meet emergencies."[3] In other words *cy pres* is the principle used by the courts to bring back to social usefulness a will or trust agreement that a changing society has outmoded.

Some legal procedure for altering the conditions of trusts is clearly desirable. In the fifteenth century, for example, a fund was established to provide "faggots for the burning of heretics," and there were "Endowments for the purpose of redeeming Christians held in slavery by Mahommedan Powers. . . ."[4] Late in the eighteenth century the John Pemberton Fund in Pennsylvania provided for the pasturing of the horses of Friends while they were attending Yearly Meeting or the Philadelphia Quarterly Meeting. In the same state a woman left funds to establish a home in perpetuity for Presbyterian ministers seventy years of age or over who did not use tobacco. And, as late as 1932, a lady named Emma A. Robinson left a sum of money to be used for providing Christmas dinners ("one bushel of oats or half a bushel of corn chops") for hungry horses in Kansas City. Julius Rosenwald, in one of the articles he wrote which argued against perpetual endowments, reported the case of a fund "which provides a baked potato at each meal for each young woman at Bryn Mawr."[5, 6]

There are numerous instances in which, even after long litigation, the courts have been unwilling or unable to change currently unreasonable conditions, and the legal principle of *cy pres* is by no means universally accepted even today. But the present tendency in American courts seems to indicate a greater flexibility in the application of the principle.

At least three of the larger present-day foundations have explicitly faced the problem of the almost inevitable obsolescence of conditions by adopting general regulations, applying to all of their permanent grants, that any initial specifications as to the use of the money be gradually relaxed as time passes. Any gift for capital purposes which the Rockefeller Foundation makes is subject to a series of liberalization provisions based on the stated desire of the foundation that "this gift, whether the income only is spent or the principal as well, shall always be regarded as available for use in the broadest ways so as best to promote the general purposes for which it is made." It is thus specifically stipulated, in connection with capital grants by the Rockefeller Foundation, that the authorities of the recipient institution are free at any time to transfer the gift, in whole or in part, to any other organization which in their judgment might make better use of the funds to serve the intended purposes; and there are relaxations of conditions after five, ten, and twenty-five years which permit a gradual use of principal as well as income, a shift to another purpose "reasonably related to the original specific purpose," and finally a shift of income or principal to any use whatsoever which has the overwhelming approval of the officers of the recipient institution.

Similarly the Ford Foundation, when it made a series of large grants (1955-56) to institutions of higher learning, arranged that after a ten-year period these grants could be used, both capital and income, for any institutional purpose. In 1946 the Carnegie Corporation provided that in the case of all endowment grants, in each year after a ten-year initial period, up to one-tenth of the capital and all uncommitted income could be used by the institution in question for any purpose.

To return to Roman times, the Justinian law specified that an endowment revert to the donor or his heirs if the will was not made effective in less than three years; and there were numerous other provisions as to what could or must not be done in connection with church endowments, together with a specification of the penalties for misdeeds.

Although he eventually changed his own ideas about certain tenets of the Christian Church, Justinian at one stage was orthodox indeed. He caused the dissolution of several endowed associations on the grounds that they sponsored heretical ideas. The most famous case was that of Plato's Academy, which had been operating for nearly six hundred years. The charge of teaching pagan doctrines led to the suppression of this organization.[7] In terminology familiar today, one could say that this academy was put out of business by the Committee on "Un-Christian Activities."

Justinian gave the bishops and abbots the right to designate the officials of charitable endowments, and throughout the medieval age the Church profited handsomely from these prerogatives. Their appointees as managers of philanthropy became in later years the Masters in Chancery, among England's most important judges.

As Henry Allen Moe has written, the medieval church was in actuality a state in itself.[8] Its courts had jurisdiction over all church property, including revenues derived from taxes imposed by ecclesiastical authority and from wills.

In England, the Saxon kings accorded the ecclesiastical foundations the near autonomy they had achieved in Roman society. The bishops and abbots continued their domination of the "spiritual trusts." After 1066, however, and with the ascent to the throne of the Norman kings, a long and bloody struggle arose to bring the foundations under secular supervision and to submit them to the usual laws of the higher courts.

CHAPTER 3

The Shift to Secular Control

Less than a century after William the Conqueror ascended to power, Henry II (1154-1189) decreed that the bishops and abbots held their possessions in trust, so to speak, for the king, and that they were answerable to the king's justice. The English monarchs were dissatisfied with the conduct of the Church functionaries in their administration of charity, and also larger issues were at stake.

Because the ecclesiastical foundations of England held one-third to one-half the public wealth of that country, economic as well as political control was involved. A comparable financial challenge would be presented to our own country at the present time only if the total endowment funds of the philanthropic foundations in the United States were well over a hundred times as great as they actually now are.[1] Another point of difference, no less significant than the quantitative one, is the fact that in medieval England the ownership of Church property was vested in a single institution, as contrasted with the wide dispersion of ownership of the assets of philanthropic foundations among the many independent entities in the United States today.

The tremendous power of the ecclesiastical foundations could not be curbed by a single edict, and not until the reigns of Henry VIII (1509-47) and Edward VI (1547-53) was the Church's financial control substantially reduced. Preceding monarchs had chipped away at the Church's domination of medieval life, but the real decline of power resulted from the dissolution of the ecclesiastical foundations and the confiscation of their wealth by Henry VIII and Edward VI.

The men of the Middle Ages gave alms as an act of piety;

14

but it was a rather self-centered type of piety, for the gifts were doubtless usually made as a kind of insurance for the future repose of the donor's soul. It is Jordan's estimate[2] that in 1480 as much as two-thirds of all benefactions were for religious purposes, whereas within seventy-five years the proportion had dropped to about 7 percent. This did not occur because of a great decline in the *volume* of charitable giving, but because of a great shift in the *auspices* of charitable giving as the control passed from the ecclesiastical courts of the official Church to secular agencies, and as the influence of the Protestant clergy increased.

A great deal of the individual giving of the Middle Ages was an indiscriminate sentimental type of charity, such as the alms to beggars at the monastery gates. But this pattern began to change, as the recognition emerged of intense and persistent poverty as a social evil rather than an individual misfortune, and an attempt was made to change the pauperism of large segments of the population; these together represented a new and broadened philanthropic concept—one which merged the Judeo-Christian and the Greco-Roman philosophies of giving. This sixteenth-century change in the character of charitable giving took place alongside, and perhaps because of, the cataclysmic religious and social upheaval known as the Reformation.

The expropriation by the state of the ecclesiastical foundations could not have occurred and held, had it not been for a climate of public opinion sanctioning the change. And the mood of consent, indeed, sometimes of jubilant endorsement, was stimulated in no small measure by a group of preachers whom the modern idiom would describe as "angry." One of these, Henry Brinkelow, a former monk and early convert to Protestantism, vociferously insisted in his writings and from his pulpit that the wealth of the Church should be used for worthy and bold social needs. Of his fellow Londoners he thundered, " 'Oh Lord God how blynde be these cytezins which take so greate care to provyde for the dead' by popish superstitions while neglecting their bounden Christian obligation to relieve those in desperate want."[3]

Another of the angry preachers, Thomas Bacon, indicted the amiable but misguided rich who had poured funds into "great monasteries for the bellied hypocrites, great colleges, chantries, and free chapels for soul-carriers and purgatory-rakers."

The attacks of these forthright and courageous, if not precisely gentle, clergymen helped set the stage for the expropriation of the funded wealth of the previously official ecclesiastical establishment. These critics were subsequently just as vigorous and acid in their condemnation of some of the ways in which the state disposed of the religious wealth it had seized. For neither Henry VIII nor Edward VI was above turning over some of this property to their aristocratic friends. A school in Wye, for example, endowed in 1447 and confiscated less than a century later by Henry VIII, was promptly granted to the secretary of one of that monarch's wives. As is so often the case, reforms must be followed by reformers of the reform.

In 1601, the forty-third year of Queen Elizabeth's long reign, a new body of law was enacted providing for the creation, control, and protection of charitable funds. Known as the Statute of Charitable Uses, this act has been recognized as the "cornerstone of Anglo-Saxon law concerning philanthropies,"[4] and as the "Magna Charta of English and American philanthropic foundations."[5]

One important portion of this statute affirmed the general principle that a charitable trust exercises a function which is jointly private and public. At the time of the issuance of the statute, this principle required that in the legal incorporation of a charitable foundation the state, or the reigning monarch, be the general founder. But the term *fundatio incipiens,* which referred to this principle, has gradually come to have the broader meaning, recognized clearly in our present laws, that the state plays an essential role in the formation of any perpetuating charitable trust.

The terms of the famous Statute of Charitable Uses have undergone considerable transformation across the centuries, but they have never been totally eclipsed. Indeed "the modern foundation in America is the lineal descendant of the charitable trust-fund provisions and practices of England."[6]

As is so often true, an outstanding event in history which seems to be the novel result of a wholly original imagination turns out, upon further study, to have had antecedents. As Dr. Henry Allen Moe has made clear in a fascinating paper, the poet William Langland well over two hundred years before the enactment of the Statute of Charitable Uses had clearly specified, as a message from a poetic character he called Truth, that wealthy merchants should take their profits

and therewith repair hospitals,
help sick people,
mend bad roads,
build up bridges that had been broken down,
help maidens to marry or to make them nuns,
find food for prisoners and poor people,
put scholars to school or to some other crafts,
help religious orders, and
ameliorate rents or taxes.[7]

The relevant portions of the Statute of Charitable Uses contain every one of these admonitions, the only changes being that the broad instruction to "help religious orders" was quite naturally trimmed down to the "repair of churches," while the assistance to help maidens become nuns was lacking.

In addition to the stimulus furnished by the Statute of Charitable Uses and the influence of the Reformation movement, other factors during the seventeenth and later centuries led to an increased sensitivity to human suffering and to a resultant increase in charitable giving. To some extent a motivation to secular giving came from the humanistic traditions of the sixteenth century. The Tudors, and particularly Elizabeth, both hated and feared poverty and vagabondage for their unsettling effects on society, somewhat as we today in the Western world dislike poverty at least partly because we realize that it furnishes a breeding ground for Communism.

Apart from the grants of the kings, however, the new endowments of sixteenth- and seventeenth-century England were small, and only through the pooling of several modest ones could sizable ones be established. Scanty records exist of philanthropic endeavors of the seventeenth century, except for those essentially restricted to relief. A library was established at Oxford in 1602, however, through a benefaction from Sir Thomas Bodley, and it is now one of the most famous in the world. Another fragment of information gives an account of one of the earliest endowments created by a private individual, Thomas Sutton. In 1612 he caused to be established a hospital and a free grammar school.

Over a century later, in 1724, the wealth of Sir Thomas Guy was devoted to the founding of Guy's Hospital in London. This act of benevolence is still a conspicuous one; it remains the only general hospital in London to bear the name of its founder. This hospital, moreover, was established by the bequest of a single donor; and it is interesting to observe that the money which created it had been derived from South Sea stock speculations which had brought both scandal and bankruptcy to some persons less fortunate or less shrewd than Sir Thomas himself. The origin of Sir Thomas Guy's fortune, and the naming of the hospital for him, "raised for the first time the 'tainted' money and egoism issues of modern philanthropy."[8]

Throughout the many centuries rapidly sketched over in the preceding pages, the emphasis in philanthropy was upon the charitable relief of need—often individual need. A large fraction of this activity was carried out by religious authorities or was in any event motivated religiously. It should not be concluded, however, that the religiously motivated response to need, or even its humane concern, went entirely without challenge. In 1705 Bernard de Mandeville wrote a book, subsequently called *The Fable of the Bees;* to emphasize his convictions, Mandeville used the subtitle "Private Vices, Public Benefits." Bronowski has said "This phrase summarizes the dominant intellectual theory of the eighteenth century, that the health of society positively requires the weakest to go to the wall. The giving of charity, and particularly the education of the poor, were actively condemned, because it was held that we disturb the dynamic balance of society if we interfere by helping the weaklings."[9] Views of this sort continue to be held by some modern critics of the welfare state, but such views apply more to the charitable alleviation of symptoms than to the deeper attack on causes.

A large part of the early giving was nevertheless undoubtedly stimulated by a desire to atone for sin or, more broadly, to please the rulers of Heaven; while another substantial portion was motivated by an urge to perpetuate the donor's name and honor. Greater social insight, more nearly selfless giving, and the vision of an effective attack upon the causes of mankind's troubles rather than relief of them when they individually occur—these aspects of philanthropy, despite the early inspirations of the Greeks, had not as yet been significantly developed.

CHAPTER 4

Early American
Philanthropic Organizations

At daybreak on Thursday, November 19, 1620[1] the lookout of the *Mayflower* sighted the highlands of Cape Cod. Two days later, after an abortive attempt to seek a location further south,[2] the vessel was anchored offshore in Provincetown Harbor.[3]

During the following month a series of reconnaissance missions were carried out by groups of about ten men, who went ashore in a small open boat. On Monday, December 21, 1620, at the location we now know as Plymouth, came the traditional "landing of the Pilgrims." William Bradford wrote in his journal: "They sounded the harbor and found it fit for shipping, and marched into land and found divers cornfields and little running brooks, a place (as they supposed) fit for situation."

The land was, indeed, ready for them; and in so many important ways they were ready for the land. They had courage and physical endurance and deep dedication. Supporting these qualities, sustaining them in whatever trials, were the religious convictions that had, to so great an extent, been the basic cause of their pilgrimage. The Mayflower Compact recorded in the most unambiguous words their purpose: "ye glorie of God, and advancemente of ye Christian Faith."[4] The most precious and significant cargo on the *Mayflower* was the set of moral convictions that dominated the lives of those aboard. A book concerned with the development of philanthropic foundations in our country must take note of the landing of this group of religious enthusiasts. As Henry Allen Moe has said, "Religion is the mother of philanthropy . . . both conceptually and procedurally."[5] The words of Jesus, as recorded in the Gospel according to Saint Luke, are completely unambiguous: "Woe unto you that are rich. . . . Give, and it shall be given unto you. . . ."[6] The other great world religions contain similar admonitions.

When John Winthrop, subsequently twelve times the governor of Massachusetts Bay Colony, same to these shores in 1630, he delivered on board ship a sermon on the theme "A Modell of Christian Charity." He made it clear that love of fellow man (and the word philanthropy comes from Greek words meaning *love of mankind*) was an essential part of the code of conduct of those "who had entered into a covenant with God."[7]

It is not intended to suggest that such concerns were prompted only by the difficult voyage or by the vision of the New World as the New Jerusalem. The England from which Winthrop sailed, in spite of all that the Puritans found fault with, was marked by tax-supported aid to the poor, by a vigorous resurgence of charitable enterprise, and by many evidences of private benevolence. Philanthropy was, for the emigrating group, an important part of their heritage from the mother country. The religious motivations of the colonists, together with the hope that conquering the wilderness would provide work for all the poor, combined to heighten a charitable concern whose roots lay deep in history.[8]

The historian Merle Curti has said:

> In ideology, the doctrine of Christian stewardship of riches was central in Puritan and Quaker thought. It was also evident in Anglican teaching. This doctrine was exemplified in such representative appeals for benevolence as John Winthrop's *A Modell of Christian Charity,* Cotton Mather's *Essays to Do Good,* and the *Magnalia,* Whitfield's exhortations for contributions to orphan asylums, as well as in the precepts of Penn, Benezet, and Woolman and in Anglican pleas for the inculcation of piety through libraries and for the conversion and nurture of Indians and Negroes.[9]

Sixty-two years after the coming of the Pilgrims, William Penn, who had been subject to strong Puritan influences in his school days in England and who had become in his teens an ardent and dedicated Quaker, was made "master of the province of Pennsylvania."[10] On September 1, 1682, he sailed from England with one hundred comrades to found the Quaker colony in Philadelphia.

The details of their religious beliefs differed from those of the Puritans, but as far as benevolence was concerned their ideas were similar.

The greatest exponent of philanthropic dynamism in Colonial America was Cotton Mather, whose "Essays to Do Good" (1710) profoundly influenced the first and second generation of settlers. Although in his youth Benjamin Franklin ridiculed Mather with an imitative character called Silence Dogood, toward the end of his days Franklin wrote to Cotton Mather's son that his own life and work had been significantly influenced by his father's writings.

Franklin, one of the most important early philanthropists, founded The American Philosophical Society in 1743, and if it had then possessed the range of means and endeavors that have accrued to it since, it would be possible to speak of it as the first philanthropic foundation in the New World. *The Foundation Directory* states that "this membership society has many of the characteristics of a foundation, including a substantial endowment, much of the income from which is devoted to grants for research in all fields of scholarship."[11]

Franklin's will provided for philanthropic bequests of one thousand pounds sterling each (then equivalent to $4444.49) to Boston and to Philadelphia, specified as being for loans of up to $267 at 5 percent "to young married artificers of good character." Franklin, himself "bred to a manual art," thought that "among artisans, good apprentices are most likely to become good citizens."

Franklin provided that the principal and interest of both these funds accumulate for one hundred years. Each fund was then to be divided into two portions—the first portion, roughly three-fourths of the total, to be devoted to public works "of the most general utility," and the second part to accumulate for another hundred years, a period which will come to a close in 1990.

With more confidence in the arithmetic of compound interest than realism concerning practicalities, Franklin estimated that in addition to $440,000 for public works in each of the two cities by 1890, over $18 million would be available for each location in 1991, of which about $13 million was to go to each of the states in question, and $5 million to each city.

Though it did not work out quite that neatly, the results are impressive. The amount released in Philadelphia in 1891 was about $90,000, rather than the $440,000 Franklin had estimated. This sum was not actually released, but was committed to a park improvement project that dragged on for so long without starting that in 1903 the courts reassigned the fund to the Franklin Institute to be used ultimately for a new building. Again there was a long delay, but by then the fund was increasing vigorously; and by the time the Franklin Institute was ready to build its fine building in 1929, the sum had grown to about a million and a half dollars.

In the case of the other municipality the arithmetic worked out rather better. After the first hundred years of accumulation the amount available for public works in Boston was $298,602.04, a sum which, after fifteen years of further growth, amounted to $432,367.29, used to construct and equip what is currently known as the Franklin Institute of Boston. The second part of the fund assigned by Franklin to Boston had a value of $2,161,734 on June 30, 1965, and will continue to accumulate until 1990.

The first part of the Franklin (Boston) Fund was eventually matched in 1904 by Andrew Carnegie, in this way starting an endowment which helps to maintain the Franklin Institute. Thus did the man who so greatly influenced the pattern for philanthropy in the twentieth-century team up with the great philanthropist of the eighteenth century.

In 1962 the Franklin Foundation obtained judicial permission, in a *cy pres* modification of the original specification for loans to young artificers, to inaugurate loans to medical students and hospital house officers; and the city of Philadelphia has similarly, and on several occasions, obtained decrees from the Orphans Court making modifications *cy pres* in the prescribed terms for personal loans from Franklin's bequest.

One of the earliest, and perhaps the first, United States foundations was the Magdalen Society. It was established in Philadelphia in 1800 as a perpetual trust "to ameliorate the distressed condition of those unhappy females who have been seduced from the paths of virtue, and are desirous of returning to a life of rectitude."[12] Difficulties arose early in the history of this laudable enterprise. There were too few candiates for redemption, and those who did volunteer often proved "insubordinate," as the minutes of the society record. Indeed the surprising nature of some of their difficulties is indicated by an entirely unamplified reference in the minutes of the Magdalen Society to one inmate of their home who was discovered to be "an impostor." It would require a moralist trained in the logic of multiple antinomies to weigh the virtue of a young woman who falsely claimed to be not virtuous!

The famous French seventeen-volume encyclopedia which appeared in the middle of the eighteenth century and which is chiefly identified with Diderot, D'Alembert, and Voltaire, contained an article on foundations written by Turgot, later the comptroller general of his country. In this discussion, written nearly a half century before the founding of the Philadelphia Magdalen Society, Turgot argued vigorously against permanently inflexible trusts of all kinds, suggesting that the eventual actual result of outmoded conditions could easily be quite inconsistent with the original purpose.

The Magdalen Society, recognizing the impracticality of the original pattern, was reorganized in 1918 as the White-Williams Foundation, and it continues now to operate a program of assistance to children and school-age youth which was begun at the time of the reorganization.

The year 1845 saw the establishment of the Smith Charities of Northampton, Massachusetts. Its charter restricted it to furnishing aid in specified localities in Massachusetts, and the assistance included "marriage portions" for poor young women about to be married.

A Havens Relief Fund Society came into being in 1870 in New York, intended for "the relief of poverty and distress, and especially the affording of temporary relief to unobtrusive suffering endured by industrious or worthy persons."[13] (This terminology, strictly interpreted, seems to exclude the consideration of suffering individuals who were *both* industrious and worthy!)

In the nineteenth and even in the eighteenth century, a number of other American funds for relief of the poor were established, often beginning as trusts for rather specifically designated purposes; and in several instances their functioning was in time shifted over to local governments or absorbed within larger organizations of more public character. Andrews cites as an example the board of directors of City Trusts, City of Philadelphia, organized in 1869. At the present time it is administering some twenty-five small trust funds all older than itself, together with over sixty trusts newer than itself.

Near the mid-point of the nineteenth century, an organization was founded which heralded in its characteristics many current American philanthropic foundations. This was the Smithsonian Institution, established in 1846 with an original half-million-dollar bequest to the United States government from James Smithson, an English inventor and scientist. It took an act of Congress to bring the Smithsonian Institution into existence, and it remains in most respects a ward of the government.

This close relationship with government distinguishes the Smithsonian Institution from the mass of foundations with which this book is concerned. But in other regards it set a pattern adopted, in general terms, by many subsequent foundations. Its purpose was, and remains, "the increase and diffusion of knowledge among men." It obviously is engaged in philanthropy, but it is not concerned with charity or with the needs and sufferings of individuals, as were so many of the eleemosynary organizations which were active in the preceding centuries. The museums, galleries, and special collections maintained by the Smithsonian Institution remind one of the benefactions of Herodes Atticus and the suggestions of Cicero. But, in addition to all that, the Smithsonian Institution used its funds to support a program of research, and to give wide distribution to the new knowledge produced by this research. This was an innovation, and a truly significant one.

The Peabody Education Fund, established by George Peabody in 1867, has the honor of being the originator of responsible accounting to the public of all its activities. It seems proper to describe, as Dr. Robert S. Morison has done, the establishment of the Peabody Education Fund, "as the beginning of the foundation as we know it."[14] This fund, of approximately $2 million, was set up to give aid to the war-devastated South. Unlike many previous benefactors, Peabody was not especially interested in the word "forever," and the charter of his fund provided that it could be dissolved after thirty years. The fund's operations were brought to a close in 1914, when the balance of its assets was transferred to the John F. Slater Fund, an 1882 newcomer to the early foundation scene with general aims paralleling those of the Peabody Fund.

Another early fund, also meriting recognition for its imaginative design, was the Baron de Hirsch Fund, created in 1891 to assist in the Americanization of Jewish immigrants.

Around 1900 two concepts of philanthropy came into great prominence, neither of them wholly without precedent, for total novelty rarely if ever occurs in the realm of ideas. But the great philanthropic concepts which we associate chiefly with the names of Carnegie and Rockefeller were given inspiring new theoretical expression and wholly new massive practical form at just about the turn of the century.

The first of these concepts was in some ways related to the Greco-Roman ideas. For, in its simplest expression, it advocated a basic attack on causes rather than on the necessarily superficial and impermanent alleviation of undesirable results. This idea involved a complete departure from the older charitable idea of a series of gifts to the needy; it recognized that as a never-ending process. For the first time, clearly formulated philosophies and tremendous resources were brought to the service of a concept of scientifically disciplined philanthropy—philanthropy which seeks the new knowledge and the new understanding which can permanently improve the condition of men. The role of education was neglected by neither man—think of the Carnegie libraries and of the General Education Board. The desirability of the enrichment of life was neglected by neither. But the attack on the problem was, so to speak, from underneath, involving fundamental study of causes.

This basic concept would not lead a foundation to contribute to the operating costs of clinics or hospitals, but rather to support research to determine the nature and cause of disease and the ways in which disease may be prevented. This concept would not lead a foundation to contribute money to buy food for the hungry, but rather to support agricultural research leading to a more abundant supply of cheaper and better foods. This concept would not lead a foundation to contribute large sums for relief to the unemployed, but rather to support studies of the ways in which our economy can be assured a vigorous and stable growth rate, ways in which automation can be properly absorbed into our economy, and so forth.

The second of the great new concepts is one which, in its full force, can effectively apply only to large foundations. It is that the mandate to the foundation be extremely broad and flexible, perhaps best exemplified by the noble, if admittedly somewhat ambitious, phrase "To promote the well-being of mankind throughout the world" which occurs in the charter of the Rockefeller Foundation. Obviously such a charge is so inclusive and general that the courts will never have to wrestle with the complications of invoking the principle of *cy pres*. But not quite so obviously, this charge presents a clear and compelling challenge to the trustees and the officers of such a foundation. They do not have the routine task of complying with specific plans laid down by the founder. Such duties could never hope to attract truly imaginative administrators, or minds of high order.

It is a challenge of a totally different sort to be told: Here is a great source of financial power, and there are the needs of the world. What do you propose to do? This kind of challenge should attract first-rate individuals. On many occasions in foundation history it has done so.

ANDREW CARNEGIE

One of the chief creators of the new vision, as we have already stated, was Andrew Carnegie. Born in Scotland in 1835, he was only eleven years old when the Smithsonian Institution was founded. His parents brought him to the United States when he was twelve, his father, a master weaver of damask, having suffered from the technological advance which replaced hand looms by steam-driven machinery. From the first, Andrew Carnegie had jobs which enabled him to help out in his family's support. He became a bobbin boy in a mill, working from dawn to dark for a dollar and twenty cents a week.

Fifty-three years after he started, penniless, his activities in the United States, his energy, shrewdness, and audacity had been so successful that he was able to sell the Carnegie Company in 1901 to the newly organized United States Steel Company for $492 million, a sum presumably equivalent to nearly five times that many present-day dollars. Almost half of the purchase price went to Carnegie himself, in first-mortagage 5-percent gold bonds.

This sale is reputed to have made Carnegie the richest man in the world at that time.[15] It enabled him at the age of sixty-five to turn to a new career, the career of philanthropist, although that term was one he disliked and one with which he never was willing to identify himself.

It would require some of Andrew Carnegie's own discipline to condense into a few sentences the power and thrust, the acumen and brilliance, with which the young Scotsman had managed to move into the front rank of industrial magnates. Carnegie himself built the businesses he sold: and Carnegie set himself apart from those contemporaries who continued accumulating up to and sometimes into their dotage. For Carnegie closed the acquisitive phase of his life at the age of sixty-five and turned to the problem of the disposition of his wealth. He did so according to a plan to which he had given much previous thought.

Not until Carnegie's death was it known that at the age of thirty-three, with some business success already in his grasp, he "had pledged himself to devote all his 'surplus' wealth to 'benevolent purposes.' "[16] This he promised on a sheet of paper, a memorandum to himself found after his death, yellow and fragile, among his keepsakes.

This early promise was delevoped into a carefully considered philosophy of giving, now always referred to as "The Gospel of Wealth,"[17] which Carnegie first published in 1889, nearly twelve years before the sale of his company. His ideas displayed a brilliant contrast between unselfishness and humility on the one hand, and totally unquestioning confidence in his own superiority on the other hand.

He took off from the proposition that "the problem of our age is the proper administration of wealth, that the ties of brotherhood may still bind together the rich and poor in harmonious relationship." There is no indication that he tried to reduce the economic margin between the rich and the poor, and indeed he seemed to have had little or no interest in the economic aspects of social reform. His essay contained the sentence "Objections to the foundations upon which society is based are not in order, because the condition of the race is better with these than it has been with any other which has been tried." So much for that!

He wished only "to provide moderately for the legitimate wants of those dependent upon him"; and the leaving of great wealth at death for public uses he considered "only a means for the disposal of wealth provided a man is content to wait until he is dead before he becomes of much good in the world." What he really believed in was that the rich should themselves administer, during their lives, their wealth for the public good. He seemed to have complete confidence in his own "superior wisdom, experience, and ability to administer, doing for them [his poorer brethren] better than they would or could do for themselves."

In a second article he urged, as a list of specific philanthropic suggestions, first, that if anyone had enough money, he should found a university. The best gift to a community he held to be a free library. Next in order he favored the founding or extension of hospitals, medical colleges, and laboratories; next parks; and then, in decreasing order, meeting and concert halls, swimming baths, and churches. In much of this the Greeks would have recognized a kindred spirit.

This was quite clearly a wonderful man, with a new clarity and depth of vision of the usefulness of wealth. For himself and his family he usually showed the Scot's dedication to "modest, unostentatious living, shunning display or extravagance," Skibo Castle being an extraordinary exception to this principle. The dramatic success of his own work and wisdom led him, quite naturally and honestly, to have a very high regard for his own judgment, and this high regard was justified. His charitable acts exhibited a new recognition of the desirability of attacking the causes of human ills and sufferings—of preventing misery rather than merely relieving it. And he had a lofty concept of "the duty of the man of wealth . . . to consider all surplus revenues which come to him simply as trust funds which he is called upon to administer, and strictly bound as a matter of duty to administer in the manner which, in his judgment, is best calculated to produce the most beneficial results for the community—the man of wealth

thus becoming the mere trustee and agent for his poorer brethren. . . . "[18]

Carnegie's large-scale giving began with grants for construction
of library buildings, each of these gifts being conditioned on the
recipient community's providing a site and guaranteeing an annual
maintenance fund of not less than 10 percent of the building costs.
When he died in 1919, he had given, directly or through the corporation, a total of 2,509 library buildings at a cost of more than
$56 million.[19]

Carnegie described as "the first use of surplus wealth"[20] his 1901
gift of $4 million "to relieve those [of his workmen] who may suffer
from accidents, and provide small pensions for those needing help
in old age [and] in addition . . . one million dollars . . . the proceeds
thereof to be used to maintain the libraries and halls I have built
for our workmen." It should be remembered that income was not
taxed in 1901 in the United States.

There promptly followed a series of major gifts: $10 million for
the Scottish Universities Trust; a total of $22 million to found the
Carnegie Institution of Washington; $3.75 million for the Dun-
fermline Trust; $1.5 million for the Palace of Peace at The Hague;
the financing of Carnegie Hero Funds; the funds for the Carnegie
Foundation for the Advancement of Teaching and for the Carnegie Endowment for International Peace. All of these came in the
period from 1901 to 1910.

In 1911 with much of his U.S. Steel bond fortune intact, Andrew
Carnegie still felt the fear of dying rich and thus disgraced. His
biographer described the situation:

> After devoting more than ten arduous years to disbursing the in-
> terest and principal of his steel bonds, Carnegie had reached an
> unanticipated impasse. The operation had not proved so simple as he
> once imagined. . . . His gospel of wealth as originally formulated
> required that the possessor of a surplus must himself dispense it in
> his own lifetime. But it now became evident that this fundamental
> article in the strange new creed would not work. With the most
> heroic efforts to expend his fortune and after a campaign of the most
> magnificent giving the world had ever known, Carnegie discovered
> that more than $150,000,000 of his steel bonds obstinately remained
> in his possession. He was seventy-six years old, and the likelihood

was remote that, in the few years remaining, so great a sum could be disposed of wisely.[21]

Convinced by Elihu Root that a handwritten will he had himself prepared might not stand up in the courts, Carnegie decided to organize a great foundation and transfer to it, while he was still alive, the bulk of his fortune.

On June 9, 1911, the legislature of the State of New York passed an act to establish the Carnegie Corporation; and to this agency Carnegie turned over first $25 million of the U.S. Steel bonds, and then shortly thereafter an additional $100 million. In this way did there come into existence what was for a time the largest "general purpose" or "general research" foundation.

At the first meeting of the trustees, Carnegie read a document which said, in part, that his purpose was

. . . 'to promote the advancement and diffusion of knowledge and understanding among the people of the United States, by aiding technical schools, institutions of higher learning, libraries, scientific research, hero funds, useful publications, and by such other agencies and means as shall from time to time be found appropriate therefor.' My desire is that the work which I have been carrying on, or similar beneficial work, shall continue during this and future generations. Conditions upon the earth inevitably change; hence, no wise man will bind Trustees forever to certain paths, causes or institutions. I disclaim any intention of doing so. On the contrary, I give my Trustees full authority to change policy or causes hitherto aided, from time to time, when this, in their opinion, has become necessary or desirable. They shall best conform to my wishes by using their own judgment. . . . My chief happiness as I write these lines lies in the thot that, even after I pass away, the welth that came to me to administer as a sacred trust for the good of my fellow men is to continue to benefit humanity for generations untold, under your devoted and sympathetic guidance and that of your successors, who cannot fail to be able and good men.[22]

As compared with perpetuities in England, the Carnegie Corporation was strikingly novel in the breadth of its concept and in the latitude permitted in the use of its funds. The new doctrine, as F. Emerson Andrews has said, regarded these resources as "the venture capital of philanthropy, best spent when invested in enterprises requiring risk and foresight . . . the usual purpose is not relief or even cure; it is research, prevention, and discovery."[23]

But, on the other hand, it must be recognized that the Carnegie Corporation, during its early years, was a personal agency. Carnegie, true to the ideas about his own competence which he had expressed in "The Gospel of Wealth," had every intention of steering the course himself. "The new agency might well have been called Andrew Carnegie, Inc. He became first president, the annual meetings were held at his home, and the executive committee, which consisted of himself, his financial secretary, Mr. Franks, and his personal secretary, Mr. Bertram, directed the expenditure of money."[24] But within four years the state of his health required that he turn over to the trustees the direction of the corporation's affairs, although he was nominally president until his death.

It is clear that Andrew Carnegie took tremendous pride in his acts of giving, and he was ever eager to be present and in the seat or procession of honor on public occasions where tribute was paid to his benefactions. Throughout his life Carnegie had acted with sure-footed, confident decisiveness. In his latter career as a benefactor there was little change in his convictions about what was right and what was wrong and what the order of importance was among values. Though deficient in formal education, Carnegie was a well-read individual. He attained through his own efforts a peerage with the great minds, aesthetes, and statesmen of his generation. The tough captain of the steel-making empire, the Lord Rector of St. Andrews University, the "Laird of Skibo," who acted as host to Rudyard Kipling, Lloyd George, the Archbishop of Canterbury, Paderewski, Woodrow Wilson, and William Osler—these are all one and the same man.

He was in simple and clear fact a self-made man. It is not surprising that in deliberating about how the community might best be benefited he became convinced that it was through "the placing of ladders upon which the aspiring can rise."[25]

JOHN D. ROCKEFELLER, SR.

The other, the second, creator of the great new vision of modern philanthrophy was John Davison Rockefeller. He was born in

1839 in the small village of Richford, about 125 miles northwest of New York City, only four years after the birth of Carnegie. It is supposed that his father, William Avery Rockefeller, was apprenticed in his youth to a doctor. Whether or not that is true, the father spent half a century of his adult life as an itinerant vendor of patent medicines and herbs, doing quite a bit of business on the side with sales of salt, fur, horses, and land. The fortunes of the family, never high, fluctuated down to rather low levels when the father was off for months at a time, and then came promptly back up when the "herbal physician" returned, temporarily flush with the proceeds of his trip. John D. Rockefeller's mother was of Scottish descent, and in contrast to her adventurous mate she was a woman of deep piety and reticence—"the soul of order and discipline . . . her ideas upon morals were precise to the point of intolerance. . . ."[26]

John received his early education at a district school near Owego, New York; at Owego Academy; then in the high school at Cleveland, Ohio (his parents had moved to nearby Strongville); and then for a brief period at Folsum's Commercial Academy in Cleveland, where at the age of sixteen he studied bookkeeping and "learned the rudiments of mercantile practice, banking, and exchange." In his school years he was, to use his own words "not an easy student," but was "sedate and earnest, preparing to meet the responsibilities of life. . . . I always got my mathematics first; arithmetic and algebra."[27]

Before entering high school he had a significant experience with one of the basic principles of finance. Having earned $50 raising turkeys, he loaned that sum to a farmer. He was deeply impressed when he received $3.50 interest at the end of a year. In his own language, "It was a good thing to let the money be my servant." His older sister, Lucy, considering his diligent schoolwork, his frugal and efficient ways, and his developing business acumen, said, "When it's raining porridge, you'll find John's dish right side up."[28] What Lucy failed to add, to complete the picture, was that a significant part of that porridge, no matter how small or large the dish, would be given to someone else.

Not until he had canvassed the larger business establishments of Cleveland twice did he locate his first real job, with a firm of commission merchants and produce shippers. For an initial trial period of three months he received, and not until the trial was completed, $3.50 a week: and subsequent to a satisfactory trial he was to receive $25 a month. During five of these initial weeks, with no pay coming in and living entirely on his savings, this sixteen-year-old boy gave $1.82 for religious and charitable purposes, this sum being meticulously recorded in his personal ledger. From the very first, the precepts of his mother and his own careful conscience made religious giving and charity an essential part of his life. By the time he was twenty-six years old his annual gifts to charity totaled over $1,000.

He remained with this firm for three and a half years, augmenting his wages through small trading ventures of his own. Then, dissatisfied with his compensation, he started a business in partnership with an Englishman who was clerk in another grain and commission house. With this move, there began the great upward spiral of the Rockefeller fortune. Six years later, by the end of the Civil War, John D. Rockefeller was a rich man. The move into the oil business started in 1862, and the Standard Oil Company was formed in 1870. Nine years after that, the properties of the Standard Oil group were valued at $70 million. By 1911 the shares of Standard, of which about a fifth were held personally by Rockefeller, were valued at some $885 million. The great pile of gold was now growing so rapidly that philanthropic gifts, even of heroic proportions, continued to leave Rockefeller with a great and vigorously increasing personal fortune.

Admittedly there were strange contrasts between the unselfish sincerity of Rockefeller's religious and charitable principles on the one hand, and, on the other, the ruthlessness of the business procedures of that time and the fact that Rockefeller seemed quite willing to play the game without questioning the rules. But his personal and his business life were also characterized by meticulous stewardship, sustained earnestness, a methodical attention to details that did not in any way hamper extraordinary leaps of the imagination.

Allan Nevins wrote that the "art of stewardship was in one sense—the deepest sense of the word—the art in which Rockefeller most excelled."[29] The Baptist minister Frederick T. Gates, who was one of Rockefeller's most influential advisors, said that he had an "almost superhuman zeal for taking pains."[30]

We tend to think of John D. Rockefeller, Sr., as the only really rich man of his period. On the contrary, 4,047 men and women were listed[31] in 1892 as being worth a million dollars or more; and substantial gifts were made by many, as we are reminded by the names of Stanford, Armour, Drexel, Newberry, Widener, Crerar, etc. But it remains true that Carnegie and Rockefeller were the massive exceptions to the otherwise almost universal rule of each rich individual's directing his gifts to his local community.[32]

The "gospel of wealth" had been embraced by Rockefeller long before Andrew Carnegie put it into print. How he had shared his small savings with church and charity in the months of his first employment has already been mentioned. Rockefeller's membership in Baptist congregations was lifelong and his generous support of their causes and campaigns unceasing. Appeals for aid came from many other sources, and they multiplied across the decades. As his wealth accumulated, the importunities of "pertinacious callers," mail, and intimates grew in volume.

Rockefeller's periodic grants to the Theological Union of Chicago, which supported the Morgan Park Theological Seminary in that city, had led to his becoming vice president of the former in 1882. In turn, this led to an interest in and correspondence with William Rainey Harper, a young professor of Hebrew who was soon to leave the seminary for an endowed professorship of biblical literature at Yale University. The closing down in 1886 of the old University of Chicago, from which students had come to the seminary, worsened the seminary's plight. Rockefeller was urged to rescue the seminary and revive the university. For several years he took no decisive measures to do either, but characteristically inquired into all aspects of this situation and met many times and for hours with Baptist educational leaders. These meetings brought Rockefeller into contact with Frederick T. Gates, formerly a Baptist minister in Minneapolis and then secretary of the American Baptist Education Society.

Gates was an extraordinary person, who realized that Rockefeller—as is sadly the case with many rich and powerful persons—had few advisors with the courage to say exactly what they believed. Gates, moreover, had the insight to realize that Rockefeller wanted competent advice, however candid it might be.

Gates became associated with Rockefeller in 1892, and his imagination, wisdom, courage, candor, and audacity played a tremendous role in the development of the Rockefeller philanthropies. This was the man who, with a voice which as Raymond B. Fosdick has said "thundered from Sinai,"[33] warned the elder Rockefeller, "Your fortune is rolling up, rolling up like an avalanche. You must keep up with it! You must distribute it faster than it grows!" This was the man who, at his last meeting of the board of trustees of the Rockefeller Foundation, passionately said to his colleagues: "When you die and come to approach the judgment of Almighty God, what do you think He will demand of you? Do you for an instant presume to believe that He will inquire into your petty failures or your trivial virtues? No! He will ask just one question: *What did you do as a trustee of the Rockefeller Foundation?*"[34]

It cannot be said that Mr. Rockefeller lacked for candid and spirited advisors. Certainly he and the two generations of John Rockefellers after him have been extremely solicitous about obtaining competent and frank advice and have been open-minded about weighing it. What Mr. Rockefeller did was greatly affected by the counsel he received. But in the last analysis the conclusions he reached were the result of the earnest, sustained, and precise thinking which he himself brought to bear.

Mr. Rockefeller differed essentially from the earlier self-seeking philanthropists, who had been chiefly interested in perpetuating their own fame and in atoning for their sins. He did make his gifts, the record indicates, as an obligation of religious duty: but, as the New York *Sun* said in 1896 about his gifts to the University of Chicago, "he has made the gifts quietly, modestly, and without in the least seeking for popular applause. . . ."

Mr. Rockefeller was without any doubt influenced by Carnegie's "Gospel of Wealth." He wrote Carnegie an enthusiastic letter of congratulation; told him, ". . . be assured, your example will bear fruits . . ."; and, when the first Rockefeller general philanthropic board was founded, Carnegie was soon made a trustee and served for eleven years.

Whether or not influenced by Carnegie's ideas on this particular point, John D. Rockefeller, Sr., did give away huge sums of money while he was alive. The original gift of $600,000, announced by Gates for the establishment of a well-equipped college at Chicago, was the precursor of endowments and payments to the university which would eventually aggregate $35 million. The Rockefeller Foundation (1913) is the largest of the four main benevolent corporations established by John D. Rockefeller. The other three are the Rockefeller Institute for Medical Research (now the Rockefeller University) (1901), the General Education Board (1903), and the Laura Spelman Rockefeller Memorial (1918), the last named uniting with the Rockefeller Foundation in 1929.

These four institutions received a total of $446,719,371.22, as calculated in terms of market value on the days when the gifts were made. John Davison Rockefeller would, without doubt, approve of the detailed accuracy of that figure.

The way in which Rockefeller established the management and control of these philanthropies seems clearly to indicate that he had advanced substantially beyond the confident assurance of Carnegie of his own "superior wisdom, experience, and ability to adminster." It was Rockefeller's idea from the first that these great funds should be vested in charitable corporations governed objectively by distinguished, able, and really independent boards of trustees and served by officers of specialized training and experience, devoting all their energies to the continuous study of opportunities for service. Scientific, disciplined, and efficient philanthropy became a reality.

At this juncture in our story it may be useful to recount two incidents. When the Rockefeller Foundation was started, there was a provision that up to 10 percent of the grants in any one year might be designated by the founder himself. Over a few early years there were such "founder's specifications." But then the practice was stopped at the request of Rockefeller himself, who indicated to the trustees that he had become convinced this was an unwise provision.

Secondly, it is, I think, interesting that in 1935, shortly before Raymond B. Fosdick became president of the Rockefeller Foundation, he called on John D. Rockefeller, Sr., at his home in

Florida. Fosdick explained that there had been some important recent developments in Rockefeller Foundation program and policy, and he quite naturally offered to tell Rockefeller as much about these new ideas as he wished to know. Rockefeller responded, in effect, that he had complete confidence in the organization and in the officers who were currently responsible. It would not be necessary to go into any detailed account.

Rockefeller was by that time an elderly man, but it is unnecessary, and probably incorrect, to interpret this episode as meaning that the founder of the Rockefeller Foundation had ever lost interest in the organization or its activities. Rockefeller had in many other connections demonstrated that he liked to chart a course, build an organization, and then depend upon trust and confidence. This did not mean that he had ceased to be interested. It did mean that he had a genius for organization and for picking men, together with that rare capacity for self-limitation which elicits from subordinates and associates the very best that is in them.

Allan Nevins said in his well-known biography of Rockefeller, "It was to be true of John D. Sr. throughout his life, as it was said of his mother, that they were 'not given to fun.' " But the biographer's comment seems completely to have missed sight of the fact, strongly emphasized to me by one of his grandsons, that for at least the last quarter century of John Davison Rockefeller's life he was a notably happy and relaxed man.

His view of philanthropy represented a new vision of the maturing relationship of a donor to the conduct of a great philanthropy. This is that vision: Our social and economic system makes possible the accumulation of a great fortune. The person who amasses that fortune makes reasonable provision for his heirs; then he turns the rest of the money back to the society which has made the fortune possible, under the administration of competent and experienced persons, who then seek to apply this money to promote understanding of the basic problems of society and to improve and enrich the lives of all men.

Carnegie also deserves the highest marks for his role. He must have liberalized his own concepts beyond the atmosphere of personal superiority which colored his 1889 statement. For, when in 1902—the same year in which Rockefeller founded the General

Education Board—Carnegie founded the Carnegie Institution of Washington, that outstanding organization was established "to encourage, in the broadest and most liberal manner, investigation, research, and discovery, and the application of knowledge to the improvement of mankind."

The noble ideas of Carnegie and Rockefeller had great impact. The Milbank Memorial Fund was established in 1905, during which year a second Carnegie board came into being—the Carnegie Foundation for the Advancement of Teaching. In 1907 the Russell Sage Foundation was created, and three years later the third Carnegie board—the Carnegie Endowment for International Peace. The Carnegie Corporation of New York, the largest and most general in scope of the Carnegie benefactions, was started in 1911; and the Rockefeller Foundation, the giant of the early foundations, in 1913. The Cleveland Foundation, first of the community trusts, was created in 1914. Clearly an effective and stimulating impetus had been given to the philanthropic concept.

The idea of charitable giving is ancient, and men have long used gifts to enhance their reputations, to preserve their fame, and to atone for their sins. Unselfishness has also played a great role, but emotionally inspired unselfishness often responds to the immediate instance of need, without attempting to weigh alternatives and without even considering the underlying problems of cause.

For hundreds and hundreds of years there have been "foundations." But it is notable that the eleventh edition of the Encyclopaedia Britannica, published in 1910, contains no reference in the index to "foundations" as the word is used in this book, while the only entries under that word refer to buildings or masonry or, very briefly, to the endowments of English colleges, monasteries, or hospitals. Philanthropic foundations, as we know them today, were just beginning to emerge in 1910. There have of course been isolated instances of earlier attempts to discipline and rationalize philanthropy. But the turn of the last century saw a combination of resource and vision that led to a new level of performance and wholly new potentialities.

CHAPTER 5

Kinds of Foundations

A wide range of institutions and organizations use the word "foundation" in their titles. Some of these, such as certain old colleges and hospitals in England, have a completely sound legal and historical right to use the word; and yet they are not at all what we now think of, in the United States, when we use the word "foundation." The terminology concerning foundations is, unfortunately, both complicated and confusing. There are many existing organizations called foundations which do not form any important part of our topic, and there are some which are very important to us which are not called "foundations" at all.

F. Emerson Andrews has suggested that an American philanthropic foundation

is nongovernmental,
is nonprofit,
has a principal fund of its own,
is managed by its own trustees and directors,
is established to maintain or aid social,
    educational, charitable, religious, or
    other activities serving the common welfare.

This book adopts the Andrews description as the best and most authoritative.

These five specifications exclude a number of organizations highly useful to society like the National Science Foundation, the National Institutes of Health, and granting agencies associated with the Department of Defense and other branches of federal, state, and even municipal governments.[1] But this book deals only with *private* philanthropy.

39

Other very useful agencies fail to meet the third condition above. Thus the Nutrition Foundation makes grants to aid biochemical and physiological studies of nutritional problems no different in any important way from others which such an organization as the Rockefeller Foundation might support. But, although the Nutrition Foundation at any one moment may have sizable assets,[2] it does not in the accepted sense have "a principal fund of its own"; it obtains its money from grants made to it by various food industries and to some lesser extent by other foundations. In a similar manner, the Conservation Foundation, has organized and supported some highly valuable studies and research projects. Such a group acts as a sort of philanthropic middle man, collecting money from individuals, industries, and foundations which do possess capital funds of their own, and then administering these funds in the field of its special interest and competence.[3] They are "funnel foundations," through which passes capital, obtained elsewhere, on its way to support certain activities.

Such organizations are nonprofit, so that gifts to them are tax-exempt. There are truly excellent examples, such as the two mentioned, of these middle-man agencies or funnel foundations.

Other organizations, some with the word "foundation" in their title, collect funds from the general public and devote their net resources (after money-raising and administrative costs) to aiding research on individual diseases or groups of diseases, assisting treatment, and sponsoring educational efforts relating to the diseases in question. Examples are the National Foundation (successor to the National Foundation for Infantile Paralysis), the Arthritis and Rheumatism Foundation, the American Foundation for the Blind, the Deafness Research Foundation, and the Allergy Foundation. These voluntary health agencies, not foundations in the sense of the Andrews definition, and are not considered here.

Still another type of organization is illustrated by the Fund for the Advancement of Education, the Council on Library Resources, and the Fund for Adult Education, now dissolved. These might be called "satellite foundations," for they are agencies with officers, staffs, and trustees of their own, but with all their financial resources coming from *another* foundation, in the cases cited from the Ford Foundation. Again they do not satisfy the third defining condition of having a principal fund of their own; and in so far as they receive any attention here they will be identified with the parent foundation of which they are satellites.

Some organizations, associations, and enterprises which do not at all correspond to the five specifications call themselves "foundations" perhaps because they consider this word to have prestige value. Some of these groups do have certain eleemosynary functions, but other groups bear little or no relation to philanthropic activity. The latter have occasioned the comment: "In a society where it is a crime to impersonate the meter reader of a gas company, one should consider the possibility that it is a considerably more heinous offense against the common weal to impersonate a philanthropy."[4]

Andrews has suggested[5] five classifications of private organizations which do, or at least can, conform to all of his specifications. With one minor change in his terminology, Andrews' five classes are:

1. General purpose foundations
2. Special purpose foundations
3. Family or personal foundations
4. Corporation (or company-sponsored) foundations
5. Community foundations

COMMUNITY FOUNDATIONS

A former president of the Cleveland Trust Company, Frederick H. Goff, is credited with conceiving and implementing a plan to assure good management of local charitable gifts made in perpetuity. Banks, serving as corporate trustees, would be given responsibility for the fiscal management of the funds, and a committee of representative community leaders would have the sole authority to decide how the funds were to be used for philanthropic purposes. The *cy pres* problem was handled by specifying that "To this group of citizens would be given the ultimate power, if literal compliance with the donor's instructions became impossible, impracticable, unnecessary, or undesirable, so to amend the specifications for the use of the funds that the donor's intent could still be carried out effectively."[6]

The first of this new type of philanthropic organization was the Cleveland Foundation, organized in 1914. Among early community foundations are the Chicago Community Trust, the Permanent Charity Fund of Boston, and the Minneapolis, Indianapolis, Youngstown, and Buffalo foundations.

These foundations are a composite of several or many individual philanthropies under common, really community, control. Their assets come from bequests, living donors, endowments, family foundations, and open-end trusts.

During the Depression of the thirties and through the years of World War II, a good many community foundations lapsed into inactivity, but in the postwar period new community foundations emerged and a few dormant ones were reactivated. The formation of the National Committee on Foundations and Trusts for Community Welfare in 1949 gave the movement impetus and stimulation, and in 1957 this committee evolved into the National Council on Community Foundations. This council, with a full-time staff, serves the existing community foundations and encourages the establishment of new ones by coordinating their activities and by furnishing information and advice. In 1964, it was reorganized and renamed the Council on Foundations, the omission of the previous word "Community" conforming to the fact that it now accepts membership from among all categories of foundations.

COMPANY-SPONSORED FOUNDATIONS

Foundations established by companies and corporations, legally separate from the parent companies but with trustees, officers, and board members mainly from their own ranks, are today the second most numerous grouping in the philanthropic fund area, with family and personal foundations the most numerous.

Company-sponsored foundations existed as far back as the late twenties. At present there are more than twenty times as many as there were in the thirties, and their giving has increased in even greater ratio. Although there were other significant influences, the levels of corporate taxation, and more particularly the excess-profits taxes, are significantly related to the sharp increases in the number of company-sponsored foundations as well as to the volume of funds granted by the existent ones. Excess-profits taxes temporarily ceased in 1945, but were resumed in mid-1950 and continued until the end of 1953 throughout American involvement in the hostilities in Korea. The latter span of three and a half years saw the establishment of nearly half the company-sponsored foundations now in existence.

FAMILY OR PERSONAL FOUNDATIONS

The family foundation is characteristically the creation of a living individual or of a group of related living persons. A family foundation may eventually be the recipient of bequests from the establishing donors, but its usual objective is to organize and regulate giving for living individuals, and to do this through a procedure which achieves tax exemption for income otherwise taxable.

Generally speaking, an individual or family establishing such a foundation obtains no greater tax advantage than if the same gifts were made directly to hospitals, churches, colleges, the Red Cross, CARE, etc. However, it is possible with a family foundation, as with the company foundation, to maintain a smoother level of annual giving than from uneven annual income. The foundation acts for the family as a reservoir into which they can put, as a *contribution to capital,* a maximum deductible gift of 20 percent of current income in any one year. The foundation, under existing statutes, must expend its income annually, but that income is the earnings on the capital gifts it has received, not the gifts themselves. Here the family foundation achieves its main purpose of serving as a channel for the founder's current giving, but in addition provides a control of the volume of giving that would not be available to the donor without loss of some tax exemption if no foundation intermediary existed.

The assets of family foundations at any given moment are not a good indicator of their potential as givers. Among the estimated 3,520 family foundations in the 1964 *Directory* listing, a fair number in 1963, for example, granted amounts several times larger than their stated current assets, this being possible because of contributions made to the foundation during the same year.

The high personal income taxes during World War II caused a great increase in the number of family foundations. Often they began small, and the great majority have remained so. At the outset only a few adopted any of the physical and organizational appurtenances of the general purpose foundations. A relatively small number have developed them since. That is to say they seldom have private office quarters, staff unrelated to the donors, or trustees with broad representation. In all but a small number of cases, the physical existence of the family foundations is to be found in a set of ledgers and files in the office of an attorney, banker, or accountant, or in the donor's business establishment.

A family foundation may start small, but it need not remain so. The Ford Foundation, the present giant among all the foundations of the world, began as a family foundation; and the Rockefeller Brothers Fund has many of the characteristics of a family foundation.

SPECIAL PURPOSE FOUNDATIONS

A foundation of rather modest size, either realizing that it cannot effectively cover the whole waterfront, or desiring to emphasize the particular interest of the founder, may pick out some special field of interest—archaeology, or creative writing, or price stabilization, or the training of religious leaders, or enzyme chemistry, or the ballet, and concentrate on that chosen field.

The existence among them of some rather silly "special purpose foundations" should surprise no one, human nature being such as it is and the decay of judgment in later years being a tragic but not unfamiliar phenomenon. There are, of course, many spectacular examples. Thomas Nash left a sum in trust to assure that the bell ringers of his church in Bath, England, ring the whole peal of bells with their clappers muffled for twelve hours each year on the anniversary of his wedding, and that each year on the anniversary of his death they ring "merry mirthful peals, unmuffled . . . in joyful commemoration of my happy release from domestic tyranny and wretchedness."

Equally ludicrous examples from recent years and from our own country could be produced. Such examples would be amusing but misleading; for many, and probably most, restricted funds serve worthwhile ends and are reasonably well managed. Among the special purpose foundations there are several medium- and even fairly large-sized institutions which have achieved considerable stature in the field of philanthropy.

The Carnegie Endowment for International Peace is one such. It spends roughly $1 million annually, this being the income on capital funds of approximately $39.7 million, together with grants from other foundations. It is an operating organization rather than a grant-making one, and, although its program covers a considerable variety of activities, it is nevertheless "special purpose" in that all of its efforts are directed to the goal of promoting international peace and understanding. It well illustrates the fact that a "special purpose" need not at all be a trivial one.

Special purpose foundations are generally what they are by reason of the terms of the will or trust instrument with which they were established. Only infrequently do they come into existence through incorporation, as do many, if not most, other foundations.

The aims of special purpose foundations are characteristically specific and sometimes narrow. They differ from organizations in the general purpose category principally in the restricted character of their missions, no significant departure from the stipulated activity ordinarily being allowed.

From time to time, an irresponsible critic will cite one or another of the small special purpose foundations in an attempt to ridicule modern philanthropy. They lend themselves to such uses by reason of the specificity of their objectives, which the passage of time often renders obsolete or even senseless. A foundation permanently dedicated to the feeding of horses looks pretty foolish by the time automobiles and trucks have taken over transport.

The disadvantages of restricted or special purpose funds do not necessarily reside in their focus on certain objectives, but more often in the rigidity of their conditions. With respect to their sometimes rather precise limitations, it is also important to recognize that a considerable number of special research foundations, assuming competent and responsible management of them, adds up from the point of view of society to the equivalent of a large and first-rate "general" foundation. Thus to a large extent the distinction between the categories 1 and 2 of page 41 is a rather artificial matter of statistics, rather than a significant one of difference in overall service to society.

GENERAL PURPOSE FOUNDATIONS

A foundation cannot effectively be general purpose unless it has:

1. Substantial size.

2. Boards or trustee bodies with representation from a number of facets of society, i.e., industry, education, research, law, commerce, public life, etc.

3. A separate staff of administrators and specialists employed to execute the board's policies by studying and evaluating proposals for aid, and by recommending these to the board for negative or positive action. In most cases the foundation makes grants to other agencies which themselves carry out the actual programs. In such cases the foundation should be described as "grant-making" and "non-operating." In other cases a staff employed by the foundation itself carries out the studies or other activities to which the foundation's resources are dedicated; such should be called "operating foundations." Or a foundation may in part be grant-making (appropriating research funds, for example, to a university) and in part operating (conducting a public health campaign in some part of the world, for example, with a staff of doctors, sanitary engineers, and so forth in the direct employ of the foundation).

4. Flexibility of program so that new areas of endeavor are regularly under consideration. These reviews sometimes lead to revised decisions concerning the employment of the foundation's resources, newer fields of emphasis replacing those to which substantial contribution has already been made. Such flexibility requires a broad mandate from the founder(s) to accommodate a range of program interests varied as well as changing; e.g., "the welfare of mankind."

These four characteristics should always apply to a general purpose foundation, but this is not universally the case.

For example, certain foundations are general purpose in the range and nature of the grants made, but this breadth does not necessarily reflect an established and publicly announced policy, or the result of careful studies by professionally competent staffs. On the contrary, the diversity may primarily reflect the personal reaction of a small number of very influential officers, or even the personal prejudices of the founder himself. This is more likely to be the case with foundations which do not issue full and informative annual or biennial reports.

General purpose foundations are sometimes referred to as "general purpose or research foundations." Concern for the useful application of existing knowledge is certainly highly desirable and laudable; but an accompanying concern for research and for the gaining of new knowledge is a hallmark of the truly great foundations.

No one of the general purpose foundations has been so naïve as to suppose that it can effectively tackle all subjects and all problems. Some, permitted by their charters to be broad in outlook, have chosen to concentrate within some one important area, such as medical education and research. Choosing the whole of some one broad area, such as all aspects of medicine and health, still permits the designation "general purpose"; whereas charter restriction to a particular disease would entail the designation "special purpose."

It will clarify all of these points if we look briefly at the primary characteristics of some of the largest organizations classified by the Foundation Library Center authorities as general purpose foundations. The fourteen largest *general purpose* foundations are also, incidentally, the fourteen largest foundations regardless of type. Although they are all officially classified as *general purpose,* some share the characteristics of special purpose and of family foundations.

THE FORD FOUNDATION

Ford has a broad program covering education, economic development and administration, public affairs, humanities and the arts, international training and research, international affairs, population, and overseas development activities including agriculture, education, public administration, family planning, and economic research. It has a broadly representational board of trustees of fifteen, eight "executive officers" with twenty-eight major assistants, thirty-three officers concerned with the administration of the various divisions of their program, and some sixty-seven additional representatives located abroad in Asia, the Middle East, Africa, Latin America, and elsewhere.

TABLE 1

THE FOURTEEN LARGEST GENERAL PURPOSE FOUNDATIONS

Foundation	Assets (millions)
1. Ford Foundation (Sept. 30, 1964)	$4097.6
2. Rockefeller Foundation	861.9
3. Duke Endowment	596.0
4. Kellogg (W. K.) Foundation (Aug. 31, 1964)	460.6
5. Mott (Charles Stewart) Foundation	418.0
6. Hartford (The John A.) Foundation, Inc.	397.0
7. Carnegie Corporation of New York (Sept. 30, 1964)	334.0
8. Sloan (Alfred P.) Foundation	297.7
9. Bishop (Bernice P.) Estate (June 30, 1964)	287.0
10. Pew Memorial Trust	264.0
11. Longwood Foundation, Inc. (Sept. 30, 1965)	251.0
12. Moody Foundation	242.0
13. Lilly Endowment	233.6
14. Rockefeller Brothers Fund	208.0

NOTE: The assets are here stated in terms of market value as of December 31, 1964, except in the cases noted.

Of the assets stated in Table 1, approximately $2,678.7 million corresponds to the foundation's holding in Ford Motor Company nonvoting stock. In the fiscal year covered in their 1964 report, the total of grants and expenses in projects administered by Ford was $234.9 million.

THE ROCKEFELLER FOUNDATION

The Rockefeller Foundation has over the years maintained a broad program in the medical sciences, public health, natural sciences, agriculture, social sciences, and humanities. At present its activities are organized in relation to five great interdisciplinary objectives: to aid in the conquest of hunger, to contribute to the understanding and solution of problems arising from the growth of world population, to help strengthen strategically located universities in developing countries, to work toward the provision of equal opportunities to all persons regardless of race, and to promote cultural activities in the United States.

The broadly representational board of trustees has twenty members, there are ten "principal officers," six of whom are corporate officers and four major program officers; thirty-eight additional program officers, twenty-five based in New York and thirteen in the field; and a professional staff numbering seventy-one. Programs are operated in Latin America, India, Africa, the Philippines, and elsewhere.

Of the assets stated in Table I, approximately $553 million (at market) are in six oil stocks. In 1964 Rockefeller made appropriations totaling $40.4 million, this being $11.3 in excess of its income for that year.

THE DUKE ENDOWMENT

The program of the Duke Endowment is indicated by the fact that during 1964 it gave over $12.2 million to four universities, three in North Carolina and one in South Carolina; $4.1 million to hospitals and orphanages in the same two states; and about a third of a million dollars for religious purposes in the same two states (the support of superannuated preachers, and the building and support of rural Methodist churches). Over half of the total grants for the years ($7.75 million) went to Duke University.

The board of trustees of fifteen includes nine associated with the Duke Power Company, and four major officers of the endowment. For the various segments of the program (educational institutions, hospitals and orphanages, and rural churches) there are committees, the members chosen from the board of trustees.

Of the assets stated in Table I, approximately $475.8 million (market) corresponds to its holding in the stock of the Duke Power Company. In the year ending December 31, 1964, this foundation made grants totaling $16.9 million, this being $1.2 million in excess of income during that year.

THE W. K. KELLOGG FOUNDATION.

The official literature states that "the Foundation itself does not have programs." The major fields in which it assists the programs of "people, agencies, institutions, communities, states, and countries with problems to solve" are medicine, hospitals, dentistry, public health, and nursing in the United States, Latin America, and Canada; education in the United States and elsewhere; and agriculture in the United States, Latin America, Scandinavia, England, and elsewhere.

The board of trustees numbers nine, plus two honorary members. Only one member of the board appears to have any direct association with the Kellogg Company. In addition to four general officers, there is a staff of seven in charge of the various divisions of activities. They rely on publicly announced professional advisory committees (in agriculture, dentistry, hospitals, medicine, and nursing), most of whose members hold important academic posts.

The Kellogg Foundation is primarily concerned "with the application of knowledge, rather than its creation through basic research."

Of the assets stated in Table 1, $413.7 million corresponds to holding of stock in the Kellogg Company. The annual level of grants is somewhat over $10 million.

THE CHARLES STEWART MOTT FOUNDATION

While the charter of this foundation is indeed broad, its concerns have been centered in Flint, Michigan, and on education and community welfare, including health and recreation services. Most of the program is operated through the Flint Board of Education. Some support has been given to universities, for the most part in the State of Michigan, and for a program of basic economic education through the Flint Board of Education and the University of Chicago.

There are six trustees, four of them members of the Mott family. The investment portfolio is diversified although heavily in the United States Sugar Corporation, and in 1963 the foundation received 1,826,421 shares of General Motors stock having a fair market value of $143 million at the close of that year.

THE JOHN A. HARTFORD FOUNDATION

The primary emphasis of the Hartford Foundation is on medical research, with a special interest in clinical research in hospitals.

Other than these medical grants it contributes to Protestant, Catholic, and Jewish charities in New York City, and makes a very occasional exceptional grant, such as to Lincoln Center for the Performing Arts. In 1964 it made sixty-six appropriations averaging slightly more than $200,000 each.

Of the ten-member board of trustees, the president and secretary are also high officers of the A. & P. Company. On the officer staff are listed three persons, one an administrative assistant and one an assistant secretary. Administrative overhead is only slightly over one percent of the annual level of grants, substantially lower than is customary.

Of the assets stated in Table 1, $346.3 million corresponds to their holding of stock in The Great Atlantic and Pacific Tea Company. The annual total of grants is about $12 million.

THE CARNEGIE CORPORATION OF NEW YORK

The primary emphasis of the Carnegie program is on education, with more than one-fourth of income, during a recent year, given for activities to improve the education of disadvantaged Americans. This foundation has been particularly concerned with the support of educational innovation—new methods, new facilities, new modes of organization; with aid to adult education; with studies of the learning process; with the education of teachers; and with the development of educational leadership. It also supports occasional projects in international affairs, and in public affairs in the United States. It supports fellowships and research in the social sciences through grants to the Social Science Research Council, and devotes 7.4 percent of its income (amounting to at least a half million dollars annually) to its Commonwealth Program, which, during the year in question, involved aid to education in eleven universities in Africa.

There are a board of trustees of fifteen, a staff of twenty-four including six general officers, one special program director with an assistant, and a number of executive associates, executive assistants, and administrative assistants.

The assets stated in Table 1 are invested in a widely diversified portfolio. The grants for the fiscal year ending September 30, 1964, totaled slightly more than $12.4 million.

THE ALFRED P. SLOAN FOUNDATION

The Sloan Foundation program includes the physical sciences, mathematics, and engineering; medical research (primarily in the cancer field); business administration and economic research; and education, with a heavy emphasis on scholarship and fellowship aid to gifted individuals, and on the freedom and flexibility of the aid to basic research. In geographical terms, the Sloan Foundation is almost completely restricted to the United States, but an occasional foreign grant is made, usually because of some relation to activities in our own country.

The board of trustees numbers eighteen; the officer staff includes six principal officers.

Of the assets stated in Table 1, approximately $116.7 million corresponds to its holding in General Motors. The total of grants in 1964 was $14.5 million.

THE BERNICE P. BISHOP ESTATE

When founded in 1884 in Hawaii, the estate was intended as a perpetual trust, initially to establish and maintain two secondary schools for public education. In 1963 the courts ruled favorably on the estate's petition to broaden its scope to include secondary scholarships, extension service aid to other schools where there are concentrations of Hawaiians, and operation of an occupational department for senior high school and more advanced students. The program remains limited to the State of Hawaii.

There are five trustees selected by a majority of the State Supreme Court; offices rotate among trustees annually.

THE PEW MEMORIAL TRUST

This foundation has as yet issued no public report. Of a total of slightly more than $3.9 million of grants made in 1964, $1.46 million went for educational purposes, $730,000 for religious purposes, $980,000 for medical research and hospitals, and $740,000 for purposes described as charitable.

Of capital holdings of $264 million (market) nearly $219 million is represented by common stock in the Sun Oil Company.

THE LONGWOOD FOUNDATION

The responsibilities and duties of the Longwood Foundation are primarily the support, management, maintenance, and development of Longwood Gardens near Kennett Square, Pennsylvania. The foundation also has a commitment toward support of the new Eleutherian Mills Historical Library near Wilmington, Delaware. Outside of these two activities the Longwood Foundation has no formally constituted program. In recent years, however, the foundation has been able to allocate funds for a few but rather infrequent one-time capital grants for educational and hospital purposes.

The foundation has seven officers and trustees, six of whom are members of the du Pont family.

The total expenditures of the Longwood Foundation for 1965 were $6.9 million. The original capital was roughly $50 million, consisting of some $33 million in Christiana Securities, Inc., plus substantial General Motors holdings. The General Motors shares were all sold, and the portfolio has been diversified.

THE MOODY FOUNDATION

This foundation has as yet issued no public report. The latest available information lists assets in 1964 of $242.0 million. Grants in the year 1964 (all within the State of Texas) are listed at $4.2 million. There is only one paid officer, and the majority of the trustees appear to be family members.

THE LILLY ENDOWMENT

About half of the annual grants of the Lilly Endowment are devoted to educational projects, with heavy emphasis on education in the State of Indiana. About one-quarter of its expenditures go to religious purposes, these grants being broadly distributed. Roughly the remaining quarter of grants is devoted to community services, nearly 70 percent within the State of Indiana.

Of the board of directors of six, three are officers of Eli Lilly & Company and three are members of the Lilly family. Of the six officers of the Lilly Endowment, the president, vice president, and treasurer are members of the Lilly family or are connected with the Lilly Company. There are three program officers, each responsible for one of the segments of the program.

Of the assets stated in Table I, $232.9 million represents holdings of stock of Eli Lilly & Company. The annual level of grants is now just over $5 million.

ROCKEFELLER BROTHERS FUND

The "General Program" of the Rockefeller Brothers Fund consists primarily of grants to more than a hundred philanthropic organizations, many of them in the New York area, which deal with "such community needs as civic improvement, cultural advancement, education, health, religion, and welfare." Its "Special Program" includes both support to and operation of experimental or new undertakings in the fields of "international relations and understanding, strengthened national life, and conservation, population, and resources."[7]

The board of trustees of eleven is almost wholly composed of members of the Rockefeller family, including, as the name would indicate, the five sons of John D. Rockefeller, Jr. The list of "Officers and Associates," in addition to Laurance S. Rockefeller, who is president, and David Rockefeller, who is vice president, includes a director and a staff of fourteen.

The capital assets of this foundation are invested in a broadly diversified portfolio. The present annual level of grants is about $8 million, the fund's program being "supported in part by annual trustee contributions."

These highly condensed descriptions make several things clear.

First, these foundations have been classified as "general purpose" to some considerable extent on the basis of the breadth of their charter provisions and hence of their *potential* breadth of program.

As regards the functional breadth of their actual programs, of the fourteen largest dealt with above, the Ford, Rockefeller, Kellog, Carnegie, and Sloan are in a first broadest category, whereas the others have chosen for themselves a somewhat less wide range of fields.

As regards the geographic spread of the programs, the Ford,

Rockefeller, Kellogg, and Carnegie are in a first widest category, the Hartford, Sloan, and Rockefeller Brothers Fund in a second, and the others in a third.

As regards the broadly representative character of the boards of trustees, the Rockefeller, Ford, Carnegie, and Sloan are in a first category, and the others are in a second.

These categorizations are in no instance intended to constitute adverse criticism. The Duke Endowment is really a "regional" foundation, as is also partly true of the Lilly. The Mott Foundation and the Rockefeller Brothers Fund have many of the characteristics of "family foundations" and the latter could well be taken as a fine model for one. The Hartford has chosen to specialize in medical research, certainly a splendid choice. The Kellogg chooses to emphasize applications rather than research; and it is a healthy thing to have at least one large foundation take this position.

All this again emphasizes the value of diversity, at the same time complicating any attempt to bring foundations under a tidy scheme of description. As the above examples illustrate, a number of "foundations," in their legal titles at least, are not specifically labeled as foundations: the Carnegie *Corporation,* the Rockefeller Brothers *Fund,* the Duke *Endowment,* the Pew Memorial *Trust,* and the Bernice P. Bishop *Estate,* to name five, each with an endowment of more than $100 million.

In his classical description Andrews states that characteristic concerns of foundations include "social, educational, charitable, religious, and other activities serving the common welfare."

This book does not attempt any comprehensive survey of the grants made by community and family foundations, giving relatively small emphasis to those whose activities are for the most part covered by the words "charitable" and "religious" (this also partly applies to company foundations). Activities of this sort are easy to understand and are hence generally understood. Furthermore, the public has demonstrated that they are, generally speaking, convinced of the desirability of such activities.

It might, at first thought, be assumed that for the reasons just stated for "charitable" and "religious," we could also minimize our attention to the word "educational." Everyone approves of education, everyone is interested in education, and almost everyone seems to think that he understands what the word means or ought to mean. Support of education, moreover, is rapidly increasing and is spreading to many agencies.

We cannot, however, afford to disregard the educational activities of foundations, partly because they are so important, partly because they are sometimes suspect, but chiefly because education and research are really inseparable.

The word "social" will merit closer and more extensive attention, for clearly one body of vigorous, and indeed sometimes vehement, criticism comes from those who think that foundations are sponsoring and promulgating improper social ideas—that is to say, social ideas which do not coincide with those of the critics.

Perhaps the most curious fact, however, is the extent to which we will be concerned with the somewhat innocuous and even mysterious word "other."

For this not very descriptive word covers a wide range of activities relating to the enrichment of life through assistance to all the creative arts, as well as a very large body of activity dedicated to the uncovering of new knowledge and to the useful application of that new knowledge in the medical, biological, agricultural, physical, and all other sciences, including basic research in the social sciences.

Although this book deals with only a very small fraction of what might be called "the American charitable dollar," it covers a substantial fraction of the financial resources held by all the private philanthropic organizations in our country. More significantly, the great general purpose foundations most clearly exemplify the broadened and deepened vision of disciplined, responsible, and sometimes venturesome philanthropy which is so largely an invention of our national culture, and which was to so great an extent launched near the turn of the century by Carnegie and Rockefeller.

CHAPTER 6

The Arithmetic, Chronological, and Geographic Facts About Foundations

You can't count chickens unless you know what a chicken is. At least partly because of the confusion as to what constitutes a foundation, there is no precise agreement as to how many there are in the United States. Representative Wright Patman has repeatedly used the figure 45,124. It is a fact that, in the year 1960, 45,124 copies of the 990-A information form, which our federal law requires of all tax-exempt organizations, were filled out. But only part of that large number are foundations in the ordinary usage of that word, and many others are civic, educational, welfare, and religious organizations. Only 200 are large foundations, and slightly more than 6,000 have substantial assets.

The Foundation Library Center is the authoritative source for many kinds of information about the philanthropic foundations of the United States. A volume which it released in January, 1964, lists and describes 6,007 American foundations.[1] The files of the center also contain information concerning roughly 9,000 additional foundations, all classed as "very small," no one having assets of as much as $100,000 or making grants of as much as $10,000 a year.[2]

Of the 6,007 foundations larger than "very small" there are 4,948 "small" foundations (with assets up to $1 million), 847 "intermediate" foundations (assets ranging from $1 million to $10 million), and 176 "large" foundations (assets more than $10 million).

Until 1950, information concerning the number of foundations in the United States was decidedly vague. The older directories,

as is now evident, omitted—simply because of lack of information
—more foundations than they listed.

Since 1950, however, nearly all parts of the information returns
which for some time foundations had been making to the Internal
Revenue Service have been open to public inspection. From this
principal source, and after much checking and cross checking, the
Foundation Library Center has by now been able to produce the
following information:[3]

TABLE 2

THE CHRONOLOGY OF THE ESTABLISHMENT OF FOUNDATIONS[4] IN THE
UNITED STATES

Decade	Number of Foundations Established
Before 1900	18
1900-1909	18
1910-1919	76
1920-1929	173
1930-1939	288
1940-1949	1,638
1950-1959	2,839
	5,050

As regards the time of creation, Figure I omits about 9,000
"very small" foundations, but their total combined assets are so
small, as compared to the assets of those listed, that no important
distortion results from their omission. This large number of very
small foundations, incidentally, is a recent phenomenon. A sampling procedure indicates that of the very small ones, less than I
percent were established before 1940, and 72 percent have been
established since 1950. The spurt in the decade following 1940
seems to be significantly due to the high tax rates resulting from
World War II, to the emergence of company-sponsored foundations, and to a new emphasis upon family foundations with living
donors.[5]

The 6,007 foundations listed in the current *Directory* are widely
but by no means uniformly distributed. As might be guessed, by far
the largest number (1,594) are located in New York State. The

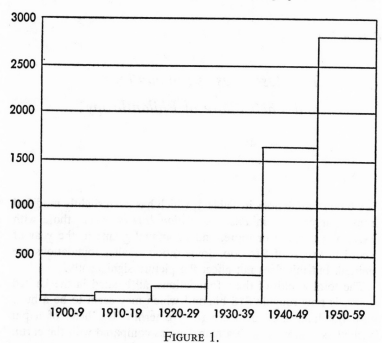

FIGURE 1.

The Number of Foundations[4]
Created in Different Decades

count of the top ten then drops abruptly to 467 in Illinois, 402 in Pennsylvania, 396 in Ohio, 376 in California, 309 in Massachusetts, 286 in Texas, 214 in Michigan, 161 in Missouri, and 161 in Wisconsin. Following Wisconsin in the list there are five more states with more than a hundred each, seven (including the District of Columbia) with more than fifty but less than a hundred, nine with twenty-five or more but less than fifty. The list goes on with a steady but slow drop in the number of foundations per state, ending up with two each in New Mexico and South Dakota, one each in Alaska and the Virgin Islands, and none in North Dakota.

CHAPTER 7

The Resources of Foundations
and Their Share of Philanthropy

The 6,007 foundations in Table 3, which has been slightly modified from a larger table in *The Foundation Directory*, are those with assets of $100,000 or more, and/or annual grants in the year of record in excess of $10,000. Some 9,000 smaller foundations are omitted, but this does not affect the picture significantly.

The total wealth of these foundations, all located in the United States, is now roughly $18 billion,[1] which may seem to be a huge sum. But large and small are relative terms. The head of a pin is small as compared with a man, tiny as compared with the earth, and almost infinitesimal as compared with the universe. Yet the head of a pin is a huge object in the world of ultimate physical particles, containing more atoms of iron than there are stars in our galaxy.

The figure of roughly $18 billion can be judged only in the framework of other national totals. Thus the permanent wealth of these six thousand foundations is somewhat less than the wealth of one single corporation—the American Telephone and Telegraph Company. Also, two years of annual national spending for tobacco would more than double the permanent endowment of all foundations, and the annual national spending for toys is just about twice the national annual expenditures of all foundations. The federally financed annual costs of research (*research,* not *research and development*) were more than five times as great as foundation expenditures in 1963, and unquestionably are still larger, relatively, now. The national annual "take" of illegal gambling has been estimated at nearly fifty billion.[2]

Table 3

The Numbers and the Financial Sizes of the Five Types of Philanthropic Foundations

Type	Number of Foundations	Percent total number	Assets (millions)	Percent total assets	Approximate annual grants (millions)	Percent total annual grants
General Purpose	190	3.1	$ 9,289	64	$384	49
Special Purpose	479	8.0	1,277	9	62	8
Community	102	1.7	425	3	18	2
Company-sponsored	1,716	28.6	1,177	8	143	19
Family and miscellaneous	3,520	58.6	2,343	16	173	22
Totals	6,007	100.0	$14,511	100	$779	100

Although general-purpose foundations comprise about 3 percent of the total number of the six thousand foundations included, they own, as Table 3 shows, nearly two-thirds of the capital assets and make one-half of all foundation grants in dollars. Thus this type of foundation forms the major sector of private foundation activity.

By far the most *numerous* are the family foundations, comprising well over half the total, but their total assets are about one-fourth and their annual grants less than one-half of the corresponding figures for the general research foundations. Next most numerous are the company-sponsored foundations, forming something more than a quarter of all foundations, with about one-twelfth of the capital but with nearly one-fifth the annual giving. The community foundations constitute from 2 to 3 percent of the totals—in number, in total assets, and in annual giving. The general-purpose foundations annually grant a total sum about 4.1 percent of their capital, indicating that these foundations make grants which depend to a major extent upon the income from their endowment. In contrast, the family foundations annually make grants totaling about 7.4 percent of their capital; and the corresponding figure for the company foundations is 12.1 percent. Thus these two types of foundations, as has been mentioned previously, are to a significant extent "in-and-out" foundations, receiving frequent additions to capital and expending these additions along with the interest on their more stable capital.

It is a source of possible confusion that the foundations with which this book deals are called *philanthropic*. For the same word is ordinarily applied to a very wide range of activity supported by individuals, groups, societies, and so on. Much of this more general activity can be designated as charitable, as religious, and as directed toward the *support* of education as contrasted to the *advance* of education. These wider activities are in general not of the sort financed by the funds of general research or special purpose foundations. The community trusts and company-sponsored foundations, however, often support educational efforts as well as the range of activities represented in a typical community fund drive, although they also, to a minor degree, support research. The giving of family foundations is difficult to categorize since it consists of so very many individual activities, most of which are

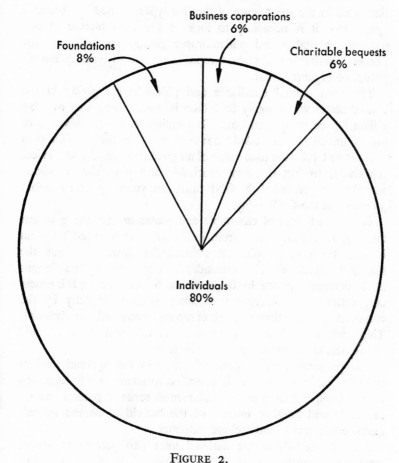

FIGURE 2.

The Sources of the Charitable
and Philanthropic Giving in the United States

not very specifically described in the formal reporting. But it seems entirely justified to assume that the family foundations cover a very wide range of purposes, including personal charity, religious and educational gifts, community services, etc., etc.

In order to judge the financial role of the foundations, using that word in the strict sense of the five types defined by Andrews (page 39), it is necessary to look at the total picture of our national charitable and philanthropic giving. We will use this phrase "charitable and philanthropic" to cover all types, personal, group, or organizational.

The total annual charitable and philanthropic giving in the United States was roughly $2 billion in 1928, something over $5 billion ten years ago, and over $10 billion in 1964. This rate of growth has slightly exceeded the rate of growth of the gross national product or GNP (the total value of all goods produced and services rendered). In fact the total charitable and philanthropic giving was about 2 percent of the GNP thirty-five years ago and is about 3 percent of the GNP today.

Of the vast total of charitable and philanthropic giving in our country, four-fifths comes from individuals, as reported by them in their tax returns (plus an estimate for those who took the standard deduction). The remainder is divided among foundations at 8 percent, charitable bequests at 6 percent, and business corporations at 6 percent (the latter as given directly by the corporation rather than through company-sponsored foundations). This crude breakdown of the sources of the total charitable and philanthropic dollar is shown in Figure 2.

The preponderance of personal giving in the national total of some ten billions of dollars is doubtless to some extent stimulated by tax laws, but in a more fundamental sense it reflects the re-markable and tangible interest of the individual person in religious, educational, and welfare activities.

Almost one-half of the national total (49 percent in 1964) went for purposes described as "religious." Nearly a fifth (17 percent in 1964) is broadly devoted to "education"; nearly a seventh (14 percent in 1964) was for "welfare"; and about one-eighth (12 percent in 1964) was for "health." Only 4 percent of the total, in 1964, was contributed toward increasing the endowments of foundations. See Figure 3.

Anyone is condemned to perpetual confusion who attempts to be absolutely precise about such categories as "education," "welfare," "health," etc. Is aid to a medical school "education" or "health" or perhaps "research" (a category not included at all

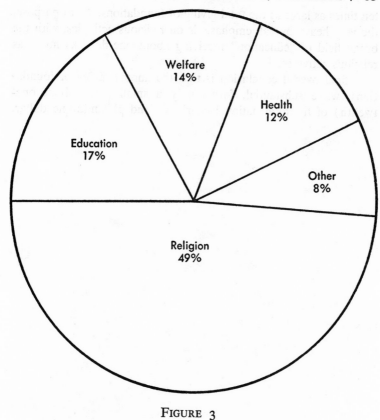

FIGURE 3

Purposes for Which Charitable and
Philanthropic Funds Are Expended in the
United States

in Figure 3)? And there is also the complication that an individual
(as a corporation) may in any one year report, on tax returns, a
"charitable gift" which is in fact not currently usable money but a
contribution to the permanent fund of some foundation.

But, apart from hair-splitting, certain general statements are
obviously valid. The bulk of charitable and philanthropic giving
comes from people. This bulk of personal philanthropy is nearly

ten times as large as the total giving of foundations. As to purpose, the very heavy overall emphasis is on religious activities, with the broad field of "education" receiving about one-third as much as religious activities.

A final overall conclusion is that the annual giving of foundations, while substantial, forms only a small part (about one-twelfth) of the total national charitable and philanthropic dollar.

CHAPTER 8

Reasons for Establishing Foundations

It is clear that there exists a numerous variety of foundations, and that they have great resources. How are these resources employed; what main factors determine the behavior of foundations; how much good do they do?

The last of these three questions—clearly the one of overriding importance—will be the central topic of the contributed chapters which form Part II of this book.

Foundations do so many things that are obviously good one might suppose they would be almost universally admired. But there have been, and are, negative critics. On four occasions during the last fifty years there have been congressional investigations of philanthropic foundations. The first of these, by now largely forgotten, occurred in 1915 and was headed by Frank P. Walsh of Montana. The three recent and well-remembered ones are associated with the names of E. Eugene Cox of Georgia (1952), B. Carroll Reece of Tennessee (1954), and Wright Patman of Texas (1962-64). Philanthropic foundations have also been unfavorably discussed in private media. Well-known books have included satirical chapters on foundations. Various facile and even gifted writers have engaged in the sport of baiting foundations and deriding philanthropy. There have been highly critical newspaper and magazine articles, in both tabloids and respected literary journals.

Such negative criticisms have tended to rely upon a few small examples, leaving the unfortunate impression that these faults are characteristic of philanthropy as a whole, paying no attention to the value which society receives from foundations. Emphasizing taxes in terms which arouse resentment—"The Big Gyp That Is

Costing You $200 a Year" or "Under an umbrella of pious charity lurks the biggest, juiciest tax dodge of all time"—they ignore the value of foundations to society.

There *are* a few bad foundations, the behavior of some having been atrocious, but their total assets are almost negligible compared with the assets of responsible foundations. Quite obviously the irresponsible foundations should be restrained, reformed, or eliminated; but, equally obviously, one does not condemn the others on their account, any more than one discards a pile of $100 bills because it is known to contain several easily identified counterfeits. Yet the good foundations have in the past been too reticent, too modest, or too unconcerned to inform the public in a clear and interesting way as to what they are doing—or when they have attempted any program of public relations, they have had limited success in communication.

It is easy to account for this lack of success. The "hard facts" of philanthropy consist of tables of hundreds and indeed thousands of grants of stated amounts of money granted to hundreds of institutions for purposes which, when phrased in the precise language of specialized scholarship, are often unintelligible or dull or both. Thus the detailed and lengthy annual reports of foundations, although exceedingly important, have a general continuing readership which is probably comparable to that of the statistical reports of government bureaus. Several of the larger foundations are now, therefore, distributing attractive and thoroughly understandable brochures, occasional statements on special subjects, and monthly or quarterly interim reports. Even so, their audience is small indeed compared with the daily readership of newspapers and the daily radio and TV audience.

The motivation behind the modesty of the great foundations has been good, and even noble; but it has also been impractical. Indeed, it has been worse than impractical; for in the absence of frequent and convincing public evidence as to the value of foundation activities, those who wish to discredit them have had the audience largely to themselves.

There are, of course, some reasonable and important challenges which foundations must face. And the public will come to correct conclusions about these questions only if it is widely and regularly informed.

What are the principal challenges that confront foundations? Doubtless the first is: *Why should these organizations be tax free?* The man in the street, acutely conscious of the range and magnitude of his own taxes, asks why it is fair that these great concentrations of wealth and power (as he views them) do not have to pay (as he understands it) a cent of taxes.

Second, *Are foundations not sometimes (or even often) used to serve selfish and private ends?* "Philanthropy" is supposed to be a noble word; but are not some supposedly public philanthropic foundations, in fact, cleverly disguised personal ventures or private businesses?

Third, *Is it a good thing for our society to permit permanent concentrations of great wealth,* with all the power and temptation which accompany such concentration? Are some of the foundations dangerously big, and is not the concentration even greater than it appears to be because of confidential collusion of several or many big foundations, creating an "establishment" which decides who get grants and who do not?

Fourth, *Is this tax-free money not being used to advance some fairly questionable ideas?* Depending on the public mood, ideas may be viewed as questionable by virtue of being too "liberal," too "radical" or even "communistic"; or of being too "conservative" and "far right"; or too "crackpot."

Fifth, *Shouldn't this tax-free money really be subject to public control,* and therefore by what right do those privately selected trustees and officers make all the decisions?

Universities, colleges, and research institutes which receive foundation aid (perhaps even more particularly some which on occasion do not) have rather more specialized concerns and complaints. Do foundations, for example, interfere with the proper internal integrity of these institutions by using money to persuade them to engage in unwise or unwanted activities? Do foundations weaken that loyalty and dedication of the professional scholars which should be concentrated on their institutions, not dissipated among external benefactors?

Individual scholars, writers, artists, and musicians have their own still more specialized questions and grievances. Are foundations interested only in supporting "projects," rather than individual persons with ideas and ability? Do you have to be hired by a famous university to have a good chance, and by some institution to have any chance at all? Is it better to live near a seacoast? Do you have to follow the current fad? Can you get money only for starting something, but never for keeping it going?

These, and a good many other similar questions, form the subject matter of the following seven chapters.

I have for over thirty years been a philanthropoid, to use the name invented by Frederick P. Keppel, the great foundation officer who headed the Carnegie Corporation from 1923 to 1941. Indeed, I have been a sort of multiple philanthropoid, with overlapping experience in about a dozen foundation or foundationlike activities. I have been exposed to a wide assortment of philanthropic experiences (even some as a recipient of aid), and have developed a good many rather definite views about foundations and the philanthropic process. These views, relating to many richly controversial topics, reflected in many of the following pages, are presented humbly. I could be mistaken, but this is the way I see it.

WHY FOUNDATIONS ARE ESTABLISHED

Any attempted piece-by-piece dissection of "why foundations are established" is bound to be an oversimplification. Almost everything that happens in the realm of human action is due not to one well-defined cause but to a complex of interrelated causes, and the noun "motivation" probably ought not to exist in the singular form.

Rarely is there a single exclusive reason for the establishment of a foundation, but even a reason of overwhelming importance may not come publicly or recognizably to the surface. It is just because there are few if any convincing voluntary disclosures of the true reasons for the creation of philanthropic foundations that so many qualifications need to accompany any discussion of motives.

Some of the more important and more easily recognized reasons for the establishment of foundations are:

Religious reasons
Egotistical reasons
The desire to thwart heirs

The desire to assure the continuance of a business
The desire to retain or at least prolong control of personal wealth
The desire efficiently to organize personal, family, or company giving
The desire on the part of a wealthy person to use money to bring his own ideas forcefully to the attention of others
The desire to aid a particular cause or to advance knowledge in a particular field
The desire to help mankind
And, in connection with perhaps all of these reasons, the attraction of serving these purposes with tax-free dollars.

The first two of these are historically the oldest reasons, and the last two are perhaps the most modern reasons. The final reason does not, of course, apply at all to the great foundations and charitable trusts established by Carnegie, Rockefeller, and others at a time when the tax-free dollar was not a consideration.

RELIGIOUS REASONS

The first chapter of this book shows how dominant was the influence of religion in earlier times. To some extent Carnegie and to a great extent Rockefeller furnished proof that the role of religion was still very heavy around 1900. The influence undoubtedly still persists, although the religious motive is much less frequently explicitly recognized. Chapter 4 quotes Henry Moe's statement that "Religion is the mother of philanthropy." Religion is now rather more accurately to be referred to as the unobtrusive great grandmother of philanthropy.

On the other hand, the more secular impression of today's philanthropy may result simply from our modern idiom; for it has been stated by two thoughtful and experienced students that ". . . no one who has examined closely the beginnings of many modern foundations is likely to escape one conclusion: most of the founders were seized by a social vision which stirred them deeply, and which was in many instances a modern expression of religious feeling."[1]

There are foundations which have a stated program interest in religion, like the Danforth Foundation and the Lilly Endowment.

EGOTISTICAL REASONS

The precepts of religion often urge personal modesty or even complete secrecy in connection with charitable giving. But increasing secularization has made philanthropy a frequent tool for advancing the social status of the donor and for satisfying egotistical yearning for wide recognition and the perpetuation of the donor's name.

Of the roughly ninety general purpose foundations with assets of $10 million or more in the United States, nearly eighty do bear the donor's name. Among the general purpose foundations with less than $10 million each, the use of the donor's name is still more frequent. The practice almost automatically proliferates: for when name foundations make grants, the gifts themselves often bear the name of the original donor.

There are excellent and completely understandable instances in which name foundations have been set up to memorialize a departed member of the donor's family. Thus the John Simon Guggenheim Memorial Foundation was created in 1925 by Senator and Mrs. Simon Guggenheim as a memorial to a son who died in 1922 before he could enter college. This admirable foundation has given more than seven thousand excellent fellowships to scholars, scientists, writers, artists, and musicians. Another such example is the Laura Spelman Rockefeller Memorial which John D. Rockefeller, Sr., created in 1918 to honor the memory of his wife. That organization originally supported projects and causes of special interest to Mrs. Rockefeller; but in 1923 it undertook a broad program in the social sciences, and in 1929 it was consolidated with the Rockefeller Foundation.

Of a rather different character are some of the cases of frankly explicit emphasis on the donor's name. One of the best-known examples concerns the support from the Duke Endowment which made possible the tremendous expansion of Trinity College in Durham, North Carolina, to form Duke University. The point is that the change of name was a condition of the support,[2] although I understand that James B. Duke, founder of the endowment, claimed that the university was named after his father, Washington Duke.

There have been instances in which insistence on the name of the donor has led to real difficulty. The ballet company which bore the name of its head, Robert Joffrey, was substantially aided for two years by the William Hale Harkness Foundation. But when, in 1964, that foundation offered $1 million of further support, and requested that the company change its name to the "Harkness Ballet," Joffrey rejected what he referred to as an "ultimatum," pointing out that "I was offered the position of artistic director, but with only vague assurances about who would exercise final control over the company's artistic policies."[3]

Although there are obvious questions of good taste involved, the use of donors' names for foundations and even for grants (assuming of course that the name does not imply improper external control) cannot, I think, be viewed as wrong or undesirable.

Reticence can be carried too far. When I joined the staff of the Rockefeller Foundation in 1932, it was the policy to underplay publicity. If a building was being dedicated and the Rockefeller Foundation was invited to send representatives, this invitation was politely declined in practically all instances. The use of the Rockefeller name for buildings and laboratories was avoided whenever this could be done gracefully, and it was suggested that any plaque stating the source of aid be modest in dimensions and wording. Indeed the criterion really was: use our name, briefly and modestly, if you think that doing so serves *your* purposes, but do not feel under any obligation whatsoever to use the name to serve *our* purposes.

On many occasions letters were received from scientists whose work had been aided by the Rockefeller Foundation. The scientist would say that he was publishing reports on his work, or perhaps a book. What sort of acknowledgment of the Rockefeller Foundation aid did we wish?

The answer always was: if you think it will be useful to you for your scientific colleagues to know that you have received Rockefeller Foundation support, we have no objection to a brief footnote which simply states this fact; but the Rockefeller Foundation does not at all ask that this acknowledgment be made, nor do we consider it in any way necessary as far as we are concerned.

This philosophy was a sort of better-mousetrap one. If we went quietly on doing good things, this would eventually become known and appreciated. A big, meticulously complete, and rather dull report was printed and widely distributed once a year, for anyone determined to find out what was going on.

It is my own opinion that such a degree of reticence is completely nonrealistic. Society cannot intelligently approve the continuance of institutions unless it first understands them. Philanthropic foundations have a clear obligation regularly and fully to disclose all fiscal and related facts. These are essential, but they do not make very glamorous reading. A foundation should also inform the public, in ways generally understandable and in an attractive and interesting form, concerning the grants it makes and why they are made; and should later inform the public about the results thus brought about. This does not need to be done with tasteless and egotistical emphasis on name or credit, but it does need to be done.

THE DESIRE TO THWART HEIRS

Whatever gifts a donor makes to a foundation are by that act irretrievably separated from his own wealth and resources, and are accordingly unavailable for distribution to heirs. "A few founders," Andrews has said, "may have been willing to thwart hopeful or aggressive relatives. . . ."[4] There have in fact been instances in which heirs have sought to restrain or annul such diversions of what they regarded as rightfully theirs. But these instances cannot constitute more than a tiny number in comparison with the cases in which heirs either concurred in or were unconcerned about the donor's decision to create a foundation.

In this section, it should be recorded that heirs sometimes take a positive position concerning the philanthropic disposition of an estate. The Danforth Foundation, for example, has recorded the desire of the Danforth heirs that the foundation, and not themselves, be chiefly remembered.

THE DESIRE TO ASSURE THE CONTINUATION OF A BUSINESS

The point under consideration here is the desire to arrange matters so that a business—normally the business responsible for the production of the wealth in question—can survive the death of the principal owner or owners. For if the business is a large and valuable one, if it is wholly or largely personally owned, and if most of the fortune of the owner or owners is invested in it, then the normal requirement to pay large inheritance taxes might easily involve a loss of control of the business, or even might necessitate that it be effectively liquidated in order to meet the cash payments of taxes.

These were in fact the circumstances in the case of the Ford Motor Company and the Ford Foundation. Through a series of gifts from Henry and Edsel Ford and from their estates, the last transfer occurring in 1950, the Ford Foundation received a total of 3,089,908 shares of nonvoting Class A stock in the Ford Motor Company. These shares represented about 88 percent of the total net assets or net worth of the Ford Motor Company, but the control of the company was vested exclusively in members of the Ford family, who held the only voting shares.

In 1956, as a result of the intent of the Ford Foundation to offer a large portion of its holdings in Ford stock to the public, the Ford Motor Company reclassified its capital stock into three categories: first, a new Class A nonvoting stock owned by the Ford Foundation, each share of the old Class A being exchanged for fifteen shares of the new Class A; second, Class B voting stock held by the Ford family and their associates, this Class B stock being assigned 40 percent of the voting rights; and third, new common stock, to which was assigned 60 percent of the voting rights, a share of the new common stock to come into being whenever a share of the new Class A stock was sold to the public or otherwise disposed of by the foundation. The three categories of stock were assigned the same equity per share and equal participation in dividends.

This reclassification thus made the Ford Foundation the owner of 46,348,620 shares of new nonvoting Class A stock. By May, 1962, the Ford Foundation had, through public and private sale and by exchange, reduced its holding to a new total of 25,394,035 shares. These shares were then split two to one, resulting in a Ford Foundation holding of 50,788,070 "new new" Class A nonvoting shares. At the end of the foundation's fiscal 1965, on September

30, 1965, its holding had been further reduced, by sale, gift, and exchange, to 39,361,465 shares, or approximately 35.5 percent of the capital stock of the Ford Motor Company. Again it should be remembered that the foundation-owned Ford Motor Company stock is all nonvoting, and that all classes of stock are assigned the same equity per share and the same participation in dividends.

Although the Class B stock held by the Ford family and associates is assigned 40 percent of the voting rights, whereas the publicly-held common stock is assigned 60 percent, it should be clear that this vast and skillfully conducted operation left the effective control of the Ford Motor Company in the hands of the Fords and their close associates, inasmuch as the common stock with voting rights now held by the public is owned by over 300,000 persons. A concentrated block of 40 percent of the voting power is clearly able to exercise effective control, since the remaining 60 percent is so widely distributed, and is in large part owned by individuals and institutions which quite naturally approve of and support the official company position. I have a few shares of the Ford common stock myself; and it never occurs to me to do anything other than sign proxy statements in such a way as to endorse the recommendations of management. Thus the turning over of the Class A nonvoting Ford Motor Company stock to the Ford Foundation did unquestionably accomplish the unimpaired continuation of the company. This was surely not the sole motive involved; but it was a perfectly legitimate motive, it accomplished the corporate purpose, and in addition it resulted in a magnificent gift to society.

Concerning this total procedure it therefore seems only fair and accurate to say in summary, first, that the Ford Foundation as such plays no role whatsoever in the control of the business of the Ford Motor Company. This is vitally important. At a later point we will be discussing the impropriety of a tax-free foundation's engaging in business activities.

Second, the procedure was strictly and meticulously in accord with law, and was carried out with full and prompt disclosure of all the facts.

Third, the procedure, quite in addition to its legality, was unquestionably ethical and desirable from the point of view of society. It permitted the efficient continuation of a great industrial establishment with all its benefits of large employment, useful production, national technical resource, and profit to its present large number of private shareholders. And, with unprecedented generosity, it dedicated a huge sum of money to serve the common good.

One must conclude that the motivation, in connection with the setting up of a philanthropic foundation, of providing for the continuing integrity of a previously private business can be a completely proper one. The legal procedures involved are straightforward and have the full approval of governmental authorities. The ethical questions involved in each individual case must be answered in terms of the nature and conduct of the foundation thus established. When, as in the case of the Ford Foundation, the philanthropic operation is totally separated from the business interests of the founding company; when the management—trustees and staff—is of high caliber, composed of able, experienced, and public-spirited individuals; and when the policies and programs are broad, sound, and flexible—then one must conclude that the procedure is not only legally impeccable, but ethically, intellectually, and socially highly desirable.

An unusual view, relating to the desire to assure the continuation of a business, has been expressed by the recently organized Bernard van Leer Stiftung in Amsterdam, a foundation set up as the recipient of a container-manufacturing business. A foundation may ensure perpetuation of an enterprise, it has said, "by avoiding the disadvantage of eventual inexpert . . . family control."[5]

THE DESIRE TO PROLONG CONTROL OF PERSONAL WEALTH

This motive, however natural it may be, seems to be an improper and unworthy one. It cannot be overemphasized that, when a philanthropic foundation is set up, the privilege of avoiding tax on the principal fund should carry with it the moral obligation that this money from that moment on be objectively and impersonally administered for the benefit of society, the decisions for the use of the money not being determined by the individual views of the person who amassed the fortune, but rather by the combined and balanced views of a group of able and broadly experienced persons, forming the officer staff and the board of trustees.

This is not to deny a living founder the right to serve as one of the trustees of the foundation he creates, nor should his ideas be disregarded. His ideas should not, however, be automatically dominant: the founder should, in an ideal case, exert precisely the influence that his ideas would merit were he not the founder.

In the case of those trustees who are themselves wealthy men with a keen realization of the effort and ability required to win a fortune and often with a close personal relation with the founder, it is understandable that their views concerning social theory and their respect and affection for the founder would lead them to think, "I will support any recommendation made by the founder, for after all this is really his money, and if he wants to use it this way that should be his privilege."

This is an understandable attitude, but I think it a wholly incorrect and improper one. The capital sum of a foundation is no longer the money of the founder: he has made it a nonpersonalized fund, the responsibility for which rests broadly yet solely on the technically trained foundation staff and ultimately on the board of trustees.

There are, of course, founders of such special intelligence, imagination, and wisdom that their views would and should be treated very seriously by the other trustees. Indeed, any board is likely to have a relatively small number of members who play leading roles in all the debates of policy, program, and choice. A founder has a perfect right to be one of these more actively influential trustees—but on the basis of his ability, not on the basis of his having been the founder.

The role of the founder appears to vary enormously from foundation to foundation. But there are superb examples that deserve wide recognition and emulation. During the time when John D. Rockefeller, Jr., was chairman of the board of trustees of the Rockefeller Foundation, he turned to the then president, Raymond B. Fosdick, near the close of a meeting of the board and asked, with characteristic modesty and courtesy, if he might have the privilege of speaking briefly to the board concerning a project in which he had a personal interest. He spoke for less than five minutes, giving a clear, precise, and illuminating description of a project. He concluded by remarking that he hoped that the Rockefeller Foundation might see fit to give that project some financial support.

After a moment of silence one of the senior members of the board stated that there could be no doubt concerning the value, interest, and desirability of the project; but that in his judgment it was not a suitable project for Rockefeller Foundation support, lying quite outside the agreed program, and offering difficulties if treated as an exception. After another brief silence a second board member indicated that he agreed.

Rockefeller at once stated that he deeply appreciated the permission granted him to discuss a personal interest not on the agenda, and that it was clear to him that he should not have done so. He thanked the board for their thoughtful consideration, and the meeting was adjourned. The real point of the story is that I have told all of it. The subject never came up again, nor were there any indirect reverberations.

The attitudes of other members of the Rockefeller family, moreover, have been consistent with the pattern set by grandfather and father. Mrs. John D. Rockefeller, Jr., on two occasions that I happen to know of, made an appointment with another president of the Rockefeller Foundation, Dr. Max Mason. She made these appointments just as would and could any other woman active in some socially-oriented enterprise. On both occasions it was explained to her why the projects for which she was seeking support were not feasible activities for the Rockefeller Foundation. Here again, that was the end of the story.

Except for a relatively brief overlap of father and eldest son beginning in 1932, there has never been more than one Rockefeller on the board of "their" foundation. Once in a while some overenthusiastic but misguided seeker-after-aid approaches one of the Rockefeller brothers other than John III. I have seen brief, courteous, but firm notes which merely referred the matter to the authorities of the Rockefeller Foundation; but not once in my twenty-eight years there did I have knowledge that any member of the family not officially concerned made any move whatsoever to influence the decisions of the officers and trustees.

There are doubtless other equally good examples. I speak of the Rockefeller Foundation simply because it is a significant example and a fine example, and because my knowledge about it is based on long personal experience. In the case of other large foundations, an attempt to enter by the side or back door by first approaching a trustee (who is at least an acquaintance of the applicant) is in effect almost a kiss of death for the application.

The desire of a founder to extend personal control of his wealth, after assigning the money to a foundation, is not the sort of motivation that comes cleanly to the surface of public evidence, and it does not seem probable that this motivation has played any general or significant role. It is my own impression that the larger foundations have seldom been plagued by difficulties of this particular sort.

THE DESIRE TO ORGANIZE EFFICIENTLY PERSONAL, FAMILY, OR BUSINESS GIVING

The convenience provided by a foundation for the efficient handling of requests for philanthropic assistance is of considerable advantage, particularly to corporations. Families with numerous members and business interests can similarly profit by channeling their giving through a foundation. Even a single wealthy individual can shield himself from the pressure and nuisance of emotional appeals, and can through the foundation mechanism provide for businesslike and, if he is so minded, expert assistance in the selection of recipients of aid. It furnishes a sort of impersonal screen —the formal policy of a legal entity—between the wealthy individual and the multitudinous persons, ranging from dedicated idealists down to overinsistent nuts, who need or want, and all of whom fervently believe they deserve, some of the donor's cash.

Improving the organization of philanthropic giving could conceivably stand alone as the basis for establishing a foundation. With increasing frequency in recent decades it has been the stated reason, and it continues to be. Not even the donor's testimony, however, wholly clarifies the point. Andrews has written, "Motives undoubtedly varied, and they are not easy to assign with assurance. We can seldom know all the complex factors that move another person to action, and he himself, with every intention of honesty, may be mistaken in their interpretation."[6]

One obvious gain in efficiency from channeling giving through a foundation results from the averaging of the rate of charitable expenditures to be achieved by an "in-and-out" or "funnel" foundation—that is, by a foundation without significant permanent endowment, but with gifts from one or more sources, which passes them on as grants. Such a foundation may receive donations, as from the earnings of a company, at an eccentrically uneven rate, but it can retain such funds to fill in the lean periods so as to expend at a more even rate. For gifts to a foundation are increases to its capital; the corpus thus created can be expended in grants at whatever rate the trustees decide and the internal rules of the foundation permit. This statement applies only to gifts to the capital structure of a foundation. The income which a foundation receives from its invested capital must under existing law be expended essentially currently, a point to be discussed later.

Whether capital, earnings, or both are being distributed as grants, the foundation procedure has much to offer to the individual who desires an efficient and convenient method of distributing his wealth. This is an easy and often very good way of avoiding the pressures of frequent appointments with solicitation agents. Such advantage is of obvious importance to corporations and large wealthy families; it is also very useful to individual donors who set up foundations. A degree of impersonality also shields them from the stubborn insistence or even the wrath of disappointed petitioners. The foundation can protect itself with a stated "policy" which would be less easy for the individual to defend and maintain. The responsibility for a turn-down or for a reduced grant falls upon the trustees or the board of directors, not solely on the individual source of the wealth.

It can be said, and has and will be said, that this partial screen between the askers and the givers is an unfair and even cowardly affair. The indignant petitioner whose request has been denied will say, "The officer said it was against their policy; but all he meant was that he didn't want to let me have the grant. And who is *he* to say that." But as one who has, for many, many years looked at and listened to the whole range of askers, and also at a wide range of givers, it is my judgment that the latter, most of whom did in fact produce the wealth by their own efforts, deserve a little protection. The great majority of reasonable and competent askers do not object to this, whereas the small minority of arrogant and incompetent askers make it highly desirable.

THE DESIRE TO PROMOTE IDEAS

In a perfect world an idea could be born, nourished, developed, made known to everyone, criticized and perfected, and put to good use without the crude fact of financial support ever entering into the process. Seldom if ever, in the practical world in which we live, does this occur.

The influence of money on ideas can be powerful; it can be good, or it can be downright vicious. The process of "giving away money" is one in which, if disaster is to be avoided, taste, knowledge, wisdom, and integrity are required. If a scientifically ignorant and wealthy man zealously but mistakenly believes that perpetual-motion machines are possible he can use his money to persuade individuals to attempt to build them. This is probably harmless; for the persons who could be so persuaded would be pretty unlikely to do anything else of a very useful character. If a wealthy person is convinced of the importance of an artificial universal language, he can doubtless find, as susceptible recipients of grants, persons with enough linguistic skill and knowledge so that they might much better be doing something else. Money can be used to lure the gullible to devote their time to spiritualism, to fanatical religions, to pseudo-science, and so on.

But one can easily proceed from these trivial examples to significant ones. It should not be assumed that the process of financial force-feeding is necessarily a bad one, for there are two ways in which using money to promote ideas may be constructive and beneficial.

First, the ideas may in fact be good ideas, not in terms of the isolated enthusiasm of eccentric individuals, but in terms of the considered judgment of society. A foundation which, in a modern liberal spirit, chooses to advance opportunity for religious education, or one which is dedicated to the service of our democratic ideas of freedom and the value of the individual, is using the power of money for the advancement of ideas which essentially all of us share and approve; and it is not only irrelevant, it is nonsensical, to object that the donor also favors the ideas.

Second, money can usefully be employed to further ideas on which we are not all agreed. We would be a drab and regimented society if it were not possible for one rich enthusiast to back his ideas about conventional art while another backs his ideas about modern nonrepresentational art. Flavor and vitality would go out of our national life if one wealthy man were not free to support studies of the value of the free enterprise system, while another sees to it that competent and vigorous expression is given to the concepts of the welfare state.

There have been numerous examples of the powerful effect of the combination of firmly held ideas backed up by ample financial support. The role of Abraham Flexner in reforming medical education is a classic and admirable example. Another outstanding example is the influence of Alan Gregg in persuading the Rockefeller Foundation to devote substantial sums, together with the merited influence of the Rockefeller Foundation reputation, to introduce psychiatry into medical education.[7]

On the other hand, there have been less felicitous examples. Educational-television research, for example, seems to have suffered somewhat from the overenthusiastic conviction of certain philanthropic foundation staff members that funds should be offered to support activities intended to prove their theories, rather than to discover the facts. In an article on research in educational television, E. G. Sherburne, Jr., has said, speaking of influences which "force our questioning into well-defined directions and restrain it from others," that

> The third bias, the philanthropic one, arises from the influence, much of it unconscious, resulting from the source of funds for educational television research. Primarily, funds for extensive research in ETV have so far come from organizations who were interested in testing very specific aspects of TV use, that is, for easing imperative school problems. While such subjects certainly needed testing, there is little doubt that most of the study grants have tended to move the development of educational television along "directed" lines rather than to explore its nature or test its range.[8]

Zealous enthusiasm of foundation staff officers can sometimes result in their canvassing institutions to see if they are "interested" in accepting a grant to carry out research in which the foundation is interested, rather than the foundation's responding to the spontaneous interests of the university or institute experts. In at least one case a grant offered by a foundation for educational television research was firmly refused by a university.

The vigor of variety has been one of the great assets in American life. What makes disagreement not only tolerable but actually beneficial, as regards the activities of philanthropic foundations, is that there are many, many foundations with a wide variety of purposes and of program orientation. Some few of the ideas they support may be bad, from one point of view or another. But the built-in diversity tends to cancel out the badness, and to bring the good to the surviving surface. The dangers which would result if this were not allowed to happen completely outweigh the very minor and occasional dangers of permitting it to happen. If money in the support of ideas comes in too massive amounts from too few sources, then there is need to worry. This is one of the strongest arguments for the existence of a large number of philanthropic foundations, and it is one of the strongest arguments for private philanthropy as a counter-influence to an excessive concentration of federal aid.

It is fortunate indeed for our sociey that there are now at least seventeen foundations each with assets of more than $125 million dollars, and that these foundations have highly varied programs.

To interrupt for a moment the primary subject matter of this section: It is somewhat unfortunate, in my judgment, that one special foundation, the Ford, has assets roughly five times those of the next-largest philanthropic foundation. The Ford Foundation has followed so broad and, with almost microscopic exception, so wise and so generally approved a program that it should be emphasized that it has clearly recognized its special obligation. Not that the Ford Foundation is too large; but rather there should be several other foundations of comparable size. Not infrequently some major plan is under discussion, and the arithmetical fact has to be faced that the magnitude of the necessary financing is such that the proponents are faced with only two alternatives— federal funds or Ford funds. This is not an ideal situation.

The Ford Foundation had, to October 1, 1965, made grants some $847.5 million in excess of its income; and it might be assumed from this that its trustees are seeking to reduce its size. In the fiscal year 1962-63 they increased the book value of the foundation's Ford stock from $28 per share to $30; and in the two succeeding years the book value was raised first to $33 and then to $36. But on September 30, 1965, when the $36 book value was reported, the closing market price of Ford common was $55.875, and its 1965 high was $62.875.

It is of course true that market value is a fluctuating figure, and that an evaluation at market value is in addition unrealistic, since a vast holding of Ford stock could not be precipitously liquidated without strongly affecting the market. It is certainly possible that the market for Ford stock may decline. But, whatever the purpose of the Ford Foundation trustees in overexpending income during the past ten years, it seems reasonably clear that the actual capital assets of the Ford Foundation have not substantially decreased. The capital assets of other foundations have increased substantially during this same period, and it would be interesting to know whether the relative position of the Ford Foundation has substantially changed over the past five or ten years. But this is a very complicated question, which does not have a simple and clear answer. The practice by foundations of listing their assets in terms of the book values of securities necessarily results in major understatements of current value during periods of high stock prices; and this procedure affects the formally stated size of various foundations in greatly differing ways, depending on the nature of their portfolios. In spite of the appropriations from capital, the record of Ford Motor stock has been such that the Ford Foundation continues to be roughly five times as large as the next-largest foundation.

The power of foundation money has of course been used, at times, to advance the ideas of the founders, or ideas enthusiastically held by influential trustees, or those sponsored by staff officers. This can be entirely proper and desirable; but it can also be highly questionable. It would be extremely bad, as well as certainly futile, to attempt to control this risk by means of legislation or rules. The danger can be minimized only by a variety which assures that competing ideas also receive support, by complete and candid reporting by each foundation as to what it is doing and by the resulting informed pressure of public opinion, and most of all by maintaining high standards for the membership of boards of trustees and of foundation staffs.

Whether or not in conscious recognition of the possible risk involved when the largest of all foundations puts money to the service of ideas, the Ford Foundation has on more than one occasion sloughed off great chunks of money for purposes that are as uncontroversial as mother love. Such, for example, was the late 1955 allotment of half a billion dollars for colleges, hospitals, and medical schools, this coming on top of a March, 1955, appropriation of $50 million to raise the salaries of college teachers.

The manner of distribution was surprisingly, and to many disappointingly, mechanical. Each of our country's 630 privately supported liberal arts colleges received a sum equal to their 1954-55 faculty payroll. Each of 3,400 nonprofit private hospitals received a sum determined by the number of births and of patient days on an average annual basis.

In favor of the grant toward teachers' salaries it can be said that an important need was dramatized at a timely moment, and that other giving was thereby encouraged, and many if not most university and college presidents would probably defend this grant.

It must be recognized, in further defense of the Ford Foundation, that the money was pouring in and that the federal laws required them to spend their income. But a distribution of this sort, based on a numerical formula, taking no account of excellence, leadership, or variations in need, employing no elements of judgment, and displaying no strategy, seems something less than one might have hoped. This kind of grant makes almost no use of an able staff: once the trustees decide on the formula, everything can be settled by a clerk with a slide rule and a standard tabulation of data. Everyone would presumably agree that it would be a stupid form of corporate suicide for the Ford Foundation to set about distributing one dollar to every person on this planet. Distributions such as these 1955 grants were a little too much like that.

In 1960, in encouraging contrast, a further series of very large grants to colleges and universities was inaugurated. These more recent grants are designated to advance the development of carefully selected recipients as regional and national centers of excellence. Not only are these grants based on excellence and on the development of leadership, they are "incentive" or "challenge" grants, which require the recipient institution to match the grants in various ratios with funds raised from other private sources. The aggregate of this series of grants as reported by the Ford Foundation in December, 1964, was $218.5 million, and the matching requirements, if all the terms are successfully met, will provide to some ten universities and forty-seven liberal arts colleges within the three- to five-year periods allowed for matching, an additional total of $556.5 million. This procedure does indeed put money at the service of ideas; but in so broad and effective a manner that none should complain.

THE DESIRE TO AID A PARTICULAR CAUSE OR TO ADVANCE
KNOWLEDGE IN A PARTICULAR FIELD

The preceding section, by using the title "The Desire to Promote Ideas," started out with a rather negatively critical attitude. But even greater emphasis should be given to the fact that those who create foundations often do so not because of any ingenuous or arrogant confidence in their own ideas, but because study and experience have soundly convinced them that certain causes deserve greater support, or that new knowledge in certain specified fields would be particularly helpful to mankind. These enthusiasms may be personal in nature, but they may have become so as the result of careful and competent thought and objective study.

This is the kind of motivation that leads a person to devote some of his wealth to such a cause as Planned Parenthood or conservation; or which induces him to support research to develop a widely available and inexpensive food.

THE DESIRE TO HELP MANKIND

As a wealthy person gets older he undoubtedly thinks more and more—as all the rest of us do—about the underlying questions of the purpose and meaning of life. As a very practical problem, he thinks about the long future, about the protection of his family and the requirements of his business or his professional activity; and quite inevitably he studies his personal problem of "estate planning." What will the inheritance taxes be; how will they be met; how, if he is wealthy, does he wish the surplus to be used?

All the overtones of the frequently used word "avoidance" seem to imply that there is something improper, unethical, even unlawful about making use of the procedures, incorporated in the laws of our land, which exempt certain capital sums of money from inheritance taxes, and which exempt certain income from income tax.

These implications are, of course, completely unwarranted. The law approves what it permits, just as explicitly as it disapproves what it forbids. And federal laws have for years quite obviously reflected an official national desire to stimulate charitable giving. This is no secret, nor is the subject in any sense a suspicious one which justifies the indiscriminate use of such pejorative words as "escape," "dodge," "avoid," and "loophole." The Federal Income Tax Form for 1964 lists conspicuously on its outside cover, and as the first item of "A Special Message for Taxpayers," the fact that the Revenue Act of 1964 provided for "Higher ceilings on charitable contributions." Indeed it is now possible to donate, free from income tax, up to 20 percent of "Total Income" for general charitable and philanthropic giving and up to ten percent additional for many types of charity; and the new law also now provides for a carry-over to as many as five future years of contributions which, in a given year, exceed the percentages stated.

It is accurate, and has been widely recognized to be accurate, to say that federal law encourages philanthropy. The limits are of course defined, and the purposes specified. When a person makes use of these provisions of the law there is, judging simply from that fact, no justification for imputing selfish, improper, or unsocial motives.

The very words "tax free" apparently arouse the loud opposition of some persons, whether or not they have any knowledge of the value of the activities supported by the tax-free money, and whatever their opinion of some of the ways in which the money would be spent if it were paid as tax. Such persons are disagreeing only incidentally with philanthropic foundations, but more fundamentally they are objecting to the basic philosophy of their own government. They have every right to question the desirability of this aspect of national philosophy—to have this right is essential to our democratic system. But with this freedom to object goes the obligation to be intelligently informed. No one has any right to object to the tax-free dollars available to philanthropy until he has made a reasonable effort to learn what these dollars accomplish.

Doubtless there have been instances of foundations, especially of the "family" type, that have been created for selfish and unsocial reasons. Doubtless there are individuals fiercely determined to use every possible means to reduce to a minimum the amount of their money which, upon their death, will go to the government. There certainly are individuals who would let their money be used for almost anything rather than for taxes.

But when these self-centered cases are all added up, they form an almost invisible, though nasty, speck in the total picture of the philanthropic activity in our country. A great deal of intelligence, compassion, and humanitarianism have accompanied whatever other forces have brought about the growth of private philanthropy in this country. The primary motive for creating a foundation certainly has been, in many, many cases, the high one of wishing to help mankind. The noble declarations to be found in the official statements of purpose of many foundations—such as the Rockefeller Foundation's phrase "To promote the well-being of mankind throughout the world"—might sound a little pretentious were it not for the fact that the solid historical record amply demonstrates that the vast majority of significant foundations are, earnestly and intelligently, trying to do just what this statement of purpose suggests.

CHAPTER 9

Legal and Financial Aspects
of Foundations

The law has a somewhat circuitous way of defining terms and thus of making its purpose clear. As a first step a law is passed, as for example the portion, to be quoted in a moment, of the Internal Revenue Code stating the types of corporations which are exempt from taxation and the requirements for exemption. Then regulations issued by the Treasury state the tests by which it can be determined whether an organization qualifies under the law. That second step, however, necessarily uses words, such as "charitable," "educational," and "scientific," whose operational meaning is different to different persons. Therefore the regulations issued by the Treasury Department undertake to define these words.

Yet certain words will remain undefined in the regulations, as for example the word "substantial" in the statement "An organization is an 'action' organization," and therefore does not qualify for exemption "if a substantial part of its activities is attempting to influence legislation by propaganda or otherwise."[1]

At that point the terms are put to practical test and begin to acquire operational meaning by virtue of rulings made by Treasury officials or by virtue of court decisions. This, as I understand it, is the way the law escapes the dilemma of circularity of definition (A means B, B means C, C means A), and also as a practical matter escapes the alternative difficulty of an infinite regression (A means B, B means C, C means D . . . and so on forever).

How do these general remarks apply to the legal aspects of philanthropy? The basic statement of the Internal Revenue Code concerning the type of organization which is to be considered philanthropic in nature and which is thus qualified for exemption from taxation is as follows:

> Corporations, and any community chest, fund, or foundation, organized and operated exclusively for religious, charitable, scientific, testing for public safety, literary, or educational purposes, or for the prevention of cruelty to children or animals, no part of the net earnings of which inures to the benefit of any private shareholder or individual, no substantial part of the activities of which is carrying on propaganda, or otherwise attempting, to influence legislation, and which does not participate in, or intervene in (including the publishing and distribution of statements), any political campaign on behalf of any candidate for public office.[2]

The Treasury regulations then go on to state that "In order to be exempt as an organization described in section 501(c)(3), an organization must be both organized and operated exclusively for one or more of the purposes specified in such section,"[3] and proceeds to set forth the organizational and operational tests to be applied in order to determine whether the foundation in question does in fact qualify for exemption.

But presently, sensing the need for defining terms, there occurs a series of subparagraphs with such titles as "Charitable defined," "Educational defined," "Scientific defined." For example:

> (2) *Charitable defined* The term "charitable" is used in section 501(c)(3) in its generally accepted legal sense and is, therefore, not to be construed as limited by the separate enumeration in section 501(c)(3) of other tax exempt purposes which may fall within the broad outlines of "charity" as developed by judicial decisions.[4]

That circularity in definition is not avoided is further illustrated by such sentences in the regulations as "For research to be 'scientific' within the meaning of Section 501(c)(3) it must be carried on in furtherance of a 'scientific purpose.'"

All this reminds one of T. S. Eliot's remark in the "Four Quartets" that in trying to use words every attempt is "a different kind of failure/Because one has only learnt to get the better of words/For the thing one no longer has to say. . . ."

It is, in fact, not surprising that the range of activity and the inevitable vagueness in assessing both purpose and value make it hard for the law to be very precise in defining proper behavior for a philanthropic organization. "Although the courts have had to decide literally thousands of individual cases by determining whether or not a particular activity or objective is 'charitable,' they have not developed more precise criteria"[5]—more precise, that is, than the very general statement that philanthropy is "that kind of 'good will to men' which induces people to give voluntarily of their money, property, time, and strength to cooperative causes and institutions which serve the welfare, the health, the character, the mind, the soul, and the advancing culture of the human race."[6]

Foundations have been, and theoretically still can be, established in three ways. The first is by a special act of Congress or of a state legislature. The Smithsonian Institution received a special charter from Congress in 1846, as did the (Rockefeller) General Education Board in 1903, the Carnegie Institution of Washington in 1904, and the Carnegie Foundation for the Advancement of Teaching in 1906. The "Carnegie Foundation" (later renamed and federally incorporated), the Rockefeller Foundation, and the Russell Sage Foundation were created through special legislative enactments in the State of New York.

This procedure of special enactment is now only very rarely followed, and at the present time some states specifically prohibit the passage of a special act to establish a philanthropic foundation.

The second way of establishing a foundation is by setting up a charitable trust. The original formation of a trust involves little contact with governmental authorities, and subsequent to its creation a trust is subject mainly or wholly to court supervision. The legal provisions for setting up charitable trusts differ from state to state, but seldom require more than the execution of a simple trust agreement. Frequently even this is dispensed with. In the case of a trust which passes title from one living person to another, no further individuals, with the exception of the tax authorities, need know anything about the matter, whereas testamentary trusts, set up by a will, are generally subject to court review.

The third way of establishing a foundation is by setting up a corporation. This must be done in compliance with the laws of the state in question, and it requires in all cases "some resort to state action and some form of registration with a state agency."[7]

There appear to be complicated and somewhat subtle differences between the legal position, particularly as this relates to personal liability, of the trustees of a trust and that of the directors of a corporation. But this is apparently neither very clear nor, as a practical matter of experience, very important. A considerable number of community foundations and a few foundations of other types are set up as trusts, but by far the commonest form of organization for all types of foundations is incorporation under the laws of some state.

A committee of the American Bar Association has drafted a Model Non-Profit Corporation Act.[8] When the secretary of state or other authorized state official grants articles of incorporation to an applicant agency they then "have a charter."[9]

The statement of purposes of a charter spells out the functional objectives, and if these are of suitable character, and if the operational tests of the Treasury are met, then the organization qualifies for tax exemption. In the case of the general foundations the statements of purpose are characteristically broad and general; i.e., "promotion of human welfare," "betterment of mankind," etc. In numerous cases the terminology directly reflects the language of the Revenue Code.

Donors' letters of gift are not legally binding but in fact they may be powerfully or even decisively persuasive, particularly in their influence on trustees. They often indicate the activities and the directions that the incorporated foundations should pursue under their broadly stated purposes. Julius Rosenwald used a letter of gift to propose the time for completing the mission of the Rosenwald Fund: "In accepting the shares of stock now offered, I ask that the Trustees do so with the understanding that the entire Fund in the hands of the Board, both income and principal, be expended within twenty-five years of the time of my death."

This request was respected, and the fund was spent out by June, 1948, sixteen years after his death.

CONDITIONS RESPECTING CAPITAL FUNDS
—ACCUMULATING FUNDS

From the point of view of the availability of their resources, foundations have operated under four types of procedure, the differences resulting from conditions set forth when the foundation was created, from policy decisions by the governing board of trustees, or from federal law.

An accumulating fund is one in which part or all of the income, together with all of the principal, is not spent for a period of time, the income thus accumulating to provide the foundation at a later time with increased resources.

In the past, many persons have been fascinated and attracted by the great potential power of the accumulative effect of compounding interest far into the future. One dollar, put out at the modest rate of 3 percent at the time of the birth of Christ, would theoretically have grown by now to about $17 million billion billion. Even in a thousand years one dollar at 3 percent would amount to nearly $7 million million. It is clear that, as a practical matter, such accumulations do not occur: something always happens to upset the theoretically possible growth—devaluation of currencies, accidents, collapse of banks or even of nations.

We have seen that Benjamin Franklin intended to cash in on this power of compound interest, and so to parlay £1,000 each to Philadelphia and Boston into very large endowments, and we have also seen that this was only very partially successful.

The Duke Endowment is a contemporary illustration of an accumulating fund. For the Indenture of James B. Duke, dated December 11, 1924, said in part:

> . . . Twenty per cent of said net amount (incomes, revenues, and profits each calendar year) shall be retained by said trustees and added to the corpus of the trust . . . for the purpose of increasing the principal . . . until the total aggregate of such additions to the corpus . . . shall be as much as Forty Million Dollars. . . .[10]

The Duke Endowment is at the moment continuing to follow an accumulative policy, although a firm decision as to the present propriety of this procedure has not as yet been announced by the Treasury authorities.

The Revenue Act of 1950 provided that philanthropic foundations must, in general, spend their income currently and not permit it to accumulate. Specifically the statute prohibited an accumulation of income which was "unreasonable in amount or duration in order to carry out the charitable, educational, or other purpose or function constituting the basis for exemption."

The difficulty here, obviously, resides in the word "unreasonable." And the difficulty is increased by the fact that the initial decision as to what is reasonable and what is unreasonable is made by authorities within the government who have demonstrated an unwillingness to define what they mean by "reasonable." Is it, for example, reasonable to spend as little as say 80 percent of income in one tax year, provided a running average, taken over a five-year period, shows income to be fully distributed?

The only clue which foundations have been able to obtain has come from four published rulings and from decisions in eight cases. The rulings have permitted partial accumulation for as much as three years for purposes approved in these specific instances. But the rulings give little hint as to the official Washington meaning of "reasonable." The case decisions, slightly more illuminating, have permitted some accumulation in instances in which the foundation in question presented a concrete and presumably reasonable plan which could not be put into effect unless the accumulation was permitted.

This requirement of currently spending income is not a matter of concern to most of the larger and more active foundations. Most of these, in fact, when not hindered by charter or deed of gift, have in recent years felt that the pressure of important opportunity justified spending each year not only all of income, but some part of capital.

Corporations make a practice of declaring only part of their current earnings as dividends, and of plowing the remainder back into expansion and into plant improvement, with resulting general upward trends in security values. A foundation could therefore interpret the expenditure of a little capital each year as the use of deferred or undeclared income, the increase in security values compensating for the minor invasion of capital, so that the latter does not reduce the total market value of the securities retained.

PERPETUITIES AND OPTIONAL
PERPETUITIES

For a foundation created either as a trust or by incorporation, the question as to whether it can spend part of its capital fund or is barred from doing so depends upon the terms set forth in the will, trust agreement, or articles of incorporation, as well as upon board policy. When it is stipulated that some or all of the capital sum— what lawyers like to call the "corpus"—be retained indefinitely, then the fund is a *perpetuity*.

If the trustees are, by the charter or trust agreement, given discretion to use or to keep capital funds as they see fit, then the fund is an *optional perpetuity*.

Perpetual (or at least theoretically perpetual) life for a philanthropic foundation does not constitute any special or unusual favor, for ordinary legal corporations also enjoy the theoretical privilege of existing forever.

When perpetuity is specified for part or all of the corpus, then this condition can be modified only by *cy pres* (see page 10 f.), or similar judicial proceedings.

More and more, over recent decades, new foundations have given their trustees discretion to use capital funds or to keep them intact as they see fit. Sometimes donors have requested the trustees to keep the endowment intact for some specified term of years, after which they are free to do as they see fit. Several of the better-known large foundations, Ford, Rockefeller, and Sloan, for example, are optional perpetuities.

LIQUIDATING FOUNDATIONS

Powerful voices in history have spoken eloquently and persuasively against the idea of a philanthropy's being allowed to continue forever. It was mentioned earlier that Turgot, who was French controller general from 1774 to 1776, argued very vigorously against perpetuities. A century later, John Stuart Mill was also inveighing against perpetual gifts; and the close of the nineteenth centutry saw the publication of *The Dead Hand*[11] by Sir Arthur Hobhouse, a classic among the philippics against perpetuities.

The well-known American merchant and philanthropist Julius Rosenwald had strong views against "forever funds." Often and forcefully he expressed his convictions on this point, and he probably caused many millions of philanthropic dollars to be expended currently. In his own letter of gift, setting up the Rosenwald Foundation, he said:

> I am not in sympathy with this policy of perpetuating endowments and believe that more good can be accomplished by expending funds as Trustees find opportunities for constructive work than by storing up large sums of money for long periods of time. By adopting a policy of using the Fund within this generation, we may avoid those tendencies toward bureaucracy and a formal or perfunctory attitude toward the work which almost inevitably develop in organizations which prolong their existence indefinitely. Coming generations can be relied upon to provide for their own needs as they arise.[12]

The Children's Fund of Michigan was liquidated in 1954 after spending $18.5 million. The founder, Senator James Couzens, had been persuaded by Rosenwald. The James Foundation was terminated in 1965, and other foundations which, for one reason or another, are now approaching the end of their measured existence include the Max C. Fleischmann Foundation of Nevada, the Houston Endowment, and the Maurice and Laura Falk Foundation.[13]

ENDOWMENTS, INCOME, AND GIFTS

Many of the large foundations, particularly those created early in the present century, were established by means of one or a few very large contributions to endowment by a living donor. The Carnegie Corporation began with $125 million, the General Education Board with $33 million over seven years, the Rockefeller Foundation with $134 million over three years, the Commonwealth Fund with $10 million, the Duke Endowment with $40 million. More recently the pattern has changed somewhat, to include cases of smaller initial amounts but recurring gifts of capital, and cases in which the bulk of the endowment comes to a foundation, previously established, after the death of the donor.

The present level of giving by foundations is not wholly to be accounted for by the income on endowment. The Treasury Report, for example, states that the net ordinary income of foundations was $580 million in 1962, whereas the grants that same year from income and capital, and including the cost of making the grants, were $1.012 billion. But the substantial excess of grants over income does not mean that the foundations decreased their total net worth during that year. For during the same period the foundations received contributions which totaled $833 million.

INVESTMENT POLICIES

At the times of the release of the annual reports of the Rockefeller Foundation back in the early and mid-thirties, it was not unusual for newspapermen to wait in the reception room to receive the report the moment it was available. One might optimistically assume that they were impatient to learn of possible changes in policy or of grants which had been made. But the practical fact is that they were eager to see whether or not the Rockefeller Foundation had made any changes in its investment portfolio.

The committee of the trustees that advised the foundation on such matters was composed of men such as Winthrop W. Aldrich, Walter W. Stewart, and, for that matter, John D. Rockefeller, Jr., himself, whose views on the sales and purchases of securities might be both revealing and significant.

When the report appeared, these financial newsmen were, I suppose, disappointed, for by and large few portfolio changes were made. The Rockefeller Foundation just maintained its huge holding of oil stock, confident that both income and market value would increase and hopeful that stock dividends and stock splits would continue. Indeed, the increase in capital endowment that resulted from stock dividends and from increases in market value enabled the Rockefeller Foundation, over the first fifty years of its existence, to make grants that exceeded income by $181.2 million, and nevertheless to end the half century with an endowment which exceeded by about $400 million the total of all the gifts made to it for endowment, valuing these gifts at the time they were made.

The holding of large amounts of stock in the company or companies which had been responsible for the personal wealth that created the foundation is an obvious characteristic of several of the larger foundations—in addition to the Rockefeller, for example, the Ford Foundation, the Duke Endowment, the Hartford Foundation, the Kellogg Foundation, the Lilly Endowment, the Sloan Foundation, and the Charles Stewart Mott Foundation.[14] In 1960 there were forty-nine foundations with assets greater than $30 million. Of the forty-five of these for which the information was available, twenty-three had the majority of their assets in a single donor-related stock, and only one in four had widely diversified portfolios.

One the other hand, two changing tendencies have characterized the investment policies of philanthropic foundations over the last decade or two. Many have diversified, or have at least started to diversify, their portfolios; and there has been a general increase of emphasis on common stocks. The Carnegie Corporation moved into a diversified investment position beginning in 1929, when the Gold Bonds of United States Steel were called and the Carnegie Corporation was paid $70 million in cash for its holding. The present portfolio of the Carnegie Corporation does not reflect the origin of its wealth.

A quarter century or more ago, many foundations depended heavily on bonds and preferred stocks—as some still do. The Rockefeller Foundation has always been strong on common stocks. Thirty years ago its portfolio consisted of about 38 percent bonds and 62 percent stock (based on ledger values, which even at that date underestimated the percentage in stock). Of their stock holding at that time roughly 70 percent was in various "Standard" oil stocks. At the end of 1964 (and now using market figures, for the ledger values would underestimate some of the stock values by a factor of four) the Rockefeller Foundation had only 5 percent in bonds and 95 percent in stocks, oils then constituting about 64 percent of the stock figure.

In terms of market values (with full recognition of the difficulties of stating market values when they not only are changeable, but are, for such huge holdings, not readily realizable) the Ford Foundation had on September 30, 1964, almost 75 percent of its total holdings in common stock, of which 90 percent was in non-voting common stock of the Ford Motor Company.

Closely related to investment policies is the matter of a philanthropic foundation's voting, or not voting, the common stock which it owns. If a foundation owns and votes a substantial fraction of all the common stock of some profit-making corporation, and especially if the remainder of the stock is widely distributed, then that foundation might easily be in effective control of the corporation. The philanthropic foundation would then in reality be in control of the management of a profit-making business enterprise. In the case of the Ford Foundation, this dilemma was met by making *nonvoting* all Ford Motor stock owned by the Ford Foundation.

In general, as is amply illustrated by the examples listed in the *Treasury Department Report on Private Foundations,* an "examination of any broad sampling of the commercial ventures of foundations reveals that several kinds of undesirable results frequently follow from them."[15] The primary objection is undoubtedly that taxable business can thus be placed at a serious competitive disadvantage.

Even though the holding of a foundation in some one stock may constitute a considerable fraction of the wealth of the foundation in question, this may constitute only a small fraction of the voting stock of the corporation in question, and thus be unobjectionable. Although the Rockefeller Foundation has, in terms of market value, roughly 46 percent of its assets invested in the common stock of Standard Oil of New Jersey, this holding represents only about 2 percent of the total outstanding common stock of SONJ, so that there is no conceivable question of the Rockefeller Foundation's exerting any effective control over the company. In the case of the Sloan Foundation, the General Motors holding amounts to about 39 percent of the total assets of the foundation, but is only about 0.4 percent of the total outstanding stock of General Motors.

Others of the large general purpose foundations do, very unfortunately it seems to me, hold large fractions of the stocks of the companies from which their wealth was derived. Thus the Duke Endowment holds 57 percent and 82 percent, respectively, of the common and the preferred stock of the Duke Power Company; the Kellogg Foundation holds 51 percent and 45 percent, respectively, of the common and preferred stock of the Kellogg Company; the

Lilly Endowment holds 45 percent of the stock of Eli Lilly and Company; the John A. Hartford Foundation holds 33 percent of the stock of the Great Atlantic and Pacific Tea Company; and the Moody Foundation holds very substantial fractions of the stock in seven corporations, including 50 percent in the Gal-Tex Hotel Corporation, 50 percent in the Silver Lake Ranches Company, and 100 percent in the Texas National Hotel Company. It should be emphasized that these figures may well be changed by the time this book appears; for they are based on the most recent public report, usually that of 1964.

My own opinions on the matter are:

1. A reasonable concentration of a foundation's assets in the company or industry within which the fortune in question was created is natural, and is unobjectionable from the point of view of society; but in no case should a philanthropic foundation, over any extended period of time, own an effectively controlling interest in a profit enterprise. For general reasons that even a rank amateur in financial affairs can appreciate, a diversified portfolio is preferable in most cases.

2. If a foundation owns an improperly large fraction of the voting stock of any company, the foundation should not be forced by government regulations to make sacrifice sales, but should be allowed reasonable time to adjust its portfolio, perhaps with some temporary provision that the degree of control of the foundation be reduced, during the period of portfolio adjustment, by its not voting all of its stock.

3. Granting a clearly noncontrolling interest, a foundation, on general grounds of responsibility and prudence, should vote its stock. A philanthropic foundation has no business indulging in a business argument with management, and it is hard to imagine circumstances in which the foundation would. If the trustees of a foundation cannot support the management of a company in which some of its funds are invested, they should shift the investment.

The fact that all of the "perpetuities" of ancient times have been wiped out, combined with the sense of special obligation that properly attaches to investments for charitable and philanthropic purposes, has inevitably favored rather conservative investment policies for most foundations. On the other hand, a very considerable part of the total assets of foundations has been concentrated in a way which—however excellent is the record of the Ford Motor Company, Standard Oil of New Jersey, General Motors, Eli Lilly and Company, The Great Atlantic & Pacific Tea Co., the Kellogg Company, the Duke Power Company, etc.—would not normally be approved by the trust officer of a bank in the case of the investment portfolio for "widows and orphans."

Aside from the normal investor's desire for safety of principal, for increase in value, and for assurance of reasonable income, there are additional considerations which affect the investment policy of philanthropic foundations. A foundation whose program includes an interest in cancer research is unlikely to invest in the stocks of the tobacco companies; nor should any foundation be concerned with the murky areas of legal and potentially profitable investment involving shrewd exploitation of the less socially sound proclivities of the public. Generally speaking, the funds of a philanthropic foundation should be invested in activities which manifestly contribute positively to society as a whole.

There is one further matter connected with the investment policies of foundations; that is the reprehensible practice of a few foundations of abusing their tax exemption by indulging in business operations, including loans which are wholly improper and quite unrelated to their philanthropic purpose.

It will be mentioned at this point only that such abuses have occurred in connection with a small handful among the thousands of other philanthropic foundations which have been meticulously ethical in all "business" aspects. The exceedingly few bad cases quite naturally got publicity, while the thousands of good cases were not news, giving the public a distorted conception of foundation integrity, and damaging the image of the social contribution of foundations. This topic will receive further treatment in Chapter 14.

It is no accident that the verbs in the preceding paragraph are in the past tense, for the shady business practices often referred to as "trading on exemption" were in large measure dealt with in 1950 by appropriate changes in the federal laws and regulations. There remains some further necessary protection against such abuses, and no one approves of such protection more fully than do the responsible great majority of foundations. These responsible foundations indeed condemn such abuses even more emphatically than do the federal agencies and the public, for they suffer more unfairly from these mistakes of a few than does anyone else. Reforms to eliminate abuses tend to place a heavy burden of complicated reporting and control; and the responsible foundations naturally are concerned that too much of their energy and resources not be diverted away from philanthropic service and consumed by administrative and legalistic busywork. Society also would lose a great asset if foundations were "regulated" to such an extent as to remove the freedom and flexibility which so largely make possible the good which they do.

It would be ridiculous to throw the baby out with the bath; and this will surely not occur. Indeed, as we shall see when we discuss the various congressional investigations, it is part of our national genius to indulge for a time in frenzied excesses of criticism and attack: and then end up by being sensible.

CHAPTER 10

The Structure, Staffing, and Procedures of Foundations

A philanthropic foundation has at its top a board of trustees or directors in which is vested all the legal authority, the power, and the ultimate responsibility for its acts. In direct relationship to that board is a group, more or less numerous, of salaried officers—the president, vice president, further officers often called directors, who are in charge of specific branches of the foundation's program, and certain general officers such as the treasurer, secretary, and controller. Supplementing and assisting all these officers is a staff ranging from messenger boys to file clerks, typists, accountants, secretaries, and individuals in charge of publications, personnel, travel, purchasing, and other services.

If the foundation in question has significant activities abroad, it may maintain offices other than its central one; and if the foundation not only makes grants to other agencies, but also carries on an "operating" program, such for example as the agricultural program of the Rockefeller Foundation, then its roster contains individuals who are not "philanthropoids," but are doctors, scientists, engineers, experts in various fields of the social sciences, etc., who are working directly for the foundation in their normal professional capacities.

The president of a foundation is in almost all cases the chief executive officer, in contrast to industries where either the president or the chairman of the board is so designated. The president of a foundation is a member of the board of trustees. In most of the larger foundations the officers other than the president are not members of the board of trustees, although the major program officers would normally be called into meetings of the board to present proposals or to discuss aspects of its program.

Falling within this general description, the number and range of personnel vary greatly in actual cases. There are some small personal or family foundations in which the donor, his lawyer, and two or three business associates, close friends, or members of his family, constitute the board of trustees and the officers, and in which the staff, using the word in the sense of the general description given above, is essentially nonexistent.

At the other extreme are large general purpose and research foundations such as the Carnegie Corporation, the Ford Foundation, the Rockefeller Foundation, and the Sloan Foundation. The boards of trustees of these four foundations are large and representative of a wide range of points of view and knowledge. Their staffs are generally well trained within their particular disciplines, whether they are philanthropoids working at headquarters or assigned to the field here or abroad.

BOARDS OF TRUSTEES

It is interesting to examine the composition of the boards of trustees of the four foundations mentioned above. As for representation of the founder or of the founding family, Carnegie, Rockefeller, and Sloan each has one such member, Ford, two. Sloan and Carnegie are rather heavy on individuals who are most naturally thought of as industrialists and financiers, Sloan having thirteen such and Carnegie seven, while Rockefeller has five and Ford four. As for academic persons or men whose principal background is academic in character, Rockefeller has ten, Sloan and Ford four, and Carnegie three. Ford has three and Rockefeller two trustees who are in the field of mass communication—newspapers, magazines, television, etc.

No one should try to associate names with all of these numbers; for the categories overlap and these men are all too able and too broadly experienced to be accurately characterized with a single label. Also I have not attempted any classification of certain outstanding figures, men of high international reputations, whom I would call "men of affairs" except for the incorrect possible implication that their colleagues are not men who are also involved in very important affairs. Men of this caliber, moreover, have such wide interests that any single characterization is wholly inadequate. How does one classify a person who is equally known as an industrialist and as a humanist; or one who is a lawyer, a financier, and a major figure in international circles?

There are other foundations with able and impressive trustees, but the four examples just characterized indicate clearly the attitude of those foundations which take a broad and serious view of their public responsibility. Such foundations place the final authority for policy and for all major decisions with a group of absolutely top-flight persons—men of experience, of special talent, of wisdom, and of integrity. These men are in no sense representatives of the founder or of the founding family. In no conceivable sense do they represent the industry identified with the fortune in question. They are representatives of the public.

The majority of the larger foundations do not pay their trustees. Of the eighty-six foundations with assets which exceed $25 million, sixty-eight do not pay their trustees, this list including the Rockefeller, Carnegie, and Sloan foundations. Five foundations pay their trustees annual fees ranging from $1,000 to $5,000, three pay $5,000, two pay roughly $15,000, and five pay somewhat over $25,000.

It is important to note that on the four boards briefly described above there is only one case of an individual who is a member of two of the boards. Carnegie and Sloan do share one trustee: in my judgment he is so extremely able that one can only be thankful that he is willing to serve society in both of these jobs. But the idea of an "interlocking directorate," or of an "establishment"—something which has actually been charged—is simply pure nonsense.

The legal authority for the acts of a philanthropic foundation rests completely and solely on the board of trustees. It is their responsibility to determine the policy and program, and, since they control the appointment of all principal officers, they also set the tone of the actual staff operation. Although they have complete control over the grants, making these by their own direct action in all the more significant instances and by delegated authority in minor instances, their role with respect to grants is normally and primarily a judicial one; they make decisions chiefly on the basis of information and recommendations furnished by the officers.

Foundation boards of trustees are normally self-perpetuating. From time to time one hears suggestions that at least part of the boards should "represent the public" and that these members should be chosen in some way by the public. Community foundations do have boards which are chosen by a public procedure, and the Bernice P. Bishop Estate's board is selected by a majority of the supreme court of the state. From a long knowledge of several of the most important self-perpetuating foundation boards I assert that they do indeed represent the public interest; and I cannot conceive of a procedure of public selection that would produce boards more intelligent, unselfish, and dedicated than those which result under the existing procedures.

On the other hand, I would agree that it would be an improvement to have trustees who, on the average, are younger, who do not normally serve for terms longer than about ten years, and who are as widely representative as possible of different elements of our society and the different parts of our country.

STAFF

For all the housekeeping activities of a foundation—the indispensable work of clerks, secretaries, accountants, purchasing agents, those dealing with transportation and with publications of all sorts, the office managers, etc.—a foundation turns to the normal employment sources. Because of the nature of the work, many foundations have exceptionally high educational requirements for all other than routine jobs. Thus a college degree, in addition to excellent secretarial training, is not an unusual condition of employment in secretarial positions.

The recruitment of the officer staff of a foundation must be handled in a very specialized and individualistic manner. It is a little like picking candidates for a first trip to the moon. Although many general characteristics are obviously desirable, one cannot advertise for individuals who have received degrees of bachelor, master, or doctor of philanthropy. There is no specifically relevant training for such positions; and therefore no one is technically qualified, although practically everyone seems to be convinced that he is.

Most of the officer personnel, especially those of the larger foundations with broad programs, are recruited from academic circles, the foundation picking persons with extensive professional training, and often with research and administrative experience in the fields within which they will continue to work for the foundation.

I have seen it suggested that foundations should not enjoy tax-free privileges unless they are efficiently managed, and that one criterion of efficiency is a low cost for "administrative overhead." It would in fact be not only inefficient but also scandalous for a foundation to pay excessive salaries to its officers. In general these salaries should be competitive with the salaries of distinguished professorships, deanships, and presidencies of academic institutions of comparable rank—for the simple and practical reason that persons of similar qualifications are required.

It does not at all follow that the ratio of "administrative overhead" to the total of grants should be automatically accepted as an indication of efficiency. A responsible officer of a foundation may exert the critically important judgments which lead to the decisions as to how hundreds of thousands, or even millions, of dollars are to be used. If an additional $10,000 of salary will obtain an officer who increases by a few percent the wisdom, and hence the practical efficiency, of the grants, this $10,000 is clearly the best investment the foundation can make.

The main variation in administrative overhead from one foundation to another is not, however, the result of salary differentials. It results from the size of staff, and this in turn results from the nature of the foundation's activities. If the foundation is completely non-operative, distributing all of its money as grants to other agencies (universities, research institutes, etc.) then the staff can be relatively small and the administrative costs relatively low.

If some of these grants go for development purposes to strengthen and improve inexperienced agencies (say some of the smaller predominantly Negro colleges, as an example) then a good deal more staff work is necessary, both in working up the basis for the grants and in furnishing helpful supervision after the grants have been made. This necessarily increases the foundation's administrative costs; but it is incorrect to label this with the pejorative word "over-head." This is a vitally necessary cost of efficient operation.

This point applies even more strongly if the foundation in question carries on semi-operating or operating activities. In the former case it is again true that the foundation must maintain, and pay salaries to, a sufficient staff to supervise and carry out the semi-operating activity in question. This might, for example, be a scholarship or fellowship program which requires a great deal of detailed attention to each individual case. And when a foundation carries on an operating program, such as for example the agricultural program of the Rockefeller Foundation, then the foundation should no more be criticized for the total of the relevant staff salaries than should a university for the total amount it pays its professors.

Percentages for administration can understandably run higher for small foundations unless they can depend partly on contributed services, or unless they utilize part-time advisors. Some foundations manage in this way to keep administrative costs down to a few percent. Thus the Lilly Endowment reports administrative costs of 3.3 percent, the Moody Foundation 3.5 percent, while the figure for the John A. Hartford Foundation is only 1.4 percent. Kellogg, Carnegie, and Rockefeller have administrative costs in the 5-7 percent range, while Duke is only slightly higher. Sloan is now operating with administrative costs slightly over 4 percent, and the administrative budget of Ford, although large on an absolute scale ($7.2 million), is less than 3 percent of its huge total of grants. Comparisons among the figures just stated are meaningless unless the individual situations are analyzed in detail.

It is doubtless natural to assume that the giving away of money is not only pleasant but very easy. This is a gross error. To give away money wisely, constructively, and effectively is very hard indeed. It involves a tremendous amount of patience, insight, courage, and hard work. It involves disappointment, regret for things that could not be done, unhappy worry over negative decisions that may have been wrong. It also involves very rich rewards, especially when some young scholar, scientist, or artist who has been helped through a foundation grant at a critical and early stage turns out later to be a great man.

Giving away money wisely is an extraordinarily subtle and difficult task, with moral, social, and intellectual complications that keep the conscience active and the mind bothered. There are so many kinds of people who legitimately need help, and so many ways of going about helping them. The philanthropoid needs intelligence, imagination, flexibility, and a large streak of unselfishness. A genuine desire to interest himself in other people's goals and ambitions is essential. There are people who cannot do this, but there are also people who can, and who find publicly unobservable, perhaps forever hidden, pleasure and satisfaction in knowing that they have helped. A good philanthropoid must be one of this latter breed.

The good philanthropoid must have a real zest and talent for understanding and dealing with people. And this enthusiasm must be tempered by that indefinable something called taste. The philanthropoid sits on one side of the desk; the applicant sits on the other. Money, and all that goes with it, sit beside the philanthropoid. These are funds, further, toward which he has clear responsibilities. But while he guards the foundation's resources he must also be able to enter into the thoughts and the aspirations of the person on the other side of the desk; he must be able, in a very delicate and sensitive way, to sit on both sides of the desk at once.

This is not to say that he must in any way direct the people who come to him for help. Anything approaching that is dangerous and can degenerate to such a level that it becomes disgraceful both intellectually and morally. The philanthropoid must never tell anyone what he ought to be interested in. He must ask questions and listen to answers. He must not plant the answers he would like to have coming back to him. He, of all persons, must never start a question by saying, "Don't you think . . ."

The problem of a good officer staff presents serious difficulties for smaller foundations, which cannot reasonably spend on administrative costs a sum large enough to hire the number and quality of officers they need. Even if a foundation chooses to work in one well-defined field—say mental disorders, just as an illustration—and even though it works only in the United States, this would normally require at least several thoroughly trained men, able and imaginative professional scientists conversant with the present state of knowledge in this field, and acquainted with, and having the respect and confidence of, active research men in this field. These men would have to travel widely and frequently, for dependable judgments rest not on paper evidence, but on direct personal knowledge.

Why is this necessary? Why not just sit at a desk in one city, read the requests that are mailed in, select the best ones for grants, and turn down the rest? There are many reasons why this will not work, or at least will not work well. Some rather mediocre persons produce elaborately impressive written requests. Some modest, shy, unassertive persons so greatly dislike the process of "asking for money" that they either refuse to do it or do it poorly. And yet they may thoroughly deserve aid. They have to be sought out.

Some colleges, universities, and research institutes have professional money-raising specialists who polish up requests until they would fairly dazzle an unsophisticated foundation officer. More serious than these difficulties is the basic fact that philanthropic decisions ought to be made only after weighing not just the request on the desk, but the possible alternative requests that might and should offer competition.

There have been instances in which a foundation has had one single top officer of such unusual insight and wisdom, and such unusual relationship with experts on whom he could call for informal advice, that he alone could do practically all the sifting of requests and possibilities, choosing those which he would take to the trustees for their approval. I believe that Fred Keppel, during the years when he was president of the Carnegie Corporation, was that kind of an officer. Abraham Flexner probably was also and his record makes it difficult to disagree with him. But the day for this kind of leadership of a great philanthropic foundation is, I think, past. The pace of advancement in all fields, the interrelationships of disciplines, international involvements—all these make it impossible for one person, contemplative in one spot, to be in touch with, to appreciate, and to weigh wisely the opportunities for philanthropic aid.

Some sizable foundations maintain an absolutely minimum permanent staff, and make use of formally constituted advisory committees for the various aspects of their programs. This seems, superficially, a very sensible and efficient procedure. It reduces the expenditures for administrative overhead, and makes possible a flexible readjustment of professional advice resources to suit changing programs or unexpected opportunities.

In actual practice, however, this procedure seems to have serious faults. Unless the advisors are very able and broadly informed, they will not be adequate; if they do have these qualifications, then they are almost certainly already overburdened with other committee, advisory, and administrative duties, so that they should not take on another such job. Many if not most of the federal agencies distributing research money make use of review, study, and advisory committees of this sort, and the good men are overworked. It is a waste of a precious national resource to require first-rate productive scientists to leave their laboratories and studies and to spend considerable time in administrative work. Because of the pressure of time, moreover, the job is often done superficially. Persons who are too junior and too inexperienced prepare summary documents and "brief" the panels of experts, this procedure being in solemn fact too brief. There is thus a real danger of accomplishing an appearance of expert judgment, whereas the actual determining forces are operating at a much more junior and inexperienced level.

Since so much of the financial support of scholarship comes from federal, foundation, and other sources outside the universities and institutes where the scholars and scientists are employed, it is necessary to recruit and train, and then to recognize, respect, and compensate properly a type of person which has been emerging over the past quarter century—the scientist-administrator, or the scholar-administrator.

The groups of highest status are, and should remain, those who personally make original and significant contributions to knowledge and art—the productive researchers, the creative artists, the penetrating and illuminating scholars. But society, and all the professional and scholarly groups, must also recognize that the role of the able scholar-administrator is creative as well as necessary. This role, at least until recently and for the most part still, has been unhonored and unsung. One of the finest and most socially useful scientists in our country said to me a few years ago, "It is rather ridiculous, but I could not be made a member of the National Academy of Sciences, and could therefore not, as an official of that organization, devote myself to broad aspects of national science problems, except for the somewhat accidental fact that, a good many years ago, I did some research in my specialty, and was elected to the Academy on the sole basis of that research." The fact is that no one could get elected to the Academy of Sciences for being expert in the precise activities for which the academy was created, namely to serve as a chief source of competent and unbiased advice to the government on all matters connected with science.

It is quite clear that a considerable number of government agencies—the National Science Foundation, the National Institutes of Health, the Atomic Energy Commission, the National Aeronautics and Space Administration, the defense agencies which support research, and now, at last, the National Foundation on the Arts and the Humanities, as well as the numerous foundations—must be administered by exceedingly capable individuals. It will not do to borrow men and women for short assignments to such duties. The familiar two-year leave is just about long enough for the person to begin to be familiar with the complications of his job. Nor will it do to depend primarily on persons who have retired from academic posts on account of age. There are uses for such persons (as the present author would quite naturally insist); but the full vigor, the elasticity, the liberalism, the imagination of younger persons is essential, as well as the direct contact with the younger ranges of contemporary intellectual life.

This new type of service to science, to scholarship, and to society must not be treated, as it has often been in the past, with faint disapproval by the elite, or with minor respect, status, and compensation by society. The foundations, being fortunately free from civil service regulations, have on the whole treated their officer staffs well. The government has not done comparably well. The attitudes of the top professional people have not, in my opinion, adjusted to the realities of the present. Just as it used to be said that those "teach" who cannot "do," so many still seem to think that the mentally anemic settle down into administrative positions at least partly because they can neither teach nor do.

Since I have said that first-rate research men should not waste their time in administrative work, the reader may incorrectly think that I am urging that second-rate persons go into administrative work, and that they should then be reclassified as first-rate persons. This is not at all what I mean. There are many ways of being first rate. Certainly the most glorious way, in my view, is to be a first-rate researcher. But there are also really first-rate persons, with eager, receptive, and excellent minds, who are not first-rate at research, but who appreciate and understand research, scholarship, and creative activity, and who are willing to spend their lives doing what it takes to make the enterprise of scholarship and learning most effective.

PROCEDURES: PROGRAMS

A philanthropic foundation has money: and it is expected, indeed it must, give its income to other persons or institutions to help them do something which otherwise presumably could not be done. But what is that something? A philanthropic foundation must decide what its purpose is, what kinds of activities it will aid. In short, it must decide what its program is.

Why cannot the foundation merely announce its existence and its willingness to receive requests and then approve the best of these and turn down the rest? Why is it necessary for a foundation to "have a program"?

In the early days of the Rockefeller Foundation, one imaginative and vigorous trustee was accustomed to say, "Our policy should be to have no policy." At times and under certain circumstances such a free-wheeling and flexible notion would work. But the modern sizable foundation needs a defined and publicly stated program, reviewed at intervals to see if changes are desirable. It would be premature to rejudge any substantial program until it had had, say, at least five years to demonstrate its strength and weakness; but it would seem wise to reconsider any program, however well it seems to be going, after each ten-year interval.

A foundation of considerable size needs a well-defined and clearly-announced program, first, because no foundation staff can be competently informed in all matters, and none should make recommendations to its board without basis in competent judgments. If a foundation selects one or more defined areas of interest and assigns relevantly trained officers to them, the first essential step is taken toward wise decisions. Second, no foundation can maintain a sense of purpose, or a staff with a conviction of accomplishment, unless it tackles definable problems within which progress can be made and recognized.

It is not only natural but proper and useful that the interests and enthusiasms of the founder and of the trustees be reflected in a stated program. The public, and particularly all the potential grant seekers, have a right to know within what areas a general foundation is operating. The declared interests of existing foundations can also play the useful role of affecting the interests of newly formed foundations, by encouraging either imitation or contrast.

I have known able scholars in universities who, resenting the fact that their own requests had been turned down because they were "outside our program," have argued that the board of trustees of a foundation has no right to decide on a program which, by approving certain areas, excludes others. Such critics seem to consider that foundation money is "public money" in the sense that all have access. Foundation money is *society's money,* in the sense that each board of trustees is responsible for using the funds they control to benefit society as a whole, but each board of trustees has the clear legal, intellectual, and moral obligation to make choices of interest and activity.

Should a foundation which has determined upon and announced a program ever depart from that plan? Many foundations do, in fact, make an occasional exception to program. If this is done for what may be called "personal" reasons, the exception is, in my judgment, improper. But, once in a long while, something comes along that fits no category, qualifies under no conceivable program or policy, but is imaginative, novel, and important. In my day at the Rockefeller Foundation we had a formula for admissible exceptions that still seems to me good.

It was this: An "exception to program" could be considered provided it met two criteria. First, the proposal had to be absolutely and unequivocally outstanding in the quality of the person or persons involved, the auspices, and all subsidiary circumstances. If "the top 5 percent" was the demand normally to be met, exceptions had to fall within the top 1 percent. Second, the project had to be truly and obviously unique so that any competition with it, then or later, seemed unlikely.

The Rockefeller boards had no recognized program in astronomy when the decision was made in the late twenties to finance the construction of the unique 200-inch telescope on Mount Palomar—a commitment which eventually required $6.55 million. That policy permitted an occasional exception without causing much trouble about precedents, but such trouble cannot be completely eliminated. When the Rockefeller Foundation, also as an exception to program, approved a large grant to assist in the building of Ernest Lawrence's 184-inch cyclotron, we then thought that an accelerator of that size would be "unique," as was the 200-inch telescope on Mount Palomar. The great optical telescope is still the largest in the world nearly twenty years after its dedication, but accelerators rather promptly become bigger and bigger. The pioneering importance of the 184-inch is not to be questioned; and accelerators have now become so costly that requests for their construction embarrass governments, rather than foundations.

The problem of program is different for smaller foundations, which can properly be more elastic in their choices. Indeed, they seem bound by circumstances to be more personal or intuitive, for they cannot afford a sizable number of highly trained specialists, whose wide travel and intimate contacts with the developing fronts of scholarship can provide an objective and logical basis for decisions.

Smaller foundations thus are almost forced to reflect the special and personal interests of the founders, the boards, and the usually rather small staffs of officers, and to reflect these interests more than a large foundation should. This seems justifiable and works well, primarily because many small foundations with a wide variety of interests and enthusiasms make possible a broad coverage of opportunities.

A small foundation can properly make a grant to, let us say, a small liberal arts college in which it has a personally-based interest. If twenty other similar small liberal arts colleges come knocking on its door (the door of its safe, presumably) the small foundation can simply say, "We made the grant to Little Ivy simply because we have a special interest in it; but we are not prepared—and indeed are obviously not able—to consider similar grants to a lot of similar fine small colleges."

A big foundation, with national or even international scope to its program and with wide and eagerly sought publicity for all its grants, cannot make that kind of reply.

The programs of foundations differ by virtue of the distinction between *external projects, operational projects,* and *self-managed projects.* A foundation may utilize one, two, or all three of these types of activity.

An external project is one to whose support the foundation contributes in full or in part, the project being carried out by a person or group in the employ of some other organization, such as a college, a university, a research institute, or an agency like the National Academy of Sciences.

When a foundation supports external projects, its own initiative is almost completely restricted to the act of decision of which projects it will turn down or approve. The wisdom of the foundation reveals itself not so much in the individual choices, for unless the foundation is overconservative and lacking in imagination (and sometimes even then!) some of the individual decisions will prove to have been mistakes. The wisdom of the foundation will reveal itself rather in the long-range pattern of these grants—whether they, as a whole, add up to an overall program with a recognizable strategy and a record for progress.

In the early and more informal stages of discussion with scholars and officers of universities, it is proper for foundation officers to contribute ideas about the project, or at least to *suggest* ideas. To the extent that these are acceptable to the institution, they will be reflected in the formal written request submitted.

But the grant once made, the foundation ought to keep its hands off if a university is to preserve its independence and freedom of action. It is as bad for a foundation to try to "run" a part of a university as it would be for the government to do so, or the alumni (for that is sometimes a threat), or the students (as happened in Latin America and as is now to some extent happening here). Once the assessment has been completed, a positive decision arrived at, and a grant made, the foundation must permit the projects to remain *external.* An attempt to have them be both *external* and *self-managed* by the foundation will almost certainly prove disastrous.

Operational projects are those activities carried out by a group of individuals chosen by the foundation and remaining under its employ and control. For example, the Rockefeller Foundation for many years carried on activities in public health (on yellow fever, malaria, hookworm, etc.) around the world. It did this *itself*, in the sense that it had a field staff of some seventy-five scientists, permanently in the employ of the Rockefeller Foundation, and supplied and serviced by the Rockefeller Foundation. In many of the actual projects, foreign governments collaborated by furnishing local assistance, but the program was essentially under the control of the Rockefeller Foundation.

This type of activity requires a large amount of money and is extremely unwise unless undertaken on a long-continued basis of stable support. When I proposed to the trustees of the Rockefeller Foundation the first move in their worldwide agricultural program in 1941, I told them not to approve the recommendation presented unless they were prepared to stand by this program for at least twenty-five years.

Such activity gives a foundation opportunity to express its own ideas and test its own capacity; but it ties up a substantial block of income for a long period. I have used here the Rockefeller Foundation program in public health as an example of an operational project: its agricultural programs in Mexico, Colombia, Chile, and India are current examples.

Good examples of self-managed programs are the Scholarship and the Basic Science programs of the Sloan Foundation. Although expert and experienced advice is sought on both programs from external personnel, the initial thinking leading to the design and the adoption of the programs was carried out, and subsequent decisions on policy and individual appointments made, by Sloan Foundation officers. On the other hand, the recipients are free to accept or refuse; no one can claim that he is externally forced in any decision which he should have a right to make for himself.

The self-managed program provides opportunity for the foundation to utilize its own wisdom and imagination. It does not "freeze" the assets and income, since it is at liberty to reduce or drop the program, if not abruptly, at least on a fairly prompt schedule of withdrawal. It has no continuing commitments to anyone.

On the other hand, the foundation is severely limited by the ideas, insight, wisdom, and imagination it can command from its staff and advisory boards. It cannot ordinarily hope or expect in such programs to put its dollars along with many other dollars from other sources; nor can it expect to employ its dollars with the tremendous efficiency to be realized when a relatively few foundation dollars are used by some exceedingly experienced, high-grade organization (usually a great university or great department of a university, or a great scholar or scientist of a university or research institute) as the critical final amount enabling them to activate their own plans, utilizing all the auxiliary resources of their own institution.

PROCEDURES: THE EVALUATION PROCESS

A large foundation cannot afford to look at a vast array of projects through a small hole in a large piece of paper, observing the attraction of a single project without seeing the competing attraction of the others. Viewed alone, a proposal may seem wonderful, unique, immensely attractive; and the man or group proposing it may seem capable of wonders. But a large foundation is obliged to think more broadly and more objectively—to look through other holes in that same piece of paper at competing alternatives. How many are there? Do they, taken together, represent a total field of activity that the foundation can or should get into? Is there any reason, strategic, social, intellectual, or moral, for preferring the opportunity seen through one particular hole to numerous others of near equal merit and urgency? Unless the large foundation is prepared to deal with more than one isolated instance, it must usually decline the invitation. Unless a project is evaluated by comparison with its natural alternatives, it is not evaluated at all.

The evaluation of proposals involves to a limited extent the weighing of ideas and plans; to a much greater and more important extent, it involves judgments about men. However elaborate and promising a plan may be, it is useless unless it is to be carried out by men and women of outstanding ability, dedication, and imagination. And if a person of proven capacity needs financial aid, it is neither important nor sensible to require from him a detailed blueprint of his possible future creations.

Years ago I recommended to the board of trustees of the Rockefeller Foundation sizable and flexible support over a substantial term of years for an outstanding chemist. In presenting the proposal I concentrated attention on the superlative record of past accomplishment of the scientist. When I was through with the presentation a very able businessman who was then on the board and whom I will call Mr. B. said, "Dr. Weaver, I am afraid that I don't understand *just what* Professor X will do over the next seven years if we provide this support." As I was somewhat frantically trying to decide how to reply, a perfect answer was provided for me by one of the scientist trustees, Dr. Herbert Gasser. Then the head of the Rockefeller Institute for Medical Research, Gasser in his answer brilliantly summarized the foolishness of attempts to overspecify the details of a future research program. He said, very gently, "Why, Mr. B., if Professor X knew just exactly what he was going to do, he wouldn't need to do it."

Another Nobel laureate, Dr. Peter J. W. Debye, has expressed the same idea. In an informal discussion reported in *Science*, Debye said, "Well, now I'm going to exaggerate, and an exaggeration is dangerous. Suppose someone submits a proposal, and in this proposal he says that he undertakes to do certain experiments and to get certain results. Since this is very clearly stated and carefully outlined, the proposal is accepted. But I claim that this should not be accepted because, if he already knows what will come out of it, then there's no point in doing it. This, you see, is the trend. What we need are proposals which the sponsors are courageous enough to support, while the investigators do not know what will come out of them."[1]

There are various ways of developing the program of a philanthropic foundation. In one procedure, the officials of the foundation (trustees, president, or officers) come to basic decisions as to the *areas* or general problems which the foundation will adopt as its interests. Thus in the natural sciences the Rockefeller Foundation, in the early 1930's, and for about a dozen years thereafter, made it clear, by their published statements and by the literally hundreds of conversations of its officers with scientists all over the world, that the Rockefeller Foundation was interested in helping support research "in which the techniques of the physical sciences are applied to basic biological problems."

From that point on, the initiative rested with the scientists and scholars, not with the officers of the foundation. As the news got around, scientists who wanted to do that sort of research turned to the Rockefeller Foundation for help.

This procedure has several disadvantages. It requires a good bit of time to develop programs. This procedure also requires officers to travel widely to hold the conversations which gradually stimulate interest on the part of the scientists themselves. It requires great patience and confidence on the part of trustees and a selfless attitude on the part of the officers. They do not *appear* to be playing an active role in the development of science; and they have to be willing to get their satisfaction out of their inner knowledge that, in actual fact, they *are* playing an important role, although it is largely behind the scenes.

In the other procedure, an officer of a foundation believes a rather specific idea ought to be activated. He approaches individuals in a university or research institute and says in effect, "I have been thinking about the desirability of. . . . This would probably take x thousands of dollars, and I think the Blank Foundation would be willing to supply the money. What do you think of the idea, and would your institution be interested?"

This second procedure also could have disadvantages. There is the risk that an officer of a university will find it impossible *not* to be interested in an idea that has a substantial amount of money attached. There is further the risk that this procedure will weaken and disturb the responsibility for planning within a university, for this responsibility ought to rest wholly *inside* the institution. In addition, it is difficult to terminate or reduce support of a development which has been more or less "wished on" an institution by a foundation. A foundation is likely to feel a moral responsibility to continue.

Certain procedures are intermediate between these two extremes. A large general purpose foundation can make a "package grant" to a smaller special purpose foundation, enabling the special purpose foundation to make a series of allocations for activities in the field in which it has special knowledge and experience. The general purpose foundation has the satisfaction of having exerted some initiative, but there is no danger of luring the special purpose foundation into a project that is not at the top of its own list of priorities. In just this way, for example, the Sloan Foundation makes a package grant to the Deafness Research Foundation. In a somewhat similar way the much larger Ford Foundation, when it has an idea it wants to develop and when a suitable special purpose foundation does not already exist, sees to it that a new special purpose foundation is created. Initially this may be a "satellite foundation" wholly supported by the originating foundation; but there is no reason why such a special purpose foundation could not later broaden the sources of its support.

This use of an intermediary agency can provide a balance between two limiting ways of developing programs. It may be important to maintain the balance. For in the case of universities or other organizations with broad and varied purposes, there ought to be, in general, great reluctance about any procedure which, however attractively put, is in fact an attempt to sell them an idea they did not generate. In the case of organizations with clearly defined and relatively narrow purpose (a deafness foundation, a conservation foundation, a cancer institute, etc.) there is essentially no risk involved in taking the initiative of asking them whether or not they would like to undertake further or enlarged activity specifically relevant to their declared purpose.

Granting that the evaluation of individual persons is the most critically important business of foundation officers, how can such evaluations be made? It must be conceded that a very few rare individuals have a natural instinct for judging ability. Such judges require no aids and no advice.

Past accomplishment is a sound guide in the case of an applicant who is old enough to have accumulated a substantial record. If his record is not excellent, but if he has been handicapped by a poor location or by too meager support, this should be taken into consideration. It is, however, of relatively routine ease, especially in highly developed disciplines, to rank the more mature persons. The challenging and significant problem is to judge younger persons. For them the foundation assistance can come at a critical time and play a significant role.

Emerging ability can be discerned in the case of young scientists, for example, in the following way: The problem is, first of all, simplified by the fact that scientists tend to blossom young. In mathematics and theoretical physics, including theoretical chemistry, which is almost indistinguishable from theoretical physics, outstanding ability is almost certainly observable by the age of twenty-five, and may be clear several years younger. This has been true in mathematics, in particular, for a long time. Galois, recognized as one of the great mathematicians of all times, was born in 1811 and died when he was only twenty-one years old. It used to be the case that chemists, especially organic chemists, who had to accumulate a great fund of experience, matured later, as did astronomers and certain types of biologists. But in the present fast-moving world, with daring and imaginative theoretical ideas leading the way in all branches of science, human leadership tends to be recognizable early.

It should be very rarely necessary, and is rarely useful, to attempt to judge the ability of scientists on the basis of formal written statements of recommendation. It should be rarely necessary, because the science officers of a foundation should travel widely to laboratories, developing informal but dependable working relationships with many scientists. Sitting on a stool in a lab, one gets to meet the young people. In long conversations in the office of the chief, one asks, "Whom do you consider the most promising young persons who are just emerging in your field?" The spontaneous answers to that kind of question, asked dozens of times in many places, form an interlaced network of invaluable information.

The formal request for a written "recommendation" rarely produces useful information. For the more conscientious an advisor is, the more likely he is to be influenced, consciously or not, by the fact that he is acting as a proponent of the candidate in question, bound to emphasize virtues and unlikely to be very candid about limitations.

The most useful information is obtained indirectly. It is not very profitable to ask, "How good do you think Dr. X is?" for this question automatically creates a prejudicial atmosphere. If instead one asks, "What are the important new leads in your field? Who is developing these? Have you recently heard especially impressive papers, at scientific meetings by young people?" then the advisor probes his memory in a completely relaxed and unforced way. It takes a lot of time and effort to build up, in this way, a broad store of information about the personnel in a field; but it is, I think, the most reliable way to do so. Ideally the science staff of a foundation, when a request is received, should already know so much about the scientists involved that the matter of further advice need not arise.

This kind of informal discussion, between foundation officers and scientists, young and mature, has important by-products. One can ask such informants, or the prospects to whom they refer, what they are interested in doing which, for a variety of reasons, they cannot now do. This is a fruitful way of drawing out useful ideas. It avoids the basic curse of putting proposals into an applicant's mouth, and at the same time it may help define the otherwise unsupported, perhaps only dreamed-of areas into which excellent people would move if they only could.

This procedure for enabling officers of a foundation to accumulate dependable information within some field is for the most part not feasible for a small foundation, unless it concentrates within a fairly narrow field and can afford at least two officers competently trained within that field. The smaller foundation must use as a basis for its decisions information both more local and more intuitive in character. This does not seem to me particularly unfortunate. Logic and objectivity are powerful tools; but many problems can be effectively approached with the more delicate and more sympathetic tools of intuition and compassion. There is ample room for both approaches.

PROCEDURES: DECISIONS

A request received by a foundation is first screened to determine whether or not it falls within the program and policy of the foundation in question. If that decision is negative, then a declination based on that fact would ordinarily be sent rather promptly.

If a submitted request does fall within the program and policy of a foundation, the normal procedure is that the officers study the proposal and obtain in various ways expert opinion as to its significance and as to the competence of the personnel involved. It is also important to judge the general setting provided by the institution involved: Will the project profit from able, efficient, and reliable management as well as from inspiring leadership? Does the institution in question furnish a suitable setting? Is there assurance that results obtained in the project will be effectively communicated and practically utilized? Are the persons involved dedicated and unselfish as well as experienced and competent? Do the past records of the persons involved justify confidence? If the project succeeds, will a real advance be thereby accomplished? Is the budget reasonable? Is there assurance of the availability of the requisite funds, equipment, and so forth not furnished by the proposed grant?

Following the studies by the appropriate officer or officers, most foundations with which I am familiar then submit proposals to a detailed and searching discussion of the entire group of foundation officers. Questions and doubts from fellow officers are fully aired. If and when a favorable consensus of the officer group is reached, the proposal is written up for formal presentation to the trustees.

Executive committees of boards of trustees of philanthropic foundations usually meet monthly, and to these executive committees is often delegated, from the full board, the authority to deal with proposals up to some stated financial size, provided the proposals fall within general policies previously approved by the entire board. Larger proposals, and questions of programs and policies, are handled by meetings of the entire board of trustees, which may occur twice a year or more often, and which may extend over more than one day.

To expedite matters and to provide greater flexibility, boards of trustees may delegate to the officers the authority to deal, between meetings of the executive committee, with certain types of smaller grants in categories previously specifically approved by the board and charged against block sums approved by the trustees. These "officer actions" in the Rockefeller Foundation, as an example, require three signatures, that of the top officer of the program area in question (assuring professional approval), that of a top financial officer (assuring that sufficient funds exist in approved categories), and that of the president (assuring overall authoritative approval). Fellowship appointments, travel grants, and so-called "grants-in-aid" are illustrations of grants handled in this way by officers acting within powers delegated to them by the trustees.

At meetings of the boards the recommendations of the officers are submitted to the trustees, normally with oral presentations to supplement the written documentation furnished to the trustees in advance. Discussion, questions, and frequently animated debates occur as the trustees probe the weaknesses and strengths of the proposals. Anyone with organization experience will, however, not be surprised at the statement that in the vast majority of instances the trustees approve the recommendations of the officers. In the twenty-eight years during which I recommended a total of many hundreds of individual actions to the trustees of the Rockefeller Foundation, the approval of the trustees was withheld on an almost negligible number, less than five of any size or consequence. In one case a recommendation was made which counsel ruled to be of questionable legality. In one case the proposed action had important and unfortunate implications neither I nor my fellow officers had sensed; the alert board skillfully and properly appreciated them. In two or perhaps three instances, weaknesses in the proposals were uncovered by the trustee debate, and I was quite properly instructed to take the proposals back and rework them to eliminate the difficulties. But the record on approvals by the trustees was well over 99 percent.

Does this mean that the board was a rubber-stamp group? It most certainly does not! The trustees were so skillful and helpful in developing and elucidating policies that the officers were working with a clear and mutually agreeable understanding of the sorts of proposals which we would bring forward. We also very well knew what sorts of proposals the trustees would consider undesirable and improper. Within this framework, legally controlled by the trustees but developed through joint efforts of the trustees and the officers, the trustees had confidence in the technical and professional judgments of the officers, and backed those judgments.

Any sensitive and sensible officer, moreover, sat through every trustee meeting with his ears and his mind wide open. The points raised by the trustees—often insights resulting from the broad and varied experience of the trustees, which the more specialized officers might well have missed—would serve as important guides for future deliberations of the officers.

With that sort of mutual respect and confidence connecting trustees with officers, it can be literally true that on the one hand the recommendations of officers are practically always approved, while on the other hand the trustees are without any possible doubt fulfilling their legal, social, and moral obligation to control all the behavior of the foundation in question.

PROCEDURES: INITIATIVE

One of the most interesting and debatable questions concerning the procedures of foundations is this: should foundation officers restrict themselves to choosing among proposals that are brought to them; or, playing a more active role, should they themselves originate projects and then try to locate individuals, groups, or institutions which are prepared to accept the foundation's financial aid and carry out the plan?

There is no single or simple answer to this question. To deny to foundations the rights to have ideas of their own, and completely to condemn them to the passive role of merely choosing among the ideas of others, would make it difficult indeed for foundations to attract competent trustees and officers, and would result in a deterioration of the entire philanthropic enterprise. But, on the other hand, it would be clearly intolerable for only moderately able persons, using the lure of financial support, to seek to influence the activities of more able persons.

If a foundation, after extended and competent study, decides that it wishes to undertake an "operating program" (for example, the eradication of a disease in some geographic area, or the improvement of crop yields in some country, or the study of some other important problem) and if the foundation is prepared to set up a staff of its own employees and take full responsibility for the entire undertaking, the foundation should certainly be completely free to do so. When it offers employment to the individuals who will carry out the project, these individuals are free agents who may accept or reject the terms of employment, exactly as though they were being offered jobs by any university, research institute, or company. The problem that money may improperly influence ideas does not arise in this type of foundation activity.

Foundations, moreover, frequently have activities which can be designated as "semi-operating." For example, a foundation may decide, after careful study, that there is a shortage of trained personnel in some special field. The foundation may, again on its own initiative, seek to alleviate that shortage by setting up a program of special fellowships open to qualified individuals who are interested in getting the training provided someone will furnish financial assistance. Then the foundation may itself administer that fellowship program, sifting the aid of candidates and choosing the recipients, perhaps with the aid of external advisors. The actual training would occur in universities and research institutes, so that the foundation does not itself carry out all portions of the program, accounting for the designation "semi-operating." The foundation, in seeking institutions to provide the actual training, must be sure that it offers terms beneficial to the institution as well as to the fellowship holder. In such a semi-operating program the foundation has a chance, and a chance which cannot be adversely criticized, to exercise initiative.

Again, a foundation can increase its initiative while decreasing the risk of undesirable or improper influence by concentrating its insight and wisdom on the problem of determining its program and policy and then announcing this publicly with clear exposition of the reasons for the choice, following which individuals, groups, and institutions are free to apply for aid under that program and policy if they desire to do so.

It is unrealistic to assume that the announcement of a "field of special interest" by a foundation does not involve any element of influence on potential recipients. Indeed, the desire of the foundation to bring new emphasis to a field would be frustrated if the announcement influenced no one. If the foundation has the intellectual resources to explain its choice attractively and persuasively, the matter may be brought to the attention of persons who are genuinely interested. No one is, after all, compelled to apply for aid.

There fortunately is, moreover, further middle ground between pure passivity and improper influence. If a foundation operates only as a post-office box into which written requests are deposited, the foundation officers merely choosing from among these requests, no one occupies the middle ground. But a good foundation does not operate in that way. A "request" should be only the opening move in a mutually profitable discussion and study, the participants in which should be the professionally competent officers of the foundation in question and the scholars or scientists (not the "development officers" or professional money raisers of the institution in question) who will be in charge of the program if it goes forward. If these two groups cannot meet on equal intellectual terms, something is wrong with one or both of the two groups. A foundation officer ought to be able and well trained enough to discuss foundation projects in his field with any academic experts in such a way as to merit the interest and respect of the applicant. I cannot fully justify the words "middle ground" at the beginning of this paragraph. For in the large majority of instances the center of special competence will be closer to the applicant than it is to the philanthropoid. But, even so, the foundation representatives ought to be able to contribute something besides money. That foundation officers do rank with top personnel in academic and other circles is clear. Academic presidents have left to become foundation officials; foundation officials have resigned to become academic deans and presidents. At the moment two cabinet positions in Washington are held by men who were previously high officers of well-known philanthropic foundations; and a previously influential officer of the government is now the president of a great foundation.

PROCEDURES: FREEDOM AND CONTROL

Generally speaking, a philanthropic foundation should make grants with a minimum of strings attached. Indeed, when a grant is made to an institution or for a person of established reputation and demonstrated competence and reliability, the granting foundation should from that moment forward leave the matter in the hands of the recipient, with that minimum of fiscal control required for legal or other formal reasons. In contrast, federal agencies must look more closely over the shoulders of the recipients of their funds, chiefly because they work within that more tightly organized system of regulation and supervision which is viewed necessary to protect public funds.

One might say that a philanthropic foundation ought not to make a grant unless it is satisfied that both the practical management and the intellectual direction of the enterprise are competent and trustworthy—and, if this is the case, why not let them alone? This remark applies with a good deal of force if the foundation is backing competence. It applies, I would suppose, to all fields. The John Simon Guggenheim Memorial Foundation, having used all possible care in selecting the persons to receive its fellowships, then gives the holders practically complete freedom to spend the fellowship period and money as they see fit.

There are, however, important exceptions. A foundation might decide to make a grant aimed at improving the accounting procedures in a large number of small and struggling colleges. Here the situation is not that of trusting competence, but of wishing to improve competence. Temporary guidance, supervision, and indeed control would clearly be called for. There are many other situations of a roughly similar sort, where help designed for remedial purposes must include more than mere money.

Other situations of a somewhat different type also require continuing supervision. Practically all foundations, wishing to aid a certain man or group in an institution, make the grant, as a formal matter, *to* the institution although *for* the man or group. If this institution is located in certain parts of the world, one cannot always be entirely confident that the money will all be properly put at the disposal of the intended recipients, and therefore some continuing supervision is necessary. Also in certain institutions the top administration has sound ideas but does not have complete control. I have known, for example, of cases in which a university president would request that the Rockefeller Foundation require that annual budgets for expenditure under a grant be approved by the foundation. We would agree to this, not at all because we wanted to exercise internal control over the institution, but simply as a means of holding up the hand and of assuring the authority of a wise administrator struggling with undisciplined elements in his own institution.

PROCEDURES: DISCLOSURE AND ACCOUNTABILITY

Until relatively recently it could be properly charged that information about philanthropic foundations, their finances and activities, was not available to the public. President Frederick P. Keppel of the Carnegie Corporation used to make frequent and indignant references to "those silent trusts,"[2] and forty years ago he wrote:

> After all, the fundamental safeguard against the unsocial use of these [foundation] funds lies, in the long run, in public opinion and the possibility of public control. The apparent immunity of those who direct them lies in the freedom from taxation which the foundations enjoy, but there is nothing irrevocable about the present exemption of such bodies, and the community, if at any time it felt so disposed, could tax an offending foundation, or all foundations, out of active existence. . . . The element of public confidence in the makeup of foundation boards is therefore of very practical importance. Even more important is as wide an understanding as possible of what they do and how they do it.[3]

Twelve years later, the Carnegie Corporation's leader returned to the subject with these words:

> . . . it would carry the writer too far afield to reenter the discussion as to the proportion of American foundations which make no public record of their activities whatsoever—thereby failing to recognize their responsibility to the public as organizations enjoying exemption from taxation, a privilege shared with religious, educational and charitable institutions. The instances in which it seems impossible to obtain pertinent information is disquietingly large. The question is not whether the funds of these silent trusts are put to useful purposes —indeed, some of the so-called family foundations are to the writer's knowledge making their grants with intelligence and discretion— it is rather whether public confidence in the foundation as a social instrument, a confidence which is in no small degree based upon the policy of complete publicity adopted by the better known foundations, may not be endangered; for as St. Paul admonished the Corinthians, ". . . whether one member suffer, all the members suffer with it; or one member be honoured, all the members rejoice with it."[4]

Keppel's colleagues in other foundations carried on the campaign against their silent brethren. Edwin R. Embree, then president of the Julius Rosenwald Fund, wrote in 1949:

> If trust funds are to continue to have the great benefit of tax exemption—which means extra taxes for all the rest of us—they

must be subject to public accounting at least as strict as that required by the Securities Exchange Commission of companies whose stocks are listed on the public marts. This does not mean that a commission would regulate the gifts of a foundation. The commission would simply require and supervise a public accounting which at a minimum would mean publication of the names of all trustees and officers, a listing of the capital holdings together with all changes in those holdings each year, a detailed statement of income and a listing of expenditures including both gifts and compensation to individuals. Pitiless publicity and objective accounting are strong forces in America.[5]

In an introduction to the volume that was in the fifties the most comprehensive study of the accountability subject, F. Emerson Andrews said:

> In return for such solid advantages [tax forgiveness], and also in view of the fact that the ultimate beneficiary is society itself, however particularly the gift may be directed, it seems wholly proper that the foundation or trust should be held accountable for its stewardship. The availability of the new social asset should be made known promptly, at least to public authorities and possibly widely. Society should have the means of protecting itself against the theft, squandering, or unreasonable withholding of this promised benefit. Finally, the operations of the exempt organization should be fully and regularly reported, with adequate provision for review by a public authority possessing power to correct abuses. This constitutes accountability.[6]

In his book *Philanthropic Foundations,* published three years years later in 1956, Andrews reaffirms the foregoing understanding of what foundation accountability is and should be, and says, "Careful distinction must be made between accountability and control." In strongly favoring the first, he believed that the legal right to impose control existed, but that "the creation of a controlling authority, with power to divert foundation funds into only such channels as might receive wide public approval at a given moment, would both discourage further gifts from thoughtful donors and threaten the freedom to experiment of existing foundations."[7]

A number of foundation officials, and others related to philanthropic funds, continued to look upon a controlling authority as a threat to their effectiveness. They have less reason to do so now that a number of significant revisions in federal accountability requirements are in effect. These new measures require additional information from the foundations and other tax-exempt organizations and they make more information publicly available from the annual tax reports (990-A's) of these organizations. In connection with the latter, the Foundation Library Center's Washington, D.C., office is now enabled to photocopy the returns of filing foundations, excepting only those data considered completely confidential, namely the names of contributors. This privilege of examining and making copies of 990-A Internal Revenue forms is available upon application to anyone.

The revised regulations for filing the 990-A, "Return of Organization Exempt from Income Tax Section 501(c)(3) of the Internal Revenue Code," require that the salary paid each officer be divulged, that data on aggregate income accumulation, allocated between ordinary income and capital gains, be furnished, and that certain information be given on corporate stocks held.

From the 990-A reports filed in 1963 (covering a fiscal year ending in 1962) and since then, it is possible to obtain five facts concerning the grants foundations made during the report year. Those facts are as follows:

- a. Name of donee (recipient—individual or institution)
- b. Address of donee
- c. Amount of grant
- d. Class or category of grant, i.e., medicine, education, etc.
- e. Beginning with 1964, the assets of the foundation at market as well as at ledger value

Ten years ago only about one hundred foundations issued public reports, three-fourths of these annually or biennially, and the others irregularly. At present over two hundred foundations issue reports, more than half of these regularly. Seven of the ten largest general general purpose foundations and seventeen of the top twenty, eight of the top ten special purpose foundations and all of the largest ten community foundations issue regular reports. "But the reporting habits of the largest family foundations mar this record, with none of the largest ten publishing annually or biennially."[8] Thirteen company-sponsored foundations issue reports, but only one of these ranks in the top ten of this category.

It must be recognized that the publishing of reports is costly, and that it requires considerable staff time. Sometimes a report will stimulate a flood of calls and requests, many of which may only waste the time of both the asker and the asked. Some foundations, moreover, undoubtedly consider the publishing of a report to be an undesirable form of self-advertising.

In addition to the 990-A's that are required from the philanthropic organizations under review here (but not of religious and purely educational organizations), and in addition to the voluntary periodic reports that many general purpose foundations publish, some *states* require reports from philanthropies. These reports vary greatly; but state records that are open to public scrutiny are, or can become, an important source of information about foundations.

From the foregoing it is evident that the secrecy that some foundations attached to their financial characteristics in the past has been almost wholly removed, in the case of the largest and most prominent foundations, by their own newer policies, and for all foundations has been substantially dissolved by the 990-A Internal Revenue reports. Some further improvements in disclosure are possible and could be achieved through additional changes in data requirements on the federal forms.

Foundation accountability has more than one aspect. Not only are there the governmental filing requirements, and the voluntary disclosure by more general foundation reports released to the public; there is also the question of the public's access to the official agency data, and the range of information included in the public reports which the funds themselves publish. The new 990-A's solve much of the problem on the first score, and the consistent, meticulous publication of periodic reports with substantive and financial information by most of the large general purpose foundations clearly points the way to what should be universal practice for all philanthropic foundations. Raymond Fosdick's "doctrine of public responsibility" is certainly the ethical imperative foundations ought to observe. As he recently wrote:

This doctrine is still valid today. Indeed with the proliferation of foundations, it has become an urgent aspect of policy. The public is entitled to know the facts—all the facts—about the operation of foundations. And most of them, I believe, have . . . nothing to hide, nothing to cover up. . . . They have a proud record, and that record should willingly be made accessible to public scrutiny. In no lesser way can the essentially public nature of the responsibilities of foundations be adequately demonstrated.[9]

PROCEDURES: FLEXIBILITY IN POLICY AND PROGRAM

A high officer of a foundation once told me that he sensed some uneasiness, on the part of his board of trustees, as to whether that particular foundation was overly dedicated to its past and present policies, and not as alive and flexible as it should be with respect to new problems, new opportunities, and changing conditions in the world.

This man had asked one of his major staff officers whether the latter had in mind any significant changes in the program of the work coming under his particular responsibility; and the officer replied, "Why change a winning game?" The policy and program which his group had been following had been useful and successful, and, therefore, he was inclined to think that patience and sustained effort rather than change were called for.

Of course, it can be pointed out that no one can hope to keep on winning any game if he always uses the same strategy. If in poker I always bluff in the same way and under the same circumstances, my strategy will not be successful for very long. The phrase "a winning game" almost necessarily connotes "a changing strategy."

It is extremely puzzling and difficult to decide in foundation activities when patience and continuity or change is preferable. Private foundations have often been more effective than federal and other agencies because private foundations have, on the whole, been able to support a more sustained effort, without the nervous and unpredictable and often irrational shifts of policy and program which continuously plague some federal agencies. A recent Philadelphia newspaper reported that a Washington official, explaining why the federal "foreign aid" program is not more successful, said, "We are asked to use five-year plans to cope with twenty-year problems using two-year personnel and one-year money." The disastrously frequent and precipitate changes in some federal foreign aid programs is illustrated by the fact that, when I went to the Philippine Islands in 1953, I was informed that the aid program had just been changed, without notice. The explanation was "We have been Stassen-ated."

On the other hand, one simply has to face the fact that individuals do often develop a kind of stubborn inertia about their own set of ideas and activities, and that vested interests do get established.

An illustration of the advantages of flexibility is the life of Billy Rose, despite the disparity between the character of his activities and those of foundation officials. Rose started life as a stenographer and acquired such expertness in shorthand that he won, at least for that time, all existing prizes for speed and accuracy. He could take 280 words a minute. As a very young man he realized that he had already reached the limit of both salary and opportunity associated with that particular talent. So he abruptly started out on a new career. He became, in succession, a successful songwriter; a successful night-club owner-manager; a theatre owner-manager; a successful investor—he was at the time of his death the largest single stockholder of A T & T, with a holding of roughly $10 million; and the donor-founder of an art museum in Jerusalem. He subsequently decided to go into a new field of activity, again connected with a theatre. His courage and imagination about dropping an activity, once he had made his own characteristic contribution and had reached a plateau of performance, constitutes a piece of personal history which officers of foundations could well reflect upon.

PROCEDURES: "BIG THINGS" AND "LITTLE THINGS," THE PROBLEM OF SIZE

Everyone who has any creative imagination and drive wants to try to do "big things," not small things. Perhaps it is worth while to examine this statement a little. What *are* big things? Which dimension—physical, financial, intellectual, or other—makes them big? How big are big things when they are first discovered?

That this is a real and long-continuing problem for foundation officers is indicated, in a small way, by the fact that my Rockefeller Foundation files contain a number of memoranda on this subject. Twenty-six years ago I wrote, for the then president of that foundation, a paper entitled "The Case for Small Projects." Twelve years ago, in a memo called "Chicken Feed," I pointed out, among other things, that chicken feed is pretty important to chickens.

Here I want to deal with the essential nature of a "big" activity. I would claim that an activity is big if it constitutes an effective attack on a really big problem.

Sometimes this culminates in a project which is both *geographically* and *institutionally* concentrated, so that one can specifically locate the activity and its sponsor; for example, the Sloan-Kettering Institute for Cancer Research, in New York City. Sometimes the activity is *institutionally* but not geographically concentrated, as would be the case if a grant were made to the National Academy of Sciences for a study related to all the colleges in the United States. In either of these two cases, a large amount of money is paid over to one recipient. This kind of "big grant" gets considerable publicity, and it is natural to call it a "big thing" as contrasted with a lot of little things.

Every one of the "big things" turns out, however, when looked at more closely, to consist of a number of "little things." Human beings come one at a time, so to speak, and one man can himself utilize only a moderate amount of support. He may need assistants (who also come one at a time), or apparatus (made of parts), or even a building) made up of rooms and containing chairs, desks, etc.). These may very well all *add up* to a big thing; but the fact remains that the activity may be entered on the books as "big" only because it is possible to draw a geographic or institutional line around the project, and find inside this line one address to which the support is sent.

An activity can be "big" even though it is not geographically, or institutionally, or financially concentrated into a single sizable package receiving one large grant. Take the important matter of giving the general public a better understanding of science, a truly "big" activity. But how can it be accomplished? No single agency can take on the job. It cannot be concentrated in a single project, for we do not as yet know enough about what will be effective to justify such a unified attack on the problem. It must be approached in a variety of ways. Therefore, this "big" thing will necessarily have to be formed out of a number of little things, each receiving its own support.

There are some big things which not only consist of a lot of parts, but which are in total of such a nature that many organizations have to club together to furnish the support. And each organization is *helping to do a big thing,* even though its own contribution is not large. For example, there are various organizations similar to the World Federation for Mental Health. Certainly mental health presents a large and important problem. Coordination of activities, interchange of knowledge and experience, assistance to emerging programs are of great value. This overall pattern of activity is significant indeed, but it consists of many, many components, and the World Federation has to elicit support from a large number of modest donors.

But a grant to such an organization is truly a little part of a big thing. Indeed, the little part works with great leverage, for a relatively small organization with relatively small support can accomplish a great deal in this way if it has the knowledge, the prestige, and the effective connection with other worldwide organizations. Large as the problem of mental health is, one can put an *effective* dent in it, even with a small grant. And great foundations ought to take real satisfaction in *helping* to do big things.

A small grant, in addition, may attract other grants and develop over the years into something big and significant. A modest Rockefeller Foundation grant made twenty-five years ago to help support Amherst's biology department "has blossomed into a research program supported by about $250,000 annually in government foundation grants (in addition to college funds)."[10] The science faculty at Amherst has grown 70 percent, and the college possesses scientific equipment "not generally found in small college laboratories."

CHAPTER 11

Foundations and Individuals

In dealing with artists, poets, musicians, writers, dramatists, and other practitioners of the creative arts and humanities, philanthropic foundations clearly have to deal with the individual persons, and often without regard to whether or not these individuals have any institutional connection. In dealing with scientists, however, it is extremely unusual for a foundation to aid an individual who is not on the staff of a recognized college, university, or research institute; and, apart from such personal assistance as a travel grant or a fellowship, aid is normally channeled through the institution. That is, the grant is made *to* the institution, but *for* the work of the individual (or group of individuals). Assistance for social scientists and for the scholarly activities of historians, lawyers, philosophers, and other humanists would also surely tend to be handled through institutions rather than directly on a personal basis.

There are persons who adversely criticize, indeed who ardently resent, this requirement of an institutional position. I have encountered individuals who classified themselves as scientists—physicists, or cosmologists, or mathematicians for instance—who held no position with a teaching or research organization, but who most earnestly felt that they should be financed by a direct personal grant from a philanthropic foundation.

Why should a foundation be so conservative, so "stuffy"? Are all geniuses professors? Are there not instances of persons of outstanding ability who do not fit into the disciplined and regimented systems of orthodox institutions?

Universities and research institutes are not as conventional as their critics often suppose. They accommodate some rather eccentric persons, providing that they are able. There may, rarely, be outstanding persons who cannot or will not get and hold a job, but foundations almost always hesitate to deal with such persons.

A foundation necessarily has a difficult problem in judging the quality of its applicants; it is most helpful and reassuring to be able to draw upon the knowledge of close associates in a reputable institution, just as it is conversely disconcerting to face the fact that an applicant has not been able to obtain and hold a good job. And under present-day circumstances the chance is exceedingly slim that a really able person would not be associated with some sort of reputable institution. A rule like this, which is easy to apply and which is correct in a very large fraction of cases, is, as a practical matter, a sound rule.

Further, every grant from a philanthropic foundation ought to have constructive by-products. If you aid a person who is part of an institution, you thereby help strengthen that institution and benefit the recipient's colleagues. Having thoroughly explored several situations, one usually discovers that the non-absorbed individual has inherent faults of personality or behavior which not only explain why he has not been absorbed, but make it evident that his future activity would continue to be handicapped.

Finally, the direct relationship of a recipient to a foundation is a risky business. It is extremely difficult to avoid developing some implied responsibility for continuing support; and the loyalty which more or less automatically accompanies support should be attached to an institution, not to a foundation.

This last-mentioned point is in my judgment a strong argument why grants to an institution for the work of an individual should not automatically be transferred if the recipient moves to another institution. This accentuates the direct tie between the recipient and the granting foundation, diminishing the role of the university or institute. And another university can consider that it is hiring a person who comes all equipped with external support. The Rockefeller Foundation not only did not shift a grant when a man moved to a new position; it did not discuss the possibility of a new grant until the man had spent a semester or so in the new position.

There could, of course, conceivably arise an exception to the rule that a foundation should aid a scientist only through a grant to an institution of which he is a staff member. We must not forget that Mendel was a monk, that Einstein evolved the special theory of relativity when he was an examiner in the patent office, that the great Indian mathematician Ramanujan never had any formal training, and that the only professional position Darwin ever held was as secretary of the Geological Society. But the person who criticizes this rule as it applies to himself is almost certainly a person to whom the rule should be applied.

In this day of teamwork and of many scientific projects requiring a sizeable group of cooperating individuals, often clustered around some huge instrumental setup, this discussion of grants to individuals may have an old-fashioned flavor. But the value of a team often depends essentially upon single leadership, and the great advances in science, particularly the important new ideas, still come from individual persons.

There is, moreover, unnecessary risk involved in a policy that mechanically prevents support to non-institutionalized individuals. Although he concedes that "in the universities" is the answer to the question, what is "the center of intellectual strength in this country?"[1] Burton Raffel, a university professor who formerly edited the news bulletin of the Foundation Library Center, thinks that foundations have become too dependent upon universities. He thinks this dependence unfortunate partly because he believes that "independently organized study" is likely to be more flexible than study carried out by a man who holds a university post. He believes "that a university post does not per se make a man objective and talented," and even holds that ". . . university posts sometimes exercise the opposite effect (in part because of the deadening effect of most graduate education, in part because of the institutional formalisms and internal policies of universities)." Raffel also objects to the dependence on universities because of his enthusiasm for scholars who are, as he puts it, "out in the great world." He considers that foundations too frequently turn to universities for studies—such as the Ford inquiry concerning the state of American humanistic learning—which involve on the part of the professors too high a degree of self-examination.

Most graduate education does not, it seems to me, have a deadening effect; on the basis of more than forty years' experience with universities and university men, I do not in the least believe that the town is more flexible and objective than is the gown. Nor do I believe that "institutional formalisms" of universities hamper foundation-assisted projects in any significant way.

It is of course true that some able, even some exceedingly able, persons who have gained deserved reputations in the world of business affairs prefer for the word "academic" the definition "visionary, unable to cope with the world of practical reality, of no practical or useful significance" (Webster), rather than the definition "scholarly, learned" (also Webster). This was a point of enthusiastic disagreement between myself and Alfred P. Sloan, Jr., a man for whom I had on other grounds the deepest respect and admiration. When I asked him how he could hold such views of academicians, and how, holding such views, he could be so enthusiastic about the Massachusetts Institute of Technology, he closed the subject with the remark that "MIT is *not* an academic institution—it is a *scientific and technological* institution."

I agree with Raffel that we should not be misled by a false "principle of university omnipotence"; but I also most deeply believe that colleges and universities remain the richest concentrations we have of scholarly competence and of dedicated capacity to increase knowledge. Without overlooking other opportunities, foundations will do well to continue to look to universities. "What social instrument is the foundation's nearest relative?" asked Frederick P. Keppel in 1930: and his answer was "I think, without any question, it is the university." That was true when said, and it continues to be true today.

In recent years, scientists and scholars have often complained that they have to spend an intolerable fraction of their time "raising money." This complaint is to a large extent justified, but it is not easy to suggest how the situation can be remedied.

The burden cannot, in my judgment at least, be shifted over to professional money raisers, or at least only a small part of it can be. No responsible foundation should base its judgments on the rapturous prose of so-called "development officers," but must have direct contact with the individual competence that is to be supported.

The application procedures are more burdensome, and certainly more protracted, in the case of federal agencies than in the case of private foundations. The latter are both informal and flexible as regards the form in which applications are made.

If federal agencies can develop democratically acceptable procedures for making larger, longer-term, and more flexible grants to colleges, universities, and research institutes, leaving many more of the details to the institutions, the burden on the individual scientist and scholar will be reduced. Some promising progress in this direction has already been made.

One aspect of the process of application is sometimes embarrassing or even unpleasant. Although a foundation welcomes its customers, some individuals take the position that they are debasing themselves by coming as suppliants—and accordingly they may decline to apply, or may apply in a manner which ranges from unpleasant groveling to overcompensating rudeness. This is an occupational disaster which the philanthropoid must accept philosophically.

One of the common complaints is that foundations are not interested in individuals or in ideas, but in "projects," by which is generally meant a plan, often a sizable one, with little emphasis on the person or persons who will carry it out.

I myself have yet to meet an experienced and respectable foundation officer who would listen very long to a dehumanized plan. Any foundation which will support a plan without prior assurance as to the capacities of the individuals who will implement it deserves both criticism and the failure the plan might easily experience.

A "project" is usually a sizable effort with an organized set of persons involved; the uneasiness about overemphasis on projects also arises because of worry that blueprints may have replaced ideas and that teams have made obsolete the individual person. Why will foundations not make bets—modest bets—on single individuals with exciting but unproved ideas?

The first answer is that some foundations do exactly this. The special fellowships which the Sloan Foundation gives to young physical scientists involve no commitment as to program or project, but are based solely on the advice of competent and informed persons that the candidate in question has ability, energy, and dedication. The Research Corporation has a fine record of having given early support to individuals with ideas; and it is in this connection relevant to record that of the sixty-seven Nobel prizes awarded from 1914 through 1962 in medicine and physiology, thirty-one, or 46 percent, had had individual assistance from the Rockefeller Foundation *prior* to their receiving the prize. The record for Nobel laureates in science is only slightly less impressive.

Foundation grants have increased substantially in their average size. Some of this increase is due to the larger number of enterprises which inherently require a considerable staff, but some of the increase is an illusory artifice, resulting from large grants made by a foundation to another agency which then uses this money to make a large number of smaller grants. The Ford Foundation has over the past years relinquished several programs of grants-to-individuals by turning these programs over to middle-man agencies.

The apparent preoccupation of larger foundations with bigness and the concomitant apparent disinterest in individual ideas—particularly fascinating but admittedly risky small ideas—will inevitably, and probably properly, bother certain individuals. It bothers some very sensible and intelligent people, particularly if they have not had much experience as philanthropoids. When he was still a professor of education at New York University, Frederick L. Redefer, in an editorial in which he expressed his concern about "the little serendipitous, imaginative ideas that inevitably get lost in foundation bureaucracy," wrote:

> What is needed, it seems to me, is a vice president for serendipity, a man whose sole job is to search for valuable and unexpected ideas. The vice president for serendipity should be given the liberty of free-wheeling and should be allowed to reach some decisions intuitively, without the assistance of experts, consultants, committees, or field generals. He should be given a sizable budget, and, while he would of course be accountable for the results, he should not be held to a specific batting average.
>
> . . . The vice president for serendipity could talk with all those time-consuming professors who have an imaginative idea that requires only small encouragement to develop.[2]

Perhaps Professor Redefer is right, but if he means literally what he says I would hate to have to sell the idea of this vice presidency to any board of foundation trustees with which I am familiar. In addition I would not want the job. I would confidently expect that the "sizable budget" would be largely wasted.

"The fury of a woman scorned" can sometimes be matched by the outrage of an applicant turned down.

In reply to a man who had sent in a proposal which was utterly irrelevant to the interests of the foundation in question and who rather insisted that he come to our offices for an oral presentation, I wrote:

"I think I ought to say to you at once that the project which you have in mind lies so completely outside of the program and policy of the —— Foundation that there would really be no point in your discussing it with any of the officers here. . . . I am sorry to send you this disappointing reply." This letter, intended to save his time, was seen and approved, before being sent, by a higher officer of the foundation.

I have omitted from the actual text of the letter quoted above only some purely neutral material which might identify the person to whom it was written. As a result of my letter, the applicant wrote to the chairman of the board of trustees and stated that he considered my letter "rude, insulting, and infantile in its concept." This applicant was by no means an irresponsible person: he had a long and impressive list of accomplishments in his entry in *Who's Who*.

A second case is more interesting and is more significant, since it concerned a person with a good university post and with, I think, a good mind. He was not a scientist, and I became involved in the matter indirectly, since his case did not fall at all under my jurisdiction. This man wrote an exploratory letter asking whether there was any reasonable prospect of a grant to furnish half his salary during a period when he wished to write a book. He stated that "this is a subject on which I have not published anything," and said that he could not be "very specific or convincing about it, since the work is at present in a rudimentary and exploratory stage." My colleague who replied, knowing the field well and the man's general reputation, wrote back that the chances would be slim indeed, stating that the enterprise did not seem to have progressed to the point where a favorable judgment was possible.

This reply demonstrates one of the dilemmas of foundation officers. The fact was that, rightly or wrongly (I have no notion which), the foundation officer did not consider the man sufficiently outstanding to justify a blind bet. Remember that an amazing number of persons "want to write a book," and are convinced that society ought to make this possible. And recognize, moreover, that a foundation officer cannot write to an applicant, and say, "In our judgment you just are not good enough to rate the grant"; and therefore the declination has to contain some less direct phraseology.

The gentleman in question was obviously displeased. His reply stated that "As I understand it, your policy is founded on distrust of the expert's judgment of the value of a research program in his own field. No doubt such distrust has some justification. However, I cannot help feeling that there is even more justification for the expert's distrust of the competence of your board to evaluate programs in his own and many other fields as well."

At that juncture I was consulted by my colleagues, for they knew that I had some knowledge about this man. He and I exchanged several letters, I writing on my own stationery and emphasizing that my letters were personal rather than official. This gave both him and me a chance to be unusually informal about expressing our views.

I explained that in view of the volume of requests sent to a philanthropic foundation and the number it must decline it is an occupational inevitability that foundation officers receive, on any mass vote, a very low score for the soundness of their judgment. Foundations, however, do not settle their problems by consulting some "current manual of procedure" (his phrase). They are delighted at the opportunity to bet on individuals of imagination, intelligence, and character, and in fact much prefer that to the overprecise packages into which "research" is sometimes almost nastily wrapped up. On the other hand, it does seem reasonable to ask a scholar, "What do you have in mind?" They certainly do not distrust the expert's judgment, but they cannot automatically accept the judgment of the applicant himself. That procedure would wipe a foundation promptly out of business, and with a final fling of activity that would be bizarre indeed.

My correspondent countered that he considered our policy an unsound one, saying, "I do not mean that you should accept the valuation of the askers at face value. I mean that your appraisal of the asker, on which you can readily obtain competent advice, should take precedence over your attempt to evaluate a project on which he, if he is really able, is likely to be by far the best judge."

How considerably this applicant misjudged the situation is illustrated by the following excerpt from one of my letters:

What, in heaven's name, inspires your phrase "the language of solemn supplication usually thought appropriate to such correspondence"? Once in a very great while we do, to be sure, encounter some oily creature who insults both our intelligence and our character by assuming that we wish to be fawned upon. Once in a while we encounter, at the other extreme, abnormally shy individuals who, desperately determined not to be a suppliant, can think of no protection other than rudeness.

But these are the exceedingly infrequent examples of the pathology of our business. The vast majority of capable and informed persons realize that foundation officers know full well that, when a grant is made, the scholar is contributing to the advance of knowledge something far more rare and precious than the mere dollars which the foundation contributes. *Our* role is the humble role, and we know it.

Your letter clearly indicates that you think that we base our decision on "projects" rather than on the ability and character of individuals.

If you struggled for months, I would defy you to produce a judgment . . . which is more inaccurate or unfair! I could cite the evidence of dozens and dozens of unambiguous published statements in our official literature. I could cite the operational evidence of hundreds of grants, involving millions of dollars, in which the central motivation was, perfectly clearly and explicitly, "This individual scholar is a person of great ability, of dedicated energy, and of creative imagination. He deserves this kind of free and flexible backing."

But now how does one come reliably to a conclusion that an individual scholar deserves such a description? This, if you will pardon me for saying so, is a question to whose answer we can apply a rather extraordinary amount of experience. Our officers travel all over the world, and on frequent schedules. We consult the most competent persons—the young and uprising ones as well as the established ones. On the basis of our record of competence and reliability we are given the most candid and complete estimates. We get the vast majority of this information, in a network that criss-crosses over all the continents, from direct conversation, not from the artificial evidence of written "recommendations."

To be sure, we also get paper evidence. And one substantial part of the latter is the written statements furnished by the scholar himself. From this, if I may emphasize this point, it is also possible to learn a good deal.

Any foundation official receives irresponsible letters. But the excerpts of correspondence of a good many years ago quoted here, written by a thoroughly trained and able man, a professor in a reputable university, illustrate the perplexing misunderstandings which sometimes arise between individual applicants and philanthropic foundations.

It was by no means uncommon during the earlier days of the Rockefeller Foundation for those who made first contacts with groups in certain foreign countries to be met with incredulity and even suspicion. What were we up to? What was our hidden but real purpose? For surely no one would give away substantial sums merely to help strangers, and without some carefully concealed plan for profit to the donor.

This misinterpretation was understandable within societies with little or no general and established tradition for unselfish benevolence on the part of the wealthy and powerful. In our own country, however, with a long record of selfless and intelligent concern for assisting the needy and for enriching our national life through the support of the arts and sciences, one could expect philanthropic foundations to be understood and appreciated.

The public reaction to philanthropic foundations is generally good, to the extent that the facts are known. It is therefore all the more surprising to discover, at certain levels of supposed sophistication, the word "foundation" the butt of sarcastic comment.

In *The House of Intellect* by Jacques Barzun, Dean of the Faculties and Provost of Columbia University, appears an extensive critique of foundations. A few excerpts illustrate the theme and tone.

". . . The very passion of philanthropy," Barzun says (p. 179), "which our forefathers kindled is now distorting judgment and superseding thought." Indeed (p. 177) ". . . intellect today, though no longer a slave, is still a mendicant friar at the mercy of philanthropy or liberal goodness." Implicitly admitting the support of the medical sciences as contrasted with the humanities, he explains (p. 176) that "A philanthropist feels much more comfortable with the sick or insane. . . ."

It is hard to get rid of money, he says (p. 180) and this explains a (supposed) tendency for foundations to prefer large demands to small. He criticizes foundations on the other hand for failing to follow a principle of concentration of their resources. He thinks this principle has (p. 180) ". . . never been acknowledged or deliberately followed." And he explains that leading institutions ". . . embracing more units, could not help receiving more support" (p. 180). The attempts of foundations to be impartial have led them to support the weaker projects.

Foundations have been (p. 182) "progressively infatuated" by a "lust for novelty," and have, in their choice of work to support, been overimpressed by emphasis on the measurable. This last view is a natural, indeed inevitable, complaint of a humanist who sees so much support given for the medical and other sciences. Indeed, Barzun bemoans the fact that (p. 182) "The humanities gave rise to no projects properly so called, were not expensive enough, and promised few social benefits."

Barzun writes that universities have been hurt, rather than assisted, by foundations. "Today, the chief beneficiaries are alarmed to see the damage done to their fabric. The levers of destruction were the matching grant and the short-term allowance for 'original' ideas" (p. 181).

He concludes by remarking that he has not been "aiming darts at any particular foundation or foundations, nor have I any of their officials in mind, save as Platonic archetypes. I have naturally disguised details while keeping strictly to the philosophic truth of the case" (pp. 182-83).

Years ago a wise dean at the University of Wisconsin advised, when some of the professors were under fire, that such an attack should usually be ignored. In the present case the reply has already been made, in an address, "The Philanthropic Foundations and

Graduate Education," given by Hugh Stott Taylor on December 8, 1960, at Cornell University. Dr. Taylor was for many years one of the leading physical chemists of this country or, for that matter, of the world. From 1945 to 1958 he was dean of the Graduate School of Princeton University, and, at the time of the speech referred to, president of the Woodrow Wilson National Fellowship Foundation.

Taylor described the benefits derived from two European foundations—the Carlsberg Foundation of Denmark, originally founded in 1876 and transformed into the New Carlsberg Foundation in 1902, and the Cecil John Rhodes trust, also dating back to the beginning of the century. He then turned to a consideration of twentieth-century American philanthropic foundations, using illustrations of activities of the Rockefeller Foundation, the Ford Foundation, and the Carnegie Corporation, and concluding:

> Enough has been said, I hope, to illustrate the many and varied opportunities for the promotion of graduate education that the philanthropic foundations have sponsored over more than a century.

Referring specifically to what he called the "ridiculous seventh chapter" of Barzun's book (the chapter quoted above), Taylor stated that in his own speech he had drawn

> ... on an academic lifetime of experience with many foundations, including the "Big Three" of Barzun's "triple image," to reach conclusions directly the reverse of those which Barzun's discussion of "the folklore of philanthropy" would seem to convey. . . . A re-reading of the chapter in question leaves me with the sense that in the "horrible examples" selected for presentation it is Intellect and its administrators that are more culpable than the philanthropic foundations.

CHAPTER 12

Foundations and Universities

This chapter will deal with the problems and criticisms that have arisen in connection with the relationship between philanthropic foundations and all the institutions within which the persons being aided by these foundations work, whether these institutions are universities, colleges, or institutes. Throughout, the discussion about "universities" (where after all the majority of foundation grantees are located) is intended to apply also to colleges and, to some lesser extent, to research institutes.

Universities properly are fiercely determined to be in command of their own internal affairs. This autonomy, so essential to free scholarship, has at times been threatened by political forces operating at local, state, or national levels, by organized external groups such as educational associations, and even by alumni. Must foundations be added to this list of invaders?

There is responsible testimony that danger can exist. "Universities," said President W. Allen Wallis of the University of Rochester, "are gradually losing control over the activities carried on within their walls."[1] "Government agencies and foundations with money to spend . . . are almost overpowering competitors for a loyalty that a university needs desperately to build and hold inviolate from within,"[2] wrote John C. Weaver, then Vice President for Instruction and Dean of the Faculties of Ohio State University. Dr. Weaver, now President of the University of Missouri, here brackets together the relatively modest funds from foundations with the astronomically large funds available to universities from government sources. But statements of this general sort, affirming the necessity of internal integrity, are to be found in the inaugural addresses of practically every new college and university official. Once in office, these officials are often too busy defending that integrity to devote more time to its oral exposition.

If a foundation merely makes it known that it is prepared to consider requests from universities, to help them do what the universities have themselves decided they want to do, one might suppose that no invasion of autonomy could result. But the matter is not as simple as that. For, after the initial approach, the foundation officers may suggest some modification of the original proposal, perhaps introducing conditions that a university would prefer to avoid but which it is willing to swallow if that is necessary in order to obtain the aid. These need not be hampering restrictions. Indeed, it may be particularly embarrassing to have the foundation be so enthusiatic that it suggests expansion of the project—an expansion which is clearly desirable except that it may upset the internal balance of the university's own plans.

If a foundation comes to a university with an idea it is prepared to finance, or at least partly finance, it is sometimes difficult for the university not to be interested, even though from its internal point of view it ought not to be.

Foundation grants are not customarily made in financial support of the normal teaching process, although grants for teachers' salaries do aid that essential function, as may unspecified grants for endowment or for general support. But most foundation grants support research, and may explicitly provide the "freedom" necessary to accomplish the research, a "freedom" usually relished by the individual grantees, liberated for a time from the burden of undergraduate teaching and the boredom of internal committee work and routine administration. But, from the point of view of the university, someone has to do these chores. The grants, however attractive to the staff members who directly benefit, may cause real headaches to the administration, and, in fact, to the university as a whole.

The Sermon on the Mount warned, "For where your treasure is, there will your heart be also"; the academic equivalent is "For where your grant applications go, there will your attention be directed also." It is almost inevitable that primary concern, even loyalty, tends to attach to the source of main financial support; and, when the main support comes from outside, the centrifugal influences tend to overbalance the centripetal ones.

These unhealthy disturbances within a university are not, I believe, as likely to result from philanthropic foundation activities as they are from activities of the federal government, which often seems to deal more directly with the individual professors than do foundations, and is hence more likely to have a disruptive influence. Further, federal activities are more likely to overemphasize public service as contrasted with the more central university functions of teaching and research. But disruptive influence can result from foundation aid also, and foundation officers and trustees should recognize that fact and guard against it.

If, on the other hand, it *were* to be conceded that foundations have invaded the autonomy of universities, luring them financially into doing things they did not really want to do, if a university *were* to accept an almost wholly unwelcome grant in order to avoid offending the potential source of a later, larger, and wholly welcome grant—would such projects hurt the universities?

I myself know of no clear and significant case of a harmful project forced on a university. Often, in fact, it has been good to crack through the rather conservative and orthdodox organizational crust of universities and inject, frankly from the outside, some fresh ideas. R. S. Morison, who combines distinguished careers inside both foundations and universities, suggests several illustrations: the Flexner reform of medical education, the General Education Board reform of admission standards and of college and university accounting practices, the Rockefeller Foundation–sponsored development of psychiatry in medical schools, the early emphasis on the behavioral sciences by the Laura Spelman Rockefeller Memorial, the role of foundations in introducing area studies and the study of exotic languages.[3]

For a quite different reason, the possible invasion of university autonomy by philanthropic foundations would today no longer be a serious threat even if foundations were less thoughtful and sensitive than they are. For foundation support of universities does not comparatively bulk nearly as large as it used to.

There was a time, nearly fifty years ago, when the Carnegie Corporation and the General Education Board were making annual grants amounting to perhaps one-fifth of the total annual income available to all colleges and universities in our country. Thirty years ago the annual grants for research of the Rockefeller Foundation constituted a sizable fraction of the total funds available for academic research in the United States.

At the present time, however, American colleges and universities require about $13 billion a year, and foundations supply only roughly 3 percent of this. The 3 percent is critically important, especially since so much of it is available for innovation; but if one scales down the 3 percent so as to include only ideas originating with foundations as contrasted with ideas which wholly represent the universities' own enthusiasms, and then scales down again to include only poor foundation ideas, he would wind up with so small a fraction of one percent of university support that the integrity of the university structure could not thereby be importantly threatened.

TEMPORARY GRANTS AND PERMANENT PROBLEMS

Foundations are customarily and properly praised for interest in new ideas, for furnishing "risk capital," for advancing "the growing edge of knowledge," for "pump priming." Lively influences of this sort are especially needed in institutions such as universities, where there is a built-in tendency to revere the past, where the influential employees settle down within the comforting stability of academic tenure.

But, from the point of view of the university administration and the professors who do not at the moment have a sparkling new idea but ardently wish to continue to work on some classic problem, this emphasis on "germinal ideas" can be a little wearisome. It is a great and exciting thing to plant new seeds; but at the same time it is essential to pay the bills for maintaining soil fertility and for upkeep on the tractor. It can also be a little boring to entertain a sequence of enthusiasts who want to attend planting ceremonies, but who are not very concerned to support any plants that survive.

This problem demands greater flexibility and more sustained interest and patience on the part of foundation officials, combined with greater strength of character on the part of university officials. A three-year grant to launch and try out a new venture, plus say a four- or five-year tapering grant to enable the university to develop permanent support and integrate the activity into the regular permanent budget, is a perfectly reasonable procedure, one which neither the foundation nor the university should initiate without being realistic about what is going to happen three years, and four to eight years, after the start.

The essential problem here is not the undesirability of temporary funds to try out innovation but is that of providing reasonably sufficient dependable and permanent funds for paying the basic bills—the salaries of staff, the maintenance and upkeep of buildings and grounds, light and heat, communication, travel, libraries, and service activities.

Philanthropic foundations on the whole can do little about these basic bills. There are exceptions at both ends of the scale of size. The Ford Foundation is large enough to make significant grants over this entire area; small foundations, which can defend local interests and hence need not be paralyzed by the fear of precedents, can make effective grants of this sort by devoting a large part of their income to one favored institution. But for all the "in between" foundations, operating with national programs, the broad basic support of colleges and universities is arithmetically impossible.

The answer, then, to the question "Who pays the regular pumping bills after the pump has been primed?" is that this has to be handled by the "regular" funds assured to the institution on a long-term basis. In part the bills can be met by annual general grants from alumni and from industrial foundations, in part, by substantial general gifts from wealthy invididuals, each of whom must be stimulated to an interest in the particular pumping operation in question. In large part such costs have, for private institutions, been met by income from endowment; this source will continue to be significant (as the success of recent great drives has shown) in spite of the spiral of costs upward and the decrease of income rates. For public institutions the basic continuing costs have to be met by public revenue. And for the private institutions, although to the older generations this seems rather unfortunate, the answer may very well increasingly turn out to be the same as for public institutions—namely, public money, probably from federal sources. We must develop still further ways in which government money can be turned over to universities so as to protect the university from threat of governmental control, while giving the government (and the public) assurance that the funds will be used effectively and properly.

MATCHING GRANTS

Abraham Flexner in the late 1920's was the great master of the matching grant, but that powerful mechanism had been used by the General Education Board before Flexner joined its staff in 1913. Matching grants involve the promise of a foundation to furnish X dollars to an institution for a certain purpose provided the institution obtained Y dollars of new money from some other source. The word "matching" is used rather flexibly. In some cases Y equals X so that the original pledge is equally matched. But in other cases Y may be two, or three, or even more times as large as X, so that the original pledge has long leverage. This technique, effectively used on many occasions, has recently had a grand revival in the series of massive Ford Foundation general university grants which require matching at the ratio of 2 or even 3 to 1.

The leverage of the matching grant has pried out a good deal of money for universities that would otherwise have gone for other purposes, even for estate taxes.

Yet the attractive lure of getting double, or even triple, for your money may lead certain universities to devote Y matching dollars of new funds to one purpose when the university has a much greater need (even two or three times as great) that new money should be used for some other purpose for which no match has been offered. The technique of a matching grant runs the possible risk of seducing a university into doing what on the criterion of overall good it has no business to do. By the same token, the matching grant may, as used by a foundation, be a tool for invading the autonomy of the university. This risk is, of course, completely removed in case the grant to be matched is for general purposes (as is the case with the recent Ford grants) and is to be wholly under the control of the university.

BRICKS AND MORTAR

One of the common, and understandable, complaints which university presidents make against philanthropic foundations is "Why are they so prejudiced against 'bricks and mortar'? Don't they understand that we *have* to have buildings within which to carry on all our various activities?" But the position of foundations (or at least the position I think they ought to take) is equally understandable when viewed from where they stand.

Buildings just as buildings—classroom buildings, administration buildings, library buildings, service buildings—however desperately needed for the broad general use of an educational institution, can properly be given aid by a foundation, at least in my judgment, only provided the foundation is big enough to give favorable consideration to all similar requests based on need (and there is no foundation big enough to do that), or if the foundation is small enough or local enough or personal enough so that it can afford to treat one institution with a favoritism it cannot extend to the others. There are such foundations. The smaller ones are apt to be more local in character, as are most family foundations, community foundations, and some company foundations. These have a perfect right to give preference to their special and local interests, and neither embarrassment to them nor objection from others should result. Thus if a small or family foundation located somewhere in Ohio wants to give a half a million or a million dollars to help build a needed building for a local college, no one in California or Oregon or Maine should be surprised, resentful, or expectant.

But if the Rockefeller Foundation announced a grant of the same size toward a new dormitory at Colgate, a new library at Pomona, a general biochemistry building at Ann Arbor, or an administration building at Tulane, the foundation telephone switchboard would be busy for the next two months. Does this mean that sizable foundations with national programs never build or help build buildings? Not at all. But they do have to restrict such aid to instances defensible with respect to their broad responsibility, cases with which they can live from the point of view of precedent.

Thus if a foundation, along one of its recognized lines of activity, wishes to help a relevant development at a university and if housing is a necessary and integral part of the development, the foundation can properly aid with the otherwise shunned "bricks and mortar." This is precisely what foundations do. The Ford Foundation invested more than $7 million in the physical plant of the Rice Research Institute, at Los Baños in the Philippines, whose activity is supported jointly by Ford and Rockefeller. They erected those beautiful and efficient buildings not just to build buildings but to house a research effort that will someday be of critical importance in feeding the Orient. In a similar manner the Sloan Foundation, in order efficiently to further its program purposes, has helped to furnish physical facilities for the advanced training of business executives at M.I.T. and at Stanford, and because of its program interest in mathematics has helped, or is helping, build buildings for that subject at the Courant Institute in New York City, at the California Institute of Technology, at Stanford University, at Dartmouth, and at Brown University.

Other foundations have done similar things. They do not rule out bricks and mortar; they restrict their building aid to defensible instances. It is not effective for a university president to come into a foundation office and say, "I have the one exceptional case: the building we need is in truth a general one, but we have a uniquely special case, a uniquely compelling need." That president only needs to listen to the taped recording of the president who preceded him and the one who follows him, for foundation officers learn, as one of their earliest lessons, that all cases are unique.

In certain senses grants to universities for general endowment may be similar to grants for general buildings. I well remember the arrogant confidence with which the president of a leading university told a great foundation that it ought to turn over fifty million of its capital to the general endowment of his institution. If a foundation decides for some reason or other to liquidate, that might be a good way to do so. But for an active foundation, with a competent staff and a board of trustees sensitive to and enthusiastic about their opportunities and responsibilities, the president's suggestion was almost exactly as attractive as would have been a suggestion to the same president that he turn over fifty million of his endowment to another university. Such a procedure does not constitute a "grant": it constitutes an abandonment of responsibility.

OVERHEAD

Another common and vigorous complaint of university presidents is that foundations are not realistic about overhead. ("Realistic" in this context is to be translated as "generous" or "willing to pay"; just as "bargaining in good faith" has in labor relations circles come to mean "making concessions to our demands.")

Foundations, these presidents say, express an interest in supporting a certain program at our institution. But they are willing to pay only the out-of-pocket costs. They can't seem to realize that for every dollar paid for the obvious support of a project (say the salaries of persons working on the project, equipment, supplies, and the like) my administration has to foot a bill of some 15–35 cents, or even more, which pays for all the background expenses of heat, light, telephone, buildings and grounds, maintenance, general adminstration, etc. The 15–35 cents I have to put up is just as real, and just as much part of the project, as the direct cost they are willing to pay. Every grant they make results in my becoming more hard up than I was before. If I accept too much grant money, I go broke. Is this reasonable or fair?

If the foundation has taken the initiative in coming to the university with a project in which the foundation has a special interest and for which they are seeking able operators, then the foundation clearly ought to pay all the bill.

If an agency (I do not say foundation, for I am now thinking more of federal agencies) wants to support work in a certain area at a university as an incidental result of a broader desire to aid the general development of the university as a whole, then again all the bill should be paid. This is one of the main reasons why federal agencies should, in normal cases, pay all of any reasonable overhead. For the federal agencies should, quite over and beyond the explicit purposes of the grant in question, be concerned to aid the broad development of universities. They are practically the only agencies that can afford to undertake that burden; in the interest of the soundness and vigor of our national life, they cannot afford not to undertake that burden. Overhead, moreover, is one of the safest and most completely "buffered" ways of introducing federal support of educational and research institutes without involving any danger of improper control.

Should foundations pay overhead in all cases? I do not think so. If a university assumes all the initiative in coming to a foundation with a plan, the foundation has a right to ask "What contribution do *you* propose to make to this project?" That contribution need not always take the explicit form of overhead. A university can well say, "The total cost of this project, overhead included, is X thousands of dollars. If the foundation will put up half (or one-third, or three-fourths, or whatever) of this, my institution accepts the responsibility of producing the remainder."

The great advantage of this procedure is not primarily the stretching of the effectiveness of the foundation's money, although that is a good thing. The more important consideration is that this sharing of costs is, or at least should be, a strong measure of protection against the danger of the foundation's invading the autonomy of the institution. If a rich uncle pays for the entire cost of a trip, you may have to go to Ireland, although you really wanted to go to Spain. But if the cost is to be shared, then you should not put up your money unless the plan suits you.

It was for precisely this reason that the Rockefeller Foundation, during the years I was there, did not pay overhead on the normal projects brought to it. We did not take the position that we were paying a university the total bill to do something we wanted them to do—we were paying part of the cost of something they themselves wanted to do; if they were not willing to assume responsibility for part of the cost, the quality of their desire was questionable.

SHOULD FOUNDATIONS HAVE IDEAS?

There are three basic reasons why foundations *must* have ideas. First, the relationship between universities (and here we must broaden the category to include *all* the persons with whom foundations deal) simply cannot be one of integrity unless this relationship is based upon mutual respect. If scientists, scholars, and artists accept money from a source whose personnel they cannot meet on equal terms, then the relationship must degenerate to a level at which the recipients become nothing better than fawning mendicants. The discussions must be carried out on each side by persons who understand the issues, who are competent in the subject matter involved, who not only have ideas but who have good ideas.

It would probably be automatically assumed that a foundation active in, let us say, the field of cancer research would have officers who are professsionally competent in that field. But there is such a thing as professional competence in all other fields, humanistic as well as scientific. The collaborating authors of Part II emphasize, at several points, that foundations must have staff officers competent in the humanities, in music, in the dance, if they are to work intelligently in those fields. Having had the advantage of working in scientific fields in which the techniques for recognizing competence are highly developed, I have seen my fellow officers suffer somewhat from the assumption that almost every person considers himself an expert in the social sciences and in education. But I am sure that this assumption is not justified. Study and experience are essential in every field. I even assume, I hope not too optimistically, that it is possible to know something about modern art.

The second basic reason why foundations must have ideas is that creative innovation is imperative in the sector of private philanthropy. If foundations are to continue to be concerned with imaginative activities, if they are to stimulate flexible new ideas in institutions that often tend to be rather conventional, if foundations are, in short, to continue to justify their position as favored social instruments, they must be something more than passive selectors among the assorted ideas brought to them.

A third reason why foundation officers have an important role apart from mere administrative choice among the ideas of others is that a great national resource of information and advice concerning universities, and advice to universities, is formed by the body of philanthropic foundation officers. They travel widely and get to know many, many institutions. They are dependent upon no one of these institutions and thus can have opinions broadly based and little prejudiced. On many occasions university administrators have told me that they knew of almost no place, other than their friends in good foundations, where they could go for information, advice, criticisms, and suggestions which would be really competent and at the same time unbiased. As one academic president has written me,

". . . officers in the large professional foundations are probably the best-informed people in the country with respect to our institutions of higher learning."

FOUNDATIONS AND DEVELOPMENT OFFICERS

When I started in the foundation business thirty-four years ago, most of my contacts were with individual professors or other members of the scientific staffs of universities and institutes. Calls on presidents were occasionally made as a formal necessity but there were few contacts with other administrative personnel. We seldom went to see deans; those modern inventions the Vice Presidents in Charge of Development and the Development Officers in Charge of Grants had not yet been thought of.

The business of obtaining grant money has by now become so extensive that a university doubtless has to have an office in which all relevant information of an administrative sort is concentrated. These officers at the mildest are sincere, polite, and earnestly enthusiastic salesmen of their own institution, and at the worst present a jumbled offering of assorted needs, expecting a foundation to pick out the ones which appeal. But they should in no instance operate as the university representative in negotiations with any intellectually and professionally competent foundation.

Only a few years ago the president of a university wrote to the president of one of the largest foundations, proposing that the university development officer come to call. The foundation president replied, in polite but unambiguous language, that he didn't want to see the development officer. If there were any men, ideas, projects, or programs for which the university was seeking support, the persons who would be directly involved were, as always, more than welcome to discuss their problems.

I think that the foundation president was completely correct. The foundation-university relationship should involve competent scholars dealing with scholars, not resistant financiers dealing with eager salesmen.

An exceedingly able college president once complained to me that the top persons in foundations "are frequently not sufficiently knowledgeable about a matter to permit them to bring their wisdom and leadership into full engagement," whereas "most of the people one encounters down the line are highly knowledgeable or are in a position to become knowledgeable about a proposal, but they are less able to be genuinely wise, bold, let alone fully responsive in their relations with customers." My answer to this is that in the best foundations the general guidance rests with the president, but to the officers directly under the president, each an expert in his field, is assigned the primary responsibility for the substantive discussion of proposals.

Another top officer of one of our largest universities, when queried on the subject of the organizational anatomy of foundations wrote,

> In general, our experience with foundations has been good as concerns projects they have wanted to support. There has not been pressure on us to accept terms or conditions prejudicial to our autonomy. Some Federal agencies, however, make requests of us that fail to take into account certain conditions vital to University interest and cooperation, namely, (a) the length of time that a faculty member can be granted leave of absence without adversely affecting his teaching and research responsibilities on the campus, (b) the opportunities for research made available to the faculty member while on leave, and (c) assurance of continuity and stability of projects to enable departments involved to make plans in recruiting participants and finding replacements for those released. Sudden requests to take on projects for which support is uncertain beyond a first step are most troublesome and most apt to have disruptive institutional effects.

There does indeed sometimes seem to be a tendency, on the part of some federal agencies, *to use* universities rather than *to aid and develop* them.

Another president of one of our best colleges wrote,

> If I were to offer any one serious criticism, it would be the tendency of foundations to support pilot projects and experimental programs. This has forced many college and university officers to lie awake nights dreaming up new and unusual projects to attract foundation attention. This has the danger of forcing us into the bizarre and peripheral at the expense of what is central to our institutional programs. I realize that there is not enough foundation money to

float all the old academic hulks which would like to keep going. I realize further the fear of foundations of getting caught in a continuing and unending commitment in support of some program or other. These are obvious dangers, but I wonder whether they may not loom larger than they need to in the eyes of most philanthropic officers.

These points are important and warranted.

What are the more important aspects of the relationships between universities and foundations?

In answering this query it will help to recognize three different types of activity of philanthropic foundations. First, there are the *basic studies* which must be carried out by highly trained scholars and which can most effectively be pursued within an institution with a stimulating and supporting atmosphere for scholarly work—library and laboratory facilities, special equipment, contacts with colleagues trained in other fields, the traditions of the intellectual life. Such basic studies would characteristically occur in all of the special fields of science, as well as, perhaps to a lesser degree, in the social and behavioral sciences and the humanities. These are the projects which, in the best traditional sense of the word, should be called "academic." These studies would, in almost all cases, come into being because university personnel, and in most and the better cases, the scholars themselves, come to a foundation, tell what they deeply wish to do, and explain what financial help would be necessary.

Second, there are projects which can roughly be called *action projects*. Certain aspects of these projects may be located on campus, but other aspects may involve work in a wide variety of other locations, like Washington, Latin America, Geneva, or Africa. These may be projects on national economies, peace efforts, international trade, means of breaking language barriers, the cultures of other lands, the training of administrative personnel in emerging nations, and as such they would largely involve experts in the social sciences and the humanities. But action projects may also involve studies of nutrition and deficiency diseases, ways of increasing food supplies, physical anthropology, power and transport needs, worldwide phenomena in meteorology and space physics, astronomy, control of worldwide diseases, population control, and these would largely involve experts in the physical, biological, medical, and engineering sciences.

These *action projects* sometimes arise because of the spontaneous interest of some academic or professional group, but they are more likely to arise "in Washington" (meaning not only the branches of the federal government but also the national agencies located in Washington, such as the National Academy of Sciences). Some originate in professional organizations such as the Brookings Institution, the National Bureau of Economic Research, the Social Science Research Council, the Council of Learned Societies, the American Council on Education, the Associated Colleges of the Mid-West, the Pacific Science Center, the National Center for Atmospheric Research at Boulder. Some of them arise in institutes located at and more or less loosely affiliated with universities. A number, however, originate within foundations. The staff of a foundation may, with skill and imagination, identify an important problem, decide the foundation is prepared to furnish financing, and then look about for persons or groups willing and interested to undertake the active conduct of the project.

Thirdly, there are *foundation operating projects*. These may, as regards subject matter and purpose, be very similar to the action projects just described. They differ essentially, however, in that the staff of the projects are employees of the foundation in question, sometimes hired for a two-year period on leave from a university position, but often (as is the usual case with the agricultural operating program of the Rockefeller Foundation) taken on for a permanent career opportunity.

These three categories do not unambiguously include all foundation projects. Hybrids overlap two categories. Fellowship programs can be thought of as primarily in the first category of basic studies. For, even though a foundation may be involved both at the level of initiation of the idea and at that of selection of the fellows, it remains true that the recipient is clearly doing something he wants to do, not something that somebody else wants him to do, and that his advanced training involves "basic study," not applied action.

Also there are projects which are not basic studies that may arise wholly and spontaneously within universities—for example, plans for major expansion of instruction and research in some field, plans for a new building, plans for increase of endowment.

In terms of these three types of projects it is possible to identify the points at which friction is likely to develop between universities and foundations.

There is relatively little chance of trouble on projects of the first category. These projects involve support, and at the best very free and flexible support, of exactly the sort of things universities ought to do and want to do. Questions about such matters as overhead and buildings tend to be peripheral and to operate largely at the university management–foundation level and not at the more basic scholar-foundation level.

There is even less chance of trouble on projects of the third (operating) category. Here the foundations do approach universities looking for persons they may hire, but they do so just as do business corporations, government, or for that matter other universities. It is an important function of universities to train men for other activities. When a foundation comes to a university professor offering him a foundation job, the university man is free to balance all the pros and cons (and there are important considerations on both sides, as I well know from having lived in both worlds) and make up his own mind.

The rub—and the friction—comes largely in the second category. This is a significant part of one of the modern problems which universities face. The university as a protected cloister for the specialized scholar who wishes to be isolated from the world around him has not wholly disappeared from the modern scene, but it has greatly shrunk from its previous dimensions. In addition to the basic traditional tasks of advancing and imparting knowledge, the universities of today have to face the challenge of public service.

This is, in its very nature, something of an invasion from without. This requires professors to leave their studies. The days of actual campus residence have, for many of the best professors, been reduced materially. It is inevitable that this puts a strain on the inner intellectual life of the faculty and students, and perhaps an even greater strain on the upper administrative levels. This strain is not made the more pleasant by the fact that an administration often, and perhaps largely for monetary reasons, simply is not able to say no.

This analysis helps to explain why a good number of the collaborating authors of Part II are so uniformly complimentary about foundation activities. They are talking chiefly about activities in the first and third categories.

These ideas also shed some light on the reservations explicit or implicit in some of the other statements, not those, however, which relate to the creative arts, for here the problems are essentially individual-foundation in character rather than university-foundation.

The strains which develop around action projects are a characteristic aspect of present-day affairs, not unlike the larger difficulties our government encounters in foreign aid. Universities must, on their side, recognize that philanthropic foundations are trying to meet their social, as well as their more purely intellectual, obligations, and that when they seek talent they must necessarily go to the great concentrations of talent in universities. Foundations on their part must never forget or ignore the basic commitments of universities to teaching and research, and the overriding importance that a university remain an intact organism, not dissipated either geographically or functionally, and in full command of its own resources. As events go inevitably forward, both universities and foundations should pay special attention to the complications and dangers of action projects.

CHAPTER 13

Foundations and Government

Fifty years ago, and to a lesser but still considerable degree twenty-five years ago, the federal government played, in the conduct of research and in the educational activities of colleges and universities, a role minuscule compared to that played today. The bulk of the income of educational institutions once came from endowment, student fees, private gifts, and, in the case of public institutions, from state funds. Fifty years ago the philanthropic foundations also played a sizable role. At that time, the annual grants of the General Education Board and the Carnegie Corporation were roughly one-fifth of the total of the annual budgets of all colleges and universities in the country; indeed, the Carnegie Corporation in 1913 spent $5.6 million, whereas the federal government's total expenditures for education in that same year amounted to $5 million.[1]

This situation is now wholly changed. The President of the United States has recently said that "Today the Federal Government is spending $15 billion annually on research and development activities, nine percent of this—$1.3 billion—being spent in our universities on research grants and contracts. . . . The impact of these federal funds is significant. They account for about two-thirds of the total research expenditure of colleges and universities."[2]

The situation is still more striking if one concentrates on the larger institutions. Gerard Piel, publisher of *Scientific American,* has said in a statement to a congressional panel, referring to the two-thirds figure quoted above, that "Federal project funds today . . . hold a still more commanding interest—exceeding 80%—in the research activities of the 10, 25, or 100 universities that receive most of the Federal funds."[3]

The huge federal support of research is perhaps not as surprising as is the present level of governmental involvement in the educational process.

After World War I it was clear that our country had to improve its position in science, and there was no prospect that the government was ready to help effectively. One of the major moves was the establishment of the National Research Council fellowships, under the financial support of the Rockefeller Foundation. In 1919, six fellows were appointed in physics and seven in chemistry. In retrospect this seems pitifully few, but those were essentially the only national fellowships in science at that time. The impact of the program was great. By 1950 1,107 men and women had held National Research Council fellowships, a group universally recognized to have played a role of outstanding leadership in the development of science in our country. This entire program, in all fields of the natural and medical sciences, required a total financing of slightly over $6.75 million from inception up to 1950.

In striking contrast to this thirty-year total of 1,107 fellowships, in the single year 1966 about 4,000 postdoctoral and career development awards and over 28,000 predoctoral awards, including 2,350 summer graduate fellowships, were available from federal sources. The cost of this program for 1966 totaled more than $194 million.[4] The government is now giving large scholarship support of a broader type; about 775,000 undergraduate and graduate students in all states and territories were expected to seek $620 million in low-interest loans under a program of the Office of Education during the year beginning July 1, 1966.[5]

It would be easy further to document the present great involvement of the federal government in education and research, but the examples given amply show that the financial aid to these fields by the philanthropic foundations is at the present time much smaller, compared with government aid, than used to be the case. This necessarily and properly raises the question: does there remain a significant role for the foundations, or should the government take over such functions entirely?

The government has given its own answer to this question. It is a clear policy of our government to encourage private giving. The tax authorities emphasize that up to 20 percent of gross adjusted income is exempt from income tax and that, indeed, an additional 10 percent may be given for specially favored purposes including colleges, universities, and medical research organizations. This policy, as must be true of any long-sustained one, reflects public opinion.

From time to time, and as a desirable part of our national governmental procedure, official question is raised as to whether philanthropic foundations are behaving properly. Such investigations tend to be sponsored by those who have doubts or even negative convictions in regard to philanthropy, rather than by those who are enthusiastic. The investigations have, however, been illuminating and in many ways useful.

CONGRESSIONAL INVESTIGATIONS

THE WALSH COMMITTEE

On August 23, 1912, the Sixty-second Congress, during the Presidency of William Howard Taft, created a Commission on Industrial Relations to "inquire into the general condition of labor in the principal industries of the United States." The chairman, Frank P. Walsh, then a lawyer from Kansas City, desired that the commission, later to be known by his name, look into the question of the "concentration of wealth and influence." Woodrow Wilson took office in March, 1913, and hearings of the commission were held during 1913-15. The hearings cited below were held in January and February of 1915.

Among the episodes of violence in the prevailing industrial unrest of the period was a strike in the plants of the Colorado Fuel and Iron Company, a corporation which Rockefeller money was understood to control. Encouraged by their success in medical fields, the Rockefeller Foundation, then a young and relatively inexperienced organization, decided to make a direct approach to certain problems of industrial relations. They engaged as the director of this project W. L. Mackenzie King, a Canadian authority on labor questions later to become the head of the Liberal party and the Prime Minister of Canada. The Rockefeller Foundation study was concurrent with the congressionally-mandated one by the Commission on

Industrial Relations, and Congress reacted with a decision to investigate the foundations.

When this first governmental investigation of private foundations in the United States was completed the findings appeared as part of Volume VIII of *Hearings and Reports, United States Commission on Industrial Relations*.[6] In the final report section, Research Director Basil Manly listed fourteen charges against the foundations. Commenting upon them and describing their outcome, John Lankford in his *Congress and the Foundations in the Twentieth Century* (which appeared in 1964) wrote:

> . . . The main line of criticism asserted that "the domination by men in whose hands the final control of a large part of American industry rests is not limited to their employees, but is being rapidly extended to control the education and 'social service' of the nation." Along with this charge of "creeping capitalism," the majority report suggested that the stocks and bonds of "dominant" American industries formed the resources of the Foundation, and therefore the policies of the Foundation "must inevitably be colored, if not controlled, to conform to the policies of such corporations." In contrast to the sweeping condemnations made by the majority, a "minority statement" came from liberal economist John R. Commons of the University of Wisconsin and New York social worker Florence Harriman. Commons and Mrs. Harriman refused to accept the polemical majority conclusions and urged that " a complete investigation of all foundations" be made before legislative actions were taken against them.
>
> . . . These reports and statements marked the zenith of anti-foundation feeling in the early twentieth century. They reflected a trend which gained strength throughout the Progressive Era. Behind the work of the Industrial Relations Commission lurked the fear of the power of big business and of the power of great wealth. By the end of the Progressive Era criticism of the foundations reached almost hysterical proportions.
>
> . . . By mid-1915 the Progressive Era was fast waning. . . . The *cause célèbre*, the labor investigation by the Rockefeller Foundation, was dropped. A large portion of the funds expended by the Rockefeller Foundation in 1915 went for Belgian relief. Congress took little interest in the *Report* of the Industrial Relations Commission.[7]

THE COX COMMITTEE

More than three and a half decades after the Walsh Commission's investigation of foundations, Congress returned to the subject. The Eighty-second Congress in 1952 established the Select Committee to Investigate Tax-Exempt Foundations and Comparable Organizations with Representative Edward Eugene Cox of Georgia as its chairman.

Harold M. Keele, counsel of the Cox Committee, made reference to the predecessor group, the Commission on Industrial Relations, in this revealing comparison (December 8, 1952):

> . . . When the Walsh investigation was on, the fear that was expressed everywhere was that the foundations would be the tool of reaction . . . that they would crush the labor unions, that they would attempt to impose a rigid form of economy on this country, which would maintain the status quo.
>
> Now, 37 years later, the expressed fear, the most articulately expressed fear, has been that the foundations have swung from that position far to the left, and now they are endangering our existing capitalistic structure.[8]

In light of fuller knowledge of the foundations, the fear of the 1950's seems no better founded than the fear of 1915. It is hard to escape the conviction that in both times the attacks were politically motivated.

Representative Cox had tried in 1951 to interest the House in an investigation, but he did not succeed until the second session of the same Eighty-second Congress, when an identical proposal emerged from the Rules Committee and went to the House on April 4, 1952, with a recommendation for approval. A sharp debate ensued and some harsh suspicions were voiced by House members opposed to the measure. Congressman Louis B. Heller of New York "summed up for a majority of the opposition when he remarked that 'this resolution is not only very broad and general, but it looks to me like it had the properties of a fishing expedition—and loaded with an ulterior motive.' "[9]

A vote of 194 to 158 carried the resolution. However, Congress did not appropriate funds until July. The requirements of a report to the House by January 1, 1953, gave the Cox Committee about six months for a task that ought to have required several times that.

The committee was "authorized and directed to conduct a full and complete investigation and study of educational and philanthropic foundations and other comparable organizations which are exempt from Federal income taxation to determine which such foundations and organizations are using their resources for purposes other than the purposes for which they were established, and especially to determine which such foundations and organizations are using their resources for un-American and subversive activities or for purposes not in the interest or tradition of the United States."[10]

Some newspapers and others expected the Cox Committee to engage in witch hunting, and, on the basis of the statements Congressman Cox made in 1951 and 1952, a firm anti-foundation position was anticipated from the investigative undertaking. Eighteen sessions (in November and December of 1952), with forty witnesses testifying, succeeded in dispelling apprehensions on this score, and more significantly the testimony made out a generally fine case for private philanthropic foundations. Not that all of the organizations involved emerged without criticism. A few were taken to task for their screening and choices of grantees. The criticism concerned foundation aid to persons and organizations listed by the Attorney General or the House Un-American Activities Committee as subversive. The record of the hearings indicated the following proportions of "questionable grants" on the part of four prominent foundations:

Whitney Foundation:	20 out of 440 grants
Carnegie Corporation:	10 or 12 out of 1,725 grants
Rockefeller Foundation:	2 organizations and 23 individuals out of 28,753 grants, and 8 scholarships out of 5,814
Carnegie Endowment:	1% of its funds[11]

Not only were the above proportions taken as evidence of the foundations' creditable handling of grants to individuals but the committee's report, assaying the evidence given in the hearings, concluded that the preponderant majority of the foundations, and certainly the large ones, were relatively innocent of the major charges made against them by the committee at the outset. On certain aspects of several of the "counts," the report qualified somewhat its bill of health for the foundations, but did so not by condemnation, but by the recommendation of greater caution and closer scrutiny.

Lankford has analyzed that the findings on the twelve original charges completely reversed the initial adverse position on three of the charges, viewed four of them as unsubstantiated, considered one criticism to apply to only a very few foundations, declined to discuss three of the charges, and recommended, in respect to one charge, that boards of trustees of foundations should be chosen more widely from the country as a whole and with less concentration on the North and Middle Atlantic States.

The Cox Committee in its report to Congress made two recommendations for congressional action on philanthropic foundations. The first of these suggested an amendment to the Revenue Code to require a more complete disclosure of financial data by the organizations, including information on administrative expenses, accumulations of resources, and full listing of contributors and grant recipients. The second recommendation importuned the Ways and Means Committee to "reexamine pertinent tax laws" to induce a greater flow of support for education and philanthropy from private sources. The first of these recommendations was clearly required and desirable; the second constituted, in summary conclusion, an overall dismissal of any significant charges that foundations were sponsoring subversion.

THE REECE COMMITTEE

On the 23rd of April, 1953, Representative B. Carroll Reece of Tennessee, since deceased, asked Congress to establish an investigatory committee with much the same mandate as that given the Cox Committee the year before. The Reece resolution used language almost identical with that which created the predecessor body, but went on to add to the central charge that foundations were using their resources for subversive activities the elaboration that they were also being used "for political purposes, progaganda or attempts to influence legislation."[12]

Following his oral presentation to the House of Representatives, Congressman Reece inserted in the *Congressional Record* an extended statement in which he combined criticism of the Cox Committee (of which he had been a member, absent for all but one session) with descriptions of the directions a new committee should follow. The latter seemed to dwell on what he termed "lopsided" support by foundations of projects of a "liberal"nature.[13]

In the House, the Reece resolution and the motivations for a new investigation of foundations were called into question with phrases as sharp as those used to suggest the kind of "subtly concealed activities" the foundations were sponsoring. By a 209-162 vote, cutting across party lines, the Reece resolution won. The conservative Chicago *Tribune* rejoiced editorially, and the liberal Washington *Post* deplored what it deemed to be a "wholly unnecessary" probing of foundations, an investigation that was "stupidly wasteful of public funds." The capital paper added that Congressman Reece had previously proved his "total incompetence to conduct" the now authorized investigation.[14]

What happened after the House appropriated $50,000 on August 1, 1953, for the Reece Committee's probe (he had asked for $125,-000) makes one of the less ennobling events in congressional annals. It took place in the shadows, as it were, because the television spotlights in Washington were at that time on the late Senator Joseph McCarthy. The public proceedings of the Reece Committee were unquestionably a show, but during those frenzied days in the capital they could not have been other than a minor sideshow.

The Reece Committee's director of research, Norman Dodd, in his testimony before the committee during the hearings, identified the principal villains in the "conspiracy" as the National Research Council, the Social Science Research Council, the American Council of Learned Societies, and the American Council on Education. "Our study of these entities," said Dodd—including additionally the League for Industrial Democracy, the Committee for Economic Development, the National Education Association, the John Dewey Society, the Parent-Teacher Associations, the National Council of Churches, and others—"and their relationship to each other seems to warrant the inference that they constitute a highly efficient and functioning whole." Dodd undoubtedly meant that all these organizations formed a sinister "establishment."

Dodd went on to testify that

> . . . the result of the development and operation of the network in which the foundations (by their support and encouragement) have played such a significant role seems to have provided this country with what is tantamout to a national system of education under the tight control of organizations and persons little known to the American public. . . . The curriculum in this tightly controlled scheme of education is designed to indoctrinate the American student from matriculation to the consummation of his education. It contrasts sharply with the freedom of the individual as the cornerstone of our social structure. For this freedom it seems to substitute the group, the will of the majority and a centralized power to enforce this will presumably in the interest of all.[15]

The late Professor Sumner H. Slichter of Harvard in an *Atlantic* article, and the *Christian Century,* the *New York Times* and the Roman Catholic *Commonweal* in editorials, all criticized in scathing terms the method and manner of the Reece Committee proceedings. As Lankford described them a decade later,

> . . . research methods used by the staff of the committee were at best crude. In effect, the staff did little beyond reading the yearbooks and reports of foundations and the available secondary literature. To these sources they applied the general "concepts" of Research Director Dodd, apparently drawn from statements of Congressman Reece. Those "concepts" were little more than the prejudices of the investigators, who did their research in order to find evidence to support them.

After the completion of Dodd's testimony, Kathryn Casey, legal analyst for the Reece Committee, presented a "Staff Memorandum" concerned with the National Education Association. She read into the record eight pages of quotations from a volume prepared by the staff of the N.E.A., upon which she had based her memorandum. This use of selected quotations was apparently "an acceptable research technique [to the Committee staff] and would prove the points at issue."[16]

Representative Wayne L. Hays, a committee member, highly

critical of the entire conduct of the investigation and specially annoyed by the tactic of taking statements out of context and using them to buttress conclusions drawn in advance, read several passages on social issues to the assistant research director Thomas McNiece. He asked McNiece what the quotations sounded like and McNiece replied that they resembled Communist thinking and writing. Congressman Hays then identified the quotations as excerpts from two Papal Encyclicals by Popes Leo XIII and Pius XI.

The Reece Committee heard a total of only nine nonstaff witnesses in the course of public hearings. Only one, Pendleton Herring, president of the Social Science Research Council, directly represented foundations. It may be significant that the public hearings were adjourned immediately after the noon recess on June 17, following a morning of testimony by Herring. The chief executive of the Social Science Research Council in his comment and answers made it plain that the empirical method of research, which had been so vigorously disapproved by the Reece Committee staff members, stands "four square in a great tradition of enquiry which is integral to American life. . . ." He assured the committee that congressional investigating committees normally follow an empirical approach. "To imply something immoral about using an empirical method of enquiry is like implying that it is evil to use syntax." In general Herring's testimony was an effective refutation of the charges against philanthropic foundations by an unbroken series of critical witnesses—concerning whom Lankford wrote later that there was "a striking coincidence . . . all except the two experts on federal tax policy, Commissioner Andrews and Assistant Commissioner Sugarman, played a part in earlier hearings on un-American activities or had very definite personal biases."[17]

The adjournment on June 1 was preceded by "turbulent" exchanges between members of the Reece Committee. Congressman Hays had persistently interrupted the committee counsel in his questioning of Herring, in what the House member described as an effort to halt the harrassment of the witness. Flare-ups between congressmen and sometimes with staff members were not uncommon during this particular investigation. Neither the private nor public sessions were ever placid for long. Harsh opinions and angry dissents punctuate the pages of the committee's report.

The June 17th "row" involved Representative Angier L. Goodwin and Hays, but none of the bipartisan committee membership escaped the controversies besetting the investigation. When Chairman Reece announced that afternoon the adjournment of the hearings until June 22 he ascribed his decision to his responsibility to protect the witnesses and the employees and members of the committee and to maintain the dignity of the House.

But the scheduled June 22nd hearing was called off and an executive session of the five members on July 2 voted, three to two, on party lines, to suspend further public sessions. The resolution said they were taking this action, "in order to expedite the investigations and develop the facts in an orderly and impartial manner." They indicated that those wishing to be heard could submit written statements to the committee, which would "proceed with the collection of further evidence and information through means other than public hearings."

Thirteen organizations did submit written statements, later published in a second volume of hearings. The first volume presented to Congress was a final report of 432 pages. Of these, 226 pages made up the majority report and 15 pages contained the minority views. The remaining pages were taken up with a special appendix of information from records of the House Un-American Affairs Committee and the Senate Internal Securities Subcommittee, records relating to individuals "cited" in the Reece Committee's hearings.

On the report itself the subsequent comment varied widely, but few had kind words for the committee's "findings." Both these and the investigation's methods came in for scathing criticism from a number of responsible journals and some of the more temperate newspapers.

"The conduct of the majority, if it was the majority, of the Reece Committee was so scandalous," wrote Robert M. Hutchins, formerly associate director of the Ford Foundation and then president of the Fund for the Republic, "that it outraged almost all the press and apparently even one of its own members. At any rate, Angier L. Goodwin of Massachusetts wrote a new kind of concurring opinion, one that disagreed with all the conclusions of the opinion with which it purported to concur."[18]

The Reece Committee felt "disinclined" to arrive at many

conclusions because their study was, in their own language, "incomplete," a fact on which there was agreement internally and externally. The report did nonetheless make several recommendations. It urged trustees to limit foundation expenses by cutting their staffs and giving up "intermediary organizations" to distribute funds. A federal law was proposed which would remove trustees who made grants to "subversive organizations," and a suggestion was made that state governments select foundation directors in order to increase trustee responsibility.

Bernard DeVoto in a *Harper's Magazine* essay entitled "Guilt by Distinction," expressed his opinion of the Reece Committee Report:

> Whether by design or inadvertently, it serves to inflame the anger of all who fear or resent the Twentieth Century. It is a denunciation of everything that has transformed the United States from a simple society, isolated from the other continents, into a complex industrial society with a necessarily powerful government and inextricably involved with world events. But its target is neither industrialization nor the process of history: it is those who try to bring intelligence to bear on them. It is an attack on inquiry, on the progress of knowledge, on education itself.[19]

DeVoto was prophetic when he wrote a decade ago:

> Most of the press has shrugged off the Reece Investigation as too idiotic to be taken seriously. I am afraid that this attitude was a mistake. The investigation was a brilliantly planned and executed attack not only on scholarly foundations but on much else besides. The Report is preposterous but it is permanently on record as the findings of a House committee. From now on it will be useful to anyone who may be interested in growing paranoia from seed.[20]

On the other hand it can be argued that the United States tolerates the expression even of absurd ideas in the interests of freedom, and then in good season gives the absurd ideas the attention they deserve.

THE PATMAN INVESTIGATION

The Patman investigation is not officially concluded. Because more charges, evidence, and conclusions may still be forthcoming it is necessary to withhold final judgments. Nonetheless, what has taken place thus far is too important to disregard here.

The activities of the Patman Committee have spanned some important changes in Treasury Department procedures, and in the regulations for reporting by foundations. Thus, whatever is said about the conduct of the Patman inquiry, the chairman and his fellow committeemen, as well as their staff, must be credited with spurring the formulation and adoption of improved practices for annual reporting by tax-exempt philanthropies.

In 1961, Representative Wright Patman, a Democrat from Texas who was chairman of the House Select Committee on Small Business, began what was essentially a one-man investigation of philanthropic foundations in the United States, presumably on the assumption that foundations were affecting small businesses. Later, in the *Congressional Record* of January 22, 1962, Patman announced that the Select Committee on Small Business had undertaken study of the impact of tax-exempt foundations on our economic structure, the committee having agreed "to carry on the study initiated by me."

Patman submitted to the House the first half of the first portion of a three-phased report on July 23, 1962. On August 20, 1962, the second half of the first report was given, again orally, to the House. Both halves were formally transmitted to his own Select Committee on Small Business on December 31, 1962.[21] None of these interim reports represented official committee action or views.

The "statistical heart of this first report was a staff analysis of the assets, liabilities and net worth, and so forth, of some 534 foundations, including most of the richest and best known."[22] The objective of his study, Congressman Patman stated, was to determine "whether legislation is needed in order to provide effective supervisory controls over tax-exempt foundations and protect the public."[23] There was vigorous criticism of the methods of the study. For example: "They are *ex parte* in nature. No public hearings were conducted in which foundation spokesmen were given a chance to present their side of the controversy; there was no participation by other members of the subcommittee. Instead the investigation was based on preconceived ideas, correlating only such unrelated and, at times, immaterial facts as supported the preconception."[24] Nevertheless it is doubtless true, as Patman said, that "Never before have the economic factors of the complex and rapidly expanding foundation business been put under the microscope of public scrutiny."[25] These factors certainly had not previously been examined in such detail. On the other hand, the vehement condemnation by Patman was insufficiently supported by the content and nature of the information collected. As a tax lawyer commented, "Patman Report Number 1 practically paralyzed the Exempt Organization Branch of the [Internal Revenue] Service, but it galvanized the upper echelons . . . into immediate activity."[26]

In his first report, Representative Patman charged, among other things, that foundations were guilty of major breaches of public trust and specific violations of federal law; that (during the 1951–60 decade) they withdrew almost $7 billion from the reach of tax collectors; and that "the rapidly increasing concentration of economic power in foundations"[27] was far more dangerous than any previous concentration of such power in our history. He attributed to the "laxness and irresponsibility" of the Internal Revenue Service a share of the blame for the foundations' continuing misbehavior. Specifically of the IRS, Patman said, "The scarcity of information on foundations and lack of supervision has made it impossible for the Treasury to determine the extent of loss to the Federal Treasury on foundation operations."[28]

The Patman Report embodied the argument that "many foundations were created to escape the payment of taxes and to retain control of large segments of American business in the hands of a family or small group."[29] Some of these modern foundations, Patman contended, resembled "the bank holding companies . . . invented by the champions of monopoly and combination in the early 1900's."[30] Elsewhere in the first installment of his report Patman said, "Now, the multimillion-dollar foundations have replaced the trusts which were broken up during the Theodore Roosevelt administration."[31]

His first report began with a strong recommendation "for an immediate moratorium on the granting of tax exemptions,"[32] and ended with seventeen recommendations, the more significant of these recommendations limiting the life of any foundation to twenty-five years, prohibiting their engaging in business or in commercial money lending or borrowing, prohibiting a foundation from holding more than 3 percent of the stock of any corporation, and providing that all contributions to a foundation and all capital gains should be considered as income, not as capital.[33]

The second installment[34] of Patman's report to his Select Committee on Small Business was made public on October 16, 1963. It focused on the Internal Revenue Service's ability to perform adequate field audits of philanthropic institutions and on the business activities of a half-dozen foundations which engaged in extensive business dealings, including transactions among themselves and with donors and their families. The foundations singled out for intensive examination (309 pages of the report were exhibits of documents and financial reports obtained from the organizations involved) were presented as case studies of exploitation of tax-exempt status. The abuses, Patman concluded, resided in the fact that these six foundations (of many hundreds!) allegedly carried on operations tantamount to those of securities dealers, business brokers, finders of credit, traders in mortgages, and other banking activities.[35]

The third and final installment[36] of Representative Patman's extraordinary contribution, a report of a chairman to his subcommittee (between the first and second installments he had vacated the position of chairman of the Select Committee on Small Business and had become chairman of Subcommittee No. 1, charged with studying foundations), appeared on March 20, 1964. It contained 330 pages of materials relating to the business activities of the Alfred I. du Pont Estate and its affiliate, the Nemours Foundation.

A total of seven days of public hearings made up the next chapter in the saga of Patman's interest in foundations. These hearings on July 21, 22, 23, August 10, 31, and September 1 and 4, 1964, were notable for the thoroughness with which the chairman extracted admissions from the chiefs of the Internal Revenue Service of sparse monitoring of foundations. Representative Patman said, "This is the most impressive record of do-nothing that I have seen in my 36 years in Congress. When it comes to the proper policing of tax-exempt foundations, the IRS appears to be totally impaled in the quicksands of absolute inertia."[37]

A year before, Patman had assailed the Treasury Department for having set up a special advisory committee on foundations that was allegedly stacked in favor of the foundations.[38] There seems little doubt that the establishment of the advisory body was prompted at least in part by the criticisms of the IRS emanating from Congressman Patman's reports and from the news stories around his reports.

There is no doubt that the illumination furnished along with the heat of Patman's spotlight has resulted in more stringent reviews of foundation conduct and important movement toward tighter regulation of the areas of permissible functioning. This is undeniably good. Patman turned up some instances of atrocious behavior on the part of a very few foundations. Their number is almost negligible as compared with the number of well-behaved foundations, but certainly the instances of bad conduct are flagrant enough to require attention.

On the other hand, the image of foundations was unfairly damaged by the sweeping charges. A number of his statements were seriously in error, and seldom were they accompanied by recognition of the superior work and record of the vast majority of the larger organizations. Patman seriously and unfairly damaged the general image of the philanthropic foundations by declining to recognize the distinction between the extremely occasional bad and the very generally good.

An attorney specializing in tax matters wrote as follows on the Patman revelations:

> There is no question that abuses appear to exist, but there is also no question that Patman's Report is not a balanced one. In certain areas his evidence is quite incomplete, or even nonexistent. He does not always carefully distinguish between situations which should receive further study and other situations where conclusions could legitimately be made on the basis of his findings. Most important, his presentation assumes that the existence of economic influence is tantamount to the abuse of this influence.[39]

In the 1964 annual report of the Carnegie Corporation its president, John Gardner, now Secretary of Health, Education and Welfare, wrote:

> Are the foundations abusing their tax exemption by engaging in improper financial and managerial practices? The answer, briefly, is

that a few foundations *are* abusing their tax exemption. Most are not. . . . Congressman Wright Patman has rendered a public service in bringing examples of such impropriety to public attention.[40]

Here are the opening paragraphs of *The Rockefeller Foundation President's Review. 1964:*

Philanthropic foundations are once again under government scrutiny.
. . . The general attitude of the Rockefeller Foundation toward these investigations is that which was expressed by one of its trustees in a recent speech: "It is easy to resent such scrutiny—even to dismiss it as unnecessary. But criticism, if objective and informed, is good for us who work to serve the public and, in any case, we must expect it. In a free society—in a changing society—every franchise is to be continually re-earned."[41]

F. Emerson Andrews, the president of the Foundation Library Center, expressed thoughts on the subject of the Patman investigation when it was initiated in 1962. Of the events of that year relative to foundations, Andrews wrote: "Newspaper headlines based on the Patman material tended toward severe exaggeration, and later factual corrections received little notice." He pointed out, nevertheless, that Patman, "using the subpoena power . . . gathered some data otherwise unavailable. His requests for information have helped alert Treasury authorities to possible and actual abuses, and have resulted in liberalization of Treasury rules on public access to information."[42]

The stimulation of the Treasury Department's closer scrutiny and its adoption of more exacting reporting standards for foundations are unquestionably in some measure attributable to Congressman Patman's investigation. This accents the positive in any comment about that investigation, just as the *New York Times* accented the negative in saying editorially that "The most glaring fault of all is Mr. Patman's studied omission of the constructive role played by foundations."[43]

Looking back on the four congressional investigations, one is led to remark that the Walsh and the Cox inquiries tend to cancel each other out, with their charges that foundations are (1) dangerously reactionary, and (2) dangerously liberal. The Reece inquiry, with its charges that foundations are forcing universities to adopt improper forms of intellectual inquiry, had almost no effect, collapsing promptly into the limbo it so obviously deserved.

Bizarre as has been the Patman inquiry in many ways, obvious as it has been that Patman picked up an issue that he thought would attract attention (as it certainly did) whether or not it had any respectable relevance to the proper concern of his committee, and equally obvious as it has been that accurate care is not Patman's forte, this inquiry nevertheless has been a good thing. It has revealed that a very few foundations have behaved badly; and that the laws and regulations should doubtless be somewhat altered to prevent such misbehavior.

Patman's own recommendations were drastic indeed; and in the judgment of responsible foundation officials and also in the judgment of treasury officials, such harsh changes need not be made.

The *Treasury Department Report on Private Foundations*,[44] issued after the third Patman Report, makes six proposals:

1) To prohibit transactions involving "self-dealing" (business transactions between the donor of a foundation and the foundation);
2) To require distribution on a reasonably current basis of a nonoperating foundation's entire net income; subject, in instances where income is abnormally low, to such additional out-payments as would lift the total distribution to a level judged by the Secretary of the Treasury to be fair on the basis of current yields on comparable institutional portfolios;
3) To impose (subject to specified conditions and limitations) a twenty per cent ceiling on any foundation's ownership of the voting stock of, or equity in, any business corporation;
4) To discourage foundation involvement in business, and especially the use of family foundations to perpetuate donor control of a private or family corporation, by severe restrictions on the deductibility of gifts—especially to a donor-controlled foundation—of corporate or other property over which the donor *retains* control;
5) To restrict foundation lending, prohibit all borrowing for investment purposes, and forbid any participation in speculative practices; and
6) To broaden the management base of the mature or maturing foundation by requiring after its twenty-fifth year that the donor

and related parties not constitute more than 25 percent of the foundation's governing body.

These recommendations, if instrumented, would without doubt help to eliminate some abuses deplored by all responsible foundations. They are surely far more reasonable and constructive than Patman's harsh proposals. The 25 percent board limitation would be difficult indeed for company-sponsored foundations, and other relaxations in the new proposed regulations could usefully be worked out. But these proposals are, at the least, headed in a constructive direction.

The congressional inquiries have served another useful purpose; they have stimulated, and perhaps in some instances the verb should be "shocked" or even "forced," foundations to take a closer and more penetrating look at themselves. Having sat out three of these investigations in a foundation chair, I am sure that although at times the reaction was one of incredulous amazement at inaccuracy or wounded resentment at unfairness the overall effect has been good. Democratic procedures have a way of being fumbling and inefficient; but they also have a way of coming out better than any other procedures.

TAXES

"Charity and conscience may be the seeds from which foundations spring, but tax exemption . . . is the nutritive soil in which they give forth their fruits."[45] Nutritive soil may seem dirty to many people, but it does make possible some valuable and attractive produce.

A great deal of the language used about foundations and taxes seems to carry double meaning—and usually unfair implications. Taxes are "avoided," they are "escaped," just as though they were morally and legally due, but have been dodged in some clever but presumably improper manner. The term "tax forgiveness" seems to connote that a crime has occurred.

Three things, thus, have to be said as clearly as possible about foundations and taxes.

First—and by now this is a point of minor historical interest— a good many of today's large foundations were established before personal income taxes existed or estate taxes were substantial.

Therefore "tax avoidance" could not have played any decisive role in the decisions to form those foundations.

Second, in "taking advantage" of the provision that an approved philanthropic foundation does not pay tax on the dividends and interest it receives from the stocks and bonds it owns, foundations are not following a formally and narrowly legal procedure, sailing just as close to the wind of impropriety as shrewdness permits; on the exact contrary, the philanthropic foundations are thereby doing exactly what the government of the United States has not only permitted but has urged them to do. In a speech to the Junior Chamber of Commerce of Cincinnati, Ohio, in 1956, Dean Rusk, then the president of the Rockefeller Foundation said,

> . . . the tax exemption privilege is a standing invitation to citizens by government itself to use private funds for public purposes. Those who take advantage of this privilege are not slipping stealthily through some obscure loophole in the law, but are acting precisely as legislatures hoped that many would, indeed, act. . . . considerations which led the Supreme Court to say, "The exemption of income devoted to charity" was "begotten from motives of public policy" and was "not to be narrowly construed."[46]

Third, it is of course not the fact that foundation money wholly escapes taxes because of the special regulations applying to charitable funds. While president of the Rockefeller Foundation, Dean Rusk analyzed the tax situation for that foundation in the year 1954, and asked

> . . . what the position would be if the Rockefeller Foundation were taxed like any business corporation.
>
> The income of the Rockefeller Foundation for the year 1954 was approximately $17,800,000. Dividends from corporate stocks accounted for about 90% of this income. On that portion of the income, the Foundation would receive the 85% dividend receipts credit, as would any other corporation, which means that only 15% of that dividend income would be taxable. In addition, the Foundation has direct operating expenses for administration and for operating programs in virus research and agriculture; these would clearly be considered deductible business expense in arriving at taxable income. Further, you would not quarrel with the claim that we should be entitled to the full 5% deduction allowed all corporations for donations to charitable purposes! . . . The net result of this analysis is

that the federal income tax of the Rockefeller Foundation, without its present exemption, would have been, in 1954, in the neighborhood of $900,000, or between 5 and 6 per cent of its income.[47]

Three sorts of taxes are primarily involved: personal or corporate income tax, inheritance tax, and capital gains tax. Excess profits taxes, prior to 1953, played an important role also. As to the first, an individual may at present deduct from his taxable income up to 20 percent of his adjusted gross income if the money is given to a foundation or charitable trust, with an additional 10 percent permitted for certain specified types of charitable gifts. The foundation or trust pays no tax on its own investment or other income unless derived from the operation of a business not related to its charitable purpose. If the donor is a corporation, the permitted upper limit free from tax is 5 percent of adjusted gross income.

Following a stamp tax on inherited personal property levied from 1797 to 1802, and an inheritance tax under the Civil War Revenue Act from 1862 to 1870, inheritance taxes were applied, at a rate of 15 percent, for a four-year period following 1898. They were resumed, at levels of from 1 percent to 10 percent, in 1916; and have been raised numerous times since then. The rates of federal tax on estates now range from 3 percent on the first $5,000 of the net estate to 77 percent on that portion of the net estate which, after an exemption of $60,000, exceeds $10 million.[48]

For two periods—1940 to 1945 and 1950 to 1953—corporations were forgiven excess profits tax on monies given to foundations. These periods have come to be known as the times of the 18-cent dollar, since corporations with high earnings could during those times turn over to any tax-exempt organization dollars of which, if they did not so donate, they could only have retained 18 cents after excess profits tax.

Corporate income tax is currently at a maximum rate of 48 percent on all earnings over $25,000; whereas personal income tax rates range up to 70 percent on amounts of taxable income in excess of $200,000 in the case of taxpayers filing a joint return. Capital gains on appreciation realized on property held over a period of more than six months is at present taxed at a maximum rate of 25 percent.

The question as to whether it is or is not *desirable* for philanthropic foundations to pay taxes on their income is a perfectly fair
question. To date the answer of our society, as expressed unequivocally and indeed enthusiastically by our government, is that it
is desirable that foundations be exempt.

> The co-ordinate privileges of tax exemption and deductibility for
> tax purposes of gifts to tax exempt organizations are remarkably well-
> conceived devices by which government can aid and stimulate private
> charitable enterprise, without subjecting it to control.
> The essence of the advantage of this system is that it is automatic.
> The government does not control the flow of funds to the various
> organizations; the receipts of each organization are determined by
> the values and the choices of private givers. The donors determine the
> direction of their own funds, and the distribution of "tax savings" as
> well. The income of each individual organization is a product of
> donations which it receives and the investment wisdom of its man-
> agers. . . .
> Similarly, under the automatic system of tax exemption and deduc-
> tions, private bodies, and not government, determine the application
> of the funds. . . . The basic premise of the system is that progress
> comes through freedom.[49]

The issue of desirability must be decided on the basis of the
record of what foundations have done and are doing with the
money, as compared with the alternative of suppressing private
initiative in the area of charitable and philanthropic giving, and
turning all the funds over to the government.

As to whether it is *wrong* for foundations to "escape" taxes,
the answer is that it is unquestionably legal and right if the foundation in question is carrying on its affairs in a proper philanthropic
manner, but is wrong if it is not.

So finally we come to the bad apple that taints the barrel of
good apples. For it is reprehensibly true that a very few foundations have abused tax-free privilege. The devices and twists known
to have been used to cheat in this matter of nontaxed gifts to
philanthropy are intricate and technical. A considerable amount
of information about such procedures has been brought to light
by the Patman inquiry.

To the present discussion should be added only two final comments. First, any improper tax dodges must be eliminated by

insistence on full public disclosure of foundation affairs and by closer regulation and stricter laws if they are required. Second, for every foundation which has cheated on tax exemption there are hundred of foundations which have conformed meticulously to the letter and spirit of the law. Moreover, these "good" foundations have been gratified at the exposure of organizations masquerading as philanthropic foundations, and the good foundations have uniformly applauded the exposure and the proposed reform.

FOUNDATIONS AND LEGISLATION

Two principal bodies of legislation relating to philanthropic foundations are under consideration at the present time. The first would activate the recommendations, described in the first part of this chapter, which the Treasury Department made as a result of its year-long study. All six of the major Treasury recommendations would presumably require new laws or new modifications of existing laws.

It is to be hoped that most of these recommendations will be dealt with promptly by Congress, and in ways that will make the new regulations promptly applicable. Two of the six recommendations, however, are of such a nature as to require legislation which permits foundations a reasonable period of adjustment. One of these is the proposed condition that no foundation be permitted to own more than 20 percent of any business unrelated to the foundation's charitable activities. This requirement, as is clear from the data presented in Section 7 of Chapter V, would require a diversification of numerous large investment portfolios, including those of the Ford, Kellogg, John A. Hartford, and Moody foundations, and the Duke and Lilly endowments. The same statement doubtless applies to various company foundations and to many family foundations. Quite obviously these foundations should be allowed a reasonable time for readjustment to prevent the necessity of forced sales.

The treasury has suggested a period of five to ten years for gradual compliance with the proposed new regulation requiring that no more than one-quarter of the governing board of trustees of any foundation come from the donor family. This seems ample.

The second body of legislation involves state rather than federal laws, and results from the conviction that the devising of an effective system of state supervision of charities would help to make unnecessary a development of federal control which some consider otherwise both inevitable and undesirable. Attorney General Louis J. Lefkowitz of the State of New York has recently drawn up a proposed state bill "to implement New York State's supervision and endorsement of certain charitable uses and purposes with respect to trusts, charitable corporations, and similar relationships." Hearings on this bill occurred in December, 1965, and favorable comment was made by representatives of the Ford Foundation, the Rockefeller Brothers Fund, and the Dean of the Columbia University Law School. The bill would require state registry of all charitable organizations and periodic accounting to the attorney general.

COLLABORATION BETWEEN FOUNDATIONS AND GOVERNMENT

One first and naïve reaction to the proposal that foundations ought to collaborate with government agencies is—of course they should! But there are special difficulties.

Much of the value to our society of philanthropic foundations comes from their independent status. They are not "government controlled" as regards their choice of projects and their freedom to say what they please. It is difficult to enter into any sort of collaboration with government, however amiably conceived, without unexpected and creeping involvement. A high officer of a major foundation was asked by the State Department to act as the chairman of a group to survey certain needs and opportunities in a foreign, underdeveloped area. The group of technical experts chosen by the foundation official were accompanied on the trip by State Department officers. Before departure, the foundation officer was quietly informed that he must take his tuxedo. Now this sounds silly, but the point is that it *was* silly. At every stop, valuable time was taken up with formalities essentially useless from the point of view of the technical experts.

Much more serious, and more subtle, involvements can occur. During the period in the early forties when the Russians were our allies, two very distinguished Russian scientists, with the enthusiastic approval of our government, visited the United States as the guests of the Rockefeller Foundation. At a farewell party, the conversation took a friendly and confidential turn. They indicated a wish to ask some questions which had been troubling them, and they were encouraged to do so. What was their first question? It was "What is the interrelation of the Rockefeller Foundation with your government?" When told that apart from a minimum of formal requirements for reporting, there simply *was* no relationship—no control, no consultation—the Russians found this hard to believe.

A prominent physicist, writing to the Sloan Foundation in praise of its fellowship program, said, "Last June when we had some prominent Soviet scientist-administrators here for a disarmament discussion, I tried to explain the Ford Foundation's support for that effort to them, with its special mixture of public responsibility and private initiative. As far as I could interpret their reactions, they just don't understand the complementarity between private and government funds, and my guess is that when they finally do we won't need disarmament conferences!"

But that lack of governmental involvement, however long it has sometimes taken for it to be fully credited, has been of inestimable value in working in foreign countries. A foundation officer is accepted as an intellectual comrade, with no complication from political formalities. The collaboration can be far stickier than the two above examples would indicate. During World War II a suggestion was made that, in certain "sensitive" geographical areas, the public health personnel of the Rockefeller Foundation could, so to speak, "keep their eyes open" and then report to our government. These medical men were highly qualified as to language and knowledge of local customs, and they were absolutely trusted by the foreign populations. But they were so trusted precisely because the trust had never been abused. However discreetly phrased, the request sought in fact to have these men act in a spying capacity.

The request for this kind of "collaboration with government" was resolutely and firmly refused. Even when the request was repeated, with more authority behind it, it was refused. And it should have been.

The issues—and the potential difficulties—raised by collaboration between foundations and government have been dramatically illustrated by the recent disclosures that the Central Intelligence Agency has used certain foundations (called funnel foundations in the earlier section dealing with types of foundations) as conduits for government money that ended up supporting a wide variety of overseas educational and cultural activities.

There were four steps to this process. First, the CIA received from the government funds over which the agency had a remarkable, if not indeed a unique, degree of unsupervised control.

Second, these funds were transferred to various foundations. The list may well not be complete, but there appear to be at least thirty-eight foundations involved in this way. Of these, twenty were concerned with only one activity, eight were involved twice, four were involved three times (The Baird, Borden, Norman, and Benjamin Rosenthal foundations), four were involved four times (The Gotham, Hobby, Price, and Rabb foundations), and two were involved six times (The J. Frederick Brown Foundation and the Pappas Charitable Trust). It seems that no one of the large and well-known foundations was involved.

These foundations, moreover, merely passed the funds along to a third set of agencies (some fifteen of them), which in turn disbursed the funds to the final recipient organizations or activities, which were very numerous. It is hard to avoid the conclusion that this complication and indirection were deliberately intended to reduce visibility.

The agencies receiving the funds from the foundations included the National Education Association, The National Student Association, The American Newspaper Guild, The American Federation of State, County and Municipal Employees, The Institute for International Labor Research, American Friends of the Middle East, and at least nine others. The final disbursers of the funds included the Association of Hungarian Students in North America, The International Commission of Jurists in Geneva, the Institute of Political Education in Costa Rica, The Center of Studies and Documentation in Mexico, and Radio Free Europe. The final activities thus supported were geographically spread over Latin America, Germany, Africa, and the Middle East. Lawyers, educators, universities, journalists, artists, writers, and students were final recipients. By the time the money emerged to the surface, the original source was pretty thoroughly concealed.

The Hobby Foundation appears to have played a double role, in that they received funds directly from the CIA which they turned over to other agencies, and that they also received funds from some five other foundations (who in turn had received the money from the CIA) and then disbursed these funds to operating agencies.

The complete and dependable details of this fantastic mishmash have not come to the surface as yet, and very probably never will. But enough has emerged to warrant several comments.

First, it appears that the vast majority of the activities ultimately aided, and perhaps all of them, were decent, constructive, and desirable. Second, it seems clear that most, if indeed not all, of the foundations, groups, and agencies were innocent of any improper intent, and in many instances were doubtless unaware of the complicated web of which they were a part. Third, this is a ridiculous and potentially a thoroughly bad way in which to finance good activities. Fourth, the role of the CIA in this matter seems deplorable indeed. If, as has been claimed, the ultimate aid went only to individuals, groups, or agencies that were approved by the CIA, then the foundations that played an intermediate role are to be severely criticized for accepting funds subject to that type of external control.

All in all, this is an example of a very bad kind of collaboration between philanthropic foundations and government.

Should government now take over all the functions of private foundations? The question, for anyone who believes in democratic procedures, almost answers itself. Freedom of action for the individual person, nurturing of private initiative, and recourse to government only when inescapable are basic principles of democracy. In many fields of activity, and certainly in the general areas of philanthropy, private institutions have always, and should always, set standards of both concept and performance. In such fields, even more than in many others, concentration and central-ization of effort almost surely means homogenization and dehumanization. The great, although often clumsy, power of the government is clearly needed for many purposes closely related to charitable action—large-scale relief, slum clearance and housing, job training, educational facilities, and many other facets of the poverty program as well as for other aspects of the drive towards the "great society." But all this will be not only inefficient, it will be basically self-defeating, if the principle of acceptance of private and individual responsibility is in any way impaired.

> Private philanthropy, and the tens of thousands of voluntary associations which are supported by it [said Dean Rusk], reflects an acceptance of responsibility by private individual citizens. They also provide a training ground for the practice of democracy by our citizens. They also help to shape by direct action the purposes and moods and spirit, the atmosphere and the standards, of our democratic society. . . . Our society would be meaner, less imaginative, less progressive, less stable, if it were not for that ability of this governing force at the bottom to make its applicable adjustments to the rapid social change and to stabilize the institutions which deserve such stability, creating the new ones where new ones had to come into being.[50]

These words were written by a man who was at that moment the president of a great foundation but who had previously had extensive and distinguished government service. He has written me that on the basis of his more recent governmental experience he reaffirms these words.

At many places in the contributed essays of Part II of this book the authors have from their direct personal experience emphasized the value of the nimbleness, the flexibility, the freedom of the support which comes from foundations. For good and indeed inevitable reasons, these qualities are not equally characteristic of governmental action. This has been widely recognized. Albert M. Sacks, Professor of Law at Harvard University, has written:

> Wherever initiative of thought and action is valued, wherever a diversity of views and approachs is thought necessary, wherever experimentation in new untried ventures is sought, the many-centered, disorderly, and even "irresponsible" private groups must be relied upon. Herein lie fundamental values. The compulsions and uniformities of government become a positive drawback. It would be unfor-

tunate, for example, to have government play an exclusive or even dominant operational role in social science research. Where private action has unique advantages but funds available only to government are needed, the no longer novel government grant may be invoked.[51]

A study of private enterprise and foreign aid was carried out for the Agency for International Development of the Department of State, by a committee of which the head was Arthur K. Watson, chairman of the I.B.M. World Trade Corporation. Their report contains the following:

> In sorting out the respective roles of the private and the public sectors in providing the resources for the aid program, this Committee believes that there are a few basic guidelines to be followed, guidelines which are derived from the experience and the convictions of the American people.
> In the first place, private organizations are generally capable of greater speed, flexibility and incisiveness than government agencies. Freed from government procedures, permitted to find their own ways of performing the tasks which are necessary for economic growth, private organizations can outperform official agencies.

The testimony from the actual recipients of both foundation and government aid eloquently emphasizes the importance of both, and often makes clear the special value of the former. In a letter to the Sloan Foundation, explaining why funds from that philanthropy would be of special importance to him, President Lee DuBridge of the California Institute of Technology wrote, in part:

> All government agencies have special missions, programs, or areas of support. Many scientific areas, including new ones, do not fit into the program of existing government agencies and find themselves without sources of government support.
> Government funds, though large in dollars, are still inadequate to meet the research requirements of all our major universities. The competition for the existing funds is extremely keen, which means that many project proposals must be declined or cut back in the funds allowed. This situation becomes especially acute for the young scientist whose standing, prestige, and research record leave him at a

disadvantage in competition with his more famous colleagues around the country for funds to support his work.

The funds of various government agencies are heavily committed to the continued support of the existing programs which they have funded, and it is extremely difficult to accommodate new projects, especially in new fields possibly unfamiliar to the staff and advisors of specific government agencies.

Government procedures for allocating funds to a proposed research project are cumbersome and often inflexible. This means it may take many months to secure funds for pursuing a new and exciting idea, and it also may take many months to secure authorized changes in a research program already financed when new ideas or new discoveries arise which make a change in direction highly desirable.

CHAPTER 14

Foundations and Society

Professor Albert M. Sacks of the Harvard Law School has written: "This notion that philanthropy, to retain its character, must remain noncontroversial represents a fundamental misunderstanding of the institution which not only perverts its historical development, but also destroys its essential values."[1] The recent Treasury Department Report, in speaking of the special role which philanthropy plays in our society, cites "dissent from prevailing attitudes" as one of the activities for which private philanthropic organizations "can be uniquely qualified."[2]

We have seen that the earliest congressional investigation (the Walsh investigation) was motivated by a fear that the overconservative and selfish power of great wealth was seeking to control our society, whereas the later Cox investigation, taking the opposite tack, attempted to prove that philanthropic foundations were left-wing and subversive agencies.

Neither of these attacks was substantiated by the evidence, but to this day it remains true that foundations are too liberal to suit some, and too conservative to suit others. The great foundations have been liberal indeed in their concern for the oppressed, whether the source of oppression was poverty, racial injustice, lack of proper food, ill health, or the more general oppression and lack of opportunity that result from ignorance. In some ways, too, the foundations are conservative. Certain of them tend to favor and defend the free enterprise system which has made possible the accumulations of wealth which have created them.

It may be difficult for a foundation to be very vigorously and successfully radical, even when it explicity and frankly sets out to do so. The historian Merle Curti, in an article titled "Subsidizing Radicalism: The American Fund for Public Service, 1921-41,"[3] has analyzed the record of one such foundation, organized by Charles Garland, a young man who was "convinced that no one has any moral right to property beyond his immediate and basic needs,"[4] and therefore refused to accept a million-dollar inheritance. The incorporators of the resulting trust included the prominent liberals Lewis Gannett of the New York *World* and Robert Morss Lovett of the University of Chicago. On the board of trustees were a number of well-known members of the liberal-labor movement.

The fund was dedicated to liberal, labor, and radical causes, and the trustees intended, in view of the founder's desires, to spend their capital promptly. Rather interestingly, the first secretary turned to the Rockefeller Foundation, the Russell Sage Foundation, and the Carnegie Foundation "for a clarification of their grant-making policies and for other regulations governing their procedure."[5] Advances of the market doubled their assets (a fact which must have displeased the group), and their opportunities to exhaust their resources were frequently thwarted by the collapse of various ventures, particularly the daily papers under labor and radical auspices, to which they might otherwise have made further grants. Indeed the directors of the fund themselves stated that much of their money "went into trying to save sinking enterprises."

This fund finally managed to exhaust itself after twenty rather tumultuous years. Its actions were vigorously criticized, not least by members of various radical movements. One of the directors of the fund "now thinks of the whole experience as a bit 'weird,' and of the results as largely negative."[6]

On the other face of the coin, foundations have recently been charged with excessively rightist tendencies. Late in 1964 the Internal Revenue Service opened a drive against certain "politically-minded organizations that enjoy tax-exempt status. Most of the fire is being concentrated on outspoken right-wing groups."[7] This effort was directed primarily against organizations few of which were in fact foundations; the Daughters of the American Revolution, the American Council of Christian Laymen, and the Circuit

Riders were included. They were "accused of putting out political propaganda while posing as a philanthropic, religious, or educational group."[8]

The Anti-Defamation League in its volume *Danger on the Right* has been concerned with the problem of the radical right as has, for that matter, the Republican party.

A very few rather noisy tax-exempt foundations have without doubt been guilty of crossing the no-man's land between education and political propaganda. The elimination of such cases should be accomplished promptly, but it will not be easy to draw the lines clearly. This would seem to require action by federal authorities within existing statutes, which should be ample to deal with such violations.

Excursions into the far left or the far right and flagrant abuses of the tax-free privilege by using the resources of philanthropic foundations for the purpose of political propaganda exist, however, in a minute fraction of cases. The "ninety and nine," or rather, the four hundred and ninety-nine, responsible foundations should not be associated, in the public mind, with the one offender, however raucous he may have been.

Further, law and regulation stringent enough to eliminate such improprieties completely would be disastrous, doing far more harm by their hobbling of the freedom of action of responsible foundations than they would do good by strict control of the rare offender. If we believe in democracy and in the right to express dissenting ideas, a small amount of pathology must be tolerated in order to maintain the health of the main social body, somewhat as protective antibodies are produced in the human body by injecting small amounts of material associated with disease. The edge of desirable experimentation must continuously be tested with vigor and variety, and can be located only by occasionally crossing it. We accept a small risk to make a large gain.

NEGLECT OF IMPORTANT FIELDS

Clear instances of important fields neglected by foundations are easily discovered—just ask persons whose foundation requests have been declined. It is easy indeed to sit on the sidelines and make superficial and irresponsible suggestions—superficial because the detailed situation has not been studied thoroughly, irresponsible because the suggester will not let himself suffer the consequences.

It is an unpleasant fact that any foundation, with necessarily limited human beings as its officers, tends to settle down into a fixed pattern of procedure. It may deserve the praiseful adjectives "sustained, courageous, determined, and patient"; but it may at times also deserve the pejorative adjectives "unimaginative, timid, dull, and disappointing."

One of the favorite games, with all the natural attraction of shooting elephants, is to tell the Ford Foundation what it ought to be doing. Most of us are tolerant of the difficulties of the new nations which have to leap-frog several centuries and move precipitately from primitive to modern-industrialized circumstances. We may forget, however, that the Rockefeller Foundation, to choose one example, had many unhurried years in which to learn the art of foundation philanthropy, whereas the Ford Foundation found itself suddenly faced with huge sums of money to be disposed of.

Philip M. Stern, himself presiding over two family foundations, has made a number of concrete suggestions to the Ford Foundation with taste, wit, good sense, and understanding.[9] His suggestions for the most part refer to opportunities of such dimensions that only Ford could deal with them. But he makes his suggestion at the other end of the spectrum that staff officers of the Ford Foundation be given authority to make, at their own discretion, small grants ranging from $50,000 in the case of vice presidents down to $5,000 in the case of junior program associates, with an aggregate ceiling for such grants.

Despite obvious dangers, this seems to me both fascinating and excellent. At one stroke it would free the Ford Foundation from its present apparent assumption that an activity is interesting and important only if the bill involves at least seven digits. It would, of course, involve the risk that some of these small grants might turn out badly: but is it so obvious that all of the big ones turn out well? As an important by-product, it would vitalize the activities of the junior officers, giving them the stimulation of direct individual decisions and personal involvement with the working levels of research.

Small grants offer real difficulties for boards of trustees. Only an unusually dedicated and otherwise unoccupied trustee could take the time to be informed about a considerable number of small grants, and, not being so informed, a trustee would be required to accept such grants wholly as a matter of confidence in the allocating officer. This confidence, in turn, would be difficult to sustain over the years necessary before many of the small grants come to fruition and demonstrate their importance, and would be virtually impossible to sustain unless the officer had, along with his duty to allocate small grants, other more general and more easily visible assignments.

The problem of small grants is a real and continuing one. Among the internal papers written in connection with foundation duties, I produced several memoranda on the subject, one going as far back as 1936 and one as recent as 1962, one of them a seventeen-page factual study of cases. Once in a while a small grant is particularly strategic in a scientific field. Early Rockefeller Foundation grants averaging only $1,900 apiece went to seven scientists, each of whom eventually became world famous. This small but essential beginning was followed up in each instance by expanding support, in some cases for ten to fifteen years. The little things became big things, and it is hard to avoid the conviction that it was important to give aid at an early stage. Similar and equally good opportunities doubtless arise in the humanities, the social sciences, the creative arts, and in all other fields.

In addition to the neglect by some foundations of significant small opportunities, certain functional areas appear to deserve more attention than they are receiving. Philip Stern suggested, as Ford-sized opportunities, the experimental and demonstration development of a model school-and-slum community center; an "educational park" as a possible solution to the urban-school-segregation dilemma; a sustained but crash program in urban transportation; the underwriting of "a massive birth-control clinic program in American poverty areas." Although foundations have, especially recently, been vigorous in support of certain educational opportunities for Negroes, they have been backward and timid indeed in the more contentious areas of civil rights and race relations. A couple of years ago there was a concerted attempt to interest the larger foundations in the problems of legal defense funds in civil rights cases, but this proved too hot a potato for them to handle. Indeed, of all the areas considered in Part II of this book, the law presents a large and very significant range of unembraced opportunity for foundation interest and aid.

In the scientific areas with which I am familiar, certain important opportunities are not as yet being vigorously developed. The two current scientific fads are the scientific attack, largely by means of huge and very costly high-energy accelerators, on the nature of physical matter, and the even more costly assault on space, with more emphasis on technology (stimulated by the concern with national prestige and defense) than upon basic science.

The opportunities not yet rigorously explored lie in the understanding of the nature of living things. It seemed clear in 1932, when the Rockefeller Foundation launched its quarter-century program in that area, that the biological and medical sciences were ready for a friendly invasion by the physical sciences. The application to the most basic problems of biology of the experimental and analytical techniques of physics, mathematics, and chemistry has resulted in the relatively recent magnificent development of molecular biology, crowned by the discovery of the structure of DNA and the unraveling of the genetic code. It seems equally clear that a next great step can be taken in molecular neuro-physiology. Just as more than thirty years ago the tools were in hand to begin an effective attack on genetics, the tools are now available for discovering, on the most disciplined and precise level of molecular actions, how man's central nervous system really operates, how he thinks, learns, remembers, and forgets. Closely allied would be studies of animal behavior, a field which also seems ready to be lifted onto a new level of significance.

Apart from the fascination of gaining some knowledge of the nature of the mind-brain-body relationship, the practical values in such studies are potentially enormous. Only thus may we gain information about our behavior of the sort that can lead to wise and beneficial control. The possibilities for improving the educational process are equally great.

Similar opportunities doubtless exist in other fields. This is a period of rapid and significant change, and social mechanisms alert and responsive to these changes are required. No mechanism of our society has proven more adept and effective in assuming imaginative new jobs than the foundations. That foundations are neglecting some important problems and fields of study is, of itself, a significant argument in favor of them.

CODES OF ETHICS

The specter of tight government control and the sincere desire of the vast majority of foundations that their behavior be as socially useful as possible, coupled with the impression made by a few bad but publicized examples, have led to the suggestion that the foundations formulate for themselves a code of ethics, with internal procedures for enforcing it.

At a recent Conference on Charitable Foundations held under the auspices of New York University in May, 1965, a session was devoted to this proposal of a foundation code of ethics. Mortimer M. Caplin, the former Commissioner of Internal Revenue, speaking on the topic "A Code of Practice Is Needed," agreed that "based upon Internal Revenue Service studies, the overall record of foundations emerges as a good one,"[10] but also referred to abuses (primarily the list given in the 1965 Treasury Report), and expressed the view that individual self-policing was not an adequate procedure. He emphasized that the Internal Revenue Service, with its limited resources, cannot hope to give individual audit to every one of the formal returns of all the exempt organizations. Caplin favors further *rules* of conduct.

John W. Riehm, Jr., formerly president of the Conference of Southwest Foundation, responded with a talk on "More Is Needed Than a Code of Practice." Emphasizing the variety of foundations and the necessary preoccupation of the Internal Revenue Service with protecting revenue, and doubting that either the foundations or the IRS could come up with an adequate solution, he proposed that some major foundation, or a group of them, furnish the financing to provide for "a detailed, in-depth study of the entire field undertaken by the American Law Institute."[11]

Donald R. Young, a sociologist who has had extensive university and foundation experience, presented a differing view:

> The often-made suggestion that a code of practice is both desirable and possible implies the existence of, first, an appreciable degree of uniformity in objectives and operations; second, a need for the development of unique standards of practice; and, third, a recognized community of interests to facilitate at least some informal self-policing. It should be noted also that an ethical implication is introduced by the word "code."[12]

Dr. Young asked whether a code is needed:

> Do philanthropic agencies known as foundations have enough in common to justify the adoption of some common core of standard practice? Are there problems of foundation management not adequately covered by the ordinary standards of good practice and proper behavior? Is it not enough to rely on the admonitory effectiveness of public disclosure of activities and somewhat strengthened government oversight?[13]

He pointed out that concise, sensible, and significant statements of good regulatory practices already exist, notably the simple but powerful list which was given by President John Gardner in the report of the Carnegie Corporation for 1964. What can possibly be required beyond the already well-recognized principles of full disclosure, of avoidance of self-dealing (the use of a foundation for the personal advantage of the donor or a member of the staff or board), of current spending of income, and of the avoidance of ownership or control of a business?

I agree with Dr. Young, and to his points I would add two. First, formal and public statements of good intentions are likely either to reflect a bad conscience, or alternatively are likely to be a little overpious. "Not every one that saith unto me, Lord, Lord, shall enter into the kingdom of heaven."[14] Second, any type of large-scale collective activity on the part of philanthropic foundations is open to the suspicion that they do in fact, as some have claimed, constitute a sort of organized conspiracy—an "establishment." Completely individual and individualistic action provides a healthier atmosphere for the vigor of variety.

BAD FOUNDATIONS

Several times in this book it has been conceded that there are a very few "bad" foundations. What is a bad foundation and what does it do?

The worst thing a foundation can do is to be incompetent—to use its money for legally impeccable purposes, but nevertheless foolishly. This constitutes intellectual poverty; but when one speaks of bad foundations one normally means legally bad, and primarily because of misuse of the tax privilege.

The Commissioner of Internal Revenue has himself given an official summary of the cardinal foundation sins: (1) self-dealing, (2) unreasonable accumulation of income, (3) speculative investments, (4) competing for interest and rental incomes, (5) manipulation of leases, (6) donation of non-income-producing property, especially where the donor holds and enjoys the donated property, (7) overevaluation of art and other properties, and (8) faulty filing of information returns.[15]

Certain of these faults, namely 4, 5, 6, and 8, would seem not only to be clearly wrong, but to involve no especially difficult or delicate judgments. Point 2 hinges primarily on the definition of "unreasonable." Point 3 also depends on a definition—in this case of an *improperly* speculative investment, since almost all investments have some aspect of risk and some hope for gain. Point 7 involves the plainly disputable matter of monetary valuations, with all the uncertainties and the variations that might naturally occur in certain fields.

But no one of these points seems to cut very deeply into the more significant ethical-intellectual problem of what makes a foundation good. Insofar as ethical issues are involved, they are involved in the above list at a rather superficial level. Only the first point goes more deeply into the problem of the relationship of the donor, trustees, and officers of a foundation to the society which they should serve.

The commissioner's list is undoubtedly proper and important from the point of view of governmental laws and regulations. But it seems to me that the essence of the matter is simply this: a foundation is bad (a) if it operates for the private gain of its donor, trustees, or officers, (b) if its privileged position is used in the furtherance of business procedures which are in any way competitive with taxed enterprises, (c) if it does not fulfill its stated philanthropic purposes either because it unreasonably accumulates its income or because it disburses its income on the basis of selfish or incompetent advice, and (d) if it fails to make reasonable public accounting of its stewardship.

The previous paragraph emphasizes foundation faults all of which are legal in nature in that they all involve violations of law or regulations. Even more significant, from the point of view of society, would be faults of stupidity, triviality, lack of imagination, unresponsiveness to the basic and long-range needs of society. These are not the shortcomings which concern most of the politicians, nor are they the faults which usually make headlines. Indeed it would take a very alert and sharp-sighted investigator or reporter to publicize these grave faults, for they are by no means common. In the total volume of criticism of foundations there have been relatively few charges relating to these qualities. The volume of competent praise far outweighs that of significant nonlegal criticism, as the second part of this book demonstrates.

A new era of clarity for recognizing irresponsible foundations began in 1950, when important substantive changes were written into the laws and regulations affecting philanthropic foundations. This came about almost as a direct consequence of disclosures about millions of dollars of business manipulations by, with, and through a cluster of New England charitable trusts. Indeed, former Internal Revenue Commissioner Caplin said that "In a response to what had been called 'trading on exemption' Congress passed legislation aimed at a number of these devices."[16] A lawyer who has written extensively on the subject of tax-exempt organizations said in 1951, ". . . the hue and the cry had been too loudly raised; Congress and the Treasury Department could or would not wait. And so the aftermath has been the passage of the Revenue Act of 1950—good in parts, bad in parts, but in any case fiendishly complicated."[17]

Certain transactions were prohibited on pain of loss of tax-exemption privileges. They were only forbidden, however, where the foundation was dealing with "its creator, a substantial contributor, family member of either, or a corporation controlled by the creator or by a substantial contributor."[18]

The following are the prohibited transactions with relation to individuals in the mentioned categories:

1. Loans of any part of its income or corpus, without the receipt of adequate security and a reasonable rate of interest.
2. Payment of any unreasonable compensation for salaries or other personal services.
3. Making any part of its services available on a preferential basis.
4. Making any substantial purchase of securities or any other property for more than adequate consideration.
5. Sale of any substantial part of its securities or other property for less than an adequate consideration.
6. Engagement in any other transaction which results in a substantial diversion of income or corpus.

The qualifying terms incorporated in the statute, as seen in the preceding chapter, constitute one of the reasons not for its being "fiendishly complicated," but for its being—doubtless necessarily from the legal point of view—vague.

These provisions applied only to dealings with the creators of or substantial contributors to a foundation, to their families, and to their corporations. Clearly these prohibitions, when made workably unambiguous, should apply to a philanthropic foundation's dealing with any person or corporate entity whatsoever.

Foundations as a group are conspicuous and attractive for their relative freedom from tight governmental regulations. They are easy to establish and a great many business-minded and/or wealthy persons (with advice and guidance from lawyers and accountants) are lured by the ease with which they can found a philanthropic corporation and enjoy numerous financial advantages within the context of actual (or, in a very few cases, presumed) charitable operations. The Revenue Act of 1950 closed the legal loopholes that made possible these misuses of foundations—in theory, at least—to a considerable extent. In practice, however, the decade

and a half since 1950 has witnessed a multiplication of foundations and almost without doubt more extensive abuse than before
—the latter by sheer increase in numbers of tax-exempt organizations rather than by any provable intensification of corruption
and chicanery.

The final report of the Patman Committee employed expressions such as "nonfeasance on the part of Treasury officials . . .
Treasury's indefensible apathy and its archaic procedures . . . 55
percent of the 546 foundations examined by the subcommittee
failed to comply with certain Treasury regulations during one or
more years. . . ."[19] Exaggerated as may be the picture such remarks
suggest, the facts seem incontestable that some of the conditions
the Revenue Act of 1950 was designed to curtail continue to
exist. Indeed, the evidence points not only to more cases, but also
to new types of abuse. The reliable available evidence, however,
compels the conclusion that only a small minority of tax-exempt
philanthropic organizations were and are involved in the prohibited practices. The February 9, 1965, *New York Times* account
of the Treasury Department's study added, "Although the Treasury
did not name the foundations that it said had abused their tax-
exempt status, officials indicated that *all or nearly all of the large
and widely known foundations had been absolved*" (emphasis
added).

Some cogent explanations have been advanced for the relative failure of the tighter IRS regulations to curb the abuses they
were promulgated to reduce if not eliminate. Caplin has ascribed
to the single inflexible punitive measure available to the Revenue
Service some responsibility for its difficulties in arresting foundation abuses. This measure is the revocation of tax exemption.

"Even after this remedial legislation, the Service continued to
suffer a series of judicial defeats during the 1950's when it attempted to enforce its interpretation of the law in the courts."[20]

Another factor that undoubtedly figured in the admittedly meager
supervision exercised over foundations was the paucity of manpower available to audit the records of the rapidly growing numbers
of foundations.

Besides revocation of tax exemption, the Treasury through its
IRS has had since 1950 the power to tax foundation income from

foundation-conducted businesses which are not related to the purposes of the foundation. But it contends that the legislation applying to unrelated business income has also proved to be full of loopholes. Finding and using the loopholes in this provision and in the wide-meshed fabric of regulations covering tax-exempt organizations has been the game of "bad" foundations.

The abuses indulged in by "bad" foundations fall for the most part into two or three general categories described by Representative Patman. The first of these is the use of foundation funds for the personal benefit of donors or donor-related persons. The second is their use for purposes unrelated to charity or social welfare. The third, for which the 1965 Treasury Report found far less confirmation, has to do with the potentially harmful effects of the economic power concentrated in foundation hands.

The Treasury Report list of six categories of problems (page 185) is in many respects similar to the IRS list. It will suffice to mention one example for each "problem," each an actual case. They cannot be called acts of illegality or statutory violations because the Treasury Department has either deemed the prohibitions not broad or precise enough to condemn the conduct, or decisions by the courts have upheld the tax-exempt organizations' defense of their propriety. It does nevertheless seem reasonable to say that no good foundation does or should do such things.

The first problem treated in the Treasury Report is "self-dealing," that is, business transactions involving the foundation on the one hand, and on the other the donor or officers or trustees of the foundation. The dozen examples cited in the report, "indicate the types of cases . . . which are being entered into and the difficulty which the Internal Revenue Service has in applying the arm's length test contained in existing law":[21]

> The A foundation made a loan to a business corporation controlled by its donor. The security for the loan consisted of an oral promise made by the donor as an officer of the corporation to execute a mortgage on certain of the real property owned by the corporation, but only if the foundation requested such a mortgage. The foundation, however, never requested the donor's corporation to execute such a mortgage. The Internal Revenue Service challenged the exemption of the foundation on the grounds that the organiza-

tion had made a loan without the receipt of "adequate" security. The Service argued that if the corporation were to become insolvent, the foundation, with only an unrecorded promise to execute a mortgage in the future, would be in the same position as any other unsecured creditor. However, the court, although recognizing that the security interest of the foundation would be ineffective if the corporation disposed of the real property, felt that a mere promise to execute a mortgage in the future constituted "adequate" security. Thus, the foundation's exemption was upheld.

"Delay in Benefit to Charity" is the name given to the second problem of the Treasury report. It has to do with the time elapsing between a foundation's receipt of contributions and its use of them in a philanthropic connection. The Treasury Report suggests that exempt status be denied to an otherwise qualifying organization for the year that its accumulated income is:

1. unreasonable in amount or duration,
2. used to a substantial degree for purposes other than those constituting the basis for the organization's exemption, or
3. invested in such a manner as to jeopardize the carrying out of the function constituting the basis for the organization's exemption.

The Treasury report illustrated this second problem with the following, one of two cases given:

The difficulty in administering current law can be illustrated by a recent Tax Court case in which a foundation with a net worth of approximately $1,000 purchased a 34-acre tract of industrial real property for $1.15 million. This purchase was financed with advance rentals of $154,000 received from a lessee and by loans of $1 million. Since the foundation used approximately 80 percent of its income for the 5 years following the purchase of the property to retire its debt, the Service revoked the foundation's exemption ruling on the grounds of an "unreasonable" accumulation. However, the Service's revocation was reversed by the court which held that the accumulation was neither "unreasonable in amount or duration" nor used to any "substantial degree for purposes or functions other than those constituting the basis for such organization's exemption."

"Foundation Involvement in Business," is a particularly vexatious problem in the realm of tax-exempt philanthropic organizations. A single foundation is given as an example of two aspects of this third problem. The aspects are the nature of the business involvement and the special benefits that accrue to a commercial but foundation-controlled enterprise, benefits which give the enterprise definite advantages over a competing business not owned by a foundation. As stated in the Treasury report:

> The E foundation controls a corporation which operates a large metropolitan department store. For its fiscal year ended January 31, 1963, the store reported gross sales of $78,395,052, gross profit of $32,062,405, and paid wages and salaries of $17,488,211. It stated the book value of its assets at that time to be $55,091,820.
>
> The dividends which the E foundation . . . has received from its department store subsidiary for the years 1960 through 1963 have ranged from less than 1 to 1½ percent of the book value of its equity in the corporation, as reflected on the corporation's February 1, 1962, balance sheet. In each of these years the store's after-tax net income has been considerably more than twice as much as the total dividends paid.

Much favored by those family foundations we think of as "bad" is the device of controlling corporate and other property. The Treasury looks upon this fourth problem as a major one. What is meant here by "controlling" would seem to furnish a major criterion for deciding whether the foundation in question is "good" or "bad." If the foundation was established to preserve intact for a donor's family a business or holding but functions in full accordance with the ethical and legal imperatives of a philanthropy, then it may well be a "good" foundation. On the other hand, it is clearly wrong if the obligations of the philanthropy are subordinated in any way to a concern for and preoccupation with the management and functioning of the donated resource.

Most of the examples of this fourth problem provided by the Treasury have to do with stock in corporations of which the donor (and often family members as well) have dominant or total ownership. Some or all of the stock may be the original corpus of the foundation, or it may have come in subsequent contributions. Complex questions of voting rights, manipulation, and dividends (declared or withheld) enter into the appraisal of whether a foundation exists to serve philanthropy or to serve selfish interests of the donor *et al.*

The following two examples, taken from the Treasury Report, typify the fourth problem:

The C and D foundations' principal donor owns all of the voting stock of the C corporation. Members of his family and he have given 106,000 shares of that corporation's class B nonvoting stock to the C foundation; they have given 80,000 shares of this stock to the D foundation.

In only 1 of the last 6 years have the C and D foundations . . . received dividends on their large holdings of nonvoting stock in a corporation controlled by their principal donor.

"Financial transactions unrelated to charitable functions" is the designation the Treasury Report gives to its fifth problem. Three classes or categories of transactions make up this problem. They are (a) foundation borrowing; (b) foundation lending; and (c) trading and speculation by foundations.

Not many foundations borrow any money. Only a few borrow heavily and repeatedly. Borrowings are estimated to account for less than 2½ percent of total foundation assets; in the Treasury's figures, $244 million of approximately $10,713 million book value.

The borrowing of money by foundations for purposes unrelated to charitable functions is frequently combined with lending to philanthropy-unconnected transactions. When the money borrowed at one rate is loaned out at a higher rate the process is referred to as "churning money." When the lending is done for other than the foundation's financial gain, the reasons are even more likely to result in Internal Revenue misgivings.

The following are examples of borrowing and lending by three foundations:

In the years 1951 through 1962 the A, B, C foundations, established and dominated by one person, borrowed money from 17 different institutions and a variety of individuals to acquire investment assets. On December 31, 1956, the total outstanding indebtedness which the foundations had incurred for this purpose appears to have been approximately $14,200,000. A recent report indicates that, during the 12-year period covered, the foundations entered into 130 separate investment borrowing transactions. Many of the transactions involved amounts of more than $100,000; several involved more than $1 million.

The A, B, and C foundations . . . all controlled by a single individual, made many loans to that individual's friends and business acquaintances. On December 31, 1956, one businessman owed these foundations $6,571,448. At the end of the years 1951 through 1961 another owed the foundations amounts ranging from $1,193,000 to $2,057,000. The indebtedness of various other businessmen to the foundations was, on the dates noted, as follows:

Individual A, Dec. 31, 1954 . . .	$138,000.00
Individual B, Oct. 27, 1954 . . .	1,519,000.00
Individual C, Dec. 31, 1961 . . .	39,210.00
Individual D, Dec. 31, 1962 . . .	80,246.92
Individual E, Dec. 31, 1962 . . .	39,027.50
Individual F, Dec. 31, 1953 . . .	247,084.75
Individual G, Dec. 31, 1962 . . .	54,000.00
Individual H, Dec. 31, 1962 . . .	50,154.32

The loans to these and other businessmen ordinarily arose through transactions in which the foundations purchased and carried (often for several years) large amounts of securities for the accounts of the borrowers. Where the documents recording the arrangements specified interest rates, the rates prescribed were sometimes as low as 3, 3½, or 4 percent. In other cases, however, the rates were higher; and in many situations the foundations were entitled to share in the profits of sales of the securities.

"Trading and speculation by foundations," the third of the three main types of dealings composing the Treasury's fifth problem of financial transactions unrelated to charitable functions, are criticized because they "ordinarily entail greater risk of loss than do prudently chosen long-term investments." When "spectacularly successful . . . they make possible both the financial empire building and the severance of a foundation from dependence upon contributors." One of the reasons for the Treasury's recommendations for changes in law to cope with this problem is that preoccupation with financial transactions of this nature on the part of foundation trustees or directors cuts in upon the time they would otherwise have for charity matters—in other words, interferes with the legitimate business of the foundation.

The same triumvirate of foundations which engaged in borrowing and lending in the examples noted above engaged in active trading of securities. The Treasury Report says of them the following:

The A, B, and C foundations carried on lively, extensive, and often speculative securities dealings. They entered into puts and calls, purchased a large volume of unlisted securities, and frequently acquired stock on margin. They agreed to a number of arrangements under which they carried securities for the accounts of individuals in exchange for the right to share in any profits which might be realized upon disposition of the securities. They sometimes sold stock within a period of from one to several days after acquiring it.

The sixth problem of the Treasury Report is referred to as "Broadening of Foundation Management" and it differs in kind from those just discussed. No supporting statistical data are furnished, and it seems questionable that any are possible of compilation. The elements of the problem are such as to "evade precise definition." But they are "more pervasive and more fundamental . . . and less susceptible of isolation." No examples are given by IRS. These are the elements:

1. Abuse potentialities of donor influence
2. Perpetual existence of foundations
3. Possibilities for narrowness of foundation management.

The first has to do, of course, with an understandable although regrettable tendency of some donors to consider that the foundations their resources created continue to be their personal property, to do with pretty much as they please. It is true that in only a small minority of cases do the things done by such foundations fall within the categories of badness dealt with in the preceding five problems. But it is clearly not appropriate that the donor should have unlimited discretionary power over wealth he has given to a philanthropic entity.

The question of how long a foundation should be permitted to exist is a most complex one. The Treasury has proposed that after twenty-five years of the organization the board or trustee body could not have more than 25 percent of its membership made up of donor and donor-related persons, presumably reasoning that such a mandatory limitation on the membership of the controlling body would have the effect of enabling "independent private parties" to review the twenty-five-year record and decide whether it justifies continuation or dissolution, either of which courses they could then command.

The "possibilities for narrowness of foundation management" are excluded by the dilution of donor influence through a proposed rule that the board of trustee body can have no less than 75 percent of its membership donor-unrelated after twenty-five years, the Treasury suggested.

It is impossible to overstate the importance to a philanthropic foundation of a broadly based board of trustees, chosen for their competence rather than for their connections. On the other hand there are special problems, such as the membership of the board of a company-sponsored foundation. It might, for example, be difficult or even illegal for a corporation to vote stockholders' funds to an organization with broad charitable purposes if that organization is not substantially controlled by the company.

Of all the examples cited, and of all the Treasury's six points except the last, I would say that they are illustrations of the occasional tendency, apparent throughout our society, of a very few persons to cheat the law—or to abuse the ambiguity of the law—for personal gain of one sort or another. But they are matters to be dealt with by the legal authorities—primarily with more efficient administration of the present laws, and with more effective laws and regulations if these are in fact necessary. In no possible sense or degree do these minuscule examples of bad foundation practice justify any poor impression of the general behavior of philanthropic foundations, nor do they justify any stringent changes in the laws that would hamper the ninety-nine and forty-four one-hundredths percent of good foundations which are unselfishly, effectively, and properly serving our society.

There are of course examples of behavior strikingly more bizarre and reprehensible than any of the examples cited above, perpetrated by outfits which in no sense deserve to use the word "foundation," although they do, and which in no conceivable sense deserve tax exemption. But again, these lurid examples are no more representative, and have no more right to blacken the public reputation of the great mass of good foundations than has the occasional scandalous episode in the choir loft to blacken the reputation of the church.

CONCENTRATION OF ECONOMIC POWER

A criticism of philanthropic foundations which is popular in some circles is that the foundations, taken as a whole, represent a vast and undesirable concentration of power.

This view depends on the combined validity of two assumptions: first, that the total sum spent by or controlled by foundations is in fact vast on a national scale; and second that in considering all foundation actions one is in fact dealing with a concentration, and a potentially bad concentration, at that.

The total wealth of all philanthropic foundations is at present upward of $18 billion and the annual grants slightly more than $1 billion.[22] Are these, on a national scale, vast figures? The total national wealth was estimated by the U.S. Department of Commerce to be roughly $1,922 billion in 1960, which, assuming a 4 percent rate of increase, would give a figure of roughly $2,430 billion in 1966. The assets of foundations are thus less than three-fourths of one percent of our national assets. In terms of national annual figures, the foundation total of slightly more than $1 billion may be compared with our present G.N.P., estimated at some $720 billion for 1966—the foundation figure in this instance being less than two-tenths of one percent—in particular, very substantially less than we are now spending annually in a frantic attempt to put a man on the moon. Even if one goes down to the total amount of money spent on charity in our country—a fraction of our economy which no one would for a moment think of as a dominating force —the foundations account for only eight cents out of each dollar.

Still, the amount of money owned by or spent by foundations might have a potentially disturbing bulk if it were indeed so concentrated as to be under some kind of unified control. But there are upwards of two hundred really large foundations, six thousand more each of which has substantial assets, and some nine thousand more small ones. They are nearly as individualistic as that many persons would be. They are interested in everything from cabbages to kings—ballet, hospital administration, Far Eastern studies, astrophysics, archaeology, etc., etc., etc. The vast majority are run by sensible persons, and the very eccentricity of the remainder constitutes just that much further proof that there never will be and never could be any concentration behind any one conspiratorial movement.

Their funds, also, are invested in so diversified a way, and their financial interest in our country's great industries are so minutely fractional that, even if several did agree on some financial campaign, although that is again unthinkable, the result would not make the Dow-Jones average flicker. The exceedingly few cases in which foundations have been in a position to use their special privileges to influence the conduct of a profit enterprise are, moreover, in the process of being eliminated by more careful administration of existing laws, and by, if necessary, more strict provisions.

Neither of the two assumptions, jointly necessary to any claim of danger of economic power, is satisfied, therefore.

DO FOUNDATIONS SERVE SOCIETY WELL?

There is little point in any reply to this question which comes personally from me. I have spent the major part of my working life in the employ of, or otherwise associated with, various foundations. I can speak from long and direct personal experience, but obviously I am prejudiced. I have a deep feeling of admiration for and loyalty to the philanthropic foundations I have worked for. I have great respect and affection for the colleagues I have had in the Rockefeller and Sloan foundations. Nowhere in university life, or in my acquaintance with government and business people, have I ever met finer, more intelligent, more socially dedicated individuals. On the basis of shorter and less-intense contacts, I have similar, though naturally less-intense, opinions about the personnel and the activities of all the other—six or more—foundation and foundation-like organizations (such as the National Science Foundation) with which I have been associated. In addition it has been my privilege to know well and to advise some of the major personnel in several more of the large foundations.

All these are staffed by exceedingly able and honest persons working to the limit of their time and strength to meet the obligation placed on them. I myself have worked longer and harder, and with far less vacation time, for foundations than I previously did for a major technical institute and a major state university.

But personal enthusiasm, I realize, is not likely to be widely impressive. Convincing proof of the value of foundation activities must come from other than foundation officials. And those balanced and unprejudiced individuals who look objectively at the entire picture come up with a view, an overall assessment, which is favorable indeed.

The Treasury Department Report of 1965, clearly issued as an official reply to the Patman Report, says at the outset:

> Private philanthrophy plays a special and vital role in our society. Beyond providing for areas into which government cannot or should not advance (such as religion), private philanthropic organizations can be uniquely qualified to initiate thought and action, experiment with new and untried ventures, dissent from prevailing attitudes, and act quickly and flexibly.[23]

Even earlier, in the introduction to the report, the Treasury carefully straightens out the record on one critical matter:

> The Department's investigation has revealed that the preponderant number of private foundations perform their functions without tax abuse.[24]

Even these statements of strong general approval coming from a high and highly qualified government agency are, however, not enough. The case for private foundations must rest not upon the opinions of foundation officers or of government officers. It must rest on the direct experience of those qualified scientists, scholars, and artists who have had first-hand contact with foundation aid.

It is for that reason that the remainder of this book is turned over to others—to eighteen world-recognized leaders in as many fields of activity. The answer to the question, Are the philanthropic foundations serving society well? must be given by them.

PART II

Judgments Concerning the Value
of Foundation Aid

Introduction to Part II:
The Difficulties of Assessment

When a food is tested by giving it to a number of experimental animals, it is also withheld from an equal number of animals of essentially identical genetic constitution, keeping all other circumstances as nearly as possible the same for the two groups. Thus one obtains convincing and objective evidence of the value of the food by comparing the results obtained with the test group and with the control group.

Unfortunately, grants of financial assistance from philanthropic foundations cannot be evaluated in any similarly neat and definitive way.

Consider, for example, the relatively simple case of a fellowship. An able young man receives the award; in later years he is apt to judge the fellowship experience as having been very beneficial indeed. But no one can be sure, in retrospect, what his development might have been if he had not received the fellowship. Even if several hundred fellowship holders are canvassed, years later (as was done, for instance, in the case of the National Research Committee fellowships), there is a natural tendency for the holders to take an almost romantically appreciative view. And one can always ask, "If you have a very careful selection process and give fellowships only to persons of great promise, how can you be sure what part of the subsequent success is due to the fellowship experience and what part to the qualities that led to the choice?"

In other words, every grant from every foundation is, in a way, an experiment that inevitably lacks controls. The results are, in a rigorous sense, unprovable; there just are no measurable indices of success that are not open to the question: "What would have happened if the grant had not been made?"

And yet the matter is not as completely elusive as these remarks might indicate. There are many, many instances, for example, in

223

which it seems convincingly clear that aid given at a critical moment brought about results that would otherwise have been seriously delayed—in some cases disastrously or even permanently; for certain opportunities have to be seized when the time is ripe or given up forever. And in a much broader sense a wise and perceptive person, thoroughly acquainted with some field of work, can look back upon his experience and can make useful and convincing judgments as to whether philanthropic assistance has or has not been of major importance to his field.

Part II of this book is made up of such professional retrospective judgments. That is to say, to get evidence as to the usefulness of foundation aid, it has seemed sensible to turn to a group of persons, each of unquestioned competence in his own realm, and to ask each of them to write a short critical summary, based on his own direct, intimate, and extensive experience, of the ways in which philanthropic aid appears to have been fruitful, and the ways in which it may have failed.

The list of these collaborators is a distinguished one, the qualifications and experience of these participants requiring no further comment. Although a few of the assisting writers have had some connection with certain foundations, they speak primarily as users of philanthropic aid, not as dispensers who might tend to defend their own decisions.

It has not been feasible to cover every field within which philanthropy has been active. For example, there is no essay on the earth sciences, on anthropology, or on many other interesting and important topics. Several otherwise very important fields, such as social welfare and research specifically directed toward various important diseases, have not been included because of the necessity to limit the subject matter of this book. Nor does any one of these essays pretend to give encyclopedic coverage. The significance rests, in each case, upon the interest and importance of the illustrative examples, chosen by their authors on the basis of their own interest and direct knowledge.

Each writer reacted to the invitation exactly as he saw fit. The length of the responses, for example, was largely of each writer's own choosing; so that the variations in length should not be interpreted as indicating any comparative judgment of importance.

CHAPTER 15

The Role of Foundations
in the Development of Modern Biology

GEORGE W. BEADLE

It could probably be clearly documented that the remarkable twentieth-century flowering of experimental biology would not have been possible without the support of private foundations in key areas and at critical times.

Without foundation support the University of Chicago could never have become a major university. William Rainey Harper's dream of what it might be was inspired by John D. Rockefeller, Sr., and came true largely through his massive personal support. But had not the Rockefeller Foundation, the General Education Board, the Ford Foundation, and other foundations continued to support, sustain, and strengthen it, the university could never have continued to play the role it did. The many contributions of its early faculty and students to biology were dependent on the university's general well-being.

The same can be said of the California Institute of Technology. Inspired to raise its sights from a not-very-lofty academic target by that astronomer of remarkable and prophetic vision, George Ellery Hale, it attracted Arthur Amos Noyes, Robert Andrews Millikan and Thomas Hunt Morgan, and in less than a decade became a major factor in American academic scholarship. This would not have been possible without the early support of the General Education Board and the Rockefeller Foundation, both of which made repeated generous grants for faculty salaries and research activities. The Division of Biology, established in 1928 by Morgan, shared handsomely in that support; in fact, it could not have come into being without it.

Examples of similar nature could be multiplied manyfold, though I know of no others where academic strength was so dramatically stimulated through foundation support.

Anything like a thorough account of the role private foundations have had in the development of specific areas of biology would require both more space than can be allotted here and a far more extensive study than anyone has so far devoted to the subject. A few examples will have to suffice.

DROSOPHILA GENETICS

Few branches of biology have developed more rapidly or had more significance to twentieth-century biology than has genetics. And no organism has contributed more to classical genetics than has *Drosophila melanogaster,* the small fruit fly so frequently to be seen hovering around a dish of fruit that has become slightly overripe.

Before he discovered the white-eyed mutant of this species in 1910 and worked out its sex-linked mode of inheritance, Thomas Hunt Morgan, then at Columbia University, regarded the new science of genetics with more than a little skepticism. Thereafter he became such an ardent advocate that he largely abandoned his first love, embryology, for a decade and a half. Up to this time Columbia University had supported the work of Morgan and his exceptional group of students and co-workers. In 1915, the Carnegie Institution of Washington granted funds for the salaries of two of the younger men, Sturtevant and Bridges, and for the maintenance of a rapidly growing number of genetic stocks of *Drosophila.* In this respect, the Carnegie Institution acted as a foundation. It continued this support for many years.

In 1928, a grant from the Rockefeller Foundation helped to make possible a move of Morgan and three of his most important co-workers to the new Division of the Biological Sciences at the California Institute of Technology. At that time Dobzhansky joined the group, first as a postdoctoral fellow of the International Education Board. He remained for a dozen years as a faculty member and contributed significantly to developmental genetics, chromosome rearrangements and population genetics.

Muller moved in 1920 from Columbia University to the University of Texas, where in 1927 he made the highly significant discovery—which resulted in a Nobel prize in 1946—that X-rays greatly increase the frequency of gene mutations in *Drosophila*. A Rockefeller Foundation grant administered by J. T. Patterson enabled him to expand this work. Leaving Texas for a stay of eight years in Berlin, the U.S.S.R., and Edinburgh, moves initially made possible by a grant from the Guggenheim Foundation, he returned to the United States in 1940 after the outbreak of World War II. At the moment of his return, he had no position and describes subsequent developments as follows: "I believe that I would have had to give up my scientific work—doubtless permanently . . . —had not the Rockefeller Foundation supported a position for me . . . at Amherst University. Equally critical for my continuance in scientific work was the support which the Rockefeller Foundation gave to Indiana University, that allowed me to be appointed a Professor there."

BIOCHEMICAL GENETICS

Shortly after the 1900 "rediscovering" of Mendel's paper on particulate inheritance in garden peas, Sir Archibald Garrod postulated that certain inborn errors of metabolism were the result of blocks in single steps in chemical reaction chains of metabolism, attributable to absence or inactivity of specific enzymes required for the catalysis of these steps, and that such enzyme changes were in turn the results of defects in genes responsible for their production. He did not use present-day terminology and was unaware of the chemical nature of both genes and enzymes. But he was essentially correct in his conclusion.

Like Mendel, Garrod was ahead of his time, for his ideas were largely unappreciated by both chemists and geneticists for a third of a century.

In 1933, Boris Ephrussi came to the California Institute of

Technology from Paris as a Rockefeller Foundation fellow to work on developmental genetics in mice and in *Drosophila*. At that time there was much talk about the nature of genes and gene action. He and I spent many hours considering what could be done about it. As a result, in 1935 I went to Ephrussi's laboratory at the Institut de Biologie Physicochimique, some years earlier established by the Rothschild Foundation, where we developed a technique for transplanting embryonic organs in *Drosophila* larvae. With less chemical evidence than Garrod had had thirty years earlier—and we were unaware of his work, so effectively had it been disregarded by geneticists—we postulated a sequence of gene-controlled reactions leading to the formation of a brown pigment of the fly's eye. It was the beginning of our adventures in chemical genetics. In the following years we attempted to identify the chemical reactions concerned, he in Paris and I at Harvard University and at Stanford, both aided by grants from the Rockefeller Foundation.

In 1937 I moved to Stanford as a young professor. Charles V. Taylor, who had revolutionized biology at Stanford with the help of a Rockefeller Foundation grant, promised me more than he had at his command. He made good. Years later I learned how. On receiving my acceptance he immediately applied for a grant from the Rockefeller Foundation to meet his commitments for me. It was made and the funds were thus available for me to invite Edward L. Tatum to join me as a collaborator. I have often wondered what C. V. would have done had the grant not been made. He was confident, persuasive, and unafraid of living dangerously.

A year later Taylor, on behalf of the group of us—Taylor, Victor C. Twitty, Arthur C. Giese, Douglas M. Whitaker, Lawrence R. Blinks, C. B. VanNiel, Willis H. Johnson, and others—applied to the Rockefeller Foundation for what at that time was a large grant for experimental biology. It was made—$200,000 for ten years, with the proviso that we not reapply for more funds for that period.

This and earlier grants from the Rockefeller Foundation enabled the eight of us to set up modern laboratories and have research assistants. Twitty's first assistant was Dietrich Bodenstein, whom he brought from Germany, where as a Diener without formal degrees Bodenstein had no visible future in science. He is now chairman of the Department of Biology at the University of

Virginia—and a member of the National Academy of Sciences.

Tatum and I did not succeed in identifying the *Drosophila* eye pigments and the reactions by which they are formed, but we and Ephrussi in Paris turned up some clues that led others later to pin them down.

Because we had trouble with eye pigment chemistry, we switched our approach. Our choice of a different organism was essentially governed by the requirements that it be favorable for genetic studies, that it synthesize within itself certain metabolic substances such as amino acids and vitamins, and that the chemistry of the biosynthesis of these compounds be reasonably well understood. *Neurospora,* an organism familiar in fact, though not in name, as red bread mold, was clearly our choice. Carl C. Lindegren had earlier worked out much of its genetics in the Caltech laboratory. We then set out to induce mutations that would block essential steps in the synthesis of the metabolites we were studying, knowing we could supply the missing metabolites through the culture medium.

We had complete faith in the one-gene-one-enzyme hypothesis that individual genes were responsible for the individual enzymes, each of which controlled a step in the biosynthesis of the metabolites in question. We were therefore confident that our genetic-chemical approach would succeed, but we succeeded beyond our most optimistic expectations. Our studies required that we obtain *Neurospora* in which certain particular genes—those which governed the particular chemical steps we were interested in—had been mutated or changed so that the organism had lost the chemical trick in question. It might have proved extremely difficult to produce these necessary mutants, but in fact it turned out to be easy. We soon had scores of so-called biochemical mutants, and it became clear that we must move at a more rapid pace than the research funds at hand would permit.

This was 1941, three years after the ten-year grant had been made. We sought more funds. I went to New York to see Frank Blair Hanson of the Rockefeller Foundation to tell him that I knew of the ten-year pact and to ask if there was any objection to my going to the Research Corporation for additional funds. Of course he said there was no objection.

On the same day, I went to see Howard Andrews Poillon at the

Research Corporation and told my story. He called in Robert E. Waterman. Not knowing he was the Waterman of Williams and Waterman vitamin B-1 fame, I retold the story. Waterman was ahead of me and tremendously enthusiastic. He and Poillon said they would give support—$10,000 right off. At that point there was a telephone call for me. It was Hanson, who said he had been thinking that, since the Rockefeller Foundation had got us started, he thought they might give added support, despite the pact. Poillon and Waterman said that was only reasonable and proper, and I should by all means go back to Hanson. They said I should send the Research Corporation a carbon copy of our application to the Rockefeller Foundation and, if the grant was not made, they would promise then and there to provide the funds.

That is a marvelous example of foundation flexibility and speed of decision. The Rockefeller Foundation made the grant without delay.

This plus further grants enabled us to invite David M. Bonner, Norman H. Horowitz and Herschel K. Mitchell to our group and to move forward with dispatch.

At this stage a Nutrition Foundation grant of $2,500 a year, that was to continue for five years at Stanford and for at least fifteen at the California Institute of Technology, made it possible to provide graduate fellowships to four students: Adrian M. Srb, now professor of plant breeding (genetics) at Cornell University; August H. Doermann, now professor of genetics at the University of Washington; David C. Regnery, now professor of biology at Stanford University; and Frank P. Hungate, now on the staff of biology at the Hanford Laboratories, Richland, Washington.

The one-gene-one-enzyme hypothesis has had its ups and downs. The low point was 1951, when there were few indeed who believed that gene action could be so simple. Today, although the view is now "one-gene-one-polypeptide chain," the number is large.

BACTERIAL VIRUS GENETICS

In 1938 Max Delbrück, a physicist interested in gene mutation and related problems in biology, went to the California Institute of Technology from Germany as a Rockefeller Foundation fellow.

He was looking for new ways to learn about genes. There he met a young biochemist, Emory L. Ellis, who introduced him to bacteriophages or bacterial viruses. Delbrück thought they had possibilities for genetic study. He was right.

Ellis had been working on cancer in mice, with support from a local benefactor of science. In the course of his work, he had occasion to make use of bacterial viruses. Working with Delbrück, he became so interested in these amazing organisms that he all but abandoned the mice. The two worked out quantitative methods for investigating the phage life cycle and soon designed a technique for studying the growth of viruses that has since become famous and is widely used for other viruses. Phage genetics was born.

Incidentally, the gentleman who supported Ellis was deeply interested in cancer and could not see what those viruses had to do with cancer. In retrospect, it is clear that the work Ellis did with viruses was enormously more important than anything he ever did with mice—and probably more significant than anything he could have done had he not deserted mice for phages.

Under the leadership of Delbrück a school of phage genetics came into being. Mutations were discovered and investigated quantitatively. Linkage and recombination were explored and genetic maps constructed. The details of the phage life cycle were rapidly worked out.

Finally, in 1952 Alfred D. Hershey and Martha Chase established (by labeling phage coat proteins with radiosulphur or, alternatively, the DNA cores with radiophosphorus) that DNA enters the bacterial host cell during phage infection but that the bulk of the protein coat does not. A major forward step in biology was the conclusion that DNA must carry the genetic information that directs the bacterial host cell to synthesize more phage particles, complete with protein coats like those that remained outside during the infection process.

Coupled with the earlier 1944 finding of Oswald T. Avery, C. M. MacLeod, and M. McCarty of the Rockefeller Institute that pure DNA from one genetic type of pneumococcal bacterium is capable of transforming cells of a different genetic type, the Hershey-Chase experiment forced reluctant biologists finally to abandon the view that the gene must be protein in nature and accept the alternative that it is DNA alone—or at least can be reduced to DNA without losing its biological potential when returned to the proper cellular environment.

PLANT AND ANIMAL VIROLOGY

The University of California, Berkeley, Virus Laboratory, now known as the Laboratory of Molecular Biology, established in 1948 and headed by Nobel Laureate Wendell M. Stanley, was very substantially aided by support from a number of foundations, including initially the Rockefeller Foundation and the National Foundation for Infantile Paralysis, and later the American Cancer Society, the Nutrition Foundation, the Corn Industries Foundation, and the Damon Runyon Memorial Fund.

The following comments by Stanley eloquently document the role of foundation support in the work of this laboratory:

> The early support by the Rockefeller Foundation made all the difference in the world in getting the laboratory started. Needless to say, it was support such as this that enabled the Virus Laboratory to make such important contributions as the following: new techniques in electron microscopy such as the now widely used shadow casting and spray drop techniques; new developments in ultracentrifugation such as the synthetic boundary cell, and new and very powerful optical systems; the first crystallization of a virus affecting animals or humans, namely, poliovirus; the first demonstration of subunits as a characteristic feature of the architecture of virus particles; the successful utilization of radioactive decay for the study of the structure, function, and replication of the genetic material of bacterial viruses and bacteria; the discovery of infectious ribonucleic acid; and the discovery of the defective nature of the Rous sarcoma virus. The exact sequence of the 158 amino acids in tobacco mosaic virus protein was also established in the Virus Laboratory. This was and still remains the largest protein whose exact structure is known. Knowledge of this structure has provided a base for extensive studies in chemical genetics using spontaneous and chemically induced mutants of tobacco mosaic virus.

In the early 1950's Renato Dulbecco of the California Institute of Technology undertook to develop a simple method for the quantitative study of animal viruses, comparable to the Ellis-

Delbrück growth-measuring technique for bacterial viruses. At the time his work and that of others was supported in part by the National Foundation for Infantile Paralysis (now the National Foundation). The proposal was to culture animal cells as monolayer tissues on glass, infect these with a dilute solution of viruses, and observe infection centers corresponding to single virus particles. The new approach was made possible by a grant from the James G. Boswell Foundation.

As a prelude, Dulbecco visited several major tissue culture and animal virology laboratories. The usual reaction was that his objective was a good idea but that for one or another of a variety of reasons it would not work.

On the first attempt, using chicken fibroblast cells and the Western equine encephalomyelitis virus, beautiful, discrete, round areas within which cells were dying and disintegrating were produced. Each such area represented a virus colony descended from a single virus particle, and there was a one-to-one relation between virus particles and plaques. This simple, rapid, quantitative method is now widely used for many different animal viruses, for example, polio virus, Rous sarcoma virus, polyoma viruses known to produce tumors in several mammals. Foundation support from several sources was decisive in its development.

THE STRUCTURE OF DNA

With the compelling evidence from the Hershey-Chase labeling experiment, it became obvious to many that an all-out attack on the detailed molecular configuration of DNA was in order. Much was known about, for example, the configuration of the four primary nucleotide building blocks, their proportions in native DNA, the helical configuration of the molecule, etc. Linus Pauling and Robert B. Corey of the California Institute of Technology had proposed a structure which later proved to be incorrect.

In 1950 James Dewey Watson, then twenty-two years of age, had gone to Copenhagen to work with Herman Kalckar as a Merck Fellow of the National Research Council. About a year later he moved from Copenhagen to Cambridge University to work with Francis H. C. Crick on the structure of DNA. Watson then informed the chairman of the Merck Fellowship Board of the move. It was the opinion of that board, not unanimous, according to the grapevine, that this was not a move likely to lead to useful progress, and the fellowship was not continued. With the encouragement and assistance of Max Delbrück, Watson was then awarded a fellowship from the National Foundation for Infantile Paralysis for the continuation of the work at Cambridge.

Using available information from all sources including X-ray diffraction data from the Maurice Wilkins group at King's College, London, the proportions of the four nucleotides found by Erwin Chargaff of Columbia University and a model-building approach, Watson and Crick had in a matter of months worked out the double helical structure which has proved to be essentially correct. This was reported in *Nature* in 1953 and was accompanied by a companion and supporting paper on X-ray diffraction data by the King's College laboratory group. The work of the King's College group, of Sir Alexander Todd, of Chargaff, as well as of a number of other contributory studies, was aided by grants from the Rockefeller Foundation.

Because it suggests how the DNA molecule can be precisely replicated, as it must be with each cell division, how it might undergo mutational change, as well as the manner in which it might carry genetic information, it has been said that the Watson-Crick structure of DNA represents the most significant advance in biology of the twentieth century.

Because of this and other significant work of the Cambridge Medical Research Council Laboratory of Molecular Biology, it is of interest to review the history of that unit in terms of foundation support. I am indebted to Dr. Max F. Perutz of that unit for supplying necessary information. He says that in his opinion the unit owes its very existence to the Rockefeller Foundation. In 1938 there was considerable unemployment among scientists in Britain. Accordingly, universities were not allowed to appoint foreigners if British subjects were available. Because Sir W. Lawrence Bragg had a grant from the Rockefeller Foundation, the Ministry of Labour allowed him to appoint Perutz as a research assistant. His initial salary was £275 per year. The foundation supported Perutz personally until 1945, when John Kendrew joined him, at which time he was given a fellowship at the University. It was only through the use of Rockefeller Foundation funds that the laboratory was able to purchase apparatus for X-ray diffraction and other work. Such funds continue to this date to support the Cambridge Medical Research Council Laboratory of Molecular Biology to the extent of about one-half of one percent of its total budget, but this kind of support is invaluable, as it is in many other laboratories, for it enables the laboratory to do highly desirable things that the Medical Research Council, being state-supported, cannot do. The essential correctness of the Watson-Crick structure has been demonstrated in a number of ways; its replication according to the original proposal of Watson and Crick has been confirmed through ingenious isotope-labeling experiments by Matthew S. Meselson and Frank Stahl, working with foundation support at the California Institute of Technology.

Replication of both native and artificial DNA has been achieved in a cell-free *in vitro* system by Arthur Kornberg and associates, who continue to have catalytic and highly useful foundation support.

PROTEIN STRUCTURE

Pioneering studies of the structure of wool fibers and other proteins, made in the early thirties and later by William T. Asbury, were supported by grants from the Rockefeller Foundation.

The sequence of amino acids (primary structure) has now been determined for a number of proteins, in many instances in laboratories either established or supported by foundations. Insulin was the first of these—worked out by Frederick Sanger of Cambridge University.

The so-called alpha helix secondary structure, first proposed by Linus Pauling and Robert B. Corey of the California Institute of Technology, has been demonstrated to be correct for a number of native proteins. The tertiary folding configurations of myoglobin and hemoglobin have been brilliantly worked out by the Perutz-Kendrew group at the Cambridge Medical Research Council Laboratory mentioned above. As already indicated, foundation support was decisively important in both laboratories.

MOLECULAR DISEASE

Sickle cell anemia is a serious disease long known to be characterized by the presence in the blood of sickle-shaped red cells. Linus Pauling and co-workers at the California Institute of Technology were the first to provide evidence that sickle cell hemoglobin, differentiated from normal hemoglobin by a single gene, may differ from normal by a relatively simple amino acid substitution. Later this provided an important clue in working out the relation of DNA structure to protein structure. More than a dozen genetically differentiated abnormal hemoglobins are now known in man, as are many other genetic diseases attributable to specific protein alterations.

PROTEIN SYNTHESIS

It is now known that cellular protein synthesis involves a transfer of DNA information to complementary ribonucleic acid (RNA), which then moves from the nucleus to the cytoplasm, where in association with submicroscopic ribosomes it serves as a template against which amino acids are ordered. The process can be followed in cell-free *in vitro* preparations containing the proper enzymes, robosomes, messenger RNA, transfer RNA, and buffer salts. Again, foundation support played an important role.

THE GENETIC CODE

The announcement of the Watson-Crick structure of DNA stimulated wide interest in the problem of the coding relation between DNA and protein. The word "code" applies here because of the evidence that the exact pattern of subunits in a small segment of DNA specifies the precise structure of a particular kind of protein molecule. Nine years later a most significant break came with the finding by Marshall W. Nirenberg and J. Heinrich Matthaei of the National Institutes of Health, making use of the *in vitro* protein-synthesizing system, that artificial messenger RNA, consisting of uracil nucleotides only, will direct the synthesis of polynucleotide chains made up solely of the amino acid phenylalanine. Together with previous evidence from the Cambridge Medical Research Council Laboratory for Molecular Biology indicating that sequences of three RNA nucleotides uncode single amino acids, this finding indicated that the RNA code "word" for phenylalanine is UUU, where U stands for the uracil nucleotide. The DNA complementary code word should accordingly be AAA, where A designates the adenine nucleotide of DNA.

This experiment could not have been made had not Severo Ochoa of New York University and his collaborators devised an *in vitro* system for the synthesis of artificial RNA. If only uracil nucleotides are present in the system, poly-U RNA results. Other such "unnatural" RNAs could be made in the same way and their use in directing synthesis of corresponding unnatural proteins identifies other code words.

Ochoa was brought to New York University in 1942 with the help of a grant from the Williams-Waterman Fund of the Research Corporation, which provided his salary, research assistants, equipment, and supplies for a number of years. His first Beckman spectrophotometer was purchased by the American Philosophical Society and came to be known as the "Philosophical" spectrophotometer. A crucial grant was made for Ochoa's work by the Rockefeller Foundation when he moved to the New Medical Sciences Building of the new New York University Medical Center. Among other essentials it provided needed equipment, including a large fifty-gallon fermenter which played a decisive role in the discovery and purification of polynucleotide phosphoralase, an enzyme essential for the preparation of artificial RNA polynucleotides of the kind used in decoding experiments.

PARAMECIUM GENETICS

Classical genetics has tended to emphasize chromosomal inheritance, in large part because it is so amenable to experimental investigation. But it has also been recognized for decades that the cytoplasm of cellular organisms is not only essential for the continued functioning of the nucleus, but is also species-specific as well as concerned with the all-important process of cellular and intracellular differentiation.

Tracy M. Sonneborn has shown that in protozoa of the genus Paramecium, cytoplasmic properties and structures have an autonomy from generation to generation that in some degree is independent of nuclear genotype. This means that in the phylogeny of cellular organisms the nucleus and the cytoplasm may follow separate evolutionary paths so long as their interactions are harmonious and selectively advantageous.

This and many other important concepts have come out of the work of Sonneborn and his co-workers. He has had foundation support for virtually all of his scientific life—from 1930 at Johns Hopkins to the present time at Indiana University. Throughout this period important support has come from the Rockefeller Foundation but more recently from the American Cancer Society as well. It is doubtful if he could ever have got started in his present career without such support.

EXPERIMENTAL PLANT ECOLOGY

Until recently most large-scale experiments with higher plants—for example, plant breeding, nutrition, physiology, ecology, etc.—were carried out under conditions in which the environment was inadequately controlled or not controlled at all. This is true of all outdoor experiments and most of those made in conventional greenhouses. Considering that every farmer, gardener, and plant lover knows that higher plants are extremely sensitive to environmental factors such as temperature, light, day length, humidity, water supply, plus physical and chemical properties of the soil, it is remarkable that not until 1937 was a greenhouse constructed within which *temperatures* were fully controlled. This was an important, but only partial, step. With funds granted by the Earhart Foundation, the Earhart Plant Research Laboratory, called unofficially the "phytotron," was constructed in 1949 at the California Institute of Technology. For the first time, temperature of air and soil, humidity, light, air movement, light-dark periods, mineral nutrition, and soil physical properties could be accurately controlled on a large scale. Many important discoveries have been made in this laboratory, thermoperiodicity, to name a single one. According to this, some plants will not develop normally if grown continuously at a constant temperature.

Many phytotrons and "biotrons" are now in use or are being built. The first one would not have been built without foundation support.

When we recognize that such scolars as H. J. Muller, Dietrich Bodenstein, Max Delbrück, Max F. Perutz, James D. Watson, Severo Ochoa and Tracy M. Sonneborn—to mention only a few— not only were aided at critical times by foundation support but might even have been unable to continue their scientific careers without it, it becomes abundantly clear that private foundations have been of tremendous significance in the rise of modern biology.

To take the single example of a major foundation which for nearly thirty years following 1932 has specially emphasized research in modern experimental biology, the Rockefeller Foundation, over that period, devoted more than $90 million to that general area of activity.

Prior to World War II, foundation funds were a major source of research support in biology, as they were in other areas of academic science. With the rapid increase in subsequent years of research support of academic science by government agencies such as the Office of Naval Research, the Atomic Energy Commission, the National Institutes of Health and the National Science Foundation, private foundation support for scientific scholarship has decreased in percentage of the total available even while increasing in absolute amount. In many of the laboratories mentioned, it now constitutes something of the order of one percent of the total support available. This marked quantitative shift could easily suggest to those not fully informed that private foundation support of this kind is no longer of sufficient significance to justify its continuation. Nothing could be further from the truth. Support from government agencies is in large part restricted and inflexible in its use. For new projects, especially those proposed by beginning academic scholars, grants from government agencies are difficult to obtain quickly. With relatively unrestricted catalytic foundation grants, new ideas can be tried out, without delay. Numerous established investigators who have government support which in total amount is *quantitatively* adequate have emphasized the point that the *nature* of support—its flexibility, its freedom, its prompt availability—is often even more important than the *amount* of the support.

I can say, as a result of fourteen postwar years of experience as chairman of the Division of Biology at Caltech, that private foundation funds enabled us to move forward with numerous new research projects without delay. In fact I can say that, with the exception of massive developments such as new buildings, centralized electron microscope laboratories, and the like, no worthy research project was held up for lack of funds. Foundation grants made it possible.

Major physical facilities such as new laboratory buildings are a different matter, especially in private academic institutions. In the early part of the century, private donors were generous with building funds. Today this does not seem to be the case. While federal funds have become available for this purpose, they are almost always on a matching basis. For private institutions matching dollars are difficult to come by. Today scientists, including some who have plenty of money to "do with" are handicapped by the lack of really adequate and properly serviced space to "do in." I suggest that foundations might well review the "no bricks and mortar" policy that once made more sense than it does today.

CHAPTER 16

Biochemistry, Chemistry, and Private Foundations

ARNE TISELIUS

The accelerating growth of scientific research today is obvious even to the layman. It is said that the amount of published material in chemistry and biochemistry is approximately doubled every ten-year period. An extrapolation a century ahead would open rather frightening perspectives: the chemists running the risk of being drowned in the wealth of material which they produce themselves.

Still, it is not so much the volume as the structure of this ever-increasing activity which falls into the eye if one wishes to look somewhat beneath the surface of what is going on. And to a certain extent a kind of "structure rationalization" is now taking place which is a necessary consequence of the expanding volume of research. It is not only government agencies, research councils, and private foundations which now discuss "priorities." Even research workers themselves have to admit that it is simply not possible to attempt to do everything which appears well worth doing. In the most advanced countries there are clear signs of a shortage of brainpower—even more than of a shortage of funds. In research, the return resulting from the use of manpower and money is to an extremely high degree dependent upon the personal quality of those who do the work. One single individual's achievements may open up new fields which yield rich harvests without much expenditure, while crowds striving in almost exhausted land may have a wasteful and little-rewarding task.

Basic research and teaching in chemistry at universities and similar institutions take place within a framework which changes only slowly. Mostly we find professorships and laboratories in divisions and subdivisions of subjects carrying names introduced perhaps a century ago: i.e., inorganic, organic, physical, analytical, and biochemistry. Most people—and especially those involved—will agree that this does not at all represent the true structure of chemistry as it appears today. The organic chemist was supposed to deal with the structure of organic matter. Today the biochemists have revealed the molecular structure of the most complicated and most significant of all substances occurring in organic matter, namely proteins and nucleic acids. In this field decisive advances have also been made by inorganic chemists, applying X-ray methods originally developed to study the structure of inorganic compounds. Physical chemistry should preferentially deal with physical laws and methods as applied to chemistry. Today all branches of chemistry not only make use of such laws and methods but also contribute to their further development. And the most significant recent advances in analytical methods did not come from analytical chemists but from biochemists, physicists, and physical chemists.

Now, if everybody tends to expand into everybody else's field, why is it so difficult to change the framework accordingly? Why not move the fences or remove them completely? I do not believe it would be just to accuse the institutions with which we deal here of undue conservatism, but there are certain factors involved which are in the way when radical changes are contemplated. An experimental science like chemistry represents large investments in building and equipment both in research and in teaching. Organizational changes or rearrangement of curricula may involve considerable expense and effort. There is another factor which (in some countries at least) tends to "conserve the chairs," not only in chemistry. There is often a rather hard competition for vacant professorships and other permanent appointments. Prospective candidates who may have worked zealously during many years with a particular chair in mind would understandably feel betrayed if the chair suddenly were to change name and character, despite the fact that the situation in the field sometimes has developed and changed greatly. I believe I am justified in saying that some of the recent years'

Nobel prize winners in chemistry would have difficulty in qualifying for the existing chairs in chemistry at the Swedish universities. (I am sure, however, that we would attempt to create special chairs for them if they wished to come.)

In and around and in between the hierarchy of well-established institutions of traditional character one finds at most universities a flourishing activity among research workers who are so engaged in their problems that they give little thought to future opportunities —or lack of opportunities. In the field of biochemistry—which is to be given particular attention in this chapter—there is now an unusual variety of new names of disciplines, as molecular biology, molecular genetics, biophysical chemistry, immunochemistry, microbiological chemistry, biomolecular structure, etc. which most people do not really know exactly where to locate in the classical catalogue of subjects. There was a few years ago a cartoon in *The New Yorker* illustrating a somewhat similar situation: a conversation between two prehistoric animals, an Archeopteryx saying to a Dinosaurius, "I know what I am but I cannot pronounce it."

Now I wish to stress particularly the point that these somewhat irregular fellows and the work they do should not just be considered as an additional headache for government officials, university administrators, and foundation officers. They represent a most valuable—perhaps *the* most valuable element—in what I would like to describe as a rationalization of the structure of a rapidly advancing science. Since science will advance anyhow, why not see to it that it does so in an efficient and rational way with a maximum output of results to the benefit of the nation and of all of mankind? I do not mean to say that advances in well-established fields should be neglected—on the contrary—but *their* chances of being taken care of within the framework of existing academic organizations are usually so much better.

New chairs and new institutes are nowadays sometimes created because some exceptionally talented research worker is available ("personal chairs") rather than because of the importance of the subject involved. This is no doubt a very rational way of expansion particularly in smaller countries where the development must to a certain extent depend upon whether first-rate candidates are available or not. Even if state and university authorities appear to show an increasingly understanding attitude in such cases, their generosity in giving continued support to the new professor or to the new institute tends to be limited because he still to them represents a special case, where one is inclined to "wait and see." A similarly cautious attitude toward new ventures is often demonstrated when one is about to organize new institutions for higher learning. Still, we live in a period of exceptional expansion of universities in most countries, the increase in the standard of living fortunately expressing itself not only in desire for new gadgets but also in an increasing ambition for higher education. We have today a chance—perhaps a unique chance—to adjust the structure of the new universities to the actual status of modern learning instead of making them into exact replicas of the old.

When new fields and new talents come forward which do not easily fit into traditional patterns, support from private foundations has played, in my view, and continues to play an essential, often a decisive role. Contrary to what some might feel, this has not been a "marginal" influence. Foundations have often managed to work at the heart of the development, helping to bring forth those new and significant achievements essential to the advance of scientific research as compared with a mere increase in output and volume. Aware of the existence of foundations and of the possibilities they represent, many research workers have been encouraged to take the risks that often go with new ventures.

My thoughts and opinions in these matters are of course based upon personal experience both in my own country—Sweden—and internationally. Such experience is necessarily limited and perhaps one-sided but I have at least the advantage of having been literally on both sides of the desk. As head of an institute I have asked for and received grants from various sources. As chairman of a research council and a member of other similar groups I have had some responsibility in deciding about grants to others. In the Nobel Foundation I have had to deal with the awards of prizes and I have received such a prize myself.

Beyond doubt one of the most striking demonstrations of what can be done is the Rockefeller Foundation program to promote unexplored fields in the basic life sciences, concerned with the "constitution, structure and function of living organisms and their component parts." This was a keen and unusually foresighted long-range project which was carried through in a most generous and successful way, with an investment of about $100 million from the beginning in the mid-thirties to the end (about 1951). I mention the end because it would seem almost as difficult, and as essential to a foundation, to be able to terminate such a far-reaching project at a convenient time as it must have been to launch it. By "a convenient time" is meant, of course, a time when it was obvious to everybody that the field was so important that sufficient support was forthcoming through other channels. Today there is almost a competition among different organizations to support especially "molecular biology." The Rockefeller Foundation officers thoroughly examined the possibilities and the resources in the field and saw to it that support was directed to strategic points where the prospects of advance appeared particularly promising.

It is a more rewarding task for a private foundation to help to start something new which appears promising. Thus, in today's perspective, it is interesting to find in the record of Rockefeller Foundation grants from the thirties, research projects such as the application of isotopes to biological problems (for example, Niels Bohr, August Krogh, Georg von Hevesy, University of Copenhagen), biological ultrastructure (W. T. Astbury, University of Leeds), biochemistry of hormones (V. du Vigneaud, Cornell University Medical College), cooperative research in biophysics, chemical biology, cell physiology (J. Runnström, University of Stockholm), ultracentrifugation, proteins (T. Svedberg, University of Uppsala). Also we find among the early projects organic chemistry in relation to biology (Linus Pauling, California Institute of Technology), physico-chemical studies of serum proteins (Edwin Cohn, Harvard), further application of isotopes to biological problems (Harold Urey, Hans T. Clarke, and others). Some early grants for developing advanced physical instruments were made within this framework, for example electron microscopes, and even cyclotrons and computers. In addition to these examples taken at random from a wealth of material, the importance and success of the fellowship program should be particularly stressed. Here it is still more difficult to single out names. It may be sufficient to point out that up to 1965 no fewer than thirty Nobel laureates had received Rockefeller Foundation fellowships before they won the prize. If one includes the names of all those Nobel prize winners who have received support in the form of grants for equipment, assistance, etc., the list approaches one hundred names (again the grants were given before the prize award in most cases). If, at the last, I may be permitted to refer to my own case as an illustration: The year 1934–35, which I spent in the U.S.A. on a Rockefeller fellowship, was a decisive influence for my whole scientific career, through the inspiration and encouragement I obtained to pursue my work on electro-phoresis, which at that time I had laid aside. A few years' work after returning home led to reasonable success. A private donor created a chair for biochemistry at my university in 1938. This would probably never have materialized if the Rockefeller Foundation (matched by the Wallenberg Foundation) had not been willing to contribute generously toward the running expenses for the first and most difficult years. And, when in 1952 we moved into the newly built Institute of Biochemistry, again the Rockefeller and Wallenberg Foundations gave valuable assistance for purchasing equipment and carried on their support for a considerable period.

There is an additional experience which I believe I share with many others: grants from foreign sources have a stimulating effect upon local generosity—both from government and private funds. This does not necessarily take the form of an agreement about "matching grants." The wide publicity given such contributions from abroad will serve its purpose simply by directing attention to a research worker and his laboratory as something deserving local support. Foundation money, wisely spent, thus often becomes "seed money." When looking through the records of some of the larger European foundations it is interesting to observe how their support of research in biochemistry and chemistry, especially during later years, has emerged out of their engagement in the advancement of health and the prevention and cure of sickness. Often they owe their origin to a desire among the donors to help mankind in such an obvious and direct way. Advisers who help the foundations in forming a policy seem to have found that such help as foundations can give may be more efficient, even if less direct, if basic research in certain fields can be promoted. We recognize

again the program of the Rockefeller Foundation discussed above.
The *Nuffield Foundation* in England, which came into being in
1943 and is one of the largest in Europe, in 1949 decided to give
preferential treatment to biology. Within such a program it has
given substantial support, for example, to J. D. Bernal of Birkbeck
College, London, Dorothy Crowfoot of Oxford, W. T. Astbury of
Leeds for their X-ray crystallographic work on proteins, viruses,
and other biological macromolecules; to the well-known work on
nucleic acids and proteins by J. T. Randall at King's College; and
to many others, including provision for buying expensive equipment, such as electron microscopes. Some very important work in
immunochemistry (e.g., R. R. Porter) has also been supported.

A similar policy has been followed by the *Wellcome Trust,*
which since 1937 has given impressive grants for buildings and
equipment to some particularly well-known laboratories in Britain
and in the commonwealth, for example, the new Laboratory of
Molecular Biology in Cambridge. It has also been active in granting
fellowships.

The *Wolfson Foundation,* London, made an especially notable
gift in 1958 for a new department of biochemistry and microbiology at the Imperial College, with Professor Ernest Chain as
head. In France private foundations apparently do not play such
a prominent role as in the U.S.A. and in England. One should
remember, however, that the Pasteur Institute, at least to begin
with, was essentially a private institution and there is no exaggeration in a recent statement by a very prominent French colleague
that French biochemistry and French microbiology essentially
originated at the Pasteur Institute. German chemical and pharma-
ceutical industry has always had particularly close connections with
academic research, involving considerable direct financial support,
and the same applies to Switzerland. In addition the new Volks-
wagen-Stiftung and the Thyssen-Stiftung should be mentioned—the
former has recently given a substantial grant to promote European
collaboration in molecular biology. The Max Planck–Gesellschaft
with its particularly well-known research institutes is not a private
enterprise (it is financed chiefly by federal and state contributions)
but seems to operate with a degree of freedom which is usually
found only in private foundations. It represents a unique and very

successful type of organization for the promotion of research. Some of the most significant German contributions to advances in chemistry and biochemistry during its fifty years of existence have come from the Max Planck Institutes.

Among the smaller countries Denmark has its well-known Carlsberg Fund, which is supporting not only the world-famed Carlsberg Laboratory, with names such a S. P. L. Sörensen and K. Linderström-Lang, but has had an impressive influence on Danish research and culture as a whole.

In Sweden the Wallenberg Foundation for many years has made substantial contributions to the advance of research in many fields, with fundamental research in medicine, biochemistry, and chemistry receiving the largest share. These funds are large compared to the population. I believe that the comparatively high standard of scientific research in these countries, particularly in the fields discussed in this chapter, is to an appreciable extent due to active and foresighted support by these foundations.

A field in which many private foundations make a very essential contribution is the support of symposia and other similar conferences, international and national. In rapidly developing areas such as those discussed in this chapter, their importance can hardly be overestimated. When one reads a scientific paper one gets to know what happened six months to a year ago. When one listens to a paper at a conference, one obtains up-to-date information, one can ask questions, and one may even find out not only what the speaker already knows, but also what he expects for the future. Planning of research today is to a large extent based upon such free and informal exchange of information in small groups. Much waste of manpower, time, and money can thus be avoided. There are foundations which devote themselves particularly or exclusively to the support of symposia and conferences, e.g., the Solvay Foundation in Brussels, the CIBA Foundation in London and the organization behind the Gordon conferences in the U.S.A. Many other foundations have engaged themselves in support of this kind of activity, thereby showing the way to government agencies who appear to have been rather reluctant to give adequate support for such purposes.

In discussions with friends both at home and abroad, I have in most cases found that they are willing to accept viewpoints like those presented here. Thus even stubborn adherents of expanding government control in most fields of human endeavor will admit that we are all heavily indebted to private foundations for their past and present contributions. But what about the future?

I believe that we should agree that it would only be to the benefit of all—both adherents and opponents—to discuss openly some tendencies which may change the outlook for private foundations more or less radically for the future and present reasons for reconsideration of their ways and means of operation. The very essence of the successful operation of a private foundation is private initiative, unhampered by the inevitable—and indeed in many respects proper—political and similar considerations affecting the activities of government agencies, which may cause an undesirable dilution of their efforts to achieve certain goals. Closely associated with this so often criticized weakness of such bodies is a reluctance to take the unavoidable risks associated with the initiation of new and far-reaching ventures. However, even government agencies may have strong and dynamic personalities among their members, willing to face certain risks and capable of persuading their colleagues to be bold. It is to be expected that governments in their own interest will find good reason to adopt, to some extent, the pattern of private foundations, for example by giving an increasing freedom of action to such agencies as (to speak of the United States) the National Science Foundation and the National Institutes of Health, which distribute federal money for the support of basic research. As a matter of fact, in most advanced countries we are already there, with entirely unpolitical research councils and similar bodies, having a membership with a majority of specialists in the fields concerned. When in 1946 I was among a group who succeeded in inducing the Swedish government to organize a Science Research Council, the overall attitude was favorable, but some objected to the idea that "such large sums" (to begin with only $200,000 per year!) were to be distributed by a number of professors entirely on their own responsibility. Today, twenty years later, such a group of professors distributes annually an amount about fifteen times as large, and the confidence in their work is shown in many ways, e.g., a 20–25 percent annual increase during the last few years in the funds at their disposal.

It must be admitted that the development of such organizations in several countries tends to make the boundaries between state and private foundations much more diffuse, at least in certain fields and in certain aspects of their activities. It seems possible that private foundations will gradually withdraw from some sectors, particularly from those where ample support is already forthcoming. I suppose no foundation would attempt today to support space or nuclear research, or to compete with government establishments or industry in projects so obviously and immediately essential to society or to national economy that they are well provided for already. I am convinced, however, that even the most progressive and research-minded government often will hesitate to give generous or even adequate support to basic research in emerging fields until it becomes convinced of their usefulness. As far as it is possible to predict, there remains here a vast field for the initiative of private foundations, if they are bold and foresighted enough, where their contributions will prove as essential to future progress as they have been to past.

I remember a typical discussion recently in a group which advises my own government in science policy affairs. What guiding principles should we apply in recommending priorities, with particular regard to the special problems in a small country? I obtained some support for the view that above all in our governmental support we should concentrate our efforts in fields in which we already are comparatively strong, the main argument being that there we have a national supply of promising young research workers and an "operation basis," which very likely would guarantee a fast output of results for the funds we spend. Most of the members agreed, but one said with some emphasis that of course we should not forget the "weak sectors" and again somebody else wished to stress particularly all those fields "in between." This was all very well and probably wise, and I assume that a similar discussion might have taken place in a meeting of the board of trustees of a private foundation. But there is the difference that the trustees would probably have found it easier to decide to follow one *or* the other alternative.

Private foundations have a great future, I believe, if they continue to concentrate upon new and emerging disciplines, not yet quite ripe to be handled through the usual channels for government support. This means of course that foundation officers must continue to be alert, they must "stop, look, and listen" when new things turn up. And foundation trustees should continue to be aware that taking risks in such matters has always been and always will be the prerogative of the private individual and of the private organization.

There may in certain cases be a competition among various forms of activity in supporting research, but I do not think that this would have to lead to conflicts. On the contrary: government organizations should realize the enormous advantage of letting private foundations explore some new fields at their own risk instead of complaining that some outsiders lay all sorts of eggs without caring about who is to hatch them. Rather it should be considered as a great advantage to enter into the picture when it only remains to pick out the golden eggs and—if one so wishes—throw the rest away.

CHAPTER 17

The Role of the Private Foundations in the Development and Growth of Physics and Astronomy in the United States

LEE A. DUBRIDGE

The sciences of physics and astronomy could hardly have emerged from the primitive state in which they found themselves in America in the first two decades of the twentieth century had it not been for the generosity of the great private foundations.

It is literally true to say that before World War I scientific research in American universities had almost no significant sources of support. University budgets seldom made provision for research, and foundation funds were only beginning to become available. Nevertheless, a few pioneers did carry forward their investigations on a shoestring. Teaching loads were also so great that there was very little time for research. The great benefactions of John D. Rockefeller to the University of Chicago and of the General Education Board to Johns Hopkins University did create two university centers in which scientific research was to be given a prominent place. Most other universities found almost no sources of research funds.

Astronomy was the first science to receive substantial gifts from private benefactors. The Harvard University Observatory and the Yerkes Observatory of the University of Chicago were two pioneering ventures in this field. But not until the founding in 1904 of the Mount Wilson Observatory in California, through the generosity of Andrew Carnegie, did large-scale astronomical study get its first major boost. Mr. Carnegie, through the Carnegie Institution of Washington, moved rapidly ahead—and soon the 60-inch and, later, the 100-inch telescopes (then and for many years the two largest in the world) were built on Mount Wilson. Their spectacular success as scientific instruments led George Ellery Hale, the director of the Mount Wilson Observatory, to envisage a colossal 200-inch telescope. The funds for this instrument were provided to the Californal Institute of Technology and came from three Rockefeller boards—the International Educational Education Board, the General Education Board, and the Rockefeller Foundation. The total funds provided amounted in the end to $6.5 million, and the great telescope—named the Hale Telescope—was dedicated on Palomar Mountain in California in 1948. Still the largest telescope in the world, it has had a spectacular history of successful investigation of the deepest reaches of the universe.

Although it has long been evident that a single 200-inch telescope is inadequate for the world of astronomy, only very recently have active moves been initiated to secure funds for other telescopes in the 180- to 200-inch size range, with one or more of them possibly to be located in the Southern Hemisphere. There is a strong hope among astronomers that at least one of these major astronomical installations can also be financed through private funds.

The support of the American foundations for work in astronomy has gone beyond the limits of the Mount Wilson and Palomar observatories, and even beyond the United States. The Rockefeller Foundation provided a half-million-dollar grant to Harvard University to aid in moving astronomical equipment from Peru to South Africa. It has provided generous grants for astronomical work to the University of Leiden, the University of Oslo in Norway, and, more recently (in 1955), three American foundations (Carnegie, Ford, and Rockefeller) made handsome grants toward the construction of one of the world's largest radio telescopes in Australia.

As in other fields of science, substantial support for work in astronomy has recently been provided by government agencies. But, for a half century, the development of American astronomy to a position of world leadership depended almost entirely upon the private foundations.

The situation in the field of physics is not greatly different, except that major support for work in this field began a few years after the initiation of the great astronomical telescope projects. But here again, as is so characteristic of foundation support, the important grants came at critical times and in critical places.

One of the most important events in the history of American science was the initiation, through funds provided by the Rockefeller Foundation, of the National Research Council fellowships beginning in the early twenties. At that time, the experience of World War I had made it clear that research in physics in the United States was far behind that of European countries. In spite of the fact that there were brilliant American physicists—such as Michelson and Millikan, the first American Nobel Prize winners —there was nothing in America to compare with the great centers of physics research then flourishing in Germany, France, Denmark, and England.

After World War I it was suggested by some that a central physics research institute be established in the United States. But a number of scientific leaders, particularly Robert A. Millikan, proposed that it would be far better to establish many research centers in many American universities, and that the urgent need was to provide opportunities for young physicists (and other scientists) to have research training following the completion of their doctor's degrees. The National Research Council fellowships provided just this opportunity to a select group of young scientists each year, who were thus enabled to pursue their studies both in American and European centers. The dividends of this farsighted program were evident twenty years later when the roll call of the outstanding physicists of this country showed that a large fraction had been National Research Council fellows during the 1920's and early 1930's. Nobel Prize winners, such as Ernest O. Lawrence, I. I. Rabi, Harold C. Urey, A. H. Compton, were on the honor roll along with scores of others who had come to occupy leading positions in American physics. There was, of course, a similar situation in the field of chemistry. Over a long period of time the National

Research Council fellowships—first established for physics and chemistry, but later extended to biology, mathematics, and the earth sciences—were solely supported by the Rockefeller Foundation.

Following the success of the University of Chicago and Johns Hopkins University as major scientific centers, the General Education Board, the Carnegie Corporation, and later the Guggenheim and Kellogg foundations combined to assist in the creation of another promising center—the California Institute of Technology in Pasadena, California—to which Robert A. Millikan had come as chief executive officer in 1920. These grants came at a key time, when the future of this budding young institution was still in the balance. They were decisive in stimulating its growth to the great center of science and engineering it has become today. As in so many other cases, the foundation grants to Caltech instigated larger gifts and bequests on the part of private individuals, and the foundations were, therefore, enabled to take advantage of the multiplying factor which has so often been the result of perceptive initial grants of "seed money."

One of the most spectacular of all the "seed money" grants was made by the Rockefeller Foundation in 1930 to Ernest O. Lawrence of the University of California at Berkeley at the time when he had developed and proved the idea of the cyclotron as a potent research tool in nuclear physics. He had obtained critically important aid from the Research Corporation, starting as early as April, 1931, and he was now seeking the large sum required to build the world's first major nuclear accelerator. The estimated cost was $1.4 million, and the Rockefeller Foundation furnished $1.15 million, the remainder being raised by the University of California with help from the Markle Foundation and, again, from the Research Corporation. A new era in the field of nuclear physics was born, the results of which are now history. One million dollars was a large sum for a single piece of physics equipment in those days, and only a large foundation could have had either the funds or the foresight to provide such an amount at just the right time.

It would be a mistake to assume that the full story of the contribution of foundations to the development of physical science occurred through these major grants. Down through the years, many foundations have made more modest grants to able individuals who were aided in making critical contributions to the advance of science. By 1948, before government research grants became available in substantial amounts, scarcely one American physicist (or other scientist) of stature had not received some sort of foundation grant in support of his work which had made the difference between being able or unable to pursue a critical or important investigation or to acquire an important piece of equipment.

Typical of such grants to individual investigators was the program adopted some twenty-five years ago by the Research Corporation. Since that time the Research Corporation has appropriated some $3,370,000 to research workers in physics, and about $526,-000 to research workers in astronomy. Many recipients were investigators in smaller institutions whose work tended to be overlooked by the larger foundations and by government agencies. For example, Professor Walter P. Dyke of Linfield College, McMinnville, Oregon, was enabled to carry out significant investigations there on electron tubes which used "field emission" techniques —and these tubes later were developed into devices with important practical applications. The first, and also critically important, philanthropic grant to Ernest Lawrence was a small grant from the Research Corporation.

Contrary to popular opinion, the role of the private foundations has not declined in the period since 1946 in spite of the great increase in the government support of science during these years. While various government agencies charged with specific missions in the fields of defense, space, atomic energy, public health, etc. have supported many large and expensive research enterprises in the physical sciences, many areas of science do not fall within the cognizance of these mission-oriented agencies. The National Science Foundation has served to supplement the other agencies and to fill in many gaps. However, its funds have never been adequate for the purpose, and they are subject to the same types of inflexibility that are characteristic of all government grants. In spite of the fact that some of the older private foundations have in recent years oriented their support more toward nonscientific fields (a very welcome and desirable development), their grants are critically important in the physical sciences. The Ford Foundation and the

Sloan Foundnation have also now entered the picture in a major way.

Since 1953 the Sloan Foundation has supported several major programs of basic research in the physical sciences. One has been a special type of fellowship consisting of grants to individual scientists to enable them to pursue their research projects. This program has grown from total awards of $200,000 to 22 research fellows in 16 universities in the year 1955-56 to $1,200,000 granted to 155 fellows in 48 universities in 1964-65. These awards have provided precisely the type of flexible and unspecified research funds that young investigators need most acutely and find most valuable and productive.

The Sloan Foundation has provided major gifts for basic research in the physical sciences, mathematics, and engineering. These included: over $1 million to the California Institute of Technology to build a new laboratory for mathematics and physics; over $3 million to New York University to provide funds toward the construction of a building to house the Courant Institute of Mathematical Sciences and to support its continuing program; a $15-million grant to the Massachusetts Institute of Technology, and a similar $5-million grant to the California Institute of Technology, for the general support of basic research in the physical sciences, mathematics, and engineering; and $1 million to Stanford University toward the creation of a new mathematics center.

The recent Ford Foundation grants in support of physical science have been international in extent and have ranged from grants for the support of the building of major astronomical telescopes to grants for supporting centers of education in the sciences.

It is frequently assumed that engineering research receives adequate support either from industry or from government agencies. Such support has been most valuable, but it has tended to support those areas where practical applications to industrial or government problems seem imminent. The more basic types of investigations, and investigations in the borderline areas between science and engineering, have often been neglected. Here again private support has provided funds for the exploration of new ideas.

As early as 1915 Daniel Guggenheim was financing the pioneering experiments of Robert Goddard on the first liquid-fueled rockets. In 1928 the Daniel Guggenheim Fund for the Promotion of Aeronautics provided a research laboratory of aeronautics at the California Institute of Technology, the first real university center for arenonautical engineering. The pioneering work of that laboratory was a major factor in putting the design of airplanes on a sound scientific basis. In the 1950's the Guggenheim Foundation provided funds for research in the new field of jet propulsion both at Caltech and at Princeton University, again stimulating basic and "undirected" research in this new field.

The educational activities of the private foundations in recent years are of great significance. During these years an active interest has been aroused throughout the country in improving school, college, and university curricula in all the scientific fields. Private foundation grants have contributed significantly to many pilot projects aimed toward the major revision and updating of high school and college curricula. The work done on these projects is spreading throughout the country and has already resulted in a significant improvement in the quality of these educational offerings in mathematics and science in high schools and colleges.

The large grants made by the Ford Foundation to a number of major universities, institutes of technology, and liberal arts colleges will contribute significantly to the educational work of these institutions in science and engineering as well as in other fields. Such grants are for purposes wholly outside the realm of government interest, and they have served as important catalysts for the raising of much larger funds for these universities from other private sources.

In engineering education, a $5-million grant from the Sloan Foundation has made possible the creation of a Center for Continuing Education in Engineering at M.I.T., providing for a new building and for operating expenses. The Sloan program of fellowships in engineering has provided critical assistance.

Private foundation grants to universities supply an element either missing from government grants or present in only occasional instances—namely, the strengthening of the university itself in order that it may be a more productive center for education and research. Only a strong university with a well-rounded faculty plus the necessary laboratory, classroom, library, and other facilities is in a position to carry on research projects suitable for government support. The private foundations have long recognized this fact and have assisted excellent universities to become better and good universities to become excellent. It is this policy, combined with the policy of understanding support of individual scientists, which has enabled the private foundations to be key factors in the extraordinary uplift in the status of the United States as a leader in scientific and engineering progress during the past forty years.

CHAPTER 18

The Role of Private Foundations
in the Development of Modern Medicine

JOSEPH C. HINSEY

In a report published in 1962,[1] Mrs. Narnie Borchardt and Dr. Herbert H. Rosenberg of the National Institutes of Health presented an analysis of foundation expenditures for medical and health-related research. They were aided by the fact that the National Science Foundation had formulated a survey dealing with the needs of both agencies in the area of private support of research and education. In the foreword of this report, Dr. Luther Terry, surgeon general of the Public Health Service, states:

A review of the current role of philanthropic organizations is, indeed, appropriate. Foundations, long the mainstay for medical research and education in this country, have played an historic role in pioneering support for these fields. Their influence goes back to the turn of the century. The Carnegie-financed Flexner Report of 1910 initiated a revolution in American medical education and inspired substantial gifts from The Rockefeller Foundation and other philanthropies for the support of faculty, facilities, and curriculum in selected schools. Through these efforts, philanthropic organizations profoundly influenced the development of the Nation's medical education system and provided the basis for present levels of achievement, and over the years we have witnessed a steady growth in the number of private foundations in the health field.

He concludes:

> Thus as the Report concludes, foundations have continued to pioneer in new areas and, at the same time, have counterbalanced and supplemented the forms and direction of support arising from governmental efforts.

Although there are more than 15,000 private philanthropic foundations in the United States, 272 of these accounted for 87 percent of the total program expenditures and 96 percent of the scientific research disbursements in 1960. Of these 272 foundations, 149 reported, for that year, expenditures for medical and health-related research and education in the amount of $72 million, of which $25 million was spent for education and $47 million for research.

Over a period of fifty years, the Rockefeller Foundation (and the predecessor organizations merged into it in 1928) has devoted[2] to the field of medicine and public health, including the development of public health services and education and the sponsorship of medical institutions, $152 million; to the investigation and control of major endemic diseases such as malaria and yellow fever, and including staff costs for such operations, $60 million; and to the medical and natural sciences some $123 million, the greater part of which was directed to various disciplines in experimental biology (genetics, biochemistry, physiology, biophysics, etc.) which are basic to medicine. Over this same half century the Rockefeller Foundation devoted $61 million to some sixteen thousand fellowships, a large fraction of which were directly or indirectly related to the physical sciences.

Since the Ford Foundation's work became nationwide in 1950, it has given more than a third of a billion dollars to assist medical schools and hospitals (of this, $100 million was given to selected private medical schools in 1956), and more than a billion dollars to the general field of education.

The W. K. Kellogg Foundation, which also makes grants for education, agriculture, and public affairs, has primarily emphasized medicine, public health, hospitals, nursing, and dentistry. A summary statement as of 1962[3] indicated a total expenditure for the medical fields just mentioned of more than $48 million; and in the following two years nearly $10 million more was devoted to the same areas.

From 1918 to 1962, the Commonwealth Fund[4] expended $109,-361,620, of which $38,566,090 was for medical education, $13,-595,497 for medical research, $15,185,508 for fellowships, $11,496,634 for community health, $8,362,975 for mental health, and $6,839,245 for rural hospitals.

In the two-year period of 1963-64, the Alfred P. Sloan Foundation[5] made grants of some $3 million in the medical field. A large portion of the Sloan Foundation support in the medical field relates to the activities of the Sloan-Kettering Institute for Cancer Research.

Each year, the Josiah Macy, Jr., Foundation expends about $1,-200,000 in the medical field and the John and Mary R. Markle Foundation about $1,400,000. Table 4 shows a listing of some twenty-two foundations with missions in the health field with a designation of some of the areas of their interests. It is clear that medical research and medical education have been heavily emphasized by philanthropy.

This interest was greatly stimulated, over a half century ago, by an episode which has by now become a classic chapter in the history of medical education in our country. Under the sponsorship of the Carnegie Foundation for the Advancement of Teaching, whose president was then Dr. Henry S. Pritchett, Abraham Flexner[6] began on December 1, 1908, a survey of medical education in the United States and Canada. This eventually involved some 155 institutions, many of which were proprietary, maintained poor quality of programs, and were without university affiliation and devoid of academic responsibility. His report,[7] published in 1910, was a significant milestone in the development of medical education because it called attention to the many inadequacies in the programs then in existence. It emphasized the importance of greater university influence, the role of the full-time system, the essential need for the research spirit in the educational programs, the role of the teaching hospital, and the need for better facilities. Deitrick and Berson[8] stated, "The decade of 1910-1920 marked the establishment of medical education as a university discipline with definite educational standards."

Two institutions, the Rockefeller Institute for Medical Research (established in 1901)[9] and the Rockefeller Foundation (established

TABLE 4

FOUNDATIONS THAT HAVE MADE SUBSTANTIAL GRANTS TO MEDICAL RESEARCH AND HEALTH-RELATED ACTIVITIES DURING RECENT YEARS

Foundation	State	Medical research	Hospitals	Medical education	Patient services	Nursing	Public health	Mental health
Avalon	N.Y.	X	X	X	X	X		
Association for Aid to Crippled Children	N.Y.	X						
China Medical Board of N.Y.	N.Y.	X	X	X		X	X	
Commonwealth Fund	N.Y.	X	X	X	X	X	X	
Duke Endowment	N.Y.	X	X	X	X			
Fleischman (Max)	Nev.	X	X	X				X
Ford	N.Y.	X	X	X				
Hartford (John A.)	N.Y.	X	X	X	X			
James	N.Y.		X	X				
Kellogg (W. K.)	Mich.	X	X	X		X	X	
Kennedy (Joseph P., Jr.)	N.Y.	X			X			X
Kresge	Mich.	X	X	X	X			
Macy (Josiah, Jr.)	N.Y.	X		X				
Markle (John & Mary B.)	N.Y.			X				
Moody	Texas		X	X				
Morris (Wm. T.)	N.Y.		X		X			
New York	N.Y.	X	X	X	X			
Pfeiffer (Gustavus Louise)	N.Y.			X				X
Reynolds (Z. Smith)	N.C.		X				X	
Rippel (Frannie E.)	N.J.	X	X		X		X	
Rockefeller	N.Y.	X		X		X	X	
Sloan	N.Y.	X		X				X

in 1913)[10] were the two most important forces to bring about the revolutionary changes called for in the Flexner report. Corner[9] has recently published a history of the Rockefeller Institute and Fosdick[10] and Shaplen[2] have reviewed the history of the various boards combined into the Rockefeller Foundation in 1928. The General Education Board was involved in the early years with the advancement of medical education in the United States. It is not possible to review here any of the details of the contributions these two organizations have made, but suffice it to say that the Rockefeller Institute provided the milieu in which medical research was nurtured and that the experiences of the early faculty members there were important in their preparation for responsibilities in a number of medical schools. A review of the list, which appears in Corner's book, of those who have been there demonstrates this. The institute's director, Dr. Simon Flexner (brother of Abraham Flexner) provided leadership, not only at the institute, but in many of the newly developing institutions. He and Dr. William H. Welch of the Johns Hopkins Medical School led and advised in many of these developments. It was fortunate that the institute was under way when the Flexner report was made, and that the General Education Board took up the challenge of the objectives set forth in it.

Later, other foundations joined to contribute to the advancement of medicine and the allied professions in the health field.

SUPPORT FOR FACILITIES AND ENDOWMENT

Starting with the Johns Hopkins Medical School in 1913, the General Education Board supported reorganizations which brought about full-time instruction in the clinical as well as in the basic science departments of the first two years of medical education at Washington University in St. Louis,[11] at Yale, and at Chicago. In 1923, a grant was made to the University of Iowa in the amount of $2,250,000 by the General Education Board and the Rockefeller Foundation. Similar grants in smaller amounts were made to the following state-supported medical schools: University of Colorado, University of Oregon, University of Virginia, and University of Georgia. An appropriation was made to the University of Cincinnati, an institution which received some of its support from municipal sources. Howard University and the Meharry Medical School were strengthened, the latter by some $8 million. The General Education Board and the Rockefeller Foundation later made substantial grants to the medical schools at Harvard, Vanderbilt,[11] Columbia,[12] Cornell,[11] Tulane, Western Reserve, Rochester,[13] Duke, Emory, and the Memorial Hospital in New York affiliated with Cornell. Fosdick[10] stated,

> It was a vast pump-priming operation, geared to an ambitious idea. The hundred million dollars contributed by the two Rockefeller boards, matched many times over by the generosity of scores of citizens like Rosenwald in Chicago, Eastman in Rochester, and Harkness in New York, took the teaching of medicine in the United States from the discreditable position it occupied in 1910 and gave it a status it shares with only a few countries in the world.

To the citizens cited by Fosdick, one could add Payne Whitney in New York, Duke and Reynolds in North Carolina, Woodruff in Atlanta, and now Hershey in Pennsylvania.

In more recent years, the Commonwealth Fund has made unrestricted endowment grants to several institutions, and the Ford Foundation distributed $100 million in 1956 to a selected group of private medical schools. Recently endowed professorships have been provided by the Macy and a number of other foundations. "Islands of excellence" have been developed as examples for others to follow. Some foundations continue to be concerned to help "pace setters" lead the way.

STAFF DEVELOPMENT

An essential ingredient for the advancement of medicine is a supply of academicians devoted as teachers, investigators, and practitioners. The role of the Rockefeller Institute in this area has been discussed. It is important to recruit the most able students for academic careers, and it is essential to make support available to them before and after graduation. Foundations have been alert to this need. The General Education Board and the Rockefeller Foundation have made appropriations to the National Research Council for fellowships to aid men and women in their preparation for careers in academic medicine. Since 1913, approximately twenty thousand Rockefeller Foundation fellowships and scholarships of one kind or another have been given, an activity which accounts for about one-tenth of the foundation's total expenditures. Thirty-two Nobel Prize winners have received General Education Board, International Education Board or Rockefeller Foundation fellow-ships or came under the National Research Council's fellowship program or a similar one sponsored by the British Medical Research Council. Seventy-three additional Nobel laureates received some form of assistance from the Rockefeller boards, such as for laboratory equipment.

The Commonwealth Fund, as reported in their publications, has supported fellowships for many years, starting in 1937, and in 1961-62, $430,000 was appropriated for this purpose.

> At present four types of awards are being made: (1) to aid candidates of unusual potential and promise who are seeking advanced or interdisciplinary training; (2) to assist in the development of new or neglected fields of activity in relation to health matters by supporting gifted persons; (3) to assist the programs of institutions or organizations of interest to the Fund by aiding qualified individuals who will occupy significant positions on their staffs; (4) to provide an opportunity to mature and creative scholars of acknowledged competence in any field of health activity to explore new ideas, review research, write, plan or otherwise engage in uninterrupted creative activities.

These awards are not of fixed amounts but are tailored to individual needs.

The Markle Scholar program[14] has been in existence now for seventeen years. Acting upon the recommendations for 945 individuals made by the medical colleges of the United States and Canada, the directors of the John and Mary R. Markle Foundation have appointed 381 scholars in 84 different medical schools. Grants in the amount of $11,329,000 have been made to support these scholars, chosen as promising young teachers, investigators, and administrators who could be helped to prepare for positions of leadership in academic medicine. Preference has been given to young men and women above the level of interns, residents, and fellows still in training who are starting their careers in academic medicine. Of the 381 men and women selected since 1948, 351 are still in academic medicine or related positions such as university presidents. A perusal of the positions held by these Markle Scholars in academic medicine demonstrates that they include many of the outstanding leaders in our medical schools. This program under the staff of the Markle Foundation, particularly its president, John M. Russell, and its secretary, Dorothy Rowden, demonstrates how a relatively small foundation has exerted and will continue to exert a marked influence on medicine by an investment in individuals, not only by a financial investment but by the provision of intellectual leadership, opportunities for communication with other scholars, and stimulation for scholarly attainment.

THE ASSOCIATION OF AMERICAN MEDICAL COLLEGES

One of the strongest influences in the forward development of medicine in this country and Canada has been the Association of American Medical Colleges, first organized in 1876. It has been important in determining what is done and what standards are followed in each of our medical schools, which, are themselves the foundations of medicine. It has been significant also internationally. Its broad objectives are:

1) The improvement and advancement of medical education by developing increasingly effective means of selecting the most able medical students for the study of medicine, 2) Experimentation in curriculum development and teaching methods, 3) Studies and programs aimed at improving the ability of students to learn and teachers to teach, 4) Efforts to improve the hospital internship and residency as educational experiences, 5) Efforts to improve and broaden the influence of continuing medical education, 6) The development of the knowledge and leadership necessary to provide for the long-range progress and stability of medical education, and 7) The creation and maintenance of effective avenues of communication between medical educators and between medical educators and the American public.

A recent study, published by Lowell Coggeshall with the support of the Commonwealth Fund[15], attempts to outline recent major trends in health care and to cite the important implications for medical education and for the Association of American Medical Colleges as the principal organization through which plans and action for medical education are considered and correlated. This report exemplifies the vitality and vision upon which the recent development of medical education in this country has depended. Since the end of World War II, this association has been helped by financial support from a number of foundations, such as the China Medical Board, the Commonwealth Fund, the Kellogg Foundation, the Macy, Markle, Rockefeller, and Sloan foundations. Some of the support has been unrestricted; some has been for special purposes. The China Medical Board and the Sloan Foundation provided most of the funds for the association's central headquarters building built on land donated by Northwestern University in Evanston.

NATIONAL CONFERENCES AND COMMITTEES

Over the years, many of the foundations have helped the work and activities of national committees. Important examples are the Rockefeller Foundation's grants to the Committee on Research on the Problems of Sex of the National Research Council, and to the National Committee for Mental Hygiene and its successor, the National Mental Health Foundation. The China Medical Board over a period of seven years financed the Conferences for Foreign Medical Graduates. The Commonwealth Fund has made grants for the work of the National Board of Medical Examiners and for that of Planned Parenthood–World Population.

EXPERIMENTS IN MEDICAL EDUCATION

The Rockefeller Foundation and the General Education Board from their inception sponsored experimentation in medical education. Despite faltering along the way and nonacceptance by those preferring to maintain the status quo, this has been one of the finest and most significant developments in American medicine. More recent experiments in medical education have had substantial assistance at Western Reserve from the Commonwealth Fund, at Northwestern from the Commonwealth Fund, at Kansas from the China Medical Board, at Rochester from the Commonwealth Fund, and at Johns Hopkins from the Rockefeller Foundation and the Commonwealth Fund. There are many others. At the present time there is widespread interest among medical institutions in making changes to meet the needs of society and to cope with the explosive increase in new information forthcoming from the greatly accelerated research activities in academic institutions. Intensive specialization in the practice of medicine has greatly improved the quality of patient care. At the same time a greater number of family physicians and doctors of all kinds are required. The greater participation of government in the care of the elderly and in categorical diseases will necessitate some important adaptations in all of medicine but particularly in medical teaching centers. Experimentation has occurred, and will continue to occur, at all levels of medical education; the voluntary foundations are the sources of the financial assistance that make much of it possible.

EXPERIMENTS IN PATIENT CARE

In the historical sketch of the Commonwealth Fund, a number of undertakings concerned with improved patient care are described. One, which began in 1922, was concerned with demonstrations in child health care. There were experiments in health services for a home care plan at the Montefiore Hospital in New York City; for the medical care of indigents by the Richmond, Virginia, Department of Public Health; for family medical care by the Health Insurance Plan of Greater New York; for the improvement of medical care in medically underprivileged areas by the Tennessee Medical Foundation; and for a program of continuing professional education by the Rochester, New York, Regional Health Council. An important project was the support of the experimental health services at the Hunterdon Medical Center in Hunterdon County, New Jersey. Grants were also made to the New York Hospital—Cornell Medical Center for research in medical education and patient care; to the University of Vermont for a regional medical care project; and to Boston University School of Medicine for an integrated program for the teaching of human ecology.

Many foundations have contributed grants for the development and continuing support of schools of public health, such as the major Rockefeller Foundation support at Johns Hopkins and at Harvard, and the Kellogg Foundation support at Michigan. Patient care has benefited from the activities of our schools of public health. Similarly, foundations have made to hospitals grants which have had profound effects upon patient care and medical education.

GRANTS FOR MEDICAL RESEARCH

Prior to World War II, the advancement of the frontiers of knowledge through medical and biological research depended largely upon income from taxes to publicly supported universities and medical schools, and from endowment income and grant support of research to privately supported institutions. Mention has been made of the importance of the Rockefeller Institute in this area. The major large foundations, particularly the Rockefeller Foundation, were primary sources of assistance. Help came through endowment grants, block grants (made to an institution, which then itself decided just how the money should be used) like the ones made by the Rockefeller Foundation in the thirties; grants to departments in a medical school; grants made for an individual staff member, and the fellowship grants already referred to. Since the beginning of World War II, the federal government has entered the field at an increased pace in a number of different directions, and at the present time the large sums available have discouraged some foundations from continuing in this field. The National Institutes of Health Report on Foundation Expeditures[1] made in 1960 concluded as follows:

In a pluralistic society, foundations provide a counterbalance to the forms and directions of support arising from governmental efforts. These latter must of necessity give strong emphasis to agency objectives, just as industry research aims at product improvement and innovations. In response to rising Federal support to established research fields and disciplines, some foundations have been able to channel support into other significant but relatively neglected or newly emerging fields of scientific inquiry. Others recognizing the concentration of Federal support in research and the deeply rooted impediments to Federal aid to education, have redirected their resources from research to education to achieve a more viable equilibrium in the national interest.

Foundations have a flexibility in their support of research that governmental agencies do not possess. This is a precious asset to the freedom of the many investigators who treasure the opportunities serendipity brings to the creative individual.

INTERNATIONAL ACTIVITIES

Under the leadership of Wickliffe Rose, Dr. Richard Pearce and Dr. Alan Gregg, the International Education Board and the Rockefeller Foundation gave grants for the improvement of a number of institutions in the British Empire, France, Belgium, Brazil, Canada, Lebanon, Southeast Asia and even in Fiji in the South Pacific Islands. The China Medical Board was created in 1914 as a Division of the Rockefeller Foundation to care for the developing interests of the foundation in China. In 1928, it was incorporated as a separate organization with an endowment provided by the Rockefeller Foundation. The funds of the board, before and after incorporation, were devoted largely to the support of the Peking Union Medical College in Peking until nationalization of the college by the Chinese Communists in 1951. Thereafter, the board embarked on a new program and enlarged its field within the geographical limits permitted by its charter, which states that its purposes are "to extend financial aid to the Peking Union Medical College and/or like institutions in the United States of America."

The Commonwealth Fund and the Kellogg Foundation have maintained fellowship programs involving students from the British Empire, Western Europe, and Latin America. At present, the Association of American Medical Colleges has an International Division which has become more important as the years have gone by. Not only have these activities involving the health sciences in the international field been of great value in international good will, in the promotion of public health, and in the work of newly emerging nations, but they have been of great value to the health of our own people. Today many foreign-trained physicians come to the United States for advanced training and many stay on for professional practice. It has been of value, therefore, that many received their undergraduate medical educations in schools whose work had been helped by an American voluntary foundation. Certain able foreign students and colleagues also have been attracted to join the ranks of our academic institutions.

SPECIAL TYPES OF GRANT SUPPORT

In writing on the subject of "Tools of Research," Fosdick[10] described a series of instances in which the Rockefeller Foundation had made grants that had resulted in important instruments for research, such as the ultracentrifuge, electrophoresis apparatus, oscilloscope, mass spectrograph, electron microscopes, and the cyclotron. Each time such a new piece of equipment is developed, new vistas open for investigation and treatment. These instrumental developments are often costly; without foundation support, they would not have been developed or would have been delayed.

In a number of instances, foundations sense the need for intensified activity in a special field and encourage its development through funding. In the 1964 Alan Gregg Lecture, Dr. Robert Morison[16] related the story of the late Dr. Alan Gregg, then director of the Medical Science Division of the Rockefeller Foundation, and his work over a number of years in the advancement of the field of psychiatry. As a result of his leadership and the support that he was able to make available, the teaching, research, and patient care in the field of mental illnesses have markedly improved. In the Rockefeller Foundation, the program in experimental biology served to stimulate work in the natural sciences of great significance today in the multidisciplinary approach to the biology of the cell. Drs. Lester Evans and Roderick Heffron did much to sponsor the contributions in the field of Exfoliative Cytology so important in cancer diagnosis made by the late George N. Papanicolaou.

The Macy Foundation, led by Drs. Willard Rappleye and Frank Fremont-Smith, made available funds that have had real influence in advancing teaching, research, and care in the field of obstetrics and gynecology and in attracting a greater number of able medical graduates. This stimulus is apparent in a report of a committee of the American Gynecological Society, entitled *The Recruitment of Talent for a Medical Specialty*.[17] The Macy Foundation also made grants to a number of medical schools to be used over a period of years to supplement salaries of younger basic science faculty members. At the end of World War II, the Kellogg Foundation sponsored a program of continuing medical education designed to meet needs of doctors who had been away in the military services. The Ford Foundation gave $10 million to the National Fund for Medical Education to be used over a period of seven years for unrestricted support of all the medical schools in the United States. The National Fund for Medical Education, organized in the late forties to raise money from corporations for the nation's medical schools, pioneered in the corporate giving for education and gathered more than $35 million. In the last few years, the Commonwealth Fund and the Kellogg Foundation have made sizable grants to aid in the planning of new medical schools and in quite a few instances for helping new two-year medical schools get under way. In 1951, the Olin Foundation, with primary interest in general education, gave $2,549,000 to the Cornell Medical College for a medical student residence, stimulating an extensive housing development in the New York–Cornell Center.

INTELLECTUAL LEADERSHIP PROVIDED BY FOUNDATION STAFFS

After Abraham Flexner completed his report, he became a member of the staff of the General Education Board, and together with his brother, Dr. Simon Flexner, of the Rockefeller Institute, and Dr. William H. Welch of the Johns Hopkins Medical School, formed a triumvirate that had a profound influence upon medicine. Wickliffe Rose, Dr. Richard Pearce, Dr. Alan Gregg, and other principal officers were not only involved in the awarding of grants for the Rockefeller Foundation, but they were counselors to heads of institutions, to lay board members, to members of staffs of medical schools and universities in the United States and abroad. They served as sounding boards, as stimulators of ideas and programs, as mediators in situations of difficulty. Barry Smith and Drs. Lester Evans and Roderick Heffron were their counterparts in the Commonwealth Fund; Drs. Willard Rappleye and Frank Fremont-Smith in the Macy Foundation; Drs. Emory Morris, Matt Kinde, and Ben Horning in the Kellogg Foundation; and John Russell and Dorothy

Rowden in the Markle Foundation. Their influence was accomplished without undue interference or domination.

FUTURE ROLE FOR FOUNDATIONS

Do foundations still have a role in light of large federal support of medical institutions? Medical educators would answer strongly in the affirmative. Many of our institutions are operating in outmoded physical facilities and, even though there are matching funds available, in many instances it has not been possible to secure the necessary support from private sources. In spite of foundation policies against providing "bricks and mortar" money, adequate physical facilities are essential for any program in medicine. In some cases, the hospitals fail to provide what is required for in- and outpatient teaching. The competition today is such that many medical schools do not have the dollars to attract and hold the best faculty members. In the years ahead, with expansion under way in established institutions and the creation of new ones, staff development will be a crucial problem. Continued experimentation to improve the entire educational system will be needed. Greater emphasis could well be placed on problems of patient care, on organization and economics of care, and on the teaching hospital and its relations with other hospitals and the community. Teaching centers are to be involved to a greater extent in international activities in all phases of their operations. Foundations will find great opportunity for "risk" research which does not have an appeal to the categorical requirements of federal agencies. As the demands in teaching centers have grown, pressures on administration have grown also, and medical education has become big business requiring a high type of administrative leadership for many of its functions. Today medical school deans are a group of harassed individuals trying to "keep many balls in the air." It is no wonder that there has been such a turnover among them. There is a great dearth of people for all branches of medical administration. One area that has fallen by the wayside with the advancement of medicine has been the proper support and development of the allied health sciences. Endowment and continuing support for nursing education has been left to the hospital in privately supported schools of nursing. Much would be gained if some foundations would take under their wings the support of educational and research activities in nursing, physical therapy, social service, occupational therapy, and the many others. Last but not least is the help required to implement the recommendations of the Coggeshall Report[15] as far as the work of the Association of American Medical Colleges is concerned.

Some of these suggestions do not have "glamor appeal" and are not spectacular but are most important in terms of human welfare and health. Possibly the time has come for more foundations to follow the lead set by some in placing greater emphasis on academic responsibilities for the organization, teaching, and application of new knowledge, and to depend on the vast federal sources for creating it.

In a discussion of the partnership of government and voluntary agencies in strengthening the organization of health services, Dr. Willard C. Rappleye[18] has stated:

The future calls for fresh approaches, new configurations that would alter—in fact they are already altering—the present patterns and responsibilities of hospitals, and a variety of health agencies in the community. The new developments are a part of the revolution of rising expectations insofar as health services are concerned. The challenges require imagination, unselfish leadership in governmental departments, medical schools, hospitals, organized labor, industry, individual practitioners and the lay community to insure satisfactory health services in the future. They present unparalleled opportunities for voluntary agencies in our democratic society to participate effectively in the guidance and administration of public functions in the health fields.

The voluntary way is one of the greatest assets Americans possess. Enterprising citizens like Rockefeller, Harkness, Kellogg, Macy, Markle, Sloan, Duke, Ford, Whitney, Hartford, Woodruff, and many others have, to our good fortune, seen fit to perpetuate their good deeds by establishing voluntary foundations dedicated to the welfare and health of mankind.

CHAPTER 19

The Foundation and Economics

GEORGE J. STIGLER

The volume and direction and quality of economic research are the product of many forces: the developments in closely related disciplines, the magnitude of the society's concern with economic problems, the organization of higher education, the values generated within the discipline, and the foundations. No one of these determinants of research has been fully isolated, let alone well measured in its effects, and the foundations (truly the *nouveau riche* of economics) because of their youth are especially difficult to assess. The underlying empirical data have not been collected and analyzed; therefore the following impressionistic survey is based only upon several decades of mostly distant and unsystematic observation of the work of the foundations. There are better weapons of scholarship than unsystematic observation and I hope some scholar will take on the task of improving our knowledge of what the foundations (and the governmental donors, who are outside the scope of this essay) have wrought, surely with the aid of a foundation grant.

Primary attention will be paid to the large foundations (such as Ford, Rockefeller, Sloan, and Carnegie). The perfect swarm of smaller but by no means poverty-stricken foundations are mostly unknown to any one person. The sample I have encountered has displayed all possible degrees of sense and skill, but generally differs from the major foundations in certain respects. The smaller foundations are usually more explicitly eager to foster particular policies and viewpoints (which they sometimes present with repellent rigidity). The smaller foundations usually seek to implement the interests of some dominant personality—usually the donor—whereas the major foundations display the varied interests of a group of professional administrators. I suspect that some donors have not recognized the fact that the problem of the intelligent disposal of wealth begins, not ends, with the creation of a foundation.

THE SPECIAL INSTITUTES

The private foundations began operating in the field of economics on a significant scale in the 1920's, and on a comparatively large scale only in the last fifteen years. It follows that the only kinds of research that the foundations could have *initiated* are those introduced since World War I. One type of research institution has in fact been created primarily by the foundations in this modern period—the private research unit independent of any university. The most prominent examples before World War II were the National Bureau of Economic Research, the Brookings Institution, and the Twentieth Century Fund; in the postwar period we must add Resources for the Future. The following observations are based upon the past performances of the institutes, and I do not seek (what would be very difficult to do) to appraise their work at the present moment.

The foundations were influential, and at least in some cases decisive, in the establishment within universities of area institutes (Russian, Near East, etc.), economic development research centers (M.I.T., Yale), institutes for the training of special groups (centers for training foreign civil servants at Stanford, Vanderbilt), interdisciplinary centers (Center for the Advanced Study of the Behavioral Sciences), and so on. Of course, substantial repackaging of traditional subjects and regular faculty members was often involved in these latter ventures—the university world is not wholly devoid of merchandising skills.

These special institutes have been built upon one of three patterns:

1. A reclassification of traditional types of academic work: for example, the historian, the economist, and the lawyer study Russia or India. The foundations surely increased the amount of material published on certain geographical areas, as, for example, the numerous studies of Russian economic life. The area institute has made no important contribution to economic theory or to research methodology, nor, in close relationship, have these institutes attracted or trained two economists of the very first rank.

This would be an appropriate place to discuss interdisciplinary projects, but only if one had more knowledge of their endeavors and achievements than I possess. The very nature of these projects is illusive: the Center for Advanced Study in the Behavioral Sciences, for example, is really a university of social science–plus–psychology with rotating faculty and no students. Are then all universities interdisciplinary projects? I know of no considerable impact upon economics of any such project, but this may merely mean that the projects are oriented to applied problems rather than disciplines.

2. The study of public policy questions: Brookings and the Twentieth Century Fund are the premier examples, but part of the program of Resources for the Future and the Committee for Economic Development, the Brookings studies of the federal farm programs in the 1930's, and Hardy's study of tax-exempt securities also demonstrate this work. It is difficult to know what criterion of success to use: the scientific purposes are incidental (and so are the achievements), and one can hardly blame Brookings, for example, because we have adhered to an unfortunate farm program! An institute (read: committee) has only one advantage in conducting research calculated to persuade Congress and the public of the virtues of efficient policies: it can offer responsible sponsorship and marshal authoritative endorsements. Seldom does this advantage outweigh the blurred formulation that a committee demands.

3. The pursuit of a special type of knowledge. The National Bureau of Economic Research is the leading example (RFF is a newer, partial example). If long association has not warped my judgment, this was the greatest scientific success of the institutes: no economist will question the immense importance of its work

on national income, and few will set a low value on the work on productivity, cyclical fluctuations, and long-term growth. In a very different direction, the Cowles Commission (a quasi-independent institute affiliated to Chicago and then to Yale) has exerted a powerful influence upon the methods of statistical research in economics. Eventually the new kinds of data are collected by the government, and the new methodologies are embraced generally, so these institutes must discover new areas of fruitful work or decline into a more pedestrian estate.

On the whole the experiments with the special institutes have been worth making. The university world, with its tenure and tradition of freedom from supervision, has not shown itself to be capable of organizing research teams, and so universities provide a weak organizational basis for a strong, program-building scientist. Such a scientist *can* make a large impact at the head of a research institute, with its definite lines of authority resting on salary control, nontenure appointments, etc. When the leader of the institute was a strong man, as in the National Bureau case, the experiment was a success; when the institute had nondescript leadership (the Twentieth Century Fund was an example), so too was the institute's work.

THE GENERAL DIRECTIONS OF
ECONOMIC RESEARCH

The nature of research in economics was undergoing an important change at the time of World War I. Up to that time the statistical method had had only a negligible role in economics, but the accumulation of data, the development of statistical techniques, and the mathematization of the theory were all favorable to statistical economics. Pioneer figures such as Mitchell and Moore began to do their most influential work around 1910-14.

The foundations began to work in economics shortly thereafter. The then ruling practice of research by the individual scholar was of course necessarily recognized, and the Rockefeller Foundation in particular had an extensive fellowship and individual grant program, mostly administered through the Social Science Research Council and research committees in major universities. I doubt whether anyone knows the effects of these programs; the oral tradition is not very complimentary.

However, the real thrust of the foundations was toward the larger project, where size is measured by personnel and dollars. Only by so concentrating funds did the foundations believe that they could achieve tangible and mention-worthy projects. Some cooperative projects (*Encyclopedia of Social Sciences,* a modest success, and *Social Science Abstracts,* an unmitigated failure) are illustrations.

The penchant for larger grants fitted in well with the growth of statistical economics. Neither the economic theorist nor the traditional economic historian nor the nonquantitative institutionalist can operate on a large scale: the basic work must be done by the scholar himself. Statistical work—the construction of national income estimates, to cite an early study of the National Bureau of Economic Research—requires extensive clerical assistance and permits "team" research.

The foundations were a major source of funds for the large quantitative research project (whether of national income, or Leontief's input-output tables, or the Harvard committee's business cycle project) and their greatest single impact on economics has been to foster this kind of work. The productivity and business cycle studies, the surveys of consumer spending and of innumerable other economic data, the analyses of price behavior, the labor market studies, and more recently the large-scale econometric models are further examples. That foundations stimulated much of this work is corroborated by the fact that such statistical work was much slower to appear abroad. (A large share of such statistical work has been taken over by the federal government.)

A second general influence of the foundations has been to support the dominant position of a relatively few major universities and research institutes in economic research.

The basic tendency in American university life has been toward the diffusion of talent and research effort. A large share of both the able economists and the significant research were located in a handful of universities before World War I. Because of the more rapid growth of support for public institutions, the degree of concentration of talent and work has probably diminished some-

TABLE 5

ARTICLES PUBLISHED BY ECONOMISTS AT VARIOUS AMERICAN UNIVERSITIES

	1912-13*			1962-63†	
Institution	Articles	Cumulative percentage	Institution	Articles	Cumulative percentage
Harvard	$13\frac{1}{4}$‡	11.4%	Chicago	$28\frac{1}{6}$	9.7%
Chicago	$8\frac{1}{4}$	18.5	Harvard	$27\frac{1}{2}$	19.1
Columbia	$7\frac{1}{4}$	24.7	M.I.T.	$19\frac{23}{24}$	25.9
Pennsylvania	6	29.9	Stanford	$15\frac{1}{2}$	31.2
Yale	6	35.1	Yale	$14\frac{5}{8}$	36.2
Illinois	5	39.4	Pennsylvania	$11\frac{1}{2}$	40.1
Cornell	4	42.8	Washington	$11\frac{1}{6}$	43.9
Wisconsin	4	46.2	Princeton	10	47.3
Johns Hopkins	$3\frac{1}{4}$	49.0	California (Berk.)	$9\frac{1}{2}$	50.6
Virginia	3	51.6	Columbia	9	53.7
Others	56	100.0	Other	$134\frac{3}{4}$	100.0
Total	116			$291\frac{7}{8}$	

* 1912-13 Journals: *American Economic Review*
  Quarterly Journal of Economics
  Journal of Political Economy
† 1962-63 Journals: Above, plus
  Econometrica
  Review of Economics and Statistics
‡ Articles with joint authors are distributed fractionally among the various schools.

what. The trend toward diffusion of capable men is obvious, but the diffusion of outstanding men is difficult to document, and in economics it has been fairly modest. For example, the share of articles in the leading American professional journals by academic authors coming from the major universities has not changed appreciably from 1912-13 to 1962-63—the leading nine schools produced about 50 percent at both dates (Harvard and Chicago together 19 percent); see Table 5. Yet a slow process of diffusion appears under way, and will be reinforced by the increasing participation of the federal government in research and teaching.

To this basic force the foundations have been a counterforce. Their penchant for larger programs, and naturally for the most distinguished scholars, has led them to concentrate a substantial

TABLE 6

DISTRIBUTION OF GRANTS IN ECONOMICS AND BUSINESS
BY FORD FOUNDATION, 1951 THROUGH FIRST QUARTER, 1965

Institution	Grants ($1000)	Percent of total
Resources for the Future	$17,822	16.9
Brookings	10,375	9.8
Population Council	7,914	7.5
Harvard	7,008	6.6
Columbia	5,645	5.3
Chicago	5,117	4.8
Yale	4,551*	4.3
National Bureau of Economic Research	4,462	4.2
Committee for Economic Development	3,553	3.4
Stanford	3,541	3.3
Carnegie Institute of Technology	2,606†	2.5
Pennsylvania	2,600	2.5
M.I.T.	2,344	2.2
Michigan	2,220	2.1
California (Berkeley)	2,190	2.1
All other	23,805	22.5
Total, all domestic recipients	$105,753	100.0

* No business school
† No economics department

fraction of their grants in the major research centers, and in particular in the private universities. The tabulation of grants of the largest foundation in economics offers some measure of this tendency (see Table 6), although the tabulation exaggerates the tendency by omitting general institutional grants. Nevertheless the distribution of grants among universities makes an interesting comparison with the measure of output in Table 5. As a result, the dispersion of research activity has been retarded although by no means stopped. Still, the pressures of political life that make for sharing grants among areas and institutions (pressures which will grow more powerful with time) are weaker in the foundation world, and their grants have exerted a concentrating counterforce —a highly beneficial one from the viewpoint of scholarship, in my opinion.

A third and lesser effect of the foundation is to increase the homogeneity of research problems: fashion is never absent from scientific work, and the foundations reinforce it. The size of their preferred grants works this way, and so too does their acceptance of dominant professional opinion (to be remarked upon below). The huge wave of work on underdeveloped economies during the past fifteen years, for example, certainly would have had a smaller crest if Ford and Rockefeller had not been caught in the enthusiasm. The fields of population and economic progress (with special reference to the production of production functions) have also received the uncertain benefits of high fashion.

SPECIFIC DIRECTIONS OF ECONOMIC RESEARCH

Let us turn to the more specific question: how have the foundations influenced particular areas of research? Any estimate of the influence of foundations must be qualified by several preliminary remarks:

First, the large foundations in general are staffed by men whose personal convictions on the proper type of research are fairly representative of the consensus of respectable professional opinion. It would be considered irresponsible or dangerous for a larger foundation to plunge on a large scale into an eccentric program, and men who seek to do this do not get on or stay on foundation staffs. This trait is probably due to the professionalization of the administration of large foundations and possibly also to their vulnerability to criticism.

Second, there is some competition among foundations, despite the fact that an economist accustomed to studying industrial concentration would say that there is excessive concentration of assets in a few of the largest foundations. The competition is in at least some part a competition for the projects of distinguished scholars, and to this degree increases the scholar's role in the formulation of projects.

Both the acceptance of general professional opinion and the competition for scholars work to reduce the directive influence of the foundations. Their influence becomes secondary to the values and goals which the science itself produces.

Economic research shows the following significant trends:

1. *The main theoretical tradition has continued very strong, and has become increasingly mathematical.* This is still one-man work, and none of the big names (Hicks and Harrod and Robbins in England; Chamberlain, Lerner, Samuelson, Solow, Friedman, Hansen, Arrow, etc.) has been significantly aided by the foundations in their theoretical researches, although most or all have been aided in financing graduate students and some have been given substantial grants. (A few economists have also led a second, empirical life: Friedman on money, for example.) At this level, however, where "publish or perish" has no cutting edge, the foundations have merely provided new alternatives, "teach or travel."

2. *The clearest impact of the foundations has been made with large grants to strong research men.* The influence of Wesley Mitchell, Simon Kuznets, Wassily Leontief, Arthur Burns, and Theodore Schultz may be cited: in each case the foundations have enabled the man to assemble a group of junior colleagues and to exert a strong influence upon their work.

3. *The foundations have tended to favor innovators over conservators of scientific tradition.* Traditional areas such as history of thought and the "older" economic history have not attracted the foundations. Graduate students have found fellowships in such areas difficult to obtain. The fact that there are more men in these areas in England than in the United States (despite our overall five- or tenfold superiority in numbers) may be due in appreciable part to the foundations.

4. *Strong foundation interest in a field* (*labor and health economics and, even more, public finance*) *or disinterest* (*public regulation and industrial organization*) *are associated with differences in the vigor of research.* Of course the causation runs both ways but the interests of foundations seem to me to reinforce the divergences in intensity of research among fields. In a sense this emphasis upon certain fields is another manifestation of the tendency of foundations to strengthen fashions.

NONRESEARCH ECONOMICS

Economics is more than the search for greater knowledge. Economics consists also of teaching students, improving the knowledge of high school teachers of economics, refreshing and enlarging the knowledge of teachers in small colleges, and reinforcing the inferiority complex of nonmathematical economists. It includes screening foreign students, creating bibliographical aids to research, putting foreign treatises into English. It consists of endeavors to instruct Congress and the public at home (Commission on Money and Credit) and abroad (the native population of India, a favorite worry of many people, has grown less rapidly than the number of foundation-financed foreign economists bent upon assisting the natives).

Everyone who counts in economics will agree that professional research is more valuable than these retailings of scientific knowledge because research determines what will be taught and applied, and is intellectually more demanding. In the scientific pecking order, the creative analyst is so far above the "journalist" and the high school textbook writer that the analyst displays curiosity rather than contempt for the work of the latter. It is indeed fortunate that everyone (the journalist and the textbook writer included) accepts this priority because it would be beyond my powers to establish it on the basis of either social utility or artistic creativity.

Whatever the order in which theorists and practitioners are admitted to heaven, on earth both have their uses. A society with a developing theory of international trade and a rapidly deteriorating scheme of exchange controls, quotas, and discriminatory trade practices has not solved the problem of bringing scientific knowledge to bear on public opinion or public policy. A new treatment of scientific literature that increases its availability and reduces unproductive forms of duplication is a genuine contribution to research.

The recent and rapid expansion of foundation activities in the dissemination of knowledge oriented to public policy and the formation of commissions and institutes with a similar orientation is creating a serious problem. There is nothing unique about public policy as an area of research and experimentation and education. It is true that in policy there is no tenable distinction between education and propaganda, or, differently put, this year's truth may be next year's blunder. The purest of research is also vulnerable to revision. Society does not think that advocates of public policy should be tax-exempt. Once the foundations purposefully and substantially enter this policy area, they invite the status of lobbyists—and it would be irrelevant to raise the truthful defense of benevolent intentions.

Economics and business have been favored relative to numerous other disciplines. Foundation grants may be responsible for the fact that academic economists' salaries are as high as, or higher than, those of any other academic department. As a bold guess, among the top two hundred economists of the country the grants average $10,000 per year. An economist must argue that this program has increased the number of able young men attracted to the field.

The program of federal governmental grants for academic economic research is expanding at a compulsive rate, but responsibility and intelligence displayed in foundation grants has, in my view, substantially exceeded that displayed in the governmental grants. A searching investigation of the nature and tendencies of this governmental program is the most important requisite for a rational reorientation of the work of the foundations.

CHAPTER 20

Philanthropic Foundations and the Law

ERWIN N. GRISWOLD

Law, legal education, and legal research have not traditionally been the subjects of extensive philanthropic activity. In the past, advances in law have come because some individual, on his own time and often at his own expense, has devoted himself to productive legal work. Of course, it may be pointed out that Blackstone gave his vastly influential lectures at Oxford on the Vinerian professorship, established there by Charles Viner for the purpose. Viner's return was surely great, for Blackstone received the sum of £200 a year for his efforts. Similarly, Jeremy Bentham carried on his reforming work largely as an individual, and without appreciable philanthropic support.

By the end of the nineteenth century much important legal writing was being done by professors of law, following a pattern set by Joseph Story shortly after he became the Dane Professor of Law at the Harvard Law School in 1829. Following him were such writers as Greenleaf, Washburn, Cooley, and Cook, and in the twentieth century Williston, Wigmore, Beale, Scott, Corbin, and others who did much to organize and systematize our peculiarly complicated law. One can have a real appreciation of what they did only if one tries to contemplate the situation which would exist if they had not written their great works.

These authors depended on philanthropy only indirectly. Except in recent years, they received no grants from any foundation, and few had allowances for expenses. They did have professorships in great universities, with the resultant opportunity for research and writing, along with a heavy assignment of teaching. They were essentially lone workers. Their research was done in libraries; and their thoughts were sharpened in discussions with their faculty colleagues and with students.

During this period law schools were developing from meager beginnings and gaining slowly in strength, with only modest philanthropic support. The Cook bequest to the University of Michigan Law School provided important new buildings and funds for research; and the Sterling bequest to Yale provided buildings for the Yale Law School. Both of these gifts came from practitioners, and not through a foundation or other philanthropic institution.

From the beginning, law schools and legal research have been conducted on what might justly be described as a shoestring. Law schools had virtually nothing for endowment; even today law school endowments remain relatively small. In 1946, the endowment of the Harvard Law School was a little over $5 million, producing about $200,000 in annual income. This was the entire accumulation in a school then 130 years old. The income available for scholarship purposes was less than $35,000 per year in a school with more than 1,500 students. There was virtually no endowment income specifically assigned for research. Nevertheless, the Harvard Law School was relatively well off. There were over 125 law schools in the country at that time, and it is doubtful if altogether they had as much as $15 million in endowment. Probably the aggregate figure was nearer $10 million. With 35,000 law students in the country, this represented an average endowment of less than $300 per student. The average endowment income of about $12 per student had to contribute toward teachers' salaries, scholarship aid to students, and expensive library facilities, among other things. It should not be surprising that there was virtually nothing available for research.

The first change in this picture came in the 1920's, when the Rockefeller Foundation and Carnegie Corporation made substantial grants to the American Law Institute to finance the production of the Restatement of the Law. This was a great undertaking, sponsored by leaders of the bar, including such great lawyers as

Elihu Root, Charles Evans Hughes, George W. Wickersham, and George Wharton Pepper. Its purpose was to produce some order out of the chaos of American law—a chaos resulting from the fact that there is no necessary similarity in the details of the law in our fifty separate states—through restating that law; that is, through undertaking to state a single coherent rule on all important questions, following the weight of authority where that was clear, and the best principle where the authorities left an appropriate freedom of choice.

The American Law Institute engaged the services of leading law professors as reporters, and they worked with a group of advisers, many of them leading lawyers and judges. Over the next twenty years, a number of volumes of excellent Restatements, were produced, covering such subjects as contracts, torts, property, trusts, conflict of laws, and judgments. The institute also produced a Model Code of Evidence. All of these works have had great influence on our law, though they cannot be said to have made our law nationally uniform.

In recent years, the institute has continued its work, with further philanthropic support from the Falk Foundation and others, as well as its original supporters. The institute played an instrumental role in the development of the Uniform Commercial Code, now adopted in nearly all of our states. It developed a Model Penal Code, and made studies of tax laws, and of the jurisdiction of the federal courts. In addition, it has undertaken to bring the Restatements down to date, through the development of the Restatement, Second—which is more than a mere second edition of the Restatement, but a complete review of every detail in an effort to bring the Restatement fully down to date.

This work, though not sponsored or directed by the law schools, has been carried out almost exclusively by law school personnel, with the actual work being done on law school premises, and with extensive use of law school facilities, such as libraries. The American Law Institute work done by faculty members has provided an excellent background for the development of further research work under the auspices of the law schools themselves.

Law schools and law teachers have special problems in the conduct of research. Much that they may do is controversial, and may sometimes involve deep emotions. Work in the area of freedom of speech may not attract donations from the usual sources of private wealth. Similarly, work done on the privilege against self-incrimination of the Fifth Amendment, during the McCarthy era, or work on birth control, or on some aspects of civil liberties may be unlikely to find philanthropic support. Legal research is always likely to disturb some person's private interest or deeply held belief. Yet legal research, if it is to be effective, cannot ignore these controversial areas. Thus the problem of financing specific types of legal research is often an especially difficult one. Though the social ills of the community may be more deeply pervasive and more costly than its physical ills, it is always relatively easy to get philanthropic support for medical research, which rarely treads on anyone's toes. Legal research, no matter how great its real importance, does not have the same appeal, and often arouses strong opposition.

Law schools are often charged with being narrow in their outlook and in their training. To a considerable extent, this is true. However, their situation must be considered. Having little or no endowment, they have had to rely on tuition income to meet their expenses. This means that they have necessarily been operated on a "box office" basis. Customarily they have relatively small faculties and large enrollments. Even today the Harvard Law School has a student-faculty ratio of about thirty to one. A generation ago it was fifty to one. Tuition income has been needed not only to pay faculty salaries and other operating expenses, but also the large expenses of building up and maintaining libraries, whose great size is the inevitable consequence of the system of separate laws, statutes, and decisions operating in each state. There was little opportunity for research and development of the law, or for law reform activities, except as each faculty member found time for such purposes while carrying a necessarily heavy teaching load.

In the years since World War II, there has been some change in this situation, thanks almost entirely to the gifts of philanthropic foundations, which have put a new life and perspective into legal education. Without them, legal education would, in large measure, have had no alternative but to proceed along its somewhat narrowly professional way—a path good in itself, as far as it goes, and from which law teachers in the past have had no means of escape.

It is not possible to list here all of these gifts for law and legal education in recent years, and no comprehensive tabulation will be attempted. The objective here is to give the general picture, and to show what an important role philanthropic gifts have played in legal education and development of the law. Small as these gifts have been in comparison to philanthropy generally, they have been of the first importance in raising the horizons of legal education, and in encouraging the many persons, in and out of law schools, who are vitally concerned with improvement in the law and its administration.

It is not surprising that the largest amount of gifts has been made by the Ford Foundation. It is almost impossible to contemplate the state in which legal education would find itself today if the Ford Foundation had not decided to devote a portion of its interest to the legal field.

In 1954, the Ford Foundation made grants aggregating more than $12 million in the field of International Legal Studies. About two-thirds of this total went to fourteen law schools in the United States. Most of these schools were endeavoring to develop their work in the international field in order to meet the needs of a world in which international contacts are developing rapidly. Some of the gifts were for professorships, and thus were capital in nature. The balance of the gifts was in the form of expendable grants for the purpose of financing research and development over a period of ten years.

In addition to these basic gifts, the Ford Foundation made other gifts for particular purposes. It made gifts to support the International Program in Taxation at the Harvard Law School, and the World Tax Series sponsored at Harvard. It made a matching gift to apply against the cost of the new building for International Legal Studies at Harvard. It gave funds to Columbia University to finance a cooperative program between Columbia, the University of Michigan Law School, and the law faculty of the University of Istanbul in Turkey. It supported a cooperative program between the Law School of the University of California at Berkeley and the University of Cologne in Germany. It financed the Indian Law Institute, in New Delhi, India, and enabled a number of American law professors to participate there. It financed an eight-year cooperative program between the law schools of Harvard, Stanford, and the

University of Michigan, with the law faculties of six Japanese universities (Chuo, Keio, Kyoto, Tohoku, Tokyo, and Waseda). A remarkably fruitful program, this has established many contacts between American and Japanese law teachers and lawyers, as well as a better understanding on each side of the laws of the other country. One of the by-products of this work is the volume on *Law in Japan,* edited by Professor Arthur T. von Mehren of Harvard, presenting the most comprehensive study available in English on the general theory and bases of Japanese law.

Altogether the Ford Foundation has made several hundred grants in the field of law, as a part of its public affairs program. One of its early moves was the provision for ten years of fellowships at Columbia, Harvard, New York University, and Yale Law Schools for American and Canadian law teachers, or prospective law teachers. Under these grants several hundred promising law teachers have had the opportunity for graduate study in law. These grants have been important not only to law teachers, and to the schools to which they have gone, but also in upgrading the graduate work at the several law schools where the fellowships were held.

The Ford Foundation has made many other relevant grants. For example, a grant of $350,000 went to the University of Pittsburgh to investigate the application of computer techniques to legal research. Several grants were made to the American Bar Foundation, some specifically for work in the area of criminal law, and some for the general work of the Foundation in law and public affairs. Grants were made to the American Society of International Law for its general support, to the Assocation of American Law Schools, and to the Institute of International Education for the purpose of strengthening African legal education; and a grant of $1.8 million was made to the Howard University Law School, where the student body is predominantly Negro, for the purpose of strengthening its work. Many of the Negro leaders in years ahead are likely to come from Howard. The Ford Foundation has also continued its grants to the American Law Institute for specific projects.

Finally, reference should be made to important grants, aggregating some $4 million, which the Ford Foundation has made to the National Legal Aid and Defender Association, to improve and expand defender and related services for defense of the accused in criminal cases. Similar, though smaller, grants have been made to the National Juvenile Court Foundation for a demonstration of the value and role of attorneys in juvenile courts, and to the National Council of Juvenile Court Judges, to study the value of attorneys in juvenile cases, and to study the treatment of nondelinquent children in juvenile courts.

Other foundations have made significant contributions in the legal area. The Carnegie Corporation, for example, has contributed a series of fruitful fellowships under which some five college teachers each year have been enabled to spend a year at the Harvard Law School, not for the purpose of becoming lawyers, but for the purpose of getting an understanding of law so that they would be able to use it in their fields of economics, history, sociology, philosophy, or whatever it might be. The Carnegie Corporation has made grants to the American Law Institute, to enable it to continue its projects in the development of the law, and a substantial grant to the Columbia University Law School, to enable it to carry on a study of the international rules of judicial procedure. Several Carnegie grants have gone to the Association of American Law Schools, to the American Society of International Law, and to the Association of the Bar of the City of New York.

The Rockefeller Foundation has for many years had a program in Legal and Political Philosophy, under which grants have been provided to nearly two hundred law teachers and other scholars. These grants aggregate nearly $1 million. A number of significant books and studies have come out of this work, as well as the general benefit received by the fellowship holders through their opportunity for study and research. The Rockefeller Foundation also supported the preparation of the Model Penal Code by the American Law Institute. It has made substantial gifts to the Yale and the Harvard law schools for the purpose of financing fellowships for advanced training and research for selected African students, perhaps forty or fifty of whom have had the opportunity for advanced training in the United States. Some of these fellowship recipients are already holding positions of considerable importance in their own countries.

The Rockefeller Foundation has also made grants to the Hague Academy of International Law, to Tulane University for a program of training in legal and social science, and to Columbia University Law School for a program in international organization. It supported the Civil Liberties Studies, prepared under the auspices of Cornell University, a number of years ago.

Other foundations which have participated in the legal area include the James Foundation, with grants aggregating $1,626,000 to seven law schools (Columbia, Cornell, Fordham, Harvard, New York University, University of Pennsylvania, and Yale) over a period of nine years. Part of this was for buildings, and the rest was for general purposes. The Falk Foundation has also made a number of grants in the legal area, notably in support of the work of the American Law Institute, particularly in support of the development of the Uniform Commercial Code.

Special reference must be made to the Walter E. Meyer Research Institute of Law, Inc., established about 1958 under the will of Walter E. Meyer. This foundation has total resources of about $2 million, which, under the terms of the donor's will, must be spent within a period of twenty years. Its grants have been made largely in aid of research projects submitted by professors in the law schools of the country. One such grant, for example, has been made to Harvard Law School, in support of the work conducted by Professor Robert E. Keeton and associates on the problem of compensation for the victims of automobile accidents. Most of the Meyer Foundation's grants have been in relatively small amounts, though a grant of $400,000 was made to the Yale Law School to aid it in its work in urban law. The Meyer Foundation has itself been the recipient of a grant from the Ford Foundation in the amount of $500,000, under which the Meyer Foundation is to act in effect as the retailer; that is, the Meyer Foundation will consider individual applications, and make grants to the applicants it regards as qualified in support of their legal research activities, thus relieving the Ford Foundation of the problem of considering and evaluating many relatively small applications for grants.

Numerous other foundations have made grants in the legal area for special purposes. A number of family foundations have supported the work of Professor and Mrs. Sheldon Glueck at the Harvard Law School in the field of juvenile delinquency. The Russell Sage Foundation, the Alfred P. Sloan Foundation, and the

Twentieth Century Fund have sponsored grants in the legal area; the Potomac Foundation, the Vera Foundation, and others, in the field of race relations and for the study of bail practices in criminal courts.

This partial list is intended to be illustrative only, and to show the extremely important role that philanthropic giving has played in the area of legal education and law development. Relatively speaking, the aggregate amount of all gifts in this area has been very small—that is, compared to gifts for other purposes, such as medicine, education generally, the natural sciences, and so on. But these gifts have in fact been just about everything that was available for the improvement of legal education and for the development of the law. Much more could be effectively utilized, and must be provided if we are to meet the challenges in this area. But the situation today would be very sorry indeed if these gifts had not been made available. There can be no doubt of the absolutely essential nature of such philanthropic gifts.

Mention should also be made of the remarkable support given to many law schools by their alumni. At the Harvard Law School, for example, the whole field of financial aid to students in obtaining their legal education has been simply transformed by alumni giving. In recent years, alumni of the school have provided, through annual giving, more than $800,000 each year, a sum which is materially greater than the amount available to the school as income on its endowment. In addition, in recent years, substantial sums have been received through bequests from alumni. Although the pattern is not clearly established at all law schools, a number of other schools have carried on successful annual giving and bequest programs. This belief by alumni in the value of the work done by their schools is very encouraging, and should be an earnest leading to even stronger support from the philanthropic foundations.

Even with generous alumni giving, and gifts from other sources, more than a third of the gifts received by the Harvard Law School in the past fifteen years have come from the Ford Foundation, and more than half of the aggregate gifts received by the school have come from the established foundations. The proportion of foundation gifts will be considerably higher at a number of other schools. It is thus readily apparent what a basic and essential part has been carried by philanthropic giving in this area. It is impossible to give too great thanks for the support which has been provided. It is only hoped that the continuing need of an area with no real backlog of strength will be recognized, and that even greater gifts will be made for legal education and law development in the future. The law and the law schools deal with a great and intractable area of human conduct and problems, and we have delayed for far too long a time a necessary systematic investigation of these matters.

We ought indeed to develop research organizations, in conjunction with law schools, so funded that they can on their own motion undertake research. At the present time there is no clear career available to a young man who wants to devote himself to legal research. He may be able to get himself a post with a research project, but ordinarily this will last for only a year or two, and then it is by no means clear what he can do next. If institutions were available to a fine and well-trained group of legal research personnel, work could be undertaken as the need for it appeared; and qualified research people could seek careers in such activity, instead of having to fall back on a teaching post or on private practice of law, as is now the case.

Thus, despite the generosity of many philanthropic donors, there is great and continuing need for free funds for research and for strengthening legal education generally. Though a number of the grants made have been given to law schools, a considerable part has been given to other legal agencies, such as the American Law Institute, the American Bar Foundation, the National Legal Aid and Defenders Association, and so on. Much of the philanthropic giving, too, has been restricted to the international area. The amount available for basic support of legal education generally has been very small and law schools have to operate on a box office basis, generally with large classes and mass production techniques, which have their merits, but which have no doubt been overdone, though this has generally been out of sheer necessity.

Law schools need buildings, library facilities, professorships, and funds for financial aid to students. The restriction often imposed by foundations against gifts for capital, either for buildings or for endowment, is self-defeating in this area where basic strength is so lacking. Happily it has often been overlooked, but this is often a problem, and foundations might well give more regard to the basic problem of strengthening legal education generally, including the broadening of its outlook, so that the schools can better train the legal scholars and researchers of the future. Law schools should be looked on, for the present, as the seed beds for development of the legal order. As law schools are strengthened, they will turn out more and better men, who will then be in a position to carry forward the work of legal education and law development.

Often in the past, a foundation having a project it wanted to carry on has invited away the man whom a law school has laboriously developed and trained to carry on work in a particular area. As a result, the work of the law school in training students in this field has come to a sorry halt, or at best has limped along until the beguiled professor has returned. What the foundations should be doing in these fields, it is suggested, is to help the law schools appoint three or four professors in these areas. Then one of them might be borrowed from time to time, and he would gain from the experience; in the meantime, the law schools would be moving ahead at their task of training students who would be available to take on such assignments in the future. The law schools should not be thought of as quarries, to be raided from time to time for good men—as the federal government sometimes does. Instead, they should be thought of as a great productive resource, to be strengthened and guarded, in order that they may produce the highly trained and qualified persons needed to carry on the projects of foundations and otherwise to advance the work of law development.

In the areas of research, the law schools should be strengthened in their general funds, so that they can move into the areas they think most need attention. In some fields, like natural science, "project research" may present no very serious problems. In the legal area, though, there has been some tendency for law school faculty members to be called on to do the research that someone else wants to have done, while funds have been scarce or wholly lacking for carrying on the research activities which the individual faculty members themselves want to do. Too often, from the point of view of the administrator, and of the faculty members themselves, foundations seek to have the law schools do what the foundations want done.

As has been indicated, the law schools have not been able to develop personnel or background or general strength to operate in this way. For the time being, what they need is basic strengthening, in personnel and other resources, so that they can really be reservoirs of talent, breadth, and vision in this important area of the adjustment of human relations. More than anything else, legal education needs general support and strengthening. If this can be done, without too much regard to immediate objectives, the potentialities for eventual development in the field of law will be greatly enhanced.

In saying this, there is no thought of detracting one particle from the great appreciation which is due to the foundations and other philanthropic givers for what they have done already in the field of law. It often takes a measure of courage to give for purposes of legal research, for the problems are sometimes controversial, and the results—indeed, any results—can rarely be guaranteed. Some foundations have shown considerable vision in the support they have given. Yet most foundations want to give for a rather specific purpose. In the case of colleges and universites, some valuable gifts have been made for general strengthening. In due course, it may be hoped that some foundation, or foundations generally, may take a long view of the field of legal education and law development, and come to see that, in an area which has traditionally been so long starved and held pretty closely to its immediate task, general support and strengthening are urgently needed in order to provide the broader-based lawyers and legal research scholars who will be badly needed to carry on essential work in this field in the future.

CHAPTER 21

The Humanities and the Foundations

WHITNEY J. OATES

Though my assignment is to address myself to the area of literature, I am taking the liberty of extending this to include not only literature but also other conventional humanistic fields, such as history, philosophy, and religion as well as those aspects of the social sciences which are humanistic in character. The creative and performing arts are indeed an integral part of the humanities, but it is surely a wise decision to consider separately philanthropic activity in connection with the arts. The problem of benefaction to the humanities, broadly defined, poses by itself difficulty enough.

All are familiar with the fact that as science burgeoned mightily in the latter part of the nineteenth century and into the twentieth even to our own day, sources of support for science, both public and private, have become abundantly available. This phenomenon can be partly attributed to the spirit of the age as well as to military and industrial needs. The humanities have surely not fared too well by comparison, though of course the financial needs of the humanist do not demand the enormously costly apparatus which is necessary for the scientist. And even more seriously, in recent years, the vast sums given to universities by government agencies for scientific research have tended to introduce an imbalance in the operation of these institutions, a cause of concern not only to humanists but to many scientists themselves. On the whole, the vast majority of humanists have not begrudged the scientists their good fortune, but rather have concentrated on ways and means whereby the humanities might attract appropriate support for their activities. Historically, humanists first attempted to adapt the so-called "scientific method" to their enterprises, but this did not succeed, for the "scientific method" can only in part be applied to the material of the humanities. Later, humanists tended to become defensive about their activities, but defensiveness, as everyone knows, can lead nowhere but to failure. In recent years, improvement has been made and the various fields of knowledge have come to be regarded as complementing one another rather than as rivals.

So much then for general background. When we look at the roles performed by three of the largest foundations vis-à-vis the humanities, we should note that in each instance this area of intellectual activity only became a sphere of interest well after the actual establishment of the foundation itself. The Rockefeller Foundation, whose first emphasis was placed upon public health, set up its Division of the Humanities in the late 1920's. The Carnegie Corporation really never operated in the territory of the humanities *per se* until the early 1950's, whereas the most recently organized foundation, the Ford, did not make the humanities a legitimate area of concern until the later 1950's. Though certain humanists may feel that foundations have not done as much as they should for the support of the humanities, from the longer historical perspective, it is a matter of great significance that these three large foundations plus several other smaller ones are officially committed to the principle that the humanities must be supported.

I propose now to discuss four instances of foundation philanthropy to the humanities of which I had some personal knowledge and which I regard as having had a profound influence in developing the humanities in this country.

THE AMERICAN COUNCIL OF LEARNED SOCIETIES

A cooperative effort of thirty-one constituent societies with a combined membership of some eighty thousand scholars, the ACLS now serves, it hopes, the best interests of the humanities and the humanistic aspects of the social sciences in this country. The story of the relations of the ACLS with various foundations should be instructive. Founded in 1919 in order to be the scholarly organization to represent the United States in the International Union of Academies, the council grew slowly in the next decade, and in the years up to World War II was supported virtually completely by grants from the Rockefeller Foundation. Perhaps it would be fair to say that in these years the ACLS concerned itself too exclusively with scholarly projects which were rather narrowly "philological," though it did undertake the combination of the very successful *Dictionary of American Biography,* aided by a gift from the *New York Times* and published by Scribner's. (Incidentally, at the present writing the D.A.B. is on a self-supporting basis, and supplement volumes will appear at regular intervals and will be financed by the royalties on current sales.) In the later thirties as the threat of war increased, Mortimer Graves of the ACLS staff was shocked at the enormous ignorance in the United States of foreign languages, in particular those of the Far East. Under the leadership of Mr. Graves, the ACLS was instrumental in producing a great number of dictionaries and textbooks dealing with these then "exotic" languages. These materials were of inestimable value when this country found itself facing Japan in a war in the Far East.

The war period, with the extra grants made to procure the language materials, was a comfortable one for the ACLS from the financial point of view. But, with the cessation of such grants, the business of the ACLS contracted and the organization received almost a lethal blow when the Rockefeller Foundation announced that its support would terminate at the end of the ensuing three years. The foundation's decision was based on its conviction that it was essentially unsound for the ACLS if it were dependent upon a single source for its support. The ACLS staff protested and even scolded in print the Rockefeller Foundation for the lack of wisdom it displayed in making this decision. However, it became evident that somehow the ACLS had lost contact with its constituent societies and their members. One foundation official (not a member of the Rockefeller staff) reported that he expected a flood of protests from irate humanists upon the announcement of the termination of the Rockefeller subvention, but he received not a single letter nor a single telephone call.

Things indeed looked bleak for the ACLS, but fortunately a new chairman of the board of directors, Howard Mumford Jones, decided that something should and could be done. With the timely aid of a small officer's grant from the Carnegie Corporation, the ACLS board set up a commission consisting of humanists, social scientists, scientists, and interested laymen, whose duty it was to explore ways by which the ACLS should be reorganized and to seek for a clarification of the objectives and goals of humane study. A new structure for the ACLS was drawn up by the commission and Professor Jones wrote what might be called a manifesto for the humanities. A renaissance for the ACLS was under way. More and more humanistic scholars became excited by the new developments, and gave the board of directors aid and suggestions concerning the basic needs of persons working in the field. Suffice it to say that in 1957 there were two handsome grants by the Carnegie Corporation and the Ford Foundation, which were renewed in 1961. Also in 1961 the Rockefeller Foundation gave the ACLS $1,000,000 for general support. This is not the place to go into details concerning the activities of the ACLS. It may, however, be worth noting that the organization disbursed in 1963-64 almost $2 million for its basic program and for other special projects supported either by the government or by foundations.

At the present time, it is safe to say that the ACLS does indeed really represent the humanists of the United States and does indeed aid them in manifold ways in the prosecution of their professions. One of the most notable methods of offering assistance is the award of postdoctoral fellowships, but it is also necessary to record here that the ACLS could grant approximately twice as many as it does now if sufficient funds were available. In addition, we should not overlook the remarkable fact in ACLS operations that it can call upon scholars from all across the spectrum of humane studies for advice, service on committees, and so on. The scholars in question gladly offer their services and uniformly without financial emolument.

A recent event gives some evidence of the current potency of the ACLS. On the initiative of its chairman, Professor Robert M. Lumiansky, the board of directors appropriated a sufficient sum to establish a National Commission on the Humanities. This action was taken with the support of the United Chapters of Phi Beta Kappa and the newly established Council of Graduate Schools in the United States. The commission, consisting of twenty members, some from academia and some distinguished laymen, under the able chairmanship of President Barnaby Keeney of Brown University, after about two years of work, produced a report recommending the establishment of a foundation to support the humanities and the arts, this foundation to complement the activity of the eminently successful National Science Foundation. The report was released on June 23, 1964, with copies widely distributed, but in particular to the members of the Congress. To the immense satisfaction of the ACLS and its co-sponsoring organizations, the idea appealed to many members of the House and Senate. Several bills were introduced in both chambers, but these bills were superseded by a version emanating from the White House which incorporated virtually all of the commission's report. At the present writing the National Foundation on the Arts and the Humanities has been operating for more than a year.

Such in brief outline is the story of the ACLS, which is what it is because the foundations have seen fit to underwrite its activities. One might even say that, though it may not have appeared to be so at the time, the decision on the part of the Rockefeller Foundation to terminate its grant proved to be a great service to the ACLS. Certainly it aroused the humanistic fraternity in this country and new vitality, imagination, and enthusiasm were stimulated and put at the service of reaching the goals toward which all humanists strive.

THE CASE OF THE WOODROW WILSON
FELLOWSHIP PROGRAM

Founded at Princeton University in the autumn of 1945, the Wilson Program was designed to recruit teachers for the academic profession by establishing a series of invitation fellowships. No one could apply, and one could become a candidate only on the nomination of a member of the academic profession. One fundamental purpose was to call the possibilities of an academic career to the attention of young people of the highest qualities of character, intellect, and personality who otherwise might never have thought of entering the profession. Also it was designed to attract those who had thought of the academic life as a possibility but were undecided. Each fellowship was for one year at a graduate school of the incumbent's choice, and gave him tuition plus an adequate living for the one-year period. At the outset, nominees were sought only from the humanities and the social sciences (only later were a small number of natural scientists accepted) because in these areas the problem of recruitment was most acute. In fact, the Wilson Program was the first systematic effort on the part of the academic profession to attract the best possible young people to embrace the career of teacher-scholar. Though this program is not confined exclusively to the humanities, its total contribution to the field well justifies its inclusion in an essay dealing with the humanities and the foundations.

For the first few years, the Wilson Program was carried on by Princeton University and Princeton supplied most of the funds needed to underwrite it. Early in its history it attracted the attention of John W. Gardner, then a junior staff officer of the Carnegie Corporation, later its distinguished president (now on leave to serve as Secretary of the Department of Health, Education, and Welfare), and through the good offices of Mr. Gardner, Princeton representatives were able to talk with Charles Dollard and Devereux Josephs, the then vice-president and president respectively of the corporation. About a year later, the corporation granted Princeton University a sum of $100,000 to be used by the program over a period of three to five years. Be it said that nominations were sought from colleges and universities other than Princeton. The program grew, the Carnegie Corporation added another grant of $50,000, and it became clear that the enterprise had become so large that it was beyond the competence of a single university to handle. It was then turned over to the Association of Graduate Schools of the Association of American Universities. More nominees were sought from a larger number of institutions of higher learning, and more fellowships were awarded. The Carnegie Corporation added $500,-000 to its prior grants and the General Education Board of the Rockefeller Foundation contributed another $500,000.

The expansion soon revealed the fact that the AGS was unequal to the task of administering the program, and that it really needed a separate organization for the purpose. At this point the Ford Foundation was approached and, after lengthy discussions, in 1957 it made a grant of $24.5 million for five years with which to establish a new organization to administer the program to be known as the National Woodrow Wilson Fellowship Foundation, a grant which was augmented in 1962 by an additional $27.5 million for another five-year period. These two extraordinary gifts have enabled the foundation since 1957 to award a thousand fellowships a year and to contribute to each graduate school where fellows matriculate a substantial "cost of education" subvention for each student admitted. The foundations' benefactions to the program (the Rockefeller Foundation with half a million dollars, the Carnegie Corporation with $650,000, and the Ford Foundation with over $50 million) constitute a telling contribution toward solving the problem of increasing the quality of people, particularly in the humanities, who are entering the academic profession. From 1945 to 1965 a total of 8,973 fellowships were awarded. Of this total 912 were awarded prior to the Ford grants and 8,061 since 1957 when the first Ford grant became available. As of the autumn of 1964, 2,124 former Wilson fellows were serving on the faculties of American colleges and universities. It is estimated that this figure represents between 70 and 75 percent of former Wilson fellows who had earned the doctorate by that time. One further statistic is worth citing. Of all persons receiving Ph.D.'s from Harvard some 61 percent enter teaching, but approximately 91 percent of Wilson fellows who have earned Harvard doctorates embark upon an academic career.

There can be no doubt that the financing of the Wilson Fellowship Program will stand out as a major achievement of significant philanthropy on the part of foundations.

THE COUNCIL OF THE HUMANITIES AT PRINCETON UNIVERSITY

In the years immediately before World War II, David Stevens, then director of the Division of the Humanities of the Rockefeller Foundation, became interested in a newly organized interdepartmental program in the humanities at Princeton and arranged for a grant which helped the operation get under way. The new program flourished, but, as is well known, activity in the humanities suffered seriously during the war years. However, in about 1950, President Dodds urged the humanists on his faculty to devise ways and means of enhancing teaching and scholarship in the humanities in the university. After two years of study, the faculty unanimously adopted a recommendation to establish a new element in the university to be called the Council of the Humanities. It should be noted here that in the years of study the experience of the Special Program in the Humanities, initially aided by the Rockefeller Foundation, proved invaluable to all those involved in the planning. The council as then constructed had three main functions: first, the appointment of fellows of the council, really distinguished professors, who were relieved of most of their teaching duties in order to carry on research, which in virtually all instances led to the enrichment of both the graduate and undergraduate curriculums; second, the supervision of graduate and undergraduate interdepartmental programs; and third, the provision of graduate fellowships, library resources, and the management of lecture and seminar programs. The council's view of the humanities is inclusive rather than exclusive, and it is committed to the proposition that every activity of the mind has its important humanistic dimensions. The council is therefore administered by an interdepartmental committee consisting of representatives of the conventional departments of the humanities plus one member each from the social sciences, the natural sciences, the School of Engineering, and the School of Architecture.

Shortly after its establishment, the council was given certain funds by the university as endowment and thus it had its very essential autonomy, even though to be sure these funds were not very extensive. A happy event in the early days came when the Carnegie Corporation, through President Gardner and the then vice president, James Perkins, were attracted by the potentialities of the council. After careful examination, the corporation on its own initiative gave the council $50,000 a year for five years, and, on the expiration of this grant, renewed it at the same rate for four more years. This was indeed inestimably helpful in enabling the council to set in motion its operations with unusual speed. A few years later, the United States Steel Foundation gave the Humanities Council $20,000 a year for five years, subsequently renewing the grant for another five-year period. Bequests to the university have added to the council's endowment, and $2 million of a James Foundation gift has been assigned to the council to help finance its activities. Also and importantly, the council received a grant of $500,000 from the Old Dominion Foundation to endow a senior fellowship of the council.

One other event is worth recording. A few years ago, representatives of the Ford Foundation's Program in the Humanities and the Arts sought out the Humanities Council to ask it to supervise a series of books in the various fields of the humanities in order to appraise humanistic scholarship in the United States in the last two or three decades. It was the hope that by such studies promising avenues—and less promising avenues—for future development might be identified. The Humanities Council agreed to undertake the project and the Ford Foundation awarded Princeton University a grant of $335,000 to finance it. The services of Richard Schlatter, now the provost of Rutgers University, were obtained to supervise the operation. More than thirty scholars from this country and abroad agreed to contribute to the series, eventually to consist of fourteen volumes. As of the spring of 1967, eleven volumes had been published. The volumes, it is hoped, will clarify the goals of humanistic scholarship, and should be useful to scholars interested in a recent evaluation of the states of affairs in territories adjacent to their own. The series also should be valuable to those who administer the new National Foundation on the Arts and Humanities. If these volumes prove successful, the Ford Foundation through the Council of the Humanities will have made a significant contribution to this area of intellectual activity.

The endowment of the council has gradually been increasing. It is expected that it will continue to help the individual growth of the humanistic scholar-teachers, and make possible the institution of new courses and programs that do not automatically fit into the compartmentalized structure of conventional departmental organization.

THE CENTER FOR HELLENIC STUDIES OF HARVARD UNIVERSITY IN WASHINGTON, D.C.

Some years ago, Harvard University was left a large piece of land immediately adjacent to the Dumbarton Oaks estate, with the stipulation that this must be used for the establishment of a center devoted to the promotion of Hellenic studies. The amount of money needed to build the buildings and to endow the operation of the center was approximately $5 million. President Pusey and the trustees for Harvard University (as the Harvard Corporation is known in Washington) took up the challenge to find this money, in the firm conviction that it was highly important for our own age to deepen its understanding of Hellenic culture, from which our culture in many significant respects has been derived. The Old Dominion Foundation, which has made numerous grants to the humanities, under the chairmanship of Paul Mellon turned a sympathetic ear to Mr. Pusey's proposal and in fact gave to Harvard the entire sum needed.

The center is now a reality. It is presided over by a director and a board of five senior fellows, each representing a department of classics of a major institution. Each year a group of junior fellows is appointed, younger classical scholars, usually eight in number, who may come from anywhere in the world. They receive an adequate stipend plus free living quarters for the year of their incumbency and devote their time uninterruptedly to a research project which will in turn enrich their teaching when they return to their own institutions. The buildings at the center consist of a home for the director, a main building containing a library, offices for the junior fellows, common rooms, and a dining room, plus five comfortable houses for married fellows and a small apartment house for those who are not married. Publications are beginning to emerge. The center will doubtless come to exert a profound influence on the Hellenists of the future.

The gift of the Old Dominion Foundation is notable, for in these days of expanding knowledge and the opening up of new fields, important as they are, it has become increasingly difficult in the humanities to find support for the time-honored conventional subjects. These in their way without doubt provide men with most significant insights as they struggle to understand the reality in which they live.

The four "cases" which have been described illustrate in their several ways how foundations have vitally aided the course of the humanities when *no other source of support* was available. The cases of the ACLS and the Wilson Fellowship Program involved operations national in scope which in a sense served the foundations as effective intermediaries in the wise disbursal of their funds. The Council of the Humanities at Princeton is an instance which shows how a foundation or foundations can assist a single institution in its effort to enhance its own educational endeavors. And finally the establishment of the Center for Hellenic Studies indicates how a foundation can support a fundamental subject where there is acute need. As someone has observed, not often in recent years has anyone given $5,000,000 to Greek studies.

Of course, there have been many other foundation grants in support of the humanities. Beyond doubt such grants in the national and the world's interest should be proliferated. In recent years in the humanities one may note numbers of gifts for the study of linguistics or of exotic languages. These are surely important, and foundations, with their limited resources (and this is true of even the largest), must experiment and engage in "pump-priming." Yet in the humanities one might dare to hope that these great philanthropic agencies would be willing to turn their attention to those subjects or areas which form the heart of the humanities, that heart from which must spring the varied relationships with the other domains of knowledge. I have in mind history, philosophy, religion, art, and literature. But, no matter what the future may hold, all humanists must be cognizant of and grateful for the role which foundations have played in the development of this central and indispensable area in the lives of men everywhere.

CHAPTER 22

American Foundations and the Theatre

BROOKS ATKINSON

When the Rockefeller Foundation several years ago made a substantial grant to help Arena Stage build a theatre in Washington I took the liberty of writing a letter of thanks. It was none of my business. But I was grateful to the Rockefeller Foundation for recognizing the worth and the validity of the Arena Stage case. Dean Rusk, who was at the head of the foundation at that time, answered with a friendly rebuke. He said that the function of a foundation is to allocate money wisely and that gratitude was beside the point, since it implied that the foundation had done someone a personal favor.

The record proved that he was right. Several other foundations also concluded that Arena Stage was performing a valuable service that should not be terminated by the loss of its old theatre. Five years later Arena Stage is a flourishing organization that provides Washington with drama on a high cultural level, has a huge list of subscribers, and consistently attracts large audiences of discriminating theatregoers. If the foundations and many individual people had not assisted Arena Stage in building a permanent home, Washington today would be without the stimulus of a cultural influence that it deeply appreciates.

My comments on foundation support of the theatre derive from two personal assumptions: (1) the theatre as an institution stimulates the life of a community; (2) foundation support has been not only extremely valuable (in some instances indispensable); it is also much more desirable than government subsidy because foundations are in a position to make artistic judgments. They can eliminate all other considerations if they want to.

Since the purpose of the commercial theatre is to show a profit it can look after itself. Let's not forget that it is a valuable institution. Although most of the commercial theatre operates on a low cultural level it has also given us our greatest dramatists—O'Neill, Wilder, Williams, Miller, Inge, Hellman, Albee, and almost all the writers of first rank. Over the years the commercial theatre, located almost exclusively in New York, has not only made the most enterprising selection of plays but has also given them the most brilliant productions. The average is low but the achievements have been high.

But the resident theatres outside New York (and one or two like the Phoenix inside New York) perform a valuable cultural service the commercial theatre of New York cannot provide. It is interesting to note that the foundations have succeeded in identifying them. The best known are those that do the best professional work and by no accident get the most foundation support—Arena Stage in Washington; the Cleveland Playhouse, which is the oldest; the Alley Theatre in Houston; the Tyrone Guthrie Theatre in Minneapolis; The Mummers in Oklahoma City; the Actors Studio; Joe Papp's free Shakespeare in New York; Jack Houseman's theatre group at the University of California at Los Angeles; and Fred Miller's theatre in Milwaukee. Since the directors of the Actors Workshop in San Francisco have come to New York to operate the Lincoln Center repertory theatre, the status of the Workshop is unsettled. There are probably other resident theatres around the country that deserve support, or at least more support than they are getting. But it seems to me that the foundations have succeeded in discovering those on the highest professional level, and have helped to raise their artistic standards.

They are not "art" theatres. They do not cultivate a coterie. But their taste is so well informed that their patrons get a more rounded cultural experience than the theatregoers of Broadway. They do not put on many new plays, as Broadway does. They produce classics and good plays that cannot be really described as classics, and they also restage plays that have recently been performed on Broadway. Occasionally, they succeed with these plays better than Broadway has, since their audiences are in some respects less rigid. Although Broadway has access to the finest talent in the theatre, the resident theatres often do brilliant work, and most of it is intelligent, enjoyable, and professional.

Since these theatres are managed by members of the community, their relation to audiences is personal; and since the box office tariff is comparatively modest, theatregoing can be more casual and frequent. During the quarter of a century when the commercial theatre has been shrinking, the resident theatres have become established institutions that stimulate the thought and imagination of their communities. For it seems to me that a city unfamiliar with Shakespeare, Shaw, Ibsen, Wilde, Kaufman, Hart, and the best of the contemporary writers is a desolate community. It is socially moribund. The cities that have flourishing local theatres are vital communities. As a businessman in the Middle West once remarked when he found out that his theatreless city was not attracting professional people: "It don't no longer pay to be dumb."

What is a theatre? Two planks and a passion, some iconoclast has said. Alfred Lunt says: "All you need are actors and an audience." Lunt on the stage would be the equivalent of Mark Hopkins on a log. Everything that is vital to theatre occurs on the stage, and that is the element that needs support by foundations. But, excepting a few special instances, like the Delacorte Theatre in New York's Central Park for summer Shakespeare, stages do have to be enclosed within walls and sheltered by a roof. That leads to the question of buildings. If it were not for foundations it would be impossible for nonprofit institutions to build theatres—like the imposing series of buildings at the Lincoln Center for the Performing Arts, the inviting Tyrone Guthrie Theatre, the brilliant little theatre plant where Arena Stage flourishes, and the attractive new building that at long last Nina Vance will have in Houston. Foundations will supply a large part of the financing for the John F. Kennedy Center for the Performing Arts in Washington.

Since buildings are tangible and can be visualized from blueprints they give foundations and individual philanthropists a feeling of confidence. The design and construction of buildings can be controlled. Donors can see what they are doing and the building becomes a permanent memorial to their taste and generosity. But theatres need something more seminal than plants. In *The Performing Arts,* the illuminating report recently published by the Rockefeller Brothers Fund, the committee makes one especially shrewd comment on foundation giving. The traditional inclination of foundations, it says, is "to support research and training rather than performance. . . . Even bricks-and-mortar grants are often justified on the ground that they provide needed facilities for training and research. But the very essence of the performing arts requires that they be viewed in another framework. A play, a piece of music, or the outline of a ballet has only a partial existence on paper. Performance before a live audience is itself part of the process of realizing a work of art. This unique characteristic of the performing arts is not widely understood as yet by philanthropic sources."

And this is the area that presents problems. In order not to waste money on futile enterprises and incompetent people, foundations have to make artistic decisions in advance of the event— namely, the performance; and they have to be willing to accept failure, as all theatres must—artistic failure as well as financial. For both kinds of failure are the common experience of the theatre, and are necessary if progress is to be made. The original production of O'Neill's *The Iceman Cometh* failed. The play was a colossal success when it was restaged a decade later. Even the commercial theatre is not a sound business. In the theatre, success is a happy accident.

Foundations like to succeed in their own field; they like to spend money in ways that augment their prestige. And in order to retain a certain flexibility most of them are reluctant to subsidize theatre performances on a continuing basis. They do not want to yield control to the beneficiary. But subsidizing performance is the most essential service a foundation can give a theatre. What the audience sees is the true genius of the theatre and it is the thing that enriches a community. The theatre building is the container. The play is the product.

Since performances are the most difficult thing to understand and evaluate I am always impressed by the grants made to the working part of the theatre. On the whole, it seems to me that the grants in this field have been intelligent. The word "subsidy" has distasteful overtones to many people; it implies endless dependence on the part of idlers. But continuing subsidy over a long period of time can widen the scope and raise the quality of performances, to say nothing of helping to pay the actors something like what they deserve. The versatile Humanities and Arts branch of the Ford Foundation is subsidizing several talented theatre operations, although the management prefers to classify its programs for specific objectives.

During the past decade or more, a significant body of opinion has been favoring government support of the arts, including the theatre. America has found itself in an ignominious position in international exchanges of art, since we have no national theatre like the Moscow Art or the Comédie Française. If it were not for the generosity of foundations and many private philanthropists we would not have been able to send abroad several interesting theatre productions—notably *Porgy and Bess*—that have given some notion of our theatrical culture abroad. To put the case on its lowest level, it would certainly be convenient if our government could send theatrical companies abroad as easily as Russia and France send us their best. Sol Hurok's contributions in this field as a manager and a public-spirited citizen should not be overlooked.

During recent years government support of the arts has begun to acquire political prestige. It can confer votes as well as kudos on politicians who promote it. But I remain among the skeptics here. If Congress appropriates money for the arts it will, quite rightly, influence or control them, and the judgments Congress makes will not be exclusively artistic. Foundations are better equipped to help the theatre, for they are represented by officers whose training and experience make artistic judgments a normal procedure.

Granted the bias of some foundations, I should imagine that the consensus of foundation points of view would be enlightened and wholesome. Most of the foundations would not be startled by reckless ideas and bizarre styles of production. If the theatre is not in advance of public taste it is a declining institution. Foundations can be more generous in their support of the theatre than the government. The Ford Foundation is already making larger grants to the theatre than any now foreseen by supporters of government subsidy. On the basis of what the foundations have already achieved in the theatre, I put my confidence in their taste and their hands.

CHAPTER 23

Philanthropic Foundations
and the Dance

ANATOLE CHUJOY

It is quite clear to people in the dance field that the professional dance in the United States—ballet and modern—could not have developed as it has during the past decade without assistance from private foundations. Most people, including many in the dance field, seem to be of the impression that foundation support of dance began with the Ford Foundation's generous program of $7,756,000, announced in December, 1963, to begin in 1964. That was and still is the most ambitious program ever conceived for dance, and, as said, it was a most generous one. The grant was also the most potent catalyst imaginable for the subsequent support of dance by foundations, and by state and municipal institutions.

But it was not the first philanthropic aid in this field. Credit for that must go to the Rockefeller Foundation, which made grants of $368,400 to dance organizations between 1953 and 1959.

Of the aid appropriated by the Rockefeller Foundation between 1953 and 1959, $151,250 went to the New York City Ballet through a grant to the New York City Center; $73,400 to the Connecticut College School of Dance and the American Dance Festival (modern dance) at New London; $37,500 to the Dance Collection of the New York Public Library for cataloguing and indexing the material in the collection; $35,000 to the Dance Notation Bureau for further development of Labanotation; $5,000 to Jacob's Pillow Scholarship Fund; $26,250 to National Ballet Guild of Canada for new productions by the National Ballet of Canada; $25,000 to San Francisco Ballet for new productions by the San Francisco Ballet; $15,000 to two writers for books on dance.

And prior to its large commitment in December, 1963, the Ford Foundation had granted $150,000 in 1959 for a three-year program to provide talented young dancers with advanced training at the School of American Ballet, the official school of the New York City Ballet, and at the school of the San Francisco Ballet. This grant also provided subsequent opportunity for the young dancers to perform with the corps de ballet of the New York City Ballet and the San Francisco Ballet.

I will return presently to a consideration of the large Ford grant of 1963, but before that, mention should be made of the support which other private foundations have given to activities in the field of the dance.

The Bethsabee de Rothschild Foundation began its activity in the dance with the sponsorship in 1953 of a two-week engagement of The American Dance Company on Broadway, in which six modern dance companies participated. In the spring and summer of 1954 that foundation underwrote a European tour of the Martha Graham Dance Company; in the winter of 1954-55 contributed toward the establishment of the Juilliard Dance Theatre, directed by the late Doris Humphrey; and in the spring of 1955 sponsored another Broadway engagement of The American Dance Company, this time for three weeks. Six modern dance companies and six solo dancers participated, the greatest assemblage up to that time of modern dancers and choreographers on one stage. Since that year the Rothschild Foundation has contributed to the support of the Martha Graham Dance Company's performances in New York, and has sponsored some of its foreign tours, furthered the production of new works, and helped to sustain the Martha Graham School of Contemporary Dance. It has also made possible the film production of *Night Journey,* Miss Graham's work based on the legend of Jocasta and Oedipus, a motion picture that won film festival awards in the U.S. as well as in Berlin, Edinburgh, and Venice. This relatively small foundation is a private activity of Bethsabee de Rothschild; its objective is to help the dancer reach a wider audience than he otherwise could.

The newest foundation active in dance is the Rebekah Harkness Foundation. The stated function of this foundation, under its president, Mrs. Rebekah Harkness, is to promote American cultural achievement and to foster recognition of such achievement throughout the world. Its first activity in dance was the sponsorship in June, 1961, of a three-month European tour of the Jerome Robbins' Ballets: U.S.A., and a three-week Broadway engagement of the company on its return from Europe.

In 1962 the Harkness Foundation sponsored the African tour of the Pearl Primus Dance Troupe, and in the summer of that year a twelve-week rehearsal and workshop period of the Robert Joffrey Ballet at Mrs. Harkness's estate at Watch Hill, in Rhode Island. A foundation grant later that summer made possible a six-day dance festival at the Delacorte (Shakespeare, open-air) Theatre, in Central Park, New York City. The American Ballet Theatre, the José Limón company, and the Alvin Ailey company participated, and the performances were free to the public. The festival was repeated with different performing groups in September, 1963, 1964, and 1965.

In 1962 and 1963 the Harkness Foundation sponsored two foreign tours of the Robert Joffrey Ballet in the Middle and Far East and in the Soviet Union, both in cooperation with the Cultural Exchange Program of the U.S. Department of State. In the spring of 1964, the relations between the Robert Joffrey company and the foundation were severed, and the Rebekah Harkness Foundation, in association with the William Hale Harkness Foundation (named after Mrs. Harkness's late husband), announced the formation of a ballet company, the Harkness Ballet. The company spent the summers of 1964 and 1965 rehearsing at Watch Hill, and had a European tour, February to May, 1965, and a U.S. tour in October-November, 1965.

Although Jerome Robbins' Ballets: U.S.A. has been the beneficiary of the Harkness Foundation, Jerome Robbins himself is the head of the Lena Robbins Foundation, which he established in 1958 and named in memory of his mother. Much as is the case with the Bethsabee de Rothschild Foundation, it is a personal activity of its head. Again, it is a small foundation, but it performs a function which a large foundation would be less likely to undertake: it assists individual young choreographers in bringing their work to the attention of the public, involving a matter of a thousand dollars, more or less, in each case—a modest amount, but without it a young choreographer would not be able to present his work. Among American choreographers who have benefited from the Lena Robbins Foundation's grants during the past few years are Anna Sokolow, Talley Beatty, Yuriko Kikuchi, Pearl Lang, Katherine Litz, and Paul Taylor.

A foundation which is very active in many areas of the arts, although less so in dance, is the Guggenheim Foundation. Its grants in dance are smaller than the dance field would hope. Among recent beneficiaries were Merce Cunningham (1954 and 1959), Pearl Lang (1960), Paul Taylor (1961-62), all for choreography. The late Doris Humphrey received a grant to write a book (*The Art of Making Dances*) on choreography.

Among the foundations whose support goes to specific organizations are the Ballet Foundation, a nonprofit organization founded in 1939 for the stated purpose of promoting ballet as a nationwide cultural movement. It is the sponsoring organization of Ballet Russe de Monte Carlo, a performing organization, now dormant. Similarly, the Ballet Theatre Foundation was established in 1947 as a nonprofit corporation for the purpose of supporting Ballet Theatre (now American Ballet Theatre) as a performing unit.

On November 25-26, 1960, Ballet Society, the parent organization of the New York City Ballet, staged a conference on the subject "Ballet—A National Movement." The organizers hopefully referred to the conference as the First National Conference; regrettably, a second has not yet been called. Among the speakers at the conference were representatives of two great foundations: for the Rockefeller, Dr. Charles B. Fahs; and for the Ford Foundation, W. McNeil Lowry.

Dr. Fahs explained that the Rockfeller Foundation's program in the arts had not been initiated until 1953, although the general program in the humanities, of which the arts are a part, was of older origin. With a total budget for the humanities, at that time, of the order of three million dollars a year, and with all fields of the humanities and all of the world to consider, it was clear that the Rockefeller Foundation could not undertake long-term support of any organization in the performing arts, but could only hope to give temporary and limited support which might enable one or another organization in the arts to develop to a new level of activity or competence, following which its continuing support would come from the public or from other sources in our society.

Indeed it is clear, Dr. Fahs said, that dance, like all art forms, needs a variety of sources of support. It is important in this country to develop greater support of the arts from the audience, as well as to get patronage—individual, social, business, and foundation—in local communities. It is also important to find ways in which the governments—municipal, state, or federal—can help build a better base for the arts. Each time that a local group develops its own resources in this manner, each time it increases the interest of the audience, and each time it enlists the interest of new patrons—each time it does any of these things, it helps build a broader base for the arts in the United States.

The activity of the Rockefeller Foundation in the dance was minimal for a time, owing primarily to a period of personnel change and program review, although there was a grant of $10,000 in 1960 to the University of Honolulu, to prepare a documentary film on classical Hawaiian dance; another of the same size to the University of Utah in 1961, to enable choreographers to participate in the dance program by Virginia Tanner; and a smaller one in 1962 to the University of California for research on the Oriental dance. In 1964 a grant of $15,000 was made to the University of Utah, to support their modern dance program, and in 1965 one of $10,200 to Connecticut College School of Dance.

However, the President's Review of the Rockfeller Foundation for 1964 states:

> During 1964, the Foundation focused its support on drama and music, and made a modest beginning in creative writing. The establishment of a program in the arts, under the direction of Norman Lloyd, formerly dean of the Oberlin College Conservatory of Music, is likely to result over the next years in expanded efforts in the

whole field of cultural development. Officers in the new program, in close collaboration with the Foundation's humanities and social sciences program, will draw on the advice of distinguished consultants who represent a wide range of creative, teaching and critical experience.

Norman Lloyd is a well-known pianist, conductor, and composer in the modern dance field. He has to his credit compositions for Martha Graham, Doris Humphrey, Hanya Holm, Charles Weidman, José Limón and several others. It is possible to speculate that the Rockefeller Foundation may find a way to make a grant to some group in the modern dance before long.

At the 1960 Conference on the Ballet W. McNeil Lowry (at that time director of the Program in Humanities and the Arts in the Ford Foundation, and now vice president for policy and planning with general administrative supervision of the Humanities and the Arts Program) stated that the Ford Foundation began its program in the arts in 1957; and said, "For the Ford Foundation, the decision in 1957 to spend two or three million dollars a year on creative artists and artistic experiments was less significant than its decision to permit a full-scale national inquiry of the economic and social positions of the arts at this point of American history, and to do so with artists and artistic directors as full participants."

"Nothing finally would be done for the arts in enlightened patronage," said Mr. Lowry, "until it is done for the art itself and not simply as icing on the cake. If art is left to be icing on the cake, it will be treated by people in power and people with influence and people with money as icing on the cake."

As is true of the budget of the Rockefeller Foundation for the arts, the budget of the Ford Foundation for the arts is a small percentage of the foundation's total budget. For the duration of the exploratory work with which the program in the arts of the Ford Foundation began, the board of trustees indicated that it would not be their policy to furnish any direct financing of any institution, organization, or association in the arts, or more generally in the humanities.

Lowry expressed the opinion, in his 1960 statement, that should the program in the arts be substantially increased in years to come it would still be mostly on a matching basis with institutions or communities. But it would not take care of deficit financing *per se*. However, in 1962 the flat prohibition of deficit financing was somewhat liberalized by limiting the prohibition to continuous deficit financing. The foundation accepted the fact that any direct support is in fact deficit financing; an organization needs financial support because it is operating at a deficit.

If Lowry knew in 1960 that he would succeed three years later in persuading the board of trustees to grant $7,756,000 "to strengthen professional ballet in the United States," he did not permit himself even the slightest hint in his talk at the conference. As a matter of fact, those who heard Lowry's speech, including this writer, were rather depressed by the lack of any sanguine expectation. However that may be, on December 16, 1963, the Ford Foundation did announce the largest one-time grant to ballet in the United States, and probably anywhere else, from any source—private, corporate, institutional, or governmental. The grant was allocated as follows:

$1,500,000 to the School of American Ballet to improve instruction and performance in local communities.

$2,425,000 to the School of American Ballet over the following ten years to strengthen it as a national ballet-training institution.

$2,000,000 to the New York City Ballet over a ten-year period; additional funds guaranteed by the City Center of Music and Drama being expected to total $1,775,000 over the same period.

$644,000 to the San Francisco Ballet over ten years, to be matched by $250,000 in new funds and a commitment by the San Francisco Ballet Guild to maintain the existing level of its contributions to the company's performing program.

$400,000 to the National Ballet, Washington, D.C., to be matched by $550,000 of other contributions over a five-year period.

$295,000 to the Pennsylvania Ballet, Philadelphia: $45,000 in assistance to the 1963–64 training and performance activities, and $250,000 to be matched by $500,000 from other contributions over a ten-year period.

$175,000 to the Utah Ballet, Salt Lake City, to be matched over a five-year period by contributions of $100,000.

$173,750 to the Houston Ballet to be matched equally by local contributions over a five-year period, the grant to go largely toward the group's training activities.

$144,000 to the Boston Ballet to assist in the development of a per-
manent professional company with four new productions in each
of the next three seasons.

The announcement of these grants evoked a lively controversy
in the dance field. Most of the opinions expressed by writers on
dance in the New York dailies and in two of the three dance publications, as well as in numerous letters to the editors of the *New
York Times* and the New York *Herald Tribune*, were critical of
the distribution of the grants. Some accused the Ford Foundation
of disregarding the modern dance, "the indigenous American dance
form"; others complained of a "collusion" between the Ford Foundation and the School of American Ballet, Ballet Society, and the
New York City Ballet—the three organizations headed by Lincoln
Kirstein and George Balanchine.

The accusation of disregarding the modern dance had no
justification, inasmuch as the foundation specifically announced
that the purpose of the grant was "to strengthen professional ballet
in the United States." This certainly did not imply disinterest in
the modern dance. It only meant that at the time the Ford Foundation had decided to do something for ballet. The complaint of
"collusion" was the result of lack of definite information by the
complainants about the research and other work of the Ford
Foundation leading to the awarding of grants to these recipients
and not to others in addition to, or in replacement of, the present
awards.

Two of the three ballet companies who applied for grants were
not eligible owing to their business structure; they were not in the
category of non-profit-making organizations, the only category to
which a foundation may award grants. The third applicant could
not furnish a proper statement of its affairs, an acceptable plan of
operation, an indication of how the funds would be expended, etc.

That these were the real reasons for not awarding any grants
to other ballet companies was proved, if proof was needed, by the
fact that on November 24, 1964, as soon as the Robert Joffrey
Ballet re-formed into a nonprofit organization, the Ford Foundation gave it a grant of $155,000.

Some ten days later, December 3, 1964, the Ford Foundation
announced another grant in the dance area: $72,000 to the Dance

Collection of the New York Public Library, for developing and employing computer techniques in connection with the production of a catalogue of the collection.

The funds appropriated by the Ford Foundation toward the performance activities of the beneficiaries have already borne fruit. Thus, the New York City Ballet was able to sign a basic agreement with the American Guild of Musical Artists (AGMA), the dancers' union, in the fall of 1964, offering the dancers compensation for fifty-two weeks, including rehearsals, lay-off weeks, and vacations. The Pennsylvania Ballet of Philadelphia succeeded in establishing a subscription series of performances in the fall of 1964, and in having additional series in the winter and spring. The Boston Ballet introduced its first season in January, 1965. The National Ballet of Washington gave performances in Washington, D.C., and had brief tours. The San Francisco Ballet and the Utah Ballet have not as yet reported any additional activity owing to the grants received. The grant to the Houston Ballet went largely toward the company's training activities.

Perhaps because performances are generally of greater interest to the public than instruction, many people in the dance community were not aware that the major part of the 1963 $7,756,000 grant ($4,098,750) went toward improving ballet *instruction* and a rather complex system of group and individual scholarships on a local, regional, and national basis.

The Ford Foundation's 1963 grants for ballet instruction dovetailed with its 1959 grant, thus making possible the continuation of the program, with some changes, practically without interruption.

The important question now, and the question will grow in importance as the Ford Foundation scholarship plan continues, is what will we do with so many good dancers and so few possibilities of employment? Lowry was aware of this problem. In the official release of the details of the 1963 grants, he wrote: "Although mounting interest of new audiences for ballet as an American dance form is apparent, two great and almost universal problems are also clear. The standards of instruction are dangerously low. And those young dancers who are fortunate enough to receive thorough training at some stage in their careers often cannot be assimilated into the few companies having any sort of artistic and financial stability."

Semiprofessional and even professional companies outside New York can absorb only a small number of dancers, mostly from their own localities, and employ guest artists to attract a public. But will many of these dancers ever be able to make a living while remaining in their cities? The answer, unfortunately, is negative.

The often-heard talk about the great strides the ballet has made in the United States, the tremendous growth of the ballet public, etc. applies mostly to the glamorous visiting companies: the Royal Ballet, the Royal Danish Ballet, the Bolshoi, the Kirov, and occasionally to the New York City Ballet. We have only one resident ballet company in New York, the New York City Ballet, and one national company, the American Ballet Theatre, the latter of which had a brilliant four-week twenty-fifth-anniversary season at the New York State Theater, March 16 to April 11, 1965, but which, during some years prior to that, appeared in New York only sporadically and occasionally missed a touring season as well.

The few large foundations which have done well in assisting dance as a performing art have before them a problem they have not yet attempted to solve. The problem is the necessary stimulus to growth of the U.S. dance public. It is perhaps a truism that theatrical dance does not exist without an audience, but it does bear repeating, for even people in the dance community forget it once in a while. The talk about "culture explosion" and similar easy catch phrases are only that; they are little more than lip service to an art form which cannot long survive—no matter how many good dancers, talented choreographers, and properly trained teachers we produce—without the active and ever-growing interest of the public, an interest which should manifest itself in the purchase of tickets to dance performances, books on dance, records, subscriptions to dance publications.

The problem, nationwide, of creating new audiences for dance, both young and mature, is so great that its solution should become a function of a great foundation. It isn't that nothing is being done in this respect at present. There is appreciable activity in this field, but it is all local, often haphazard, casual, and nearly always empirical. It should come as no surprise that most of the activity in this field is centered in New York, city and state. John Guttman, assistant general manager of the Metropolitan Opera, has initiated free performances and lecture-demonstrations of the Metropolitan

326 / *U.S. Philanthropic Foundations*

Opera Ballet, directed by Dame Alicia Markova, in the city's high schools and on occasion at Town Hall for students assembled from several schools. Ballet Society in collaboration with the New York City Ballet has been offering free lecture-demonstrations by the company's outstanding dancers in New York high schools, usually attended by the entire student body. The New York State Council on the Arts has supported performances of the New York City Ballet, the American Ballet Theatre and several modern dance companies, all at minimum admission prices, and has presented free lecture-demonstrations throughout the state. As mentioned earlier in this chapter, the Rebekah Harkness Foundation sponsored in the summers of 1962, 1963, 1964, and 1965 free series of six performances each at the Delacorte (Shakespeare, open air) Theatre in Central Park, New York City.

For the season 1965-66 the Lincoln Center Student Program offered performances of the New York City Ballet and Juilliard Artists in schools at a very low cost to the schools. The New York City Ballet, on its own, is offering lecture-performances on the stage of the New York State Theater, the company's home, for student groups during regular school hours. These programs are designed to show students the principle of dance through examples presented in the atmosphere of the theatre. Other educational services of the company include photographs for school exhibitions, printed material on dance, and a ballet film entitled *Watching Ballet*.

In neighboring New Jersey, Fred Danieli and his Garden State Ballet, a regional (civic) company with headquarters in Newark, have been doing pioneering work in introducing ballet to thousands of students in schools in the area, in collaboration with the board of education. And most of the more than one hundred active civic ballets have been doing their bit toward increasing the interest in ballet in their regions. But what they have done and are doing and how effective their efforts are or have been is not known; also not known is the result of the manifold, occasionally duplicative, and very often overlapping activities of the organizations in and around New York.

In view of this, it would seem that the initial activity of a large foundation would be to institute a thorough investigation of what is being done in the country, mainly by civic and regional, i.e., nonprofessional and semiprofessional, companies, or their sponsoring bodies, by some of the state and municipal councils on the arts, or whatever other titles they bear; and what have been or are the palpable, measurable results.

A subsequent analysis of the methods used and results achieved would offer an indication of whether a nationwide approach to the solution of the problem of creating a large dance audience is feasible, and if so, what the most effective method of solving the problem would be; or, if a nationwide approach is not feasible, how the regional or local activities should be conducted.

In summary, dance owes a great deal to a number of philanthropic foundations. The small and rather personalized foundations interested in dance are likely to be well informed and have strong and definite likes and dislikes. They are also likely to have erudite, volunteer advice from people sharing the taste of the heads of the foundations. These foundations act rather like the wealthy patrons of former times, and quite naturally support what appeals to them.

It is, however, also very important that a few large foundations should make use of really competent and experienced persons as consultants.

An example of less than careful selection of advisory and in this case writing personnel is the recently published book *The Performing Arts: Problems and Prospects* (the Rockefeller panel report on the future of theatre, dance, music in America). The chapter on "The Performing Arts—Today and Tomorrow" contains a section on dance which begins as follows:

> From the standpoint of finance, administration, and organization, the dance world is close to chaos. There is only one theatre devoted exclusively to the dance—at Jacob's Pillow in Massachusetts, which is open only three months a year. At the moment not more than five or six dance companies can claim both a national reputation and a relatively stable institutional setup capable of surviving a crisis. . . .

The writer of the above paragraph completely missed the importance of the Ted Shawn Theatre at Jacob's Pillow. The theatre was especially designed as a summer theatre by Joseph Franz, the architect who had previously designed the orchestra shell at Tanglewood for the Berkshire Music Festival. It is the only theatre devoted exclusively to dance in the United States as well as in Europe, and the Jacob's Pillow Dance Festival, now in its 33rd year (the 24th in this theatre), is the longest dance festival anywhere in the world.

The judgments as to which are the five or six companies with national reputations and which "can claim a relatively stable institutional setup capable of surviving a crisis" are neither explicit nor clear. Nor are they made more impressive when one examines the "Papers Prepared for the Study." Here one finds only two papers relating to the dance, and although I have been active in the dance field since 1936, I have never heard of the experts who prepared these studies.

CHAPTER 24

Foundations and Serious Music

DONALD L. ENGLE

The field of music is a relatively new interest for foundations. Although some have been promoting cultural activities in this country and abroad for more than three decades, only within the last ten years or so have philanthropies begun to show much concern for the musical arts.

Some of this apparent increase in interest can be attributed to better reporting, but much is also directly related to the recent and rather sudden national awareness of the performing arts generally. The personal and overt interest of President and Mrs. John F. Kennedy and their "official family," the impressive new cultural complexes for the performing arts now in planning or under construction in more than thirty cities, and the passing of legislation which for the first time will make federal funds available directly to a wide variety of artistic endeavors are among the many manifestations of awareness which have been as obvious to foundation officials as to the general public.

In a less dramatic but more direct way, the 1965 panel report by the Rockefeller Brothers Fund, *The Performing Arts: Problems and Prospects,* has helped focus attention on the needs which must be met if the performing arts are to fulfill their role in the nation's cultural development. A correlative but more detailed study of the economics of the performing arts, now in progress as a project of the Twentieth Century Fund, will make available much essential information for assessing and providing for the financial health of performing ensembles and their participants.

One indication of this increasing interest can be seen in the semiannual summaries of grants in music reported in *Foundation News,* the bulletin of the Foundation Library Center. In the first listing in September, 1960, there were eight grants reported under music; but in the March, 1965, issue there were fifty-three of $10,-000 or more included under the same heading. The latter figures, moreover, do not include any of the separately listed contributions to the building or operating programs of cultural centers, from which music will be an indirect but substantial beneficiary.

In looking through the grants announced in *Foundation News,* or referred to in other sources readily available, one notes that the spread of interest in the musical arts has been particularly marked among the smaller foundations. With the especially notable exception of the Ford Foundation, and to a lesser degree the Rockefeller and Avalon foundations, the large general purpose philanthropies have as yet not extended sustained support to the field of serious music, or to the performing arts generally.

In the past few years there have been a surprising and gratifying number of grants from personal, family, or corporate foundations to local symphony orchestras, opera companies, and music schools. Although their gifts may reflect more interest in civic welfare than in music *per se,* the very fact that such foundations are beginning to recognize the value of music in the community is encouraging and to their credit. Some of them, such as the Kulas Foundation in Cleveland and the Hartford Foundation for Public Giving, have extended aid to several musical organizations and educational institutions within their geographical areas, for both general support and special purposes. With the matching provisions stipulated in the grants of major foundations and the new federal legislation for aid to the arts, these community-oriented philanthropies may expect to be called upon increasingly to meet the requirements of leverage imposed or offered from outside resources. They are performing just the role recommended for them in the Rockefeller panel report: to provide the continuing support of local institutions, leaving to their larger national counterparts the demonstration projects which they may be called upon only indirectly to augment.

Among the major philanthropies, the Ford Foundation has come to occupy by far the dominant position. As part of a massive, long-range program of aid for the arts and humanities, begun in 1957, it has mounted an extensive series of experiments and pilot projects, intended "to aid talented individuals, strengthen the institutions which are their outlets, and develop musical resources at various levels through the nation." This broad program is being carried out through projects to aid both individuals and organizations, usually in blocks whereby a number of grants for a single purpose are made simultaneously.

Its most recent appropriation of $85 million for strengthening the position of the country's leading symphony orchestras has so far surpassed any previous consideration for the performing arts that the initial reaction of many orchestra boards must have been one of stunned but pleasurable disbelief. Actually the program was in the planning stage for several years; its coming on the heels of approval of federal aid was coincidental, and was in no sense an effort to outdo Uncle Sam. Taking into account the funds the orchestras must raise to match funds from the foundation, the action is expected to result in a total of $165 million in new support for symphonic development in the United States. Some fifty professional orchestras (those with annual budgets in excess of $100,-000) will be considered in the course of implementing the program. Amounts for each orchestra will range from $600,000 to $2.5 million, in a combination of outright grants and endowments to be matched over a period of several years.

In administering assistance to or for individuals, the Ford Foundation normally does not entertain applications directly, but relies on recommendations from professionals in the area under consideration. Grants have been made to aid groups of concert and opera singers, composers, choral directors, administrative interns, and other specialists such as editors, critics, and musical scholars. The foundation has also supported many institutional projects for developing individual professional skills and experience.

Major grants have also been made directly to a number of training and performing units for strengthening their position by extending periods of operation, employment, repertoire, facilities, curriculum, etc. The foundation has not hesitated to continue or extend the programs which have been successful; a few which were less so have at least suggested other approaches or answered questions of viability. In short, the impact of its participation has been felt in virtually every facet of the musical arts in this country, to a degree that, more than any other single force, has caused a most encouraging note in the national musical scene.

The Rockefeller Foundation has also been a prime mover in certain areas of music. A grant of $400,000 in 1953 to the Louisville Orchestra for a ten-year project for commissioning, performing, and recording new works was an early and bold step in support of contemporary music. To its credit, the Louisville Orchestra has continued the project since termination of the grant. Two important summer conductor institutes, under auspices of the American Symphony Orchestra League, were launched with another long-range grant at about the same time, and have also been continued through other means.

After a period of relative inactivity, the Rockefeller Foundation in 1964 announced it was establishing a program in the arts, which in the next years may be expected to result in expanded projects in music. Although a few grants have recently been made directly to profesional organizations, the 1964 annual report indicated that the foundation would deal primarily with educational institutions as the preferred channel for its interest in developing professional skills of young musicians, providing them with opportunities to perform, and collaborating with other community organizations.

Some major grants have already been made under this policy. The University of Chicago, through a five-year $250,000 grant, is establishing a Center for Music, whose program includes postgraduate composers and musicologists who are also instrumentalists. They will be the nucleus of a chamber group for rehearsing and performing new works. A gift of $200,000 made possible a Center for the Performing and Creative Arts at the State University of New York at Buffalo, with twenty annual grants to "creative associates" included in its diversified program. Reflecting its concern over the present state of symphonic music in the United States, the Rockefeller Foundation has begun what may extend to a four-year program, with disbursements of up to $500,000, through which selected symphony orchestras may extend their seasons with rehearsals and first performances of new works by young American composers in residence at neighboring educational institutions. In most instances the grants will be made to the universities rather than the orchestras, but they will still bring closer collaboration between town and gown.

Reference was made above to the Avalon Foundation, which in recent years has shown a broad interest in musical activities. Among its recipients have been such diverse groups as the American Opera Society, the Brevard Music Foundation, the Cantata Singers, the Santa Fe Opera, the Manhattan School of Music, and the City Center of Music and Drama. Several general purpose foundations have contributed to Young Audiences, Inc., a national organization through which concerts by small ensembles of local musicians are presented to school children in literally hundreds of communities. Others have shown interest in summer music camps and festivals, as has particularly the Kresge Foundation in the expansion of facilities at the National Music Camp and in the founding of the Meadow Brook Musical Festival at Michigan's new Oakland University.

Between the poles of the large and smaller general purpose philanthropies are a number of special purpose foundations, whose community of interest results from their common focus of interest. Some are substantial in size, with professional staffs. Many are making vital contributions in ways or areas their general purpose brethren have found impractical. As one might expect, they are inclined and equipped to maintain a continuing interest in certain musical activities or repertoire.

One characteristic of these special agencies is their ability to deal with individuals in response to direct applications. A rather popular objective is to help talented young persons toward a professional career, through study, performing experience, and sometimes living expenses to permit time for developing skills. Some foundations select their individual recipients through periodic competitions, with cash awards, study scholarships, and performance opportunities as prizes. The Edgar M. Leventritt Foundation, now in its twenty-fourth year of such contests, the Walter W. Naumberg Foundation, and the Kosciuszko Foundation with its Chopin competitions have each given artists a step up the ladder through recognition and financial awards.

Several foundations offer study grants directly to young musicians, usually after selective auditions, which are given less publicity than certain widely-announced competitions. The William Matheus Sullivan Musical Foundation, Inc., and the John Hay Whitney Foundation, through its opportunity fellowships, have been mainstays in this area. It is gratifying to note that several distinguished artists and musicians have announced or established foundations to assist a younger generation: Blanche Thebom, Marian Anderson, Lauritz Melchior, and Leonard Bernstein are some who come to mind.

In contrast to the several programs in which a limited number of prizes or scholarships are given periodically, the Martha Baird Rockefeller Fund for Music, Inc., averages about one hundred grants annually in a continuing program of assistance to young artists and other specialists on a noncompetitive basis. Grants are made according to individual need for a number of purposes related to advancing their careers, without firm limits on age or number of grants. The fund also extends assistance to individuals collectively through grants to performing, training, and professional service organizations.

Another area in which a few foundations have done a great service to the music profession is charitable aid for retired or unemployed musicians. The welfare programs of the Bagby Music Lovers Foundation, the Musicians' Foundation, the Musicians Emergency Fund, and the Presser Foundation have been particularly effective over a long period.

Though composers sometimes complain that performers receive more attention and support than they, a number of special purpose foundations are now directing at least a portion of their resources toward aiding creative talents in music. Aid is generally available in four forms: direct grants, peaceful retreats for concentrated work, awards and fellowships, and performance of new works by contemporary music groups. Commissions are indirectly a form of assistance, though they should preferably be regarded as payments for a product to be furnished on order.

Composers have long regarded the John Simon Guggenheim

Memorial Foundation grants as a great boon. Fellowships are awarded to about ten to fifteen composers annually, and also to two or three musical scholars or theorists. The Fromm Foundation has acquired a distinctive position in its support of contemporary music in various ways, including commissions, a performance laboratory at the Berkshire Music Center, and a periodic journal called *Perspectives in New Music*.

The Koussevitzky Music Foundation and the Elizabeth Sprague Coolidge Foundation have also done much to assist composers through commissions, as have others on an occasional basis. The Alice M. Ditson Fund of Columbia University follows a broad and sympathetic program for composers in sponsoring contemporary music concerts, recordings, and publications of new works, and forums for performance and discussion of new music. Until its regrettable closing recently, the hospitality of the Huntington Hartford Foundation's retreat near Los Angeles had been extended to several composers through its fellowships for fostering the creative arts. The Yaddo Foundation in New York State and the MacDowell Colony in New Hampshire have also extended a similar cordial welcome to composers among their creative guests.

A new turn in foundation support was initiated recently when Francis Thorne, a musician and composer himself, established The Thorne Music Fund for aiding composers. An initial grant of $10,500 to Ben Weber for a three-year period is expected to set a pattern for an annual award. The idea quite properly attracted considerable attention for its novelty and its charitable spirit toward fellow composers.

A few special purpose foundations have still other interests. The Coolidge Foundation, for example, has pioneered in encouraging interest in chamber music. Though their charters permit support of broad musical interests, the Mary Louise Curtis Bok Foundation and the Juilliard Musical Foundation are primarily concerned with maintenance of the Curtis Institute of Music and the Juilliard School of Music respectively. The Presser Foundation no longer provides communities with auditoriums as Theodore Presser's beneficence did for many years, but grants are made for facilities and other purposes to promote music education. The Kathryn Long Trust, originally created to foster interest in grand opera in the

United States, places its funds at the disposal of the Metropolitan Opera Association for training promising artists.

Any comment on foundations and music, however brief, should not omit reference to a unique type of corporate support, the Music Performance Trust Fund, created in 1949 as part of the settlement in a protracted strike by the American Federation of Musicians against the recording industry. Through payments from recording companies of 1 to 1.5 percent of the total dollar volume of record sales at "suggested retail price" levels, the trust fund has disbursed more than $5 million annually in recent years for free concerts in all parts of the country. Beginning in 1964, the receipts are being divided equally between free concerts and payments to the musicians who played the original recordings.

Impressive as is this increasing interest by foundations generally, support for musicians and musical organizations, on the basis of the incomplete information available, has been estimated at about one percent of total annual foundation giving. (The mammoth appropriation of the Ford Foundation for symphony orchestras of course completely upsets the statistics for 1965). There has thus been some justification for the perplexed queries by musicians about the vast sums available in other fields and the minuscule consideration given their circumstances.

Actually there are several reasons for this apparent unconcern which representatives for artistic endeavors have either not recognized or have not attempted to change. Many foundations, having long experience at dealing with the needs of the mind through education and the body through welfare and charitable projects, have simply not broadened their outlook to consider ministering to the spirit through the arts. Many do not have staff help capable of screening or evaluating the requests of artists or arts organizations. Many reflect the interest or preferences of patrons who apparently find no satisfaction in backing artistic endeavors.

Furthermore, it has been pointed out that in the view of a general purpose foundation, musical organizations are rather fragile entities compared with welfare and educational enterprises. They seldom own property, they depend to a great extent on volunteer help, they involve amateur and professional personnel in an often bewildering mixture, and except for the largest units they are seasonal. Musicians and composers as individuals also seem to be considered more dubious risks for aid than their counterparts in other professions or the sciences, possibly because the nature of artistic and musical talent has been less well understood or its supposed quixotic characteristics are more exaggerated.

Whatever the reasons for lack of more joint understanding heretofore, it is apparent that only through better understanding of objectives and methods of operation on each side can music, and the performing arts generally, receive philanthropic aid in amounts proportionate to an increasing importance in the nation's social fabric.

These and other difficulties of communication and understanding between patrons and petitioners can and will be overcome. With the tremendous government support now available in their traditional areas of education and welfare, foundations have both an opportunity and an inducement to give more attention to music and its sister performing arts. One observer has even noted that the arts are becoming a status symbol for foundation patronage. This may be a motive for some of the grants to cultural centers now arising across the country; even more important is the next step, to support the activities taking place within them, and to back the artistic and administrative leadership on which their value depends.

CHAPTER 25

Foundation Philanthropy
and the Visual Arts

RICHARD MCLANATHAN

Foundations provide less than 10 percent of all philanthropy. Yet this percentage is no index of the importance of foundation giving, not only because of the frequent policy that grants depend upon matching funds (which effectively multiplies the foundation's grant by a factor of two or more), but also because of the leadership demonstrated in the selection of projects for foundation support. Through recent decades, major foundations have thus made contributions far beyond the actual size of their grants, though these have in a number of cases been very large, particularly in welfare, health, and education.

But, despite several individual programs of great value, foundations have, in general, been as slow in assistance to the arts as have been other elements of the community. There is reason for optimism, however, in the sudden recognition of the difficult situation of the performing arts, analyzed in the recent Rockefeller panel report, *The Performing Arts: Problems and Prospects*. With the giant strides taken at Lincoln Center, which concentrates on the performing arts, and with the mushroom growth of art centers across the country and the development of promoting and supporting agencies, such as art councils, an increasing number of which receive foundation assistance, there is now hope that a wider en-

338

joyment of the arts throughout the nation may be approaching realization.

Though the visual arts have shared in the tremendous recent increase in interest in the arts in general, only a very small percentage of American painters and sculptors derive even the major part of their living expenses from the practice of their art, contrary to the impression one might gain from the spectacular successes of a much-discussed few. And, in spite of the bullish tendencies of the art market, the average income from sales is negligible. Since the percentage of the nation's citizens today designated as "artists" is larger than it has ever been before, questions might be raised regarding sheer quantity as well as standards of quality. But American artists are generally recognized as leaders in the world of art, and such a position has not been won without powerful abilities, whatever one's opinion may be about the forms in which those creative powers are expressed.

At a recent national conference of the Arts Councils of America and the American Symphony Orchestra League, Governor Rockefeller, whose pioneering statesmanship in founding the New York State Council on the Arts has led government into taking the first steps into the field of culture, remarked that he "felt that the public was way ahead of the politicians." It might also be said that the public is ahead of the major foundations, which allocate less than one percent of their grants to the visual arts. The second largest of them gave no support whatsoever to the visual arts in 1963, out of a year's expenditure of some $30 million. With the stipulation that one percent of the budgeted cost of new construction in the Philadelphia area go to painting, sculpture, or other artistic embellishment of the resulting buildings, the politicians are definitely out ahead of the foundations. But under the circumstances theirs is a cheap victory. What is needed in the terms of the Rockefeller panel report is for foundations "to increase their interest in the arts and in so doing to recognize the necessarily speculative element . . . and give particular encouragement to the bold and the venturesome." The report goes on to state that this is "an encouragement they are especially equipped to provide," though there has been a disappointing lack of evidence of their fulfillment of this function in the case of the arts. In medicine and

340 / *U.S. Philanthropic Foundations*

science, needs are more obvious, and there are recognized standards of judgment that seem more susceptible of objective analysis, so that in those areas a consensus of expert opinion and public approval is more easily achieved.

There have, however, been important exceptions to the general disregard by major foundations of the visual arts. The Carnegie Corporation and the Ford Foundation have performed pioneering functions in programs whose importance bears little relation to the size of the comparatively small grants involved. The Carnegie program of a number of years ago, which supplied sets of art books and slides to libraries and colleges, was of widespread influence in calling attention to and giving information about the arts in communities lacking adequate cultural resources; and the corporation's grants for tuition and scholarship to selected art schools show a continuing concern with the broadening of opportunity. The more recent gifts by the Kress Foundation of works of art to museums across the country has done much to arouse a public interest in the visual arts, even though the artistic importance of these works has sometimes been overestimated.

The Ford Foundation's program of circulating well-catalogued, one-man shows of the work of leading artists who deserve but who have not received such recognition, as well as their substantial grants to leading museums to strengthen their educational programs, accomplished almost as much by calling attention and lending prestige to the causes as by the actual and much-needed financial support. Kress's grants for the production of catalogues of museum collections, and Ford's, following the earlier lead of the Carnegie Corporation, for the training of museum personnel, and its recognition of the importance of professional art schools by support through scholarships and in related areas, are also significant.

The massive foundation grants received by many educational institutions for general educational programs have indirectly also benefited the visual arts through strengthening faculties and making possible increased offerings of courses and studio experience to increased numbers of students, and in bringing creative personalities to the campuses of the nation.

One of the limitations of the large foundations is their size, which, they feel, necessitates their thinking and acting on a national if not a global level. Such is not the case with the specialized or the local foundations, both of which have significantly assisted various cultural agencies to continue functioning. The margin between successful existence and failure of such cultural agencies is, as anyone experienced in any field of the arts is only too aware, small indeed. Thus annual foundation grants of $10,000 to $20,-000, or in a few cases considerably more, have added incalculably to the nation's artistic resources.

As the instrument of an individual's enthusiasm and interest, the smaller foundation may be capable of great diversity. The Kaplan Foundation's concept of buying loft buildings in New York to rent to artists who have difficulty in finding living and working space in the city, and its financing of the work of a leading contemporary sculptor in designing a children's playground; the Spaeth Foundation's sponsorship of important traveling exhibitions of religious art; and the List Foundation's making possible, in a program carried out by the American Federation of Arts, the commissioning, for Lincoln Center and for museums throughout the country, of posters from the world's leading artists, are but a few examples of the greater latitude and freer imagination possible for the smaller foundation. It appears that such foundations may increasingly take a lead in exploring new areas in which the more general and larger foundations might become interested.

As imaginative programs in the field of the arts have adequately proven, it is perhaps less the size of the grants than the form they take, the special encouragement they offer, that gives them their value and significance. Thus the more than forty years of grants, mostly of less than $10,000, in the form of awards and fellowships to creative individuals by the John Simon Guggenheim Memorial Foundation, and also to a somewhat lesser degree grants by such other foundations as the Danforth, Hartford, Graham, and a few others, have done much to change the artistic climate by encouraging gifted persons and making possible their pursuit of a creative life.

Though many foundations grant fellowships in other fields, few act to benefit the artist directly except the handful that, like the

Longview Foundation, make possible purchases of works of art, though a number carry on programs that ultimately influence the artist's career. In general, it is still the individual, the collector and the museum curator, who give the artist what small income he derives from the sale of his work, and a number of collectors have established foundations as a means for the pursuit of their interest.

Since, thanks to the tax laws as well as to an increased sense of social responsibility, most private collections are destined for eventual public ownership or possession by institutions of public service, the significant factor is not the foundation but the purpose of the collector. By far the most generous benefactions in the arts —the Morgan gifts to the Metropolitan Museum and the foundation of the Morgan Library; the magnificent generosity of a Mellon, a Widener, or a du Pont; the incalculable enrichment of such collections open to the public as those in museums in Washington, Philadelphia, Cleveland, Chicago, and Boston, to mention but a few of the institutions that have thus benefited—have been the result of personal gift and bequest, often without the medium of a foundation. Only in comparatively recent times has it proven expedient to use the foundation as an instrument of benefaction in the arts.

Similarly, the newest significant factor in artistic patronage today, namely business, has as often played its part directly as through corporate foundations. Thus it is unimportant whether the Johnson Wax Company collected and made possible the circulation of its collection of contemporary American art through a foundation or not. The important element is the belated but strongly increasing entrance of business into the world of the arts, in what Dr. Frank Stanton, President of CBS, has called "essentially a democratizing movement." The purchase of large numbers of contemporary paintings and sculptures by such corporations as the Chase Manhattan Bank and CBS, to name but two out of many, has been of immediate advantage to the artistic community.

A recent series of advertisements featuring works of art especially commissioned from leading artists for the Container Corporation of America, the circulation of exhibits by IBM, the annual exhibition of contemporary paintings from the southeastern United States by the Mead Paper Company, the sale of works of art by

Sears, Roebuck and Korvette, and the offering of works by lead-ing modern painters as premiums by the King Korn Stamp Com-pany are among the many recent ventures of business into art that may have done as much for the artist and for bringing art to the general public as many foundation programs.

Thus the place of foundations in fostering the arts must be seen in the perspective of a larger picture in which other elements are of equal if not greater importance. And the most important of all remains the private donor, who, besieged by demands for innu-merable causes, provides more than 75 percent of the nation's annual charitable support. To remedy the fact that less than 2 percent of that support goes to the arts requires education and promotion, made all the more necessary by the keenness of the competition. In this process of education the foundations, as well as other cultural institutions, have not yet played a sufficient role. Since it is less a matter of amount than of thoughtful and imagina-tive planning that will enable the growing public enthusiasm for the arts to receive something approaching the quality as well as the quantity that it demands, the field is open for the same leader-ship by foundations that has already been shown by the far too small though significant minority among them, and by the few imaginative programs sponsored by individuals, whether working through a foundation or by themselves.

There are areas still insufficiently explored where foundations might play a decisive part. Art education and art experience for children are largely neglected, as is art as therapy, significant though it has proven to be in treatment of the mentally and emo-tionally disturbed and the handicapped. Though the Woodward Foundation and the Museum of Modern Art make possible the display of works of art in American embassies throughout the world, there is insufficient support of traveling exhibits of Ameri-can art abroad and of the arts of other countries in the United States, and there are no agencies responsible for the continuing representation of America in the great art exhibitions such as take place regularly at Venice and São Paulo. And, though agencies do exist, more opportunities for the exchange of artists might be provided.

In an age of increasing leisure, people are turning to the arts as a source of fulfillment. There are thus standards to be established and maintained, efforts to be directed and aided, and experiments to be tried. People are eager for an experience of the arts, and imaginative programs for amateurs of all ages are needed, for without the dedicated amateur the professional loses a major part of the critical and informed public necessary for his own growth and for a genuine flourishing of the arts. Some increase in the presently small number of foundation administrators with a knowledge and experience of the arts would assist in exploring the possibilities in this area.

America's museums have in recent years evolved into leading institutions of public education in the arts, and annually attract astronomical numbers of visitors and students. In many communities they have had to assume responsibilities properly in the domain of public education. In recognition of this, legislation has been recommended to the State of New York to grant public funds to strengthen the educational departments of the museums of the state, on the grounds that their programs are already established and of proven quality, and that such supplements to their budgets would provide satisfactory public education in the arts, and eliminate the vast increase in cost needed to duplicate their efforts within the public education system. Yet, despite their contribution to the cultural life of the nation, a survey conducted by the American Association of Museums has concluded that "funds coming from foundations, corporations, and federal, state, and county-level government are estimated to represent less than two percent of the total annual income of all museums." In the last annual report of the Philadelphia Museum, the director states that this distinguished institution has "a planned and budgeted deficit of $155,000 . . . to carry out the museum's relatively modest program this season."

Yet foundations, especially the smaller ones, are becoming aware of the importance and the needs of museums, and in the last few years have set an example that might be more widely followed. Recent grants have been made to such institutions in Denver, Atlanta, Phoenix, and Allentown, Pennsylvania, by the Bay Foundation, and the sum of $100,000 was provided for the Art Institute of Chicago by the Schermerhorn Charitable Trust, to name but two. The recent successful drive for the enlargement of the Museum of Modern Art and the construction of the Los Angeles County Museum, as events of national importance, brought forth broad foundation support. And there have long been a small number of foundations that use their funds either entirely or predominantly for the support of a single cultural institution or a group of institutions. Among these are the Nelson Trust, chief benefactor of the William Rockhill Nelson Gallery of Art in St. Louis; the Winterthur Foundation, which supports the Delaware museum of the same name that houses the extraordinary collection of American arts formed by Henry F. du Pont; and the Solomon R. Guggenheim Foundation, which sponsors the Guggenheim Museum in New York.

The Ford Foundation's artist in residence program, administered by the American Federation of Arts, and its program of purchases of works of art, as well as as that anonymously financed through the federation, making it possible for art centers, smaller museums, colleges, and universities across the country to add significantly to their collections, have had a success which could lead to further experiment. Such programs assist the artist as well as the public, because new audiences and supporters are won, standards are raised, and lives are enriched. And those who neglect the support of the visual arts might ponder that, while distinguished visitors come and go, and such vital contacts are of immeasurable value to the persons experiencing them, when a work of art becomes a part of a collection serving the public, its value is of continuing duration.

A nation such as ours should be well able to support its just share of all the arts, performing and visual, if we are convinced, with the authors of the Rockefeller panel report, that "the arts are not for a privileged few but for the many, that their place is not on the periphery of society but at its center, that they are not jus a form of recreation but are of central importance to our well-being and happiness." It might well be that the most significant contribution foundations could make to the arts lies in a dramatic increase in the venturesome leadership now assumed by only a few, and by a larger number of dedicated private citizens, some working through foundations and some without.

CHAPTER 26

Contributions of Philanthropic
Foundations to World Health

BROCK CHISHOLM

The vast extent, in time, space, and subject matter, of the contribution of charitable foundations and organizations to health on a world basis dwarfs any attempt even to describe it in a limited article. Until shortly before the First World War most of such efforts were undertaken by religious missionary groups, usually on a sectarian, and sometimes even on a competitive basis. In general, they provided little if any technical or administrative training for the people with whom they worked, and consequently their effects were limited. Treatment of disease, as an introduction for religious instruction, was usually given precedence over prevention of disease and health education. Though the total effort was large, the effect was to keep the people in a state of tutelage and dependence, which in turn justified the continuing of the mission.

In extending the hookworm control programs they had developed in the southern U.S.A. to some fifty-two other countries and many islands, the Rockefeller Foundation in 1913 initiated an approach to world health problems which became highly effective. The fact promptly emerged that most of the countries where their teams were working were simply not equipped to carry on the techniques that were being introduced. The basic knowledge and experience necessary to adapt and adopt new techniques did not exist. This was found to be true even in the southern U.S.A. The recognition of this fact led to the foundation's financing of the building and endowing of the School of Hygiene and Public Health at the Johns Hopkins University, an event of world importance, demonstrating a new and necessary pattern for the control of many widespread diseases which could never be controlled by treatment. The foundation followed this by assisting in the development of schools of public health and related institutions in many other countries. This great effort was supported by a system of fellowships to bring promising students from most of the world to such institutions for study. From these demonstrations many governments learned the possibility and the value of the control of disease, and in many cases themselves developed related services and institutions, often with the advice and assistance of the Rockefeller Foundation, which had become, in effect, a world organization.

The Health Organization of the League of Nations also owed much to the Rockefeller Foundation, which during its early years provided nearly half its budget. Also the research work done in disease control by the foundation formed a base for much of the work of the Health Organization's expert committees and for its technical advice to governments.

Since the World Health Organization was established, as an interim commission in 1946 and as a full-fledged specialized agency of the United Nations in 1948, the Rockefeller Foundation has been most helpful on many occasions and in many ways. As samples of the types of effective cooperation several may be quoted:

In 1950 a committee of experts was set up in Italy, with members from the WHO and from the Rockefeller Foundation, to examine the state of public health services in that country and to make recommendations for their reorganization. This committee was presided over by the Italian High Commissioner for Hygiene and Public Health, and was composed of local specialists in public health and the external experts provided by the WHO and the foundation. The WHO established a field office in Italy to provide necessary services for this committee for the term of its existence. The information and recommendations of the committee formed the basis of many long-term as well as emergency programs of the government.

During the same year, 1950, the Rockefeller Foundation also cooperated with the government of the Netherlands and with WHO in a seminar for European sanitary engineers, attended by engineers from fifteen countries.

In 1951 a Demonstration and Training Centre for Rural Public Health Service problems was inaugurated at Soissons, France, organized by the French Government in cooperation with the International Children's Centre, the Rockefeller Foundation, and WHO. This center was designed to train students from other countries as well as from France. In 1951 a second seminar for European sanitary engineers was held in Rome under the auspices of the Italian government, the Rockefeller Foundation, and WHO. Participants came from sixteen European countries and numbered sixty-eight; some ten selected university students in engineering from Italy attended as observers. In 1955 and 1956, the Rockefeller Foundation assigned Dr. J. Austin Kerr, former director of the Virus Research Center, Poona, India, to work with the Pan American Sanitary Bureau, Regional Office of the WHO for the Americas, as a special advisor in the study of yellow fever and related virus diseases. This was a very extensive study in many countries of Central and South America.

Since its establishment in 1949, the Institute of Nutrition of Central America and Panama in Guatemala City has been doing extensive research and training for the relief of the many problems of nutrition in those countries. Collaborating with the governments concerned and with the Pan American Sanitary Bureau are the Massachusetts Institute of Technology, the W. K. Kellogg Foundation, and the Rockefeller Foundation. The Food and Agricultural Organization of the United Nations maintains close liaison with this work because of its implications for similar problems in many other countries.

Since the establishment of WHO, consultations between its specialists and administrators and appropriate persons of the Rockefeller Foundation have been frequent and rewarding. The long and detailed experience of the foundation has been freely made available to WHO, without any formality or reluctance. The foundation released Dr. Fred Soper, of its staff, to become director of the PASB and of the Regional Office for the Americas of WHO. His unique experience and knowledge were of great value in these positions until his retirement.

It has been in the fields of control of malaria and of yellow fever that perhaps the most valuable work of the Rockefeller Foundation has been done, though much work in the control of typhus, influenza, rabies, yaws, bilharziasis, syphilis, tuberculosis, and amoebic dysentery has also been of great international significance. Like the work on hookworm, that on malaria began in the U.S.A. but spread to Brazil in 1938. A vast antimalarial campaign was organized and directed by the foundation so successfully that by the end of 1940 *Anopheles gambiae,* the most important vector, had been eradicated from a 12,000-square-mile area, terminating the most severe epidemic of malaria which had ever occurred in the Americas. In 1942, *Anopheles gambiae* invaded Egypt, producing an intense epidemic, which by 1944 had caused 135,000 deaths. At the request of the government of Egypt, the Rockefeller Foundation organized and directed another campaign of extermination which was completely successful within two years. The methods developed and demonstrated during these two great operations provided much of the experience on the basis of which the nations of the world instructed the WHO to engage in a worldwide ten-year program of malaria eradication, which program is now being carried on.

In the control of yellow fever the Rockefeller Foundation has been providing leadership on a world basis since 1915, with large staffs of scientists working in New York, Africa, and Latin America. Several of these contracted yellow fever, and six died of it. In 1935, the foundation at last succeeded in developing the vaccine which is now in global use, and which has brought yellow fever under effective control. A Nobel prize recognized this great work.

The Rockefeller Foundation is still breaking new ground in its continuing studies of arthropod-borne and other viruses, for which it maintained a central laboratory from 1928 to 1964 in New York City, located on the premises (but not an integral part of) the Rockefeller Institute. This group has now been moved to Yale University, where it has been absorbed into the School of Medicine; it is located in a new building, for which part of the funds were furnished by the Rockefeller Foundation, constructed for the Department of Epidemiology and Public Health. This unit is now known as the Yale Arbovirus Research Unit, and it continues to receive financial assistance from the Rockefeller Foundation.

In addition to this central laboratory, the Rockefeller Foundation maintains a field laboratory in California and, in cooperation with local governments, virus laboratories in Brazil, Colombia, India, and Trinidad. The WHO and its expert committees look to these laboratories for the development of new knowledge and experience, as do many of the world's governments.

Since 1913 the Rockefeller Foundation has substantially influenced world health problems by aiding medical education outside the United States, first in establishing the China Medical Board, which built the Peking Union Medical College, now expanded and carried on by the government of that country. The foundation expended some $47 million to improve medical teaching and practice in China. In 1919 assistance to medical education expanded greatly, with strong support provided by the foundation to improve medical teaching in Belgium, France, Germany, Great Britain, Canada, Brazil, Lebanon, the Pacific islands and Southeast Asia, as well as for emergency measures to restore medical services disrupted by the First World War.

The early work on penicillin in England by Florey, Chain, and others, on the basis of Alexander Fleming's accidental discovery in 1928, was supported at a critical early stage by a grant of $5,000 a year for five years from the Rockefeller Foundation. This work proved penicillin so revolutionary and valuable that large investments by governments and drug manufacturers produced great results before the end of the Second World War.

The health of most of the world's people has benefited by the many years of productive work of the Rockefeller Foundation. Public health practice and the practice of medicine throughout the world would have been poorer without these great contributions. The control of many of the world's most damaging diseases owes much to this foundation and its research and demonstration, as well as to its direction of preventive work and its extensive advice to institutions and governments.

The W. K. Kellogg Foundation began in 1949 a program of cooperation with the Council of the Institute of Nutrition of Central

America and Panama, with the Rockefeller Foundation, the Pan American Sanitary Bureau, the Massachusetts Institute of Technology, and the FAO of the United Nations. The work of this institute has been of great value in dealing with many of the serious problems of Central America, a large number of which are nutritional. Among them are endemic goiter, kwashiorkor (multiple deficiency syndrome in children), avitaminosis A, anemia, atherosclerosis and pellagra. Training courses are provided and an extensive publication program is carried on in the medical journals of the member countries and the U.S.A and in the official bulletin of the Sanitary Bureau. The Kellogg Foundation engages also in many other programs of assistance in national and international health work.

There are many foundations and other types of voluntary organizations active in world health. To illustrate the variety a few may be mentioned:

The *Milbank Memorial Fund* has been responsible for excellent work, particularly in nutrition, which has helped many countries. Recently, along with the Population Council and the Ford and Rockefeller foundations, the Milbank Fund has made aid available to many countries for studies of population problems and their health aspects, and for planning to take effective steps to deal with them.

CIBA, established in London in 1947 by the great Swiss drug-manufacturing firm, does extensive work in medical research, study groups, symposia, publications, bursaries, awards, libraries, and other facilities.

CARE has, since the Second World War, provided vast amounts of medical and welfare supplies, often in consultation with WHO, and often to relieve desperate situations of infants' needs, maternity needs, hospital supply shortages, and many other such emergencies.

The Ittleson Foundation, The Grant Foundation, The Josiah Macy Junior Foundation, The Samuel Z. Levine Foundation for International Child Health, Inc. (concentrating on improvement of technical and leadership qualities in developing countries), and others, have contributed to international health work, some of them through voluntary organizations and others directly.

Some sixty-five international nongovernmental organizations are in official relationships with the World Health Organization, and many or most of them are supported or partly supported by foundations. This adds up to a very large amount and variety of international health work on many aspects of health. The definition of health agreed on by the members of the World Health Organization—and thus by almost all the nations of the world—as "a state of complete physical, mental and social well-being and not merely the absence of disease or infirmity" allows for official relations with a wide variety of international organizations, each with its special interests. These organizations are a fruitful source of strength and inspiration to the WHO and to its member governments. Many of them make proposals to the WHO through the director-general and the executive board, which if approved may be incorporated into the program of WHO.

CHAPTER 27

The Problem of the World's Food Supply and the Role of Philanthropy

LORD BOYD-ORR

The value of the work done by private philanthropic organizations for the elimination of hunger will be better appreciated if considered in the light of the role played by food in the evolution of human society.

FOOD AND POPULATION

Food is a main factor in determining the rate of growth and size of the population. Before the discovery, about fifteen thousand years ago, that food could be grown, prehistoric man like other animals had to hunt for food from natural sources, and the human population probably then never exceeded 5 million. After the discovery, the population increased as the food supply increased. By A.D. 1 it had reached about 200 million, and by 1700 about 600 million.

Then about two hundred years ago there began a rapid increase in the food supply in Europe, owing to the advance of agriculture and to imports from the new continents of the Americas and Australasia. By 1900 England was importing two-thirds of the food it consumed, and the population had increased from 4 million in 1800 to 34 million in 1900, to take no account of the millions who had emigrated. The rate of increase was accelerated by the control of killing diseases, especially in the latter part of the nineteenth century, reducing the death rate without a corresponding reduction in the birth rate.

As Malthus explained in 1798, population has always increased faster than the food supply. Hence in a food shortage due to bad harvests, famines reduce the population. Famines have occurred in every densely populated country. The last one in Europe was in Ireland, where nearly a million died because of the failure of the potato crop. Since then, owing to the easily available imports, there has been in Europe neither famine nor the fear of famine, except what was caused by war. Since the beginning of the present century, with a rise in the standard of living and education, the birth rate in Western Europe began to fall and it looked as if the explosive phase of population growth had passed. In the densely populated countries of Asia, however, agriculture continued primitive, with a marginal food supply which decreased after bad harvests, so that famines resulted. One of the biggest was in 1876-78, when 14 million perished in parts of India and China.

In the present century preventive medicine began to be applied in the poor countries, reducing the death rate. But since there was no reduction in the birth rate in these countries, the explosion of population passed from European countries to the colored nations. By 1946 world population growth had reached the alarming rate of about 20 million a year. In the nineteenth century the average rate, even with the increase in Western Europe, had been only about 8 million. The rate was increased by the activities of the World Health Organization, organized in 1946. By 1960 the rate of increase of world population had reached 60 million a year, and it is still rising. In the next forty years the present population of 3,300 million will be doubled and, if the rate continues, it will be doubled again in the succeeding thirty years.

However, it is doubtful whether the present rate of growth will continue. With contraceptives, legalized abortion, and other measures, the birth rate has begun to fall in countries where it was highest. In Japan it has fallen by over 40 percent since 1949. A big decrease has also taken place in Hong Kong, Singapore, and Puerto Rico.

An account of the worldwide movements to control the birth rate will be found in the next chapter. In spite of these efforts, however, it seems to me unlikely that stability will be reached before the world population reaches six billion, which will probably occur about the end of the present century. The urgent question is whether the food supply can be increased to sustain such a huge population.

To maintain the present consumption of food per head, the world food supply would need to be doubled in the next forty years. But, in addition, between a half and two-thirds of the people in the world are, at present levels of consumption, ill nourished. To bring them up to the level needed for health the present supply would need to be nearly doubled, the biggest increase needed being in the more expensive protein- and vitamin-rich foods. For adequate nutrition for six billion, food production would need to be increased to nearly four times the present level. With modern agricultural and engineering science that is physically possible, but it could only be done by the cooperation of all nations, including the food-deficit countries, in a worldwide food production project.

In 1934, there was widespread unemployment in industrialized countries, with over ten million unemployed in America, six million in Germany and three million in Britain. Governments were taking measures to reduce production of food in order to raise prices. On the other hand, the League of Nations appointed committees with members from both America and Russia to consider international collaboration in a World Food Plan based on human needs as a means of increasing world trade and reducing unemployment. It was estimated that this would mean nearly doubling the then world food supply. This would have required such enormous quantities of fertilizers, agricultural equipment, and other industrial products for water-control projects for irrigation, for food storage, and for transport, that the world market for industrial products would have been increased to such an extent that there would have been worldwide economic prosperity with a great reduction in unemployment. The reports of the League committees were approved, and by 1938 delegates from twenty-two leading nations were meeting in conference to work out this plan in greater detail. The outbreak of war in 1939 put an end to this attempt to bring about a new era of economic prosperity.

President Roosevelt later revived the project at the Hot Springs Conference with the wider objectives of allaying social unrest in food-deficit countries, and of bringing about world unity and peace by the collaboration of all nations for their mutual benefit. From this initiative there arose the Food and Agricultural Organization, which was able to get the nations to collaborate to deal with the postwar food crisis, although there unfortunately was no comparable success in the effort to get the great powers to cooperate in the long-range objectives.

Since then both Western and Communist countries have given financial aid and technical assistance on a large number of projects in food-deficit countries, by far the largest amount being given by the United States; and the United Nations had provided funds for technical assistance in a variety of projects. It is difficult to find out how much of the aid was given for humanitarian reasons and for the basic purpose of supplying food or industrial products needed to increase food production, and how much was given to win allies in the cold war, to arrest the march of Communism, or on the other hand to undermine the power of the capitalist countries. But, whatever the motives, the aid did increase food production. The increase, however, occurred in the Western industrialized countries where surplus food had already become an economic embarrassment.

Food-deficit countries were not so fortunate. In Asia and the Far East, for example, between 1955 and 1961 production increased by 3.6 percent per annum while the population increased by 2.4 percent, closing the gap between food and population by only 1.2 percent per annum, a gain which, even if continued, gave little hope to the present generation of hungry people. But even that meager improvement has not continued. Since 1961 food has increased by only 0.5 percent while population has continued to increase by 2.4 percent. The position is somewhat similar in all food-deficit countries, which contain about two-thirds of the world's population. In the last two or three years total world food production has not kept pace with population growth. There is little wonder that experts think that the threatened world food shortage is as great a danger to the survival of world civilization as a nuclear war which may never occur.

WORK BY PRIVATE ORGANIZATIONS

By far the most important work by private organizations for the elimination of hunger is that done by foundations in the United States. These were established by wealthy philanthropists who had high ideals concerning the enrichment of life through improvements in education, through the gaining of new knowledge, and through the application of this knowledge to basic and world-wide problems. During recent years certain of these great foundations, notably the Rockefeller Foundation and the Ford Foundation, have given great emphasis to the practical aspects of the conquest of hunger.

The modus operandi of the foundations is different from that of governments or of the United Nations. Governments frequently furnish economic aid or shipments of food grains under such programs as the "Food for Peace" or "Freedom from Hunger." These commendable and necessary relief measures furnish only temporary help, however, terminating when the food grains are consumed. The importation and purchase of food supplies by countries that are struggling to improve their agricultural and total economy also may cause substantial financial distortion in the developing economies. For example, the several billion dollars of surplus food sold to India by the United States since 1956, under the Public Law 480 program, has generated American rupee credits that represent a substantial part of the total rupee funds in circulation in India. The governments of both the United States and India are concerned about measures that will enable India to achieve *self*-sufficiency in food grain production.

The governments of America, Britain, and some other countries, in addition to the immediate aid of giving food also give technical assistance, and the United Nations as well provides funds for technical aid through organizations such as the FAO. This type of assistance is valuable in developing large industries, but is less effective in the immediate increase of food. The technical assistance projects are too often of short duration and are frequently devoted to attempts to transfer American or other "know-how" to agricultural situations where the climatic, soil, and other conditions may be very different from those in which the technical advisors gained their experience.

The Rockefeller Foundation program in the agricultural sciences, which was initiated in 1943, has demonstrated that agricultural productivity can be increased substantially through well-ordered, cooperative projects in research and education. The major effort in the cooperating programs in Mexico, Colombia, Chile, and India has been given to research to improve the production of the basic food crops of these countries, with concurrent attention to the improvement of varieties, better management of soil fertility and water, the effective control of diseases and pests, and better practices for the storage and preservation of the harvested crop. An integral part of this research effort, which is conducted in co-operation with the ministries of agriculture of the host countries, is the in-service training and scientific education of the cooperating local personnel. As the corps of trained scientists grows, to furnish the base for indigenous leadership, attention is given to the development of stable institutions for research and education. The Rockefeller Foundation experience in Mexico is indicative of what may be achieved through well-planned and sustained technical assistance concentrating on research and education. Mexico, which once imported substantial quantities of corn and wheat, has now become self-sufficient with respect to both of these food grains. Perhaps no country can point to more remarkable progress in the increase of a single food crop than has been achieved in Mexico's production of wheat. The national average yields of about 11.5 bushels per acre in 1943 were increased to 39 bushels per acre in 1964. Total wheat production in the country climbed from 300,000 tons in 1943 to over 2,100,000 tons in 1964. The cooperative training and education program, which supplied in-service experience for 700 young agriculturalists, also has supported 156 young scientists through the M.S. degree and 70 through the Ph.D. degree. With this group of well-trained and experienced scientists Mexico has proceeded to develop, with the assistance of the Rockefeller Foundation, the Ford Foundation, the U.S. Agency for International Development and the Inter-American Development

Bank, a center for coordinated attention to agricultural research, education, and extension near Mexico City at Chapingo.

The Chapingo center is now under construction and should serve not only the future development of Mexican agriculture but also is destined to be increasingly important in agricultural research and education on an international basis. For example, since 1961 a total of thirty young scientists working on wheat and barley improvement in twelve countries of the Near East region have spent up to one year in Mexico gaining first-hand experience in wheat research. This project has been supported by the Rockefeller Foundation in collaboration with the FAO and the government of Mexico. Steps are being taken to insure the continued cooperation of these young scientists in the Near East Wheat and Barley Improvement Program, under FAO auspices, by the arrangement of biennial planning and review conferences that will foster continuous interchange of materials and ideas.

The method of beginning at the grass roots and building from below upward is the most economical and effective method of assisting the natives in countries with primitive agricultural systems to improve their conditions by their own efforts. This foundation method is completely free from political involvements and, therefore, easily gains the confidence of the cooperating local personnel. Further, plans can be fluid and adjusted according to experience, without waiting for the approval of governments or treasury officials. A still further advantage is that the foundation activities, while flexible, are stably sustained over long enough periods of time to be effective, with highly trained agricultural scientists devoting their lives to this work, in contrast to the government personnel who often are on short assignments.

The work of the Rockefeller Foundation in Mexico is of extreme importance to the Latin American countries, where the population between 1930 and 1960 increased by 66 percent, while the production of food grains increased by only 42 percent. The population in some countries of Latin America is increasing at a rate of 3.2 to 3.6 percent annually, which will double the number of people in twenty years. The threat of hunger and possible starvation is, therefore, imminent.

The food shortages of Latin America have not yet reached the critical stage of the food deficit in India, where the population has increased by 33.8 million during the past three years and where the annual production of food grains has leveled off at approximately 80 million tons. In spite of the expansion of food imports from the U.S. and elsewhere, India's food deficit problem continues to increase.

The Rockefeller Foundation's cooperative program in India, initiated in 1956, has not been in operation for a sufficient time to match the accomplishments in Mexico but substantial progress has been made. The research efforts have been directed toward the improvement of production of maize, sorghums, and millets. It has been estimated that the nine improved maize hybrids developed for Indian conditions since 1961 could double the production of this crop in India in the next five years even if only 50 percent of the maize acreage were planted with the improved seed. Similarly, new sorghum hybrids have been released that are adapted to about 14 million of the 40 million acres of this crop grown in India, and it is calculated that these hybrids, grown with improved cultural practices, could increase production of sorghums by 25 to 50 percent in five years' time.

The Post Graduate School, developed with Rockefeller Foundation assistance at the Indian Agricultural Research Institute, was inaugurated in 1958 and by March, 1965, had awarded 395 M.S. degrees and 132 Ph.D. degrees. The Post Graduate School has a continuing enrollment of four hundred students and should make an effective impact on Indian agriculture as this trained human resource directs attention to the factors that limit agricultural output in the country. The principles and improved teaching procedures established in the Post Graduate School are now serving to guide the new agricultural universities that are being established by the several state governments of India. These universities are receiving major support and guidance from U.S. land-grant colleges and universities, with financing from the U.S. AID program.

Almost from the day of India's independence her scientists and government leaders have given continuous attention to the organization of research and education activities. Steps are now being taken to reorganize the Indian Council of Agricultural Research in order to ensure more effective use of the central government and state government resources for agricultural research and education.

It is particularly encouraging to see the responsiveness of Indian leadership to proposals for change in the research, education, and development activities, with the purpose of modernizing one of the world's most primitive agricultural societies.

The Ford Foundation program in agriculture has been concerned largely with the development of educational institutions, research to increase production and levels of nutrition, and education-demonstration programs at the village level, with accent on rural self-help. The Ford Foundation initiated cooperation in India in 1952 by helping to develop extension training in Indian agricultural colleges, at the beginning of the government's first five-year plan. The Allahabad Agricultural Institute had already started extension work when the Ford Foundation grant in 1952 helped to establish a full-fledged extension department to specialize in village work. Subsequent grants were made to eight other colleges. The need for such practical training is great since few Indian students have had farm experience.

The Ford Foundation contribution of $12 million to India's community development program is supporting the most ambitious national program of rural improvement ever undertaken by any country. It is destined to raise the living standards of the 375,000,-000 people living in villages.

In addition to the two Indian programs concerned with education at the professional level, and education plus extension at the subprofessional level on a massive scale, the Ford Foundation has initiated a cooperative effort aimed at an immediate increase in food supplies. This "intensive agricultural district program" is designed to demonstrate the benefits from application of several essential measures—adequate and timely supplies of fertilizer, pesticides, improved seeds, farm tools, and other production aids; cooperative farm credit to buy these supplies; storage, drainage, and other public works; education and assistance in farm management; and individual farm planning. In the first crop season of 1961-62 in the Shahabad district the demonstration plots produced yields of rice that were 84 percent higher than on the control plots, wheat yields that were 100-150 percent above the standard plots, and potato yields that ranged 78-200 percent more than with common practices.

The total Ford Foundation support for agricultural and village development projects abroad between 1952 and 1964 was $39.6 million, or about 17.8 percent of the funds spent by the foundation in its overseas development program.

Particularly interesting and promising is the International Rice Research Institute, started by the Rockefeller Foundation and supported by that foundation and by the Ford Foundation. Roughly two-thirds of the people in the world derive 80-90 percent of the calories of their diet from carbohydrates, chiefly grain; one authority has said, "Rice is the most important food in the world. Although surpassed by wheat in total acreage in the world as a whole, the volume of food produced by the world rice crop is 10 to 20 percent greater than that of wheat."[1] It has in fact been estimated that for about 60 percent of the world's population, something like 80 percent of the calory intake comes from rice.

In 1952 the Rockefeller Foundation began considering the possibility of setting up an institute for the study of rice. After a series of exploratory studies, and extensive trips throughout the Orient by experienced agricultural scientists, the project was inaugurated in 1959. The government of the Philippines furnished the necessary land and cooperated in other ways. The Ford Foundation appropriated over $7 million for the capital plant, and the Rockefeller Foundation undertook the scientific and financial responsibility for operation.

This has by now grown into a truly international center for research on all aspects of rice improvement and cultivation, with departments of varietal improvement, plant physiology, agronomy and soils, plant protection, agricultural engineering, chemistry, statistics, etc. A staff totaling roughly one hundred persons, including highly trained scientists from the Philippines, India, Japan, Taiwan, Thailand, Burma, etc., have physical facilities of the finest sort with which to seek to improve the yields and the quality of the rice grown in all parts of Asia, and indeed all parts of the world. The support is now shared by the Rockefeller and Ford foundations, and the government of the Philippines has steadily increased its participation. Training of personnel is an important part of the program.

This is a long-range project of the sort which would be difficult, if not indeed impossible, to start or to continue under the restrictions and complications of government aid. Although still in its developing stages, it has every promise of eventually making a major contribution to the world's food problem.

Other U.S. foundations, including the W. K. Kellogg Foundation, have assisted with grants for research and particularly for education and extension. The Milbank Foundation, whose late director was Dr. Boudreau, one of the pioneers in the League of Nations program for doubling world food production, has promoted and given grants to support investigations on food requirements, to furnish guides in deciding which foods were most urgently needed to prevent malnutrition.

Research, education, and extension projects to increase crop production have been undertaken in nearly every food-deficit country. The resulting increases in food production have staved off threatened famines in the past and if continued and expanded could go far in solving the problems of food and population throughout the world.

Similar work in helping the natives of the hungry nations to increase their wealth by their own efforts is now being done by other organizations. The FAO campaign against hunger has raised about $15 million, not for the immediate relief of hunger but for increasing food production. The money is being devoted to specific measures to increase food production with a little technical assistance to ensure the success of each project. Of other means of help, one of the most interesting is that of the Northern Dairies, a north of England company which devotes part of its profits to social purposes. It has already raised £38,000 of its £50,000 target from its employees and directors for the establishment in Hyderabad in India of a modern dairy, which will increase milk production and supply clean, safe milk. Thus, the example of the great American philanthropic foundations for relieving the world of hunger is being followed by other people of the world. It would be a help in promoting further work of this kind if the achievements of foundations in enabling people to increase food by their own efforts were better known.

The Oxfam Organization in England devotes over $6 million a year to the relief of hunger and distress, a commendable and necessary program, but the main effort should be directed to helping persons to help themselves. Many people in the wealthy countries are keen to help their fellow world citizens in the poor countries. The methods adopted by the great philanthropic organizations show the way help can be given.

Some might suggest that all these organizations along with FAO might be brought together under a common council. This would be a mistake. The individual organizations might lose their initiative and power to make quick decisions for changes in programs without waiting for permission from a central authority. As a matter of fact, as has been shown above, they do cooperate if and when such joint effort seems desirable.

As the president of the Ford Foundation has pointed out, the world is spending the equivalent of $120 billion a year on military budgets, twenty times as much as the capitalist countries give for overseas aid, only part of which is devoted to increasing food production. If part of this vast amount spent on arms could be channeled into the organizations working to avoid a world food crisis, it would do more for the good of the people and for the peace of the world than all the expenditure on armaments.

This inadequate account of the vitally important work being done by these organizations shows the enormous importance of their work in creating a better human society. The vision and philanthropic impulses of the men who founded these organizations, of those who direct them, and of other like-minded people, point the only way to a new and better world. Unless their great objectives are attained there is little hope for the survival of our civilization. The foundations deserve and urgently need the financial and moral support of all those interested in the kind of world our children shall inherit.

CHAPTER 28

American Foundations
and Population Problems

FREDERICK OSBORN

Shortly after World War II demographers—as we now call professional students of population—noted that a rapid fall in death rates was taking place all over the world, particularly in the underdeveloped countries where traditionally death rates had been high. But birth rates were not falling, and it was obvious that as death rates went down populations were increasing at an unprecedented speed. Widely publicized, the phenomenon became popularly known as the population explosion. Next to the threat of an atomic war, the population explosion has come to be thought of as the greatest danger threatening the future of mankind. As governments became aware of what was happening, the demographers who had warned of the danger were called on to develop plans for averting it. And in great majority the demographers were Americans or men trained with American money. They were numerous and they were ready. There had been none thirty-five years ago. Where had they come from?

The first students of population were provided by the census. They were well trained in their specialty of census taking, but with few exceptions they did not go into population theory or the broader field of the causes underlying the growth of populations. Then, as life insurance developed a scientific base, a new group of actuarial specialists moved into the field of demography to develop life tables, group survival rates, and more extensive analyses of births and deaths. By 1920 the limited fields of census taking and life insurance were well provided with trained men, but the larger aspects of population growth and change were being neglected. Work in population was not offered in any of our colleges or universities.

In 1922 the Scripps Foundation for Research in Population Problems was established by the late E. W. Scripps. Warren S. Thompson was employed as director, and P. K. Whelpton was brought in as assistant in 1924. These were the first of the new breed of demographer. Supported with foundation funds, they applied themselves to the broader political and social implications of growth and change in world populations, and to the study of the differential growth and replacement of socio-economic groups in the United States. In 1929 Thompson published *Danger Spots in World Population,* and for forty years these two men, Thompson and Whelpton, with a varying staff of assistants, and with the help of grants from other foundations, developed population studies and methodology. They were responsible for over three hundred publications, besides taking an active part in national and international conferences and in the development of large-scale research programs.

In 1928 the Milbank Memorial Fund brought Frank W. Notestein to its Division of Research to be concerned largely with problems of population. This Division of Research cooperated with the Bureau of the Census in analyzing the returns for a large sample of women in the enumeration of the 1910 census. It developed the field of differential fertility with the help of Clyde Kiser, who became one of the country's leading specialists. Notestein, with the collaboration of Regine Stix, opened up for the first time the subject of the differential use and effectiveness of contraception, a subject till then considered too "dangerous" for study outside clinical circles. Notestein's early studies of contraceptive practice are landmarks in a field which only recently has become respectable. With support from the Milbank Fund, Raymond Pearl's studies of contraceptive practice demonstrated the "birth control" interpretation of class differences in fertility as opposed to his previously held "biological" interpretation.

By 1936 it was clear that the study of population and of the factors making for change and growth in different areas and among different peoples offered a field for research which might become of the greatest practical importance. But it still was not a widely accepted field of study, and would not become so until it was accepted as a proper field by some recognized university. To meet this situation, the Milbank Fund in 1936 made a grant of $250,000 to Princeton University for the establishment of the Office of Population Research at Princeton University. Notestein was made director, and fellowships were provided by the Milbank Fund and later by grants from the Rockefeller Foundation. Other universities offered courses in population, and in an increasing number of places it became possible for fellows to receive training appropriate for work overseas. But facilities in the United States were limited until 1961 and the three years following, when the Ford Foundation made grants totaling over $3 million to the University of Pennsylvania, Cornell, Johns Hopkins, Harvard, Michigan, and Chicago for strengthening their programs in training and research in population.

Meantime, the Rockefeller Foundation had commenced a series of studies on the biological processes associated with reproduction. Its first grant was made in 1931 to the Committee for Research in Problems of Sex of the National Research Council, and a total of over $2 million had been contributed by the time the program was terminated in 1961. Between 1937 and 1943 it gave over $76,000 to the National Committee on Maternal Health for its studies relating to fertility. It supported the International Union for the Scientific Study of Population in its critical early years. In addition, five major universities, originally supported by the National Research Council, were aided directly by the Rockefeller Foundation to the extent of another million dollars. Beginning in 1932 the Macy Foundation made a series of grants in the field of reproduction, commencing with a grant to Dr. Gregory Pincus for studies of ovulation. These grants by the Rockefeller and Macy foundations broke new ground in supporting work on reproductive endocrinology in the United States, and prepared the field for the important developments which came when problems of population became acute.

During the early years the Rockefeller Foundation, the Milbank Fund, and the Carnegie Corporation made a number of small grants opening up new approaches to population studies, or giving support to new organizations badly in need of help. As early as 1931 the Carnegie Corporation was supporting the International Union for the Scientific Study of Population with a grant of $2,500 for its International Conference, repeating a grant of the same amount in 1937. A grant of $2,000 to the Population Association of America in 1938 helped the new organization of professional demographers with its publication program. A grant of $5,700 to the Population Investigation Committee in London helped carry out a piece of research on population problems in the British West Indies, perhaps the first such study made in a country directly threatened by the too-rapid growth of its people. The Carnegie Corporation's largest contributions were $75,000 in 1942 and $150,000 in 1956, which, with help from the Milbank Fund, made possible first the Indianapolis Study, and later the so-called Princeton Study, both notable contributions to knowledge of the dynamic factors of population growth.

The Rockefeller Brothers Fund first contributed to the Planned Parenthood Federation of America in 1941, reaching a total of $269,000 in annual contributions in the following twenty-four years.

By the end of 1952 American foundations had contributed something over $3 million to the field of population study. A beginning had been made in almost every area: contraception; the physiology of reproduction; the attitudes of people toward child bearing, toward size of family, and toward the social and economic conditions which would help determine the number of their children; as well as more formal studies of trends in births and deaths, migration, and net rates of increase. A considerable number of competent students had been trained. The sum of money involved had not been large, but it had been made available at a critically important time. This aid prepared the field for larger developments, and saved ten years or more which would have been lost if the foundations had shown less initiative and courage in a field not yet respectable in the eyes of the public or the professions. And time was beginning to be important, for by 1952 world population was increasing at a rate to double every forty years, and it was hard to see how per capita consumption of food and goods could be maintained, let alone increased, to keep up with such a rate of growth.

A few people recognized the danger as early as 1952. One of these was John D. Rockefeller 3rd. After a preliminary meeting with relevant experts in Williamsburg, he organized a new foundation, The Population Council, charged with hastening the development of the scientific knowledge and the trained personnel which were a prerequisite to effective solutions of national and international population problems. Financed at the start by gifts from Rockefeller, The Population Council drew for its staff on the trained personnel developed during the thirties and forties. It started immediately with grants for fellowships and aid to training centers. It boldly entered the field of the physiology of reproduction, seeking clues to new methods of contraception, and carrying out extensive clinical tests of the methods then known, particularly those known for their effectiveness in actual use among various types of populations. It attracted the interest of the larger foundations, which were beginning to be alerted to the urgency of population problems. The Rockefeller Brothers Fund made a grant of $120,-000 to The Population Council in 1956, and annual grants in larger amounts thereafter reached a total of over $2,000,000 by 1965. The Ford Foundation made it a grant of $600,000 in 1954 and of $1,000,000 in 1957, and increasingly larger grants in later years. The Population Council was prepared and staffed for the work in hand, and other foundations and interested individuals turned to it as the only organization at that time properly equipped for work with governments overseas. In 1954-55 it sent a mission to advise on India's program of fertility control. It supplied technical advisors and research programs for the early years, preparatory to the greatly enlarged and important program of the Ford Foundation in that country.

The Population Council's income rose from $370,000 in 1956 to $1.036 million in 1959, to something over $5 million in the year 1964. Of the total of $28 million in gifts and grants received by the council by the end of 1964, over $19 million was from foundations, and approximately $9 million from individuals. With this growing income it was able to increase the number of its fellowships in demography and its medical fellowships in the physiology of reproduction from four or five a year, with which it started in 1954, to over fifty a year by 1964. These young men and women came from countries all over the world; some were trained in the United States, some in Europe, many of the demographers in the regional training centers which had been set up in Santiago, Chile, and in Bombay, India, by the United Nations with the help of grants and technical assistance from The Population Council. These trained personnel, returning to their own countries, supplied needed help to the census and other government agencies and stimulated recognition of the dangers of the too-rapid growth of local populations. A number of governments responded by asking The Population Council to give them advice on setting up programs of control. Pakistan made family planning a part of its second five-year plan, and in 1962 instituted a large-scale action program. South Korea started a National Family Planning Program in 1961, with a budget of $83 million. In Malaysia, Ceylon, Barbados, and Hong Kong governments are helping finance family planning organizations. The governments of Taiwan, Tunisia, Thailand, and the United Arab Republic have set up experimental or pilot projects with the help of qualified consultants, looking toward setting up countrywide programs for reducing birth rates. In the great majority of these programs the consultants were supplied by The Population Council or were men who had received Population Council fellowships.

During the 1950's, on grants from American foundations and in one case with help from Sweden, large-scale research projects were carried out in underdeveloped countries on the use and effectiveness of various forms of birth control. It was found that no existing method known at that time was for long effective with agricultural and poorly educated populations. Even after considerable training and indoctrination, such populations would not continue the old methods for long, though other studies had shown that the great majority of these women did not want more than three or four children. Evidently other methods must be developed.

The first breakthrough was an oral contraceptive, the famous "pill." It was developed at the Worcester Foundation of Experimental Biology by Drs. Pincus, Rock, and Chang. It provided for the first time a safe and highly effective method of contraception on a planned basis, not related to the timing of the sexual act. It came quickly into wide use in the United States and Europe. It attained notable success with the least educated groups and those at the lowest economic levels. It is making an important contribution toward reducing the births of illegitimate and unwanted children in the United States. But its cost and the need for daily administration made it unsuitable for use in less-industrialized countries. Other methods, immunization, or means for preventing fertilization or insemination, were still in the developmental stage. It looked as though the actual control of fertility on a large scale would be delayed for a long time.

Then in 1961 The Population Council began investigating the plastic intra-uterine devices, then being developed independently in this country and abroad. These were successors to the old Graefenberg ring, long known in Europe and America. But the metal ring was in poor repute and there would need to be strong evidence that the polyethyline devices were harmless, safe, and effective, in order to convince a properly conservative medical profession that their use could be approved. The Population Council accordingly conducted a major program of investigation. In three years it sponsored more than forty research projects in medical schools, clinics, hospitals, and research institutions here and abroad, dealing with the safety, effectiveness, acceptability, and mode of action of intra-uterine devices. Conducted under the direction and supervision of leading medical men and research workers in this country, the study cost The Population Council almost $2 million. It proved, as conclusively as was possible in that period of time, that the intra-uterine plastic device was the most effective means of contraception yet discovered and that it was not harmful, and did not show any indication of being injurious over the long run. When the results of these studies became known in 1963-64, the devices came into immediate large-scale use in the underdeveloped countries. In Taiwan over 50,000 devices had been inserted by the end of 1964; in South Korea 100,000 devices were inserted in 1964 alone. The government of Tunisia has decided to make extensive use of the intra-uterine device in its national birth control program; it is laying plans for national manufacture and hopes to supply a great number of women with the device each year. India, Pakistan, and other countries are commencing its use on a larger scale.

The plastic coil is, in effect, a form of reversible sterilization, costing only a few cents, easily inserted, causing no discomfort, usually staying in place a number of years, highly acceptable, especially to agricultural populations and those of low literacy. It does not require repeated diligence to prevent pregnancy as other methods do. Most important of all it provides an effective vehicle for governmental programs of fertility control, which can now be carried out at per capita costs not much higher than the cost of the highly successful government programs for controlling malaria and contagious disease. From all present indications, the intra-uterine devices will, until better methods are devised, provide the means for a worldwide reduction in births in the critical period just ahead.

These important developments could not have taken place if there had not been an increase in public understanding. Discussion of population problems in the press and on the radio increased rapidly after 1952. Credit for this is due to the work of the Planned Parenthood Federation of America, and to the Population Reference Bureau of Washington, a small foundation engaged in compiling information on population growth and change, and giving the figures wide public circulation through press releases, *The Population Bulletin,* and other media. The Population Reference Bureau had foundation support as early as 1952, when it received its first grant from the Ford Foundation. By 1962 it had an annual income of approximately $200,000 a year, in part from subscriptions and individual gifts, but most of it from continuing foundation grants. Through their early support of this agency the foundations helped arouse public opinion, which in turn awoke a greater interest among other foundation trustees and staffs, and resulted in more and larger grants in this field.

The tempo of foundation giving increased rapidly after 1952. Previous to that date the Rockefeller Foundation had given some $900,000 to work in population and substantially more to medical studies in reproduction. Between 1952 and December, 1962,

Rockefeller Foundation grants in this field totaled over $2,250,000, and during 1963 and 1964 it made grants totaling $3,397,800, of which $2,250,000 was to The Population Council, $600,000 to Harvard toward the development of a center for population studies, $500,000 to the Population Reference Bureau. The Carnegie Corporation, one of the earliest in the field, made grants totaling $305,000 in the period 1954-63. Finally, in the same period, the Ford Foundation made the field of population one of its major interests. From 1954 through 1964 it gave $15,145,000 to training and research in population and $5,364,000 to technical assistance to Family Planning Programs. It gave $816,000 to dissemination of information on population, and a total of $18,-459,000 in grants in reproductive biology for training programs, research, the recruitment of scientists, and for other purposes. The Rockefeller Brothers Fund, as noted above, contributed $120,000 in 1956, and its grants to The Population Council alone through 1964 totaled over $2,000,000. Other foundations contributing to work in population were the Markle Fund, The Commonwealth Fund, the Old Dominion Fund, the Alfred P. Sloan Foundation, the New York Foundation, the Henry Nias Foundation, the Smith, Kline & French Foundation, The Ottinger Foundation, Inc., the Gleich Foundation, The Pathfinder Fund, the Salisbury Community Fund, the Sunnen Foundation, the John Lindsley Fund, the Larned Johnson Foundation, and The Rosenstock Foundation, Inc.

In the United States early work in population had little support except from American foundations. No funds of the government or of the universities went into the pioneering work. It was different in Europe, where governments, particularly in the Scandinavian countries and in France, supported extensive research in population problems. But when the world was suddenly threatened with an increase in numbers so rapid as to endanger the future of man, the United States and not Europe was prepared to meet it. It was to the United States that the countries of Southeast Asia and the Middle East turned for help when they found that their hard-won economic gains were being eaten up by ever-greater increases in the number of their people. The technical advisors and consultants who were asked to help with national programs of fertility control in India, in Pakistan, Taiwan, South Korea, Turkey, and

Egypt were trained in the United States or in centers financed by American foundations overseas, or in the demographic training centers of the United Nations, to which American foundations had contributed the major part of the costs. The most effective methods of control, and the know-how for their manufacture abroad, came from the United States, tested with money contributed by American foundations. Even as this goes to press, national research and training programs, demographic and medical, are going forward in a dozen countries overseas with the help of monies given by American foundations at the request of the governments concerned.

The role of the foundations in the field of population is far from over, but they have already performed their most vital functions of innovation and stimulus. The central governments of many Asian and African countries have now committed themselves to government-financed programs of fertility control. The American government itself is helping, when asked, with counterpart and AID funds. In the United States, state and local authorities are beginning to take responsibility for birth control activities in hospitals and clinics. We can foresee the time when all over the world the control of births is as much the accepted responsibility of governments as is at present their responsibility for the public health. In this field at least the innovating role of the foundations was performed at a most vital time.

CHAPTER 29

International Affairs

PHILIP E. MOSELY

Almost against its will, the United States emerged in the twentieth century from a self-imposed isolation to become one of the decisive forces of world power and change. Twice in a span of less than thirty years it found itself driven to mobilize its potentially immense resources of economic and military power in support of impoverished political goals. How and why this decisive shift occurred, and what it portends for the future shape of a world whose dimensions have been vastly shrunk by jet travel, Telstar, and the intercontinental missile, provides the focus of an increasingly intensive intellectual effort which, for lack of a better term, is called "international affairs."

Over these same few decades the scholarly community has responded to this seismic shift by putting forth great and varied efforts to analyze, interpret, and predict the course of world affairs. These efforts, in turn, have been made possible in very large measure, indeed primarily, through the understanding, encouragement, and support provided by American foundations. Without their recognition of the need and their assistance in meeting it, the process of intellectual initiation, experimentation, and diversification in international studies would still be limping along not far from the starting line. Without that understanding and support, the United States would, in truth, be poorly equipped intellectually to comprehend and fulfill its responsibilities as a member of the unruly family of nations.

The practical bent of the American mind, including the minds of philanthropists and statesmen, inevitably leads many people to question the value of this greatly expanded effort. Is it not premature for either scholars or those who back their efforts to pause to congratulate themselves at a time when peace seems poised on a threat of mutual annihilation, if not of a regression to barbarism, and at a time in history when painful differences among nations in their power and well-being—differences that were previously repressed or concealed by the colonial system—have re-emerged to clamor for new and presently unattainable solutions? Of course it is. On the other hand, to blame the unsatisfactory state of the world on the few scores or hundreds of innovating scholars who study these problems implies that the scholars, and the foundations who have helped them, are either incompetent miracle workers or perhaps malevolent witch doctors. The scholars are, in fact, only slightly abler and better trained than their fellow citizens, endowed like them with good will and a hope for a more peaceful world. What sets them somewhat apart is their confidence that in the long run it may be useful to provide statesmen and their nations with a more systematic understanding of the world environment in which we live.

Like most fields of social science research,[1] the study of international affairs derives from the optimistic and rationalist assumptions of moral philosophy, the dominant strain of Western thought in the eighteenth and nineteenth centuries. The search for ways to put an end to wars was stimulated by the liberating philosophy of the American and French revolutions, as formulated by many thinkers from Rousseau and Jefferson to Cobbett and Mazzini and restated by Woodrow Wilson. The searchers for peace can be divided roughly between those who believe, with Wilson and Karl Marx, that peace can be achieved only through effecting basic changes in human institutions, and those who look, as do most schools of pacifism, to the purifying of the human heart and mind as the first and crucial change that must be brought about. Whatever the diversity of philosophical assumptions that motivated them, for an entire century the "peace movement" in America centered its efforts directly on the goal it sought, in the same spirit of practical idealism that made realities of the demands for universal education, equal rights for women, and a respected status for the working classes.[2] The peace enthusiasts felt that there was only a relatively short step to take from the expression of a devoutly held moral purpose to its practical fulfillment. They were therefore little inclined to delay or complicate their appeals for action by elaborate schemes of prior investigation and rigorous analysis.

Something of this flavor of impatience influenced two major and lasting philanthropic acts of the early twentieth century in the field of international affairs. In establishing the Carnegie Endowment for International Peace in 1910, Andrew Carnegie sincerely believed that the permanent elimination of wars and the prospect of wars might well be achieved in the lifetime of men then living. And he directed the trustees, when that happy state had been achieved, to apply the endowment's resources to solve other major problems of mankind. In establishing the World Peace Foundation, Edwin Ginn took a similarly optimistic view. Both these foundations, which develop and operate educational, research, and other programs of their own (in distinction to non-operating or grant-making foundations), have continued to exhibit intellectual vigor and courage and to make many valuable contributions, especially in the fields of international organization and education of citizen opinion. Both have set high standards through their research, books, and periodicals. Both have been able to enlist the support of major grant-making foundations for some of their larger projects.

The impact of World War I and the abortive peace that followed it stimulated the development of important new institutions in the field of international affairs. The twin decisions to create the Council on Foreign Relations and the Royal Institute of International Affairs (Chatham House) were taken by small groups of foreign policy experts, largely university scholars, in the midst of the Paris peace conference in 1919. They were created in recognition of the urgent necessity to continue and deepen, in a time of troubled peace, the work of analytical and policy study that had been hastily improvised in the House Inquiry of 1917-18 and in a somewhat parallel effort in Great Britain. From the beginning each institution provided an off-the-record forum for frequent and intimate discussions of foreign-policy problems by people of political, business, and scholarly backgrounds; each established an important journal.

Perhaps because of the then absence of international affairs studies from the curricula of British universities (except for a lonely chair at the University of Aberystwyth), the Royal Institute preceded the Council by more than a decade in setting up an extensive program of research (predominantly, however, of background to policy, rather than of policy alternatives). The research program of the Council on Foreign Relations was launched cautiously but effectively on a continuing basis in the 1930's, received a great impetus from its off-the-record War and Peace Studies Program, 1940-45, and, since World War II, has enlarged very substantially the coverage of both world areas and problems, to cite only its recently completed programs on Communist China and U.S. policy in Asia and on U.S. policy and the Atlantic Community.

The example and experience of the Royal Institute led, in the 1930's and later, to the creation of sister institutions in major Commonwealth countries, and also to the establishment, often with significant support from major American foundations, of institutes on Commonwealth affairs, Africa, and strategic studies. Both the Royal Institute and the Council have developed substantial and reliable sources of nonfoundation support. Yet it must be noted that each important new advance they have pioneered in developing programs and methods of research has been made possible in major part through foundation grants (Rockefeller and Ford for both Institute and Council, Carnegie for certain Council programs).

The experience of World War I also stimulated the Brookings Institution to devote major attention to international, particularly economic, problems; many of its post-1918 studies on war debts, commercial policy, and international finance were very influential. With the support of major grants from the larger foundations Brookings, since World War II, has expanded its program effectively to embrace such fields as United Nations affairs, economic development, commercial policy, foreign aid, foreign operations of the federal government, and numerous other fields.

The creation of the Foreign Policy Association in 1918 was directly stimulated by the recognition of the great need for an improved flow of information about world affairs to potentially influential groups throughout the country. For almost five decades, FPA has pressed its search for important audiences and for the best ways to reach them. More than half its modest resources, from the beginning, have come from major foundations and, to some extent, from smaller ones.

Out of the same impetus to create a better-informed public opinion has developed a network of World Affairs Councils, numbering some sixty-five today. Some are extremely effective, with a wide regional impact; others remain rather quiescent. After supporting their development by substantial funds, the major foundations, in accordance with the basic foundation concept of supplying "venture capital" for new initiatives, have generally let the regional councils find their own level of locally generated financing, apart from support for some experimental projects to strengthen their work. Family, business, and regional foundations, however, are often an important source of continuing support for World Affairs Councils.

One center of international affairs interest, influential in the 1920's but then fading from the scene, was the Williamstown Institute, which attracted important statesmen and scholars to its annual sessions. Its example led to a widespread pattern of similar institutes and conferences on foreign affairs.

The first postwar decade saw the creation of important international affairs institutions, each cultivating some major part of this large field. This expansion took place outside a university setting. In contrast, the second of the interwar decades witnessed the first major development of the study of international affairs as a recognized part of the interests and operations of several major universities and leading colleges. The creation of an interdisciplinary graduate program by the Committee on International Relations at the University of Chicago was followed by the establishment of similar programs at Harvard and Columbia. Of central significance was the formation of the research-oriented Institute of International Studies, at Yale University (transferred in the main to Princeton University in the late 1940's), under the leadership of the late Frederick S. Dunn, Arnold Wolfers, and others. These were the first major experiments in organizing the systematic study of world affairs within the academic curriculum.

The research efforts of several of these new enterprises were supported primarily by foundation grants; the instructional programs were generally a part of the university budget. Except for the institute at Yale, which also devoted special attention to problems of international economic policy, the university efforts developed largely within the hospitable and permissive discipline of political science, with a strong assist from the vigorous field of diplomatic history.

It is perhaps symbolic of the practical bent of the American approach to new problems that the establishment of professional schools for the training of young diplomats actually preceded any clearcut and general definition of international affairs as a distinctive focus of intellectual training and research. The pioneer in this effort, the School of Foreign Service of Georgetown University, was joined in the early 1930's by the Fletcher School of Law and Diplomacy of Tufts University, the Woodrow Wilson School of Public and International Affairs at Princeton, and the Woodrow Wilson Department of Foreign Affairs at the University of Virginia. The late 1930's also saw the founding of the School of Advanced International Studies in Washington, which later became affiliated with the Johns Hopkins University.

The relatively late emergence of international affairs or world politics as a recognized discipline or subdiscipline was due, in part, to the traditional strength and high prestige of international law; in part, to the burgeoning of the study of diplomatic history after World War I; and, in some degree, to the post-1920 enthusiasm for studies of international organization. Each of these three fields, even though they covered only a part of "world politics," attracted many talents and much support. Each had its luminaries, who in turn attracted and shaped able younger scholars, whereas for quite a while no one seemed quite sure what "international politics" was or where it fitted in among the long-established disciplines and departments. Actually, in the interwar decades the strongest single center for the study of world politics was the Graduate Institute of International Studies at Geneva, established by the prestigious William E. Rappard, and largely supported for many years by Rockefeller Foundation and other American grants. A surprisingly large number of American pioneers in international affairs, in fact, received a crucial part of their training and stimulation either at the Geneva Institute or at the Ecole Libre des Sciences Politiques, in Paris.

In the 1920's and 1930's the primacy of international law within the field of international affairs was still unchallenged. Many of its great pioneering achievements grew out of the national program which was conducted by the Harvard Bureau of Research on International Law, inspired by the late Manley O. Hudson and strongly supported by grants of major foundations. Relying on rigorous criticism in well-organized committees and seminars, the Harvard Bureau saw through to completion a remarkable and influential series of treatises on the law of treaties, territorial waters, nationality, government immunity, neutrality, and many other central themes.[3] American scholars also took an active part in the programs of the Hague Academy of International Law and the International Studies Conference, the latter sponsored by the Institute of Intellectual Cooperation in Paris; both institutions relied heavily on the support of American foundations.

The World War of 1914-18 had as one minor effect the stimulation of a very strong interest in analyzing the origins of the catastrophe which so few had foreseen. This effort, in turn, was greatly assisted by the prompt and large-scale publication of diplomatic collections. The study of almost contemporary diplomatic history provided a strong underpinning for a more probing examination of the international states system, alliances, causes of war, and conditions of peace. Finally, the establishment of the League of Nations, the International Labor Organization, and the Permanent Court of International Justice encouraged the writing of books and the introduction of courses in the new field of international organization. Indeed, until the late 1930's the new international institutions received greater emphasis in most courses on international affairs than did the study of international conflict.[4]

It was not until the mid-1930's that the study of international politics emerged from under the deep shadows cast by vigorous disciplines of history and law, and set about discovering and defining its particular role. The publication of a number of systematic textbooks focused on world politics helped open the way for the introduction of undergraduate courses. With the acquisition of an academic constituency, international affairs could now win curricular and budgetary status. The normal academic flow of energies from teaching undergraduates (with opportunities for the employment of trained specialists), systematic graduate training (to meet this demand), and opportunities for postdoctoral research (and nonacademic experience) was at last being established in the field of international affairs just as World War II began. After a wartime hiatus in academic development, the field of international affairs entered upon an almost explosive growth in volume and variety of effort.

Unlike the intensive and relatively brief effort that World War I had demanded of the United States—an episode that a majority of Americans were inclined to forget in a return to the psychological comfort of isolation—World War II left a legacy of almost universal concern with the nature and prospects of world politics. In addition, the second war involved much larger numbers of scholars, with far greater responsibilities, in the problems of achieving victory and thinking about the peace which proved so difficult to establish. The war effort demanded the application of old skills and the development of new talents. Psychologists, sociologists, economists, anthropologists, historians, philosophers—and even the small array of students of international affairs—were, to the amazement of "practical men," indispensable to the winning of the war.

There is no need here to review the crucial role played by wartime demands and wartime experiences on the development of non-Western studies.[5] Before the war these fields of studies had not attracted the interest and cooperation of many social scientists, except historians. The war and the postwar years changed this. Political scientists, economists, sociologists, and also geographers, jurists, and psychologists joined with linguists, students of literature, and historians to develop interdisciplinary training and research in the long-neglected areas that lie outside North America and Western Europe. The challenge to mount an effective response to the new and vast responsibilities that, unsought, devolved upon the people of the United States during and after World War II evoked a remarkable upsurge of academic innovation. By far the largest part of that effort was financed for two decades by the large-scale and imaginative decisions of major foundations. In the last few years government support has taken over a substantial part of this responsibility, but the scholarly community looks still to the foundations for support of new, untried, and experimental ideas.

The growth of area studies has greatly broadened and strengthened the field of international affairs since World War II. For one thing, international politics holds an important place in most programs of regional studies. Teaching, government, and business now recognize the need for broadly trained students of Russian, Chinese, African, Middle East, and other varieties of international politics. Even more important has been the impact of area studies on the approach of postwar scholars to international affairs. Today no student of world affairs would assume that one state is very much like any other state, that France and the Soviet Union, Communist China and India, Ghana and Brazil are likely to behave according to a single or classical pattern just because they are all described as "states." The experience and concepts of political development, of elites and their recruitment, of patterns of communication between national units—these and many other new conceptual and research tools have their applications to the study of international affairs; they would hardly be familiar to the student of world politics were it not for the close communication and cooperation developed out of a common fund of experience shared by both area studies and international relations. The study of the international behavior of states and other actors on the international scene can no longer be compartmented off from the study of the domestic sources of that behavior.

A second major expansion of the scope of international affairs, similarly stimulated by the experiences of World War II, has been the emphasis on policy studies—on the analysis of possible, feasible, alternative, and desirable courses of national and international action. The worldwide range of wartime and postwar policy problems gave rise, almost overnight, to a demand for the comprehensive and dispassionate examination of the nature of probable constellations of forces in the postwar world and for fresh definitions of U.S. national interests. This urgent concern was reflected in policy studies carried on by the Council on Foreign

Relations and the Brookings Institution, in the discussion of future international organizations by several private expert groups, and, on a broader scale, in the postwar planning carried on within the government, to a very large extent by scholars summoned to national service. The range of study was a broad one. It included, for example, food and agriculture, monetary and economic reconstruction, refugees, relief and rehabilitation, treatment of defeated countries, territorial settlements, and also the planning for the institutions and early postwar programs of the United Nations, the International Bank and the International Monetary Fund, the Food and Agriculture Organization, UNESCO, and other international bodies. The wartime efforts, in both the United States and Britain, to pave the way for a "better world" were far more comprehensive and expert than those of World War I.

The experience of harnessing the insights of many disciplines to the task of defining possible and useful policies has been reflected in the postwar emphasis on international affairs as a "policy science." True, the scholars who have participated in this effort during and since the war have not expected any utopias to emerge full-blown from committees and memoranda. They have constantly been aware of the gap between analysis and decision, and they have not expected the social scientists to take over the responsibilities of the statesmen. However, their efforts have demonstrated that political leaders are often able to act more intelligently, and to better long-range effect, when they have available the findings of expert and independent policy research to check against their curbstone hunches and sometimes to moderate their expectations.

The policy approach, as one aspect of the study of international affairs, continues to provide a strong link between university and other private research, on the one hand, and policy analysis and planning within government, on the other. Because of this substantial degree of shared intellectual responsibility, policy researchers have continued to move with a good deal of flexibility between government service and nongovernmental research, in a way that seems incredible in most other countries. Even in Western Europe there is usually a sharp gap between the tight-lipped professional civil servants and the rather un-policy-oriented academics, who often view even the larger policy concerns of governments from a great distance. Moreover, so long as the government feels a need to call on the services of noncareer but expert men of affairs or scholarship, it is indispensable for the latter to acquire training in policy thinking in advance of actual service as part-time or temporary officers of government. That experience is best provided by independent policy-study centers or institutions, which, without being financed or dominated by government, offer both an exposure to "real" problems and an opportunity to sharpen policy thinking. Without these contributions by the private sector, governmental bodies would find great difficulty in replenishing their ranks and in conducting a continuing canvass of emerging policy problems and exploring possible ways to cope with them.

In response to the continuing pressure for unremitting intellectual efforts in the field of policy research, long-established organizations, such as the Council on Foreign Relations and the Brookings Institution, have expanded and systematized their programs of policy research, and have extended them into new fields of strategy, social psychology, arms control, economic and political development, and others. Many newly-created centers have made extensive and important contributions to the flow of policy studies. Among them special mention should be made of the Center for International Affairs at Harvard University, the Center for International Studies at the Massachusetts Institute of Technology, the Economic Growth Center at Yale University, the Institute of War and Peace Studies and the Institute of Atomic Age Studies at Columbia University, the Center for International Studies at the Woodrow Wilson School of Princeton University, the Foreign Policy Research Institute at the University of Pennsylvania, the Washington Center for Foreign Policy Research at the School for Advanced International Studies of the Johns Hopkins University, the Center for Strategic Studies at Georgetown University, the Rule of Law Research Center at Duke University, the Mershon Center for Education in National Security at Ohio State University, the Committee on International Relations at the University of Chicago, the Social Science Foundation at the University of Denver, and the Institute for International Studies at the University of California (Berkeley). This incomplete listing does not include, of course, the even more numerous centers of regional or world area studies, a substantial part of whose work deals with problems of world politics.

The universities have by and large provided the indispensable setting and backing for most of this remarkable development. They offer the conveniences of proximity for cooperation among a variety of disciplines. They provide the senior scholars with stability of tenure, a precondition of any long-range intellectual effort. They furnish massive library and other research resources, and they draw in and train able graduate students, who in turn are attracted to new and developing fields of inquiry. The financial contributions of universities have been large, stable, and indispensable, for support of research by foundations, and even more so by government grants, is often unpredictable. In sum, the universities provide the essential elements of continuity and independence.

The foundations have in turn made available by far the major part of the new, mobile, and large resources needed for this farflung and ramified effort. They have been alert to recognize new needs and new approaches; they have given support to a variety of intellectual innovations and have fostered intellectual competition. The provision of government support has, on balance, followed later. Quite often it has supported the application of already tested methods of analysis to new problems and has been less willing than foundations to back experimental efforts. Because of the universities' almost universal insistence on conducting research primarily for the advancement of science through publication and dissemination of the results, very few of the government grants have been in the field of classified research. Here again, the availability of sympathetic and effective foundation interest in developing the study of international affairs, as a source alternative to governmental support, has greatly strengthened the independence and integrity of the scholarly community in meeting governmental needs in this relatively new field.

STRATEGIC STUDIES

A third major innovation of the postwar decades has been the large-scale development of strategic studies and their integration into the general field of international studies. This has been brought about primarily through the creation of important research centers supported by continuing grants of federal funds but operating with varying degrees of intellectual independence from policy control by their sponsors. The first of the new postwar "think tanks" has been the RAND Corporation.[6]

Like many creative innovations, the "RAND idea" seems simple and inevitable in retrospect. Research and development (the meaning of the word RAND) have been indispensable to the revolutionary development of military technology, for carefully analyzed choices among numerous possibilities must be made as early as feasible in the development of advanced military instruments; in turn, the uses to which those instruments may be put five, ten, or fifteen years later can be defined only in terms of the defense systems they are designed to serve. Finally, military power, in its broadest sense, is inseparable from the role it may play, whether in actual use or in reserve, in projecting and supporting national political purposes in a rapidly changing world environment. Thus, after the war, RAND added economists, psychologists, political scientists, and historians to its always much larger staff of physicists, mathematicians, and engineers. What was more important, RAND pioneered in developing an even broader range of interdisciplinary cooperation, thus learning by trial and error to blend and harness the joint efforts of, for example, strategists and political scientists, physicists and economists, in analyzing problems of tremendous import and baffling complexity.

To pursue the RAND experience a little further—RAND people early saw, for example, the great importance of making the clearest possible analysis of the structure, resources, and trends of the Soviet economy. How much of its resources could and would the Soviet Union devote to building up its military power? No one university would have more than one well-trained expert, at most, on the Soviet economy; indeed, such experts could be counted on the fingers of one hand. By bringing together the scanty research resources available, by promoting the retraining of economists to work in the Russian field, and by establishing a carefully planned program, the RAND studies of the Soviet economy carried through a comprehensive and penetrating analysis of the Soviet economic system and set a standard of rigorous objectivity. No one university could have organized this effort effectively, and no one foundation would have been willing to devote to this single field the substantial resources that it required.

Over the past two decades, however, the most important contributions made by RAND and a number of similar organizations have not been made in the fields of economic research, in social and political development studies, in analyses of conflict and crisis management, in studies of subversive and antisubversive warfare, or in similar fields. It has been, rather, in the comprehensive examination of the nature of power and the role of power in political strategy. Prior to World War II, the study of international affairs generally made a quick bow to the notion of power, which is as old as Thucydides, and then hastened on to examine diplomatic, institutional, and other problems that are more accessible to the political scientist and more congenial to him. The stark facts of the postwar world have made the study of power, in its many ramifications, an indispensable part of the field of international affairs. In this development, government-supported policy-advisory corporations, usually guided at least loosely by boards of trustees of high public and intellectual standing, have played a decisive role. And, as one consequence of their efforts, strategic studies, broadly defined, have also come, twenty years after the war, to occupy an important place in the academic curriculum, in graduate studies, and in the research efforts of university and other nongovernmental institutions. The success of RAND and similar bodies has eroded their original status of near-monopoly in the field of strategic studies.

One condition for the continuing intellectual effectiveness of a government-financed policy-advisory corporation is its ability, when necessary, to act independently of its sponsor in identifying and exploring untrodden avenues of investigation, perhaps before the sponsor has understood their potential significance; in having adequate access to the relevant data, whether classified or not; and in its ability to work through to conclusions and recommendations that may be displeasing to the traditional or perceived interests of the sponsor. A corollary requirement is the ability to publish important and innovative studies, subject of course to some essential restrictions on the dissemination of classified information, defined as narrowly as possible. Integrity of research means that methods and findings shall be subjected promptly to scrutiny by the community of scholars and experts, and that its broad conclusions be made available to the attentive segment of public opinion, which in turn sets broad limits of public support for national purposes and policies. In these respects, too, RAND has been a pace setter, with the intelligent support of the U.S. Air Force, which has recognized its broader than single-service responsibility in a democracy. In part because RAND has served these needs with imagination and integrity, its example and its success have been contagious. Government-sponsored research corporations have become a prominent feature of the policy-making process. The Stanford Research Institute, the Institute for Defense Analyses, the Research Analysis Corporation, the Franklin Institute, and other bodies have tackled many new and complex problems.

In general, this major development, unlike most of the growth of international studies, has taken place independently of the role of foundations. For obvious reasons, foundations are extremely reluctant to "mingle" their "venture capital" with government funds, if only for fear of involving research institutions in dual and conflicting responsibilities to the donors. Because of their tradition of full and complete accountability to the public, foundations cannot—or at least certainly should not—give support to classified, i.e., unpublishable, research. On the other hand, through their support of independent or non-governmental research in strategic studies, the foundations have done a great deal to hasten the otherwise slow process of integrating these studies into the academic environment and have provided alternative opportunities for research by "strategists" in a congenial atmosphere of unquestioned scholarly independence. Both the standing and the product of the government-financed research corporations have been greatly strengthened by the foundation-supported growth of smaller but independent centers within universities. Thus in this field, as in others, the relative importance and impact of the contributions that have been made by government and by foundations cannot be measured primarily in financial terms.

INTERNATIONAL STUDIES

Within the broad and somewhat amorphous field of international affairs, older and newer trends coexist in friendly and often cooperative rivalry. Among older disciplines, the well-defined field of international law has continued an orderly and effective expansion of its interests and methodologies. This renewed vitality has been stimulated in part by the intellectual and political challenges raised in the almost twenty years of its work by the United Nations Commission on the Codification of International Law, as well as by international conferences, and sometimes by agreements, on a wide range of subjects, including, among others, telecommunications, international civil aviation, the status of the Antarctic and outer space, diplomatic immunities, and the law of territorial waters. In this area of international affairs the role of scholars has long been of decisive intellectual importance. Most of this private effort has been financed by foundation grants to universities, to the programs of the American Society of International Law and the International Law Association, to the Institute of Air and Space Law at McGill University, and, of course, to the Hague Academy of International Law. The discipline of international law, which sometimes felt neglected by foundations in the postwar years, has recently displayed great vigor. The support of numerous smaller foundations, as well as special attention by the Ford Foundation, has contributed to its healthy growth.

Under the stimulus of the many problems that have confronted the United Nations as well as other international organizations, both scholars and research centers concerned with their problems have also risen actively to the challenge. Whereas before World War II studies of international organization were typically rather general and somewhat legal or institutional in treatment, today questions of pressure groups, bloc voting, financing of the United Nations, the role of the secretary general, and specific case studies of international operations hold a central position. Scholars in this field have drawn on the accumulated experience of national studies of lobbying, decision making, and so forth to enlarge their armory of research tools.

While the field of diplomatic history continues to show strength, its role is less prominent than it was in the interwar decades. Much of the new development has been directed toward case studies of conflict, bargaining, psychological values, and similar concrete analyses, which in turn have benefited from the recent enrichment of political science by adaptions from other disciplines.[7] Thus, to a considerable extent the historical method, within international affairs, is now applied not so much to reconstruct the record of diplomacy but rather to test new hypotheses and interpretations against that record, not so much to examine the history of diplomatic tranactions among governments regarded as more or less similar to one another but rather to trace in greater depth the interaction of political systems exercising varying degrees of power and motivated by diverse and contradictory value structures. Despite the growth of strategic studies, by far the largest part of scholarly production within international affairs derives from the case study or modified historical tradition which has so long been central to it.

Many innovations of concept and method are emerging within international studies, many of them derived from quantitative, psychological, and political science insights. Limitations of space make it necessary to mention them only briefly here. Able scholars are expanding the tool kit of quantitative research, following the patterns set by economics and, to some extent, by sociology and social psychology. Model building of international systems, including alliance systems and adversary patterns, has been greatly stimulated. Decision making has emerged as a distinct subfield and is refining its tools. Political war gaming, on the model of strategic war games first developed by RAND, is being tested intensively in a number of leading centers. Studies of conflict resolution attempt to integrate the insights of social psychology into a newly defined subfield. The role of elites and of mass opinion is being studied against the background of international as well as national policy making. Political, ethnic, religious, and economic interest groups are under study. A small but vigorous effort is being devoted to the study of the integration and disintegration of larger-than-national communities.

In sum, the somewhat static approach of the prewar decades has given way to dynamic inquiry into many new problems and the elaboration of new methodologies with which to tackle them. Foundations have not been loath to "take a flier" on almost any of the newer currents of research. Indeed, on balance they are anxious not to "miss a bet" and are willing to give each potential line of innovation a fair run for "their" money.

In the postwar years important new journals have been founded, offering channels for a more rapid circulation of new ideas and research suggestions than is possible through the publication only of books. Several journals continue the tradition of a broad coverage of international affairs; others plow more deeply a special segment of the field; and still others stress particular, sometimes particularistic, schools of methodology. Foundations have often assisted the launching of new journals when they could be considered an integral part of the process of research, from conception of new ideas through their dissemination. Much to the disappointment of editors or would-be editors, foundations are seldom able to provide continuing support to any particular journal without falling under accusation of damaging unsubsidized competitors.

In the long run the existence of a vigorous and growing field of international affairs only in the United States, together with some participation by the scholarly communities in Canada, Britain, Scandinavia, and the Low Countries, with little being accomplished elsewhere, works counter to the requirements for a broadly based international community of scholarship. Accordingly, several major American foundations have devoted much thought and large funds to supporting new initiatives abroad. Because of the lead established by American scholarship in international affairs, there have been transitional and probably transitory outcries against American "intellectual imperialism." Actually the foundations' efforts have been devoted to shortening the transition to self-development and therefore self-respect. Two of the main obstacles to achieving this fervently desired condition are entirely of non-American origin: the extreme rigidity of university administration and the traditional separatism among disciplines in Western Europe and Latin America; and the complete, or almost complete, absence of "venture capital" from private or governmental sources.

Mention has been made earlier of the extensive support which the Rockefeller Foundation provided for the pre-1939 development of international studies in Europe. This tradition has been continued, now mainly by the Ford Foundation. The Graduate Institute of International Studies, Chatham House, St. Antony's, and many other institutions receive, like so many American institutions, a great, often the greatest, part of their maneuverable research funds from American foundations. Since the war important new centers of foreign policy research have also been created in Germany and France, and others are getting under way in Italy and Austria, again with the partial support of American foundations. The development of area studies in Western Europe also owes a great deal to American support, which withdraws eagerly as soon as local support has been mustered. An international Institute for Strategic Studies located in London has done a great deal to domesticate new methods of modern strategic studies in the continent where they originated long ago.

The development of international and area studies in Asia, Africa, and Latin America has been stimulated by foundation support, which provides advanced training, library collections, travel, and conferences, and, where applicable, supports well-organized programs. The efforts to develop international and area studies outside the Atlantic area are only a small part of the total effort in which foundations, governments, and international organizations are engaged with the aim of equipping newly independent and ambitious nations with the necessary instruments for generating their own advancement to full intellectual stature in the world community.

ROLE OF FOUNDATIONS

American foundations have played a central, indispensable, but not determining role in the growth of international studies. Since early in the twentieth century they have seen their proper function not in political advocacy or propaganda, but in promoting systematic research along many lines and in a variety of institutional settings. They have responded imaginatively to intellectual initiatives presented by individuals and small groups. They have promoted the interchange of ideas and experiences, rather than attempting to impose strong preferences or initiatives of their own. When governments have shown a willingness to take over the basic support of tested programs, they have gladly shifted their own funds to encourage the new and untried, though not necessarily the completely untried. They have made great efforts to promote the development of an international community of scholars engaged in international studies.

In the postwar years important changes have taken place in the relative roles of major foundations. The Rockefeller Foundation, for several decades the strongest source of support for international studies, has greatly curtailed its activities in order to concentrate on other goals that are also of worldwide importance. In recent years the Carnegie Corporation of New York has similarly shifted the center of its concerns away from international affairs. The Ford Foundation, through two of its major divisions, has greatly expanded its contributions to both international studies and area research. And, in a very healthy development, numerous smaller foundations—smaller than the three large ones cited here—have substantially increased their own participation in this development. In doing so, they are demonstrating how much relatively small investments, as well as very substantial support, can do in fostering dynamic development and experimentation in a field in which careful, imaginative, and objective research may hope to make some measurable contributions to equipping mankind to cope with the crucial problems of war and peace.

CHAPTER 30

The Role of the Foundations
in Non-Western Studies

GEORGE M. BECKMANN

The foundations have played a decisive and continue to play a crucial role in support of the development of non-Western studies as an integral part of American higher education. Foundation grants not only have assisted universities in developing the essential resources for graduate training and for research, but have also, as a result, helped to generate a much-needed and long-overdue revolution in American education as a whole. In brief, they have improved the capacity of American universities and colleges, and consequently of society as a whole, to meet the educational challenges of a rapidly and dynamically changing world and at the same time to broaden the cultural horizons of the American people.

The foundations have provided and continue to provide the venture capital for the development of non-Western studies that the universities and colleges lacked themselves, and which the government has been for the most part reluctant to offer. Compared with other sources of support, the record of the foundations has been impressive. Looked at with the advantage of hindsight, however, in the light of national need, the foundations started too late and let their interests develop too slowly. They are, moreover, still doing too little, and there is the danger that they will stop what they are doing too soon.

The Rockefeller Foundation was the first large national foundation to recognize the need to develop non-Western studies as an integral part of American higher education, and it was the only major foundation that was active in this field until after World War II. The Rockefeller Foundation pioneered support of Slavic, East Asian, Near Eastern, and Latin American language and area studies at universities and colleges, and of scholarly activities in these areas sponsored by organizations like the American Council of Learned Societies. Its grants, however, were modest in size and totaled less than $1 million in the period from 1934 to 1942. In addition, Rockefeller fellowship programs provided funds to help train a relatively small number of young men and women in various disciplinary aspects of non-Western studies. These dollars were well invested as they helped to create the kind of competence that was so sorely needed during the period of World War II. But not enough money was invested for these purposes by American philanthropy as a whole. The demands of fighting a global war and of planning for the peace made it increasingly apparent that our society did not have adequate knowledge about many foreign areas or about the personnel and materials for training and research on them. Between 1943 and 1945, the Rockefeller Foundation, therefore, increased its support of university programs, used primarily for training and research by the military, by an amount in excess of the total of all its grants in the previous decade.

The responsibilities that accompanied the new position of power and leadership held by the United States after World War II created even greater demands for increased competence in global terms. American society desperately needed more knowledge and more trained personnel. Among the major foundations, the Rockefeller Foundation was again the first to assist a small number of scholars and their universities to expand existing or create new graduate-training and research programs in Slavic, East European, East Asian, Indian, or Near Eastern language and area studies. It set a precedent followed later by other national foundations with its grant in 1945 of $250,000 to Columbia University for the establishment of a Russian Institute in the newly created School of International Affairs. The first of its kind and a model for others, the Russian Institute had two basic objectives: one, to train area specialists with competence in the various aspects of Russian life and command of the Russian language; and, two, to improve American knowledge of the Soviet Union through research. In all, the Rockefeller Foundation invested another $1 million in university programs and in activities sponsored by the American Council of Learned Societies in the two-year period from 1946 through 1947 and another several million dollars in the period down to 1951.

The Carnegie Corporation was the second major foundation to provide support for the development of non-Western studies. In 1947, after several years of planning, it made a series of relatively modest five-year grants to a dozen or so universities in support of area institutes for graduate training and research on Japan, India, the Near East, Southeast Asia, and Latin America. The largest grant was for $155,000, and the smallest for $56,000. A year later, the Carnegie Corporation made two grants with an especially important impact upon the whole effort to develop non-Western language and area studies programs. One was a grant of $740,000, an unprecedented sum, to the newly established Russian Research Center at Harvard for study of all phases of Russian life through utilization of all the available tools of the social sciences. The second was a grant of $130,000, subsequently renewed, to the Social Science Research Council for a program of national fellowships for graduate-level training in foreign area studies. In all, the Carnegie Corporation made grants in support of non-Western studies totaling some $2.5 million in the period from 1947 to 1951.

The Rockefeller Foundation and Carnegie Corporation grants, while not generally large, brought handsome returns. First, they helped universities to establish or strengthen non-Western language and area studies programs at a time when university finances and facilities were strained under pressures both old and new. This was important because these grants not only helped to expand non-Western studies in the disciplines and to establish a firm base for language instruction, but also assisted a new approach to graduate training and research to obtain a secure foothold in the academic community. The concept and practice of combining discipline and multi-disciplinary area studies training was accepted more rapidly as a result. Second, the grants helped to increase the number of young men and women competent in non-Western areas. For example, the Foreign Area Training Fellowship Program administered by the Social Science Research Council made more than two hundred awards between 1947 and 1953.

The Ford Foundation, shortly after its reorganization as a national philanthropy in 1951, recognized the need to improve the capabilities of the United States in meeting its responsibilities in world affairs—especially for maintaining the strength of the non-Communist nations and for assisting the social and economic development of the emerging countries. Its International Training and Research Program therefore followed the lead of the Rockefeller Foundation and the Carnegie Corporation in spending part of its substantial resources, vast when compared to other foundations, to assist American higher education to equip itself with the men, knowledge, and organization necessary to respond more effectively to the demands upon it.

Since 1952 the Ford Foundation has allocated $138 million for grants designed to improve American competence to deal with international problems by narrowing the gap between the needs for and the supply of trained personnel and knowledge. Approximately half of that total has been used to strengthen non-Western language and area studies in American universities and colleges. Over the same period, the Rockefeller Foundation and the Carnegie Corporation expended for the same purpose approximately $5 million and $4 million, respectively. Recently, however, the latter two foundations have begun to change their roles. The Rockefeller Foundation has increasingly moved away from supporting American institutions of higher education in world affairs and has followed the path of developmental assistance to selected universities in the underdeveloped countries. The Carnegie Corporation continues its active interest in American higher education and world affairs, but, with its relatively smaller funds, plays more of an innovating role.

GRADUATE TRAINING AND RESEARCH PROGRAMS

The bulk of the Ford funds have been used to improve and consolidate existing language and area training and research programs in the major universities and to establish new programs where they were needed. In the case of existing programs, this permitted an expansion of graduate training and research. It also made possible a change in the very character of area studies through the addition of new staff in the social sciences. This was important because it gave language and area studies programs a broader disciplinary base, which could provide for more attention to modern and contemporary problems. In the case of hitherto neglected areas, there was an expansion of language and area studies programs on Southeast Asia and Africa. In all, by 1959, some twenty-one language and area studies programs were receiving foundation support.

During the past five years, an important change has occurred in the pattern of Ford Foundation grants to universities in support of non-Western language and area studies programs. With the growth of institutional competence there has been a shift from short- or medium-term grants, originally given to support specific graduate training and research programs, to broader, long-term—usually for ten years—assistance to *university-wide* efforts to develop non-Western language and area programs, as well as other international studies. Through long-term grants the Ford Foundation has sought to encourage the country's major university centers to take an institution-wide approach to their international interests and to incorporate non-Western language and area studies as permanent features. From 1959 to 1963 it made grants to fifteen universities, divided almost equally between private and state institutions, in an amount totaling $42 million. It designated $26 million of that total for support of non-Western language and area studies, to include provision for faculty and library-staff salaries, expansion of library holdings for research, individual, or group research projects, and graduate-student fellowships. The fifteen universities are Columbia, Harvard, Chicago, California, Cornell, Michigan, Washington, Princeton, Yale, Indiana, Pennsylvania,

Wisconsin, Northwestern, Stanford, and Boston. They have led the way in the development of non-Western language and area studies and, in most cases, have substantial other international interests. They have a large number of the country's most distinguished scholars, libraries with strong research collections, and imaginative and effective instructional programs. In summary, through this single-grant approach, the Ford Foundation is supporting some forty-four non-Western language and area studies programs for graduate training and research: East Asian, 12; Slavic or East European, 10; South or Southeast Asian, 8; Near Eastern, 7; and African, 7. And it also is providing limited developmental support to stimulate interest in Latin American studies at six of the above universities.

The Ford Foundation is not confining its support of non-Western language and area studies programs to grants to these fifteen universities. On the contrary, it recognizes that, viewed in terms of national need, the collective resources of the fifteen universities account for only a small fraction of the country's student population, faculty interests and competences, overseas programs, and visiting foreign students and scholars. The Ford Foundation is seeking, therefore, to encourage additional private, state, and land-grant universities to enlarge and consolidate their resources for graduate training, research, and developmental activities in the international field. To date, it has made grants, usually for a five-year period, totaling approximately $6 million, to the following universities: Oregon, Washington at St. Louis, Kansas, Syracuse, Illinois, Pittsburgh, and Michigan State. Each of these grants includes support of non-Western language and area studies programs for graduate training and research.

FOREIGN AREA FELLOWSHIP PROGRAMS

The foundations have provided support for the training of individuals, as well as the development of university language and area programs, because personnel continues to be inadequate in view of the needs of American society as a whole and of higher education more specifically. The continued expansion of existing university programs, for example, depends upon increasing the supply of first-rate, well-trained young scholars. The creation of new faculty positions in discipline departments at other institutions and the establishment of new language and area programs at some of them were similarly dependent upon the availability of competent personnel. Talent had to be recruited systematically and trained over a period sufficiently long to guarantee linguistic and research competence. The Rockefeller Foundation and the Carnegie Corporation had begun to attack this problem in the 1930's and 1940's through limited support of fellowship programs. The problem was so great in the decade of the 1950's that a crash effort was needed, and among the foundations only Ford had the resources for such an approach.

The Foreign Area Fellowship Program, funded by the Ford Foundation since its inception in 1952, has made and continues to make the single most effective contribution to solution of the problem of the shortage of first-rate, well-trained personnel. It was administered directly by the Ford Foundation from 1952 to 1962 and since that time by a joint committee of the American Council of Learned Societies and the Social Science Research Council. Over the past twelve years, the Fellowship Program has awarded a total of approximately $10 million in grants to 1,214 individuals, of whom some 984 have completed periods of training averaging from two to three years in length. The bulk of the grants have gone to advanced graduate students and young scholars in the training stages of their careers rather than to established scholars. Their training programs have in most cases combined the regular requirements of a discipline or professional field, intensive language study, and a multi-disciplinary approach to a foreign culture, and have often included field language-training and research for the doctoral dissertation. At first, fellowships were offered only for the study of Asia and the Near East; however, in 1954 the program was enlarged to include the Soviet Union, Eastern Europe, and Africa. Later, in 1961, fellowships were offered for Latin American studies, and in 1964 for West European studies. The breakdown of the area concentrations of the fellows is as follows: East Asia, 237; the Near East, 148; South Asia, 141; Southeast Asia, 105; the Soviet Union and Eastern Europe, 348; Africa, 171; Latin America, 37; and International Relations, 27.

A few more statistics will demonstrate just how successful this program has been in strengthening American higher education. Of the 984 former fellows, 550 hold faculty positions in 181 colleges and universities in 38 states. This has had two important results, one of which is clearly indicated by the figures and a second which is not. The fellowship program has helped to provide personnel for colleges and universities which have become interested in non-Western studies. Young men and women have joined their faculties largely as historians, political scientists, anthropologists, and economists and to a lesser extent as teachers of critical languages and literature, sociologists, and geographers. They have enabled discipline departments to expand their course offerings, and some of them have provided the necessary leadership for the establishment of new language and area programs. Yet, at the same time, there has been some concentration of former fellows at universities, thereby adding strength to existing programs while providing a broader base for new ones. Twenty-nine universities have employed five or more fellows, and ten universities have employed ten or more. In addition to academic and teaching careers, eighty-two former fellows are now in government service, thirty-eight have joined philanthropic or nonprofit organizations, and forty-five are in business or the professions. Many former fellows have added to our knowledge of the non-Western world through the publication of the results of research. Altogether they have published 373 books and over 3,000 articles and short monographs; moreover, they have edited or contributed to another 516 volumes.

INDIVIDUAL AND GROUP RESEARCH PROJECTS

Foundations have also been the major source of support of research projects conceived by individual scholars, especially those at institutions where there is no foundation-supported program, or by groups of scholars with common or complementary interests that require large-scale funding.

Grants have sometimes been made directly to individual researchers by foundations, but more often they have been made through existing academic or scholarly channels, such as the various committees of the American Council of Learned Societies or the Social Science Research Council. For example, five committees—on Africa, Contemporary China, Latin America, the Near East, and Comparative Politics—of the Social Science Research Council made grants to more than three hundred scholars in the period from 1955 to 1964. And the Asian Committee and the Slavic and East European Committee of the American Council of Learned Societies have made grants to another three hundred scholars over much the same period. Another foundation-supported program deserving particular mention in this context is the study and research program in the Soviet Union under the auspices of an interuniversity committee, which now has a membership of thirty-eight American universities. By 1964 well over two hundred American scholars had participated in it. Although group projects tend to get more publicity, the foundations have not ignored the individual scholar. And, in many cases, group projects have been nothing more than the coordination of the common interests of individual scholars.

The following examples of grants to group projects will give some idea of the variety of kinds of projects and approaches to knowledge that have been supported by the Rockefeller, Carnegie, and Ford foundations: $420,000 to Columbia University for research on the political evolution of modern China (1955), $277,000 to Harvard University for research on the economy of China in modern times (1955), $200,000 to the Massachusetts Institute of Technology for a study of economic development and social change in sub-Saharan Africa (1959), $200,000 to the University of Michigan for research on the political modernization of Japan (1961), $130,000 to the University of Florida for studies of the historical and contemporary forces shaping the territories and nations of the Caribbean (1961), $910,000 to the Social Science Research Council for research on the economy of Communist China (1961), $240,000 to the University of Chicago for research on education and socio-economic development of transitional societies (1962), and $250,000 to Northwestern University for research on intercultural relations (1962).

The foundation approach in support of research has also included grants to foreign scholars and institutions in order to broaden the base of our knowledge of areas and cultures of the non-Western world. For example, the foundations have assisted research carried on by scholars associated with Toyo Bunko in Tokyo, the Academia Sinica on Taiwan, and the Asiatic Research Center of Korea University in Seoul. And they have made possible fruitful collaboration between American and indigenous foreign scholars, especially in the case of Japanese and Indian studies.

UNDERGRADUATE EDUCATION

The foundations have played a crucial role in encouraging and assisting liberal arts colleges, either independent or in universities, to make basic changes in their approach to liberal learning through the integration of an international dimension, especially non-Western studies. The Carnegie Corporation led the way in the late 1940's and 1950's with a relatively small number of experimental grants to Columbia, Chicago, Michigan, and eight other universities and colleges for the development of new general education courses on non-Western areas. And since 1959 the Ford Foundation has made grants, totaling about $6 million, to help approximately one hundred colleges make non-Western studies a permanent part of undergraduate education. In order to maximize impact, the Ford Foundation has made grants for the most part to support various kinds of cooperative approaches to the development of adequate teaching resources involving groups of liberal arts colleges.

Space limitations permit only a brief listing of the variety of foundation efforts which have helped to implant non-Western studies in undergraduate education. They include the much enlarged reservoir of scholarly personnel now teaching undergraduates in several hundred colleges and universities; curricular planning and experimentation; the substantial materials which have been prepared for use in general education courses; the addition of a non-Western area dimension to the competence of existing college faculty members, either through special advanced study programs at major university foreign-area centers or through on-campus faculty seminars and other similar means; and the expansion of library holdings for teaching purposes, following such specialized guidelines as the select bibliography on Asia, Africa, Russia and Eastern Europe, and Latin America prepared by the American Universities Field Staff.

The demands upon the United States arising out of its involvement in world affairs show no signs of lessening in the decade ahead. If anything, a greater effort will be required to produce the personnel, knowledge, and understanding required for the tasks at hand and in prospect. One important task for American higher education is to build a broader base of competence on non-Western areas in order to expand the capacity for teaching, research, and service in the international realm.

In response to this challenge many American universities and colleges are currently undergoing a revolutionary transformation in adding a new international dimension to their activities and integrating it with their educational programs. They are endeavoring to reconceive their international roles, to innovate in their programs and organization, and to establish new relationships with one another, the government, and overseas institutions. Two recent reports have focused upon this important advance—*The University and World Affairs* and *The College and World Affairs*.[1]

This kind of development in American higher education requires not only leadership from within but also financial and other support from various sectors of society. The federal government, entering upon fields pioneered earlier by the foundations, is a potential source of massive support. So far it has played a limited but expanding role in supporting certain language and area activities of American universities through the NDEA, in using universities in development programs through the Agency for International Development (AID), and in strengthening educational institutions in the United States and overseas through the State Department exchange programs. State governments are only now beginning to recognize that their own vital interests are served by great state universities which help to meet needs in the field of world affairs, with which the individual states, as well as the nation, are profoundly and directly concerned. Foundations, business, and other private agencies continue to provide the indispensable support without which the American higher educational establishment would

406 / *U.S. Philanthropic Foundations*

lose its characteristic pluralism, flexibility, and freedom in responding to new social demands with new scholarly approaches and new educational programs.

It is essential that those foundations already devoting part of their resources to broadening the basis of international competence throughout American higher education continue to assist selected training and research programs on non-Western areas. It is equally important that they support the full range of the international activities. It is also necessary that other national foundations and, even more important, local foundations allocate some of their resources for these purposes.

More specifically, foundation resources will be required for the following:

1. *Personnel.* Because of the increased pressures and complexity of international events and the increased awareness of the existing and potential roles of the universities and colleges, the gap in American competence cannot be said to have been closed, despite the resource development that has taken place. There must be an increase in the number of persons with non-Western area competence. To this end, programs like the graduate-level Ford-supported Foreign Area Fellowship Program must be continued if not expanded. There is need, moreover, for more postdoctoral fellowship opportunities, especially for training on Africa and Latin America, and for more imaginative approaches to the training of a select number of able and committed undergraduates.

2. *Research.* Continued and expanded support of individual and group research projects by the foundations is essential in order to keep abreast of all kinds of demands for new knowledge. There will be increasing need for studies on problems relating to the process of development, or concerned with intercultural relations, which can build upon area and social science knowledge already obtained. But these studies should not be supported at the expense of basic research on specific non-Western countries and areas. Foundation support of research must not be confined to projects geared only to problem solving or to increasing knowledge of contemporary society. The recently published *Report of The Commission on the Humanities* in suggesting a reordering of foundation priorities noted as follows:

Everyone knows it is easy to persuade the board to give $950,000 to young economists working over the meager data on China's present economy, difficult to get $120,000 for a seven-year project in the humanities (her pre-modern history) involving all the senior Chinese scholars in the country.[2]

There is much in recent foundation policy and actions to warrant such a complaint.

3. *Graduate training and research centers*. The foundations must persist in their support of existing graduate language and area programs until they are accepted as a permanent and normal part of a university's total educational effort. The universities on their part must reciprocate by showing greater evidence of their commitment. And there is more that the foundations can do. The present development of language and area centers provides uneven coverage of the important non-Western countries and regions, and in some cases there is scarcely any systematic coverage at all. For example, it is essential that the United States have at least one first-rate training program and research center on Korea, the Philippines, and Vietnam, and that there be an effective division of labor in African and Latin American studies. It is especially important that the foundations make a vigorous effort to help support a long-overdue expansion of Latin American studies. Latin American studies were among the earliest of area studies programs to be established. There are at present Latin American course offerings at more than thirty American universities, but in none of them is to be found the quality of scholarship which has become increasingly common among non-Western area studies centers. The country needs a minimum of ten to twelve major graduate training and research centers, each with at least one very strong disciplinary base in addition to multi-disciplinary resources. It is hoped that the current program of the Ford Foundation to improve Latin American competence will be the harbinger of similar activity by other foundations. And finally it is essential that foundations help to encourage and assist the development of closer relationships and more effective collaboration between the academic social sciences and those professions or applied social sciences most heavily involved in overseas developmental activities in Africa, the Near East, Latin America, and South and Southeast Asia.

4. *Interinstitutional cooperation to develop and share scarce resources.* Foundations should help stimulate joint planning by universities and assist them to develop joint programs along the lines of the intensive summer Chinese- and Japanese-language program of the Committee on Institutional Cooperation or the Interuniversity Language Centers in Tokyo and Taipeh. Foundations should also encourage and assist cooperative programs between universities and colleges such as the Indiana statewide non-Western studies program or the cooperative critical languages program involving Princeton and over fifty liberal arts colleges. Foundations also have a special responsibilty for encouraging American universities to increase and regularize their contacts with training and research institutions in their geographic areas of interest. This can be done through faculty exchange and through arrangements for collaboration on research projects with scholars in the foreign area. Although there are recognized difficulties in such ventures, the prospective results over the long run are so promising that foundations not only should seize upon opportunities as they appear but also should not draw back from making their institutional support grants conditional on them.

5. *Undergraduate education.* A substantial number of colleges are developing a clear and unequivocal institutional commitment to include non-Western studies, not as an extra, but rather as an integral part of their educational programs. Many want to experiment with new curricular approaches. The central problem for them will be teaching resources. They will need assistance especially to strengthen faculty competence. They will also need to make limited resources go farther by cooperating when feasible with other institutions—sharing faculty and library resources; developing programs, such as overseas study, jointly; and working out a division of labor in non-Western language and area studies—and by taking advantage of the experience and resources of nearby universities. Foundation grants should continue to seek to stimulate and assist various kinds of cooperative approaches to faculty development and curricular revision by groups of colleges; cooperation between universities and colleges, especially in mobilizing scarce resources for non-Western language and area studies; faculty development and curricular experimentation at, at least, a

select number of colleges; and the preparation of teaching materials.

Clearly then, the contribution of the foundations to the development of non-Western studies in universities and colleges has been impressive. Yet, despite remarkable progress in the creation of new resources, the gap is widening instead of narrowing between the demands of American society for more well-trained personnel and new kinds of knowledge and the capacity of American higher education to supply them.

CHAPTER 31

The Foundations and Education

FRED M. HECHINGER

Education always runs at a deficit. Often, the higher the quality of education, the greater the deficit. No school or college budget ever could be termed satisfactory. The money available is never "enough." If more money were available, more could be done. There is no such thing as a fixed production goal in education.

The gap between a local school budget and the ideal aims of education is infinite. It is the difference between reality and what might be. Even in less utopian terms, the gap between the hard cash represented by tuition income and endowment interest on the one hand and the budget of a college or university is merely a practical device to tell those essential private donors that the enterprise they support is, and will always be, a deficit operation.

This is why the foundations are of such crucial importance to education. It is simply impossible to persuade local school boards and taxpayers that, since there is not even enough money for the routine operation, funds should be made available for experimentation, research, and innovation. Higher education faces much the same difficulty. Meeting the regular payroll leaves too little energy for inventiveness. It has been American education's good fortune to be able to rely on substantial and steadily growing contributions from the foundations—contributions which have often made the difference between routine operations and the vital effort to blaze new and unconventional trails.

Major foundation grants currently amount to well over half a billion dollars a year, and at the most recent count, in 1964, about one-third of the total was reported to have been in support of education. Even that impressive proportion tells too little of the full story of education support: many of the other categories, such as health, international activities, and the humanities, are in fact also in support of education and educational institutions. It would probably be more realistic to say that around $300 million of annual foundation money goes to the support of education.

The concept of such foundation efforts dates back to the last century. It was then that the great oil, steel and other industrial magnates began to divert some of their giant fortunes to the support of education. Two years after the beginning of the new century, John D. Rockefeller's millions helped to set the pace for future action through creation of the General Education Board, with its aim of the general furthering of education "without distinction of sex, race or creed." While these goals of nondiscrimination were undoubtedly linked to the politics of the post-Civil War period, it is inviting to think of them as the far-sighted forerunner of today's crucial concern of the major foundations with the issue of school integration and educational upgrading of the ethnic minorities.

But there are other important parallels between the actions taken by the General Education Board at the beginning of the twentieth century and the concern of the modern foundations. Colleges had mushroomed across the country; but many of them were precariously based, without proper quality controls and adequate financial backing. The board, realizing the dangers to the future of American education, set itself up as an unofficial watchdog of quality. Its dollar gifts were used as carrot and stick, in an effort to put a stop to chaos and aimlessness. Rather than dispensing charity, the board demanded proof that the college which sought financial aid stood ready to move in the direction of quality and stability.

In the first quarter of the century, the General Education Board in this strong-minded fashion distributed about $60 million. An indication of the real significance of this amount at the time may be gained from the fact that the federal government's total education expenditure for education in 1913 was only $5 million.

At the same time, the board established another pattern which has become the trademark of foundation support of education— the requirement to match its gifts, not merely on an equal basis but often by a two- or three-to-one ratio. Thus, the recipient of foundation grants is, in effect, told to approach its own friends and supporters, with the understanding that their efforts are needed to turn the foundation promise into reality. The tradition has been preserved. Among recent Ford Foundation grants have been $25-million gifts to Stanford and New York universities, each requiring the institution to raise $75 million for a total of $100 million resulting directly or indirectly from the foundation grant.

Perhaps the most widely noted foundation effort at quality control of education was the appointment of Abraham Flexner as an investigator of medical education. American medicals schools had been scandalously lax. Many of them were little more than diploma mills. Most serious students of medicine, if they could afford it, went to Europe for much of their professional training.

The Flexner report of 1910 came as a bombshell. It recommended that 80 percent of all existing medical schools be scrapped. It called for huge expenditures for the upgrading of medical education, a recommendation heeded both by John D. Rockefeller as a personal donor and by the Rockefeller Foundation. Its was also the beginning of the rise of American medical education and medicine itself to world leadership.

During the same era, the Carnegie Foundation for the Advancement of Teaching spent much money and effort to raise the salaries and pensions of college teachers. Significantly, it linked its financial underpinning of higher education with the establishment of qualitative yardsticks by which the content of a college curriculum might be measured. Carnegie "units" remained the measurable ingredients of a student's course work or of a teacher's classroom functions.

In the 1920's, moreover, Frederick P. Keppel, the father of Francis Keppel, the United States Commissioner of Education in the Kennedy and Johnson administrations, shaped the Carnegie Corporation of New York into an important instrument of foundation support of education. Earlier, the corporation had been merely a personal tool to help Andrew Carnegie in his bookkeeping of his charitable acts and deeds; now it was rapidly being transformed into a future-oriented foundation. Along with other foundations, notably that organized by Lessing Rosenwald, it threw its support behind attempts to infuse new blood into the liberal arts colleges. Institutions which broke with the sterile, German-inspired lecture system and moved instead toward independent study and faculty-led seminars were nursed along. Swarthmore, Bennington, Antioch and other so-called experimental colleges were major beneficiaries of such support. In the years ahead, their revolutionary departures from the beaten path exerted a vital, rejuvenating influence on all of the country's higher education.

The post–World War II period opened a distinctly new chapter in the foundation's role in supporting American education. The purposes of education had undergone vast changes. Although mass education had always been the nation's ideal, the true nature of the huge enterprise was revealed only after the G.I. Bill of Rights expanded the aspirations of college going beyond anything that had ever been thought possible. At the turn of the century, even high school attendance had still been the prerogative of the privileged; now college attendance was skyrocketing; by the mid-sixties, about half of the high school graduating classes went on to higher education. Coupled with the birth-rate boom, education at all levels had to face unprecedented demands for expansion.

But the question of numbers—challenging as it might have been by itself—was only part of the postwar story. There were rumblings of discontent over the curriculum as well. The nation was moving out of its phase of youthful optimism. The unlimited faith in the intellectual laissez faire was being questioned. Warning voices were heard urging educators to give up the sentimental idea that there would always be enough talent to go around, even if youth were to go through school at a leisurely, permissive pace. The demands of science and technology along with a new competition for world markets reminded educators that the self-satisfied Fortress America posture, which had already been shattered militarily, was increasingly difficult to justify in the world of learning. Even before education was recognized as the all-important key to full equality in the Negroes' civil rights struggle, the schools' part in the nation's and the individual's future began to undergo critical reappraisal.

Quality control, within an unprecedented mass-education system, became the challenge of the postwar era. It was therefore also the challenge to the foundations. And it is important to remember that it was at this stage—in 1950—that the nation's largest education-oriented foundation, the Ford Foundation, became a national force.

Perhaps the theme for this new stage in education—and foundation concern—was written by the Rockefeller Brothers Fund in its report on education, significantly entitled *The Pursuit of Excellence*. It was prepared for the panel of experts by the man who had already begun to be considered the symbol of the new look in foundation activities, John W. Gardner, president of the Carnegie Corporation and of the Carnegie Foundation for the Advancement of Teaching. Subsequently, he further underlined the new theme of reform and quality control in education when he wrote his book, *Excellence,* and asked in the subtitle: "Can We Be Equal and Excellent, Too?"

The foundations at this point sensed that the reforms of the schools could not rely on the improvement of the colleges alone. With mass education now a reality, the changes had to be sponsored on the school level. Nor was it sufficient to support existing efforts since many programs which later were to become important were still largely nonexistent.

A typical example of the prescience with which the foundation-sponsored school reform movement got under way was the establishment of the Commission on Mathematics with a Carnegie grant in 1955. Even though the nationwide mathematics and science reforms did not attain general support until the first Soviet Sputnik in 1957 and, more specifically, until the passage of the National Defense Education Act in 1958, the foresight of the Carnegie Corporation mobilized school and university talent and provided the basis for general improvement. The wide variety of "new mathematics" curriculums was built on that foundation.

Similarly, the foundation's support of the new advanced placement programs offered a subtle and inexpensive device to accomplish a dual purpose of reform: to give bright students in high school the opportunity to stretch their talents by taking part in virtually college-level instruction in some subjects; and to establish a natural bridge between school and college teachers at the very point where they ought to enter into partnership most readily.

Probably the most daring attacks on stagnation in the public schools were mounted in the early 1950's by an agency of the Ford Foundation, the Fund for the Advancement of Education. Under the leadership of Clarence Faust and Alvin C. Eurich, a small but lively group of innovators showed marked impatience with the "business as usual" approach to curriculum and organization. Often against the opposition of the established profession, they coaxed, pleaded—and offered money—to achieve departures from stale tradition. Much of the fund's battle was directed against the traditionalism which made every classroom the organizational replica of every other classroom, with the teacher's special talents largely unutilized. Through the fund's inventiveness a host of experiments were launched. These included the introduction of team teaching, the use of teacher aides, the attempt to let housewives, as "contract readers," help English teachers in grading compositions (a scheme supported also by the Educational Testing Service) and a variety of other educational regroupings. Out of the fund's belief that, in the words of former Newton, Massachusetts, school superintendent Harold B. Gores, the traditional schoolhouse fostered the "egg crate" confinement of learning, the foundation encouraged less restricting school and college architecture. Buildings themselves were planned in a way that would encourage a curriculum composed of large-group instruction, side by side with small seminars and even individual study. Out of this new form of foundation pioneering emerged a Ford Foundation subsidiary, the Educational Facilities Laboratories.

At the same time, the foundations realized that the schools were about to overlook the uses of the new medium of television just as they had largely wasted the potential of radio and even of film. The Fund for the Advancement of Education launched the first large-scale instructional television project when it helped equip the entire school district of Washington County, with headquarters in Hagerstown, Maryland, with a network of closed-circuit TV. It became the testing ground and has since remained the demonstration laboratory for educators all over the country and from many parts of the world.

At about the same time, in the late 1950's, the Carnegie Corporation made a bold attempt to repeat the Flexner success with the reform of medical education, but this time in the area of the public schools. This was how the remarkable mission of Dr. James B. Conant, former president of Harvard University, was born.

Supported by a minimum of research staff, the one-man reform mission was turned into a key in the reformation of American public education. Out of it, in 1959, came the historic book *The American High School Today,* generally known as the Conant Report. It was followed by a critique of the junior high schools, a report on the problem of the urban schools and the plight of the Negro minorities (*Slums and Suburbs*), a major volume on the reform of teacher training (*The Education of American Teachers*), and a series of proposals for the improvement of educational leadership at the state level (*Shaping Educational Policy*).

Despite the foundation's new enthusiasm for public school experimentation, higher education once again required attention. Here, too, the earlier experiences served as a guide. Carnegie and Rockefeller had been deeply interested in improving the working conditions and job security of college faculty members; now the Ford Foundation went a step beyond when, in 1955, it made the largest single grant in foundation history—$260 million for the improvement of faculty salaries. It was given to more than six hundred institutions. (In fact, the foundation encountered its most severe criticism over its departure from past foundation practice: it failed to ask the institutions to match funds or to use the grants offered for imaginative new approaches to academic salaries. Thus, it was charged by some, a great deal of money was so widely scattered as to make relatively little impact on pay patterns. Nevertheless, the publicity value of the giant gift, at a time when faculty salaries were still critically low and when few private donors were aware of this grave deficiency, was widely credited with a rapid and dramatic change in the situation. Subsequently, many colleges reported, it became far easier to solicit gifts specifically for the raising of faculty pay.)

Meanwhile, the Ford Foundation also turned to the support of higher education in the more conventional way, along patterns established earlier by the General Education Board. Over a period of less than a decade, the foundation distributed more than $200 million—all with stiff matching provisions and each grant based on the institution's demonstrated ability to chart its educational course for a number of years ahead. The stated purpose was to establish "regional centers of excellence."

Other foundations, with more limited funds, joined in the task of improving the quality of higher education. For example, the Danforth Foundation sponsored summer workshops for professors to improve teaching techniques, as well as fellowships for future college teachers. It also put the spotlight on good classroom teaching, possibly as an antidote to the trend toward greater rewards for research and publication, by selecting an annual group of outstanding college teachers. They were rewarded with free-wheeling, foundation-supported sabbaticals.

Increasingly, the foundations have directed their attention to educational research. It is here that relatively limited funds can accomplish a great deal; yet the operational limitations on school and college budgets make it most difficult to find funds for exploration of new techniques and ideas. It is unlikely, for example, that any progress would have been made in such novel areas as programmed instruction (teaching machines) without foundation help. Who but a foundation—in this instance it happened to be Carnegie—would offer funds for experiments to predict students' artistic ability? Who would attempt to find out objectively the effects of parochial school education on American Catholics? How would it be possible to put to the test the effectiveness of such new pedagogical approaches as the teaching of reading via the augmented Roman alphabet?

Vital attempts to increase the effectiveness and reduce the cost of higher education have been made through cooperation among colleges and universities. Foundations became the indispensable catalysts in these efforts, whether they aimed at cooperation among groups of liberal arts colleges or at the establishment of a mid-Western Academic Common Market—an option for graduate students to complete part of their work at various member institutions within the pact.

While experimentation often began with the work of a particular scholar, attempts to spread the results of such work throughout the network of American mass education frequently required a certain amount of institutionalizing of the successful individual work. Thus, Dr. Jerrold R. Zacharias, the Massachusetts Institute of Technology physicist, started out virtually single-handedly in reforming the high school physics curriculum. Dr. Bentley Glass undertook a similar task in biology. Others pioneered in advanced foreign languages study and brought the beginning of foreign language teaching to the elementary schools.

Yet, as the curriculum reforms began to spread and as new fields were crying out to be swept along, the personal efforts of individuals, no matter how devoted and gifted, proved inadequate.

This was how such institutions as Educational Services Incorporated were born. Although millions of dollars have been contributed by the government, particularly the National Science Foundation (over $11 million) since its inception in 1958, the organization's specific educational research assignments have received major assistance from the Ford Foundation and the Alfred P. Sloan Foundation. Indeed, one of the special functions of this type of educational research and development agency is to act as a reservoir for foundation funds for pinpointed school improvement. While ESI was the child of the physics reform movement, it has since branched out into curriculum research in all the sciences and mathematics, the social sciences, engineering and other areas. About 350 scholars from over 200 colleges and universities as well as several hundred elementary and high school teachers have worked full- and part-time at ESI, supported by a variety of foundation grants, in efforts to infuse new ideas into the curriculum. Over 200 films have been produced in ESI studios. Ten nations in Africa are currently using 23 special texts prepared for their schools by ESI researchers.

In similar fashion, the Greater Cleveland Research Council and a number of other new educational research organizations have been adding a new dimension to national efforts to improve schooling on all levels.

In the postwar world, it became abundantly clear that American education had an obligation far beyond its national borders. The pacification of formerly war-torn areas and the build-up of the new and developing nations depended almost as much on educational as on economic investment. The foundations' tradition of international educational involvement was firmly established. In the early days of organized philanthropy, at the beginning of the century, Andrew Carnegie launched significant education programs in Scotland, Britain, and the British Commonwealth. In 1910 he established the Carnegie Endowment for International Peace, and that foundation often, in the years to come, linked its international goals with those of academia. In the 1950's, for example, it sponsored important studies of the stress on international affairs and understanding in the American college curriculum, found that there was too little of it, particularly with a view of the non-Western world, and thus was an important instrument in the gradual reform of that vital aspect of higher education.

Born one year before the outbreak of World War I, the Rockefeller Foundation inevitably developed a sense of the critical importance of international understanding. Although much of its effort has always been aimed specifically at preventive medicine, health studies, and medical research, its leadership has also been sharply aware of the close link between the general physical welfare of nations and the strength of their academic institutions. Its donations to universities abroad have become an important adjunct to American intellectual influence. In England there were large grants at Oxford, Cambridge, and the University of London. There were similarly substantial grants at Paris, Strasbourg, and Lyons; at Göttingen and Munich in Germany; at Copenhagen, Uppsala, and Oslo in Scandinavia. In the most recent program of the Rockefeller Foundation it has undertaken to assist in the general development of the University of Valle, Colombia, the University of East Africa, the University of Ibadan in Nigeria, and at other strategically chosen places.

The Carnegie Corporation of New York decided early in the 1960's to demonstrate in Africa the close interrelationship between education and the economic development of nations which had recently gained their independence. By making educational and manpower projections the heart of national planning in such countries, the foundation put the spotlight on education's importance, not only for the developing countries but also for the highly developed industrial nations, such as the United States itself. Moreover, these studies attempted to form natural scholarly links among the universities of Africa, Great Britain, and the United States.

Although most recent, the Ford Foundation quickly became the giant in the international education field. It launched a vast Overseas Development Program and an International Training and Research Program. Its influence extended over wide areas in Asia, the Middle East, Africa, Latin America, and parts of Europe. In its first decade of operations, the foundation made grants in excess of $210 million in the international field, much of the total devoted to education. The foundation's own report said: "This assistance was largely in support of educational, training and research institutions and activities essential to the recipient countries' own programs of social, economic, and educational advancement."

The Foundation Library Center's statistics for 1964 report that all the foundations together (counting only gifts of over $10,000) in their international activities during that year made 164 grants to education, amounting to over $17 million. Actually, this figure tells only part of the story. For example, another $28 million for international studies, over $4 million for the exchange of persons and $12 million for technical assistance were, in effect, also actions in support of education, educational planning and training.

The special importance of the foundations' international educational contribution transcends the actual dollar value. Often such aid is given in places where similar governmental action might be suspect as a form of neo-colonialism. Elsewhere, as in some areas behind the Iron Curtain, the foundations can keep alive the often fading contact between the United States and the oppressed people of the satellite countries. Such intellectual forays are not without their risks. Abroad, anti-American voices decry them as mere subterfuge, camouflaging dollar diplomacy and imperialism. At home, some ultra-conservatives attack such involvement with charges which stand in ironic contrast to the foreign left-wing criticism. The descendants of the isolationist wing of American opinion moreover complain that American money is being used to support foreign ventures when it might be given to education at home.

George Eastman, whose family-industrial foundation has taken part in the support of educational ventures abroad, replied that such grants were only a fraction of the contributions made to domestic enterprises. Yet, he added, "My money has been made in the Kodak business, which is carried on all over the world."

Henry T. Heald, as president of the Ford Foundation, said, ". . . The resolution of our domestic problems would be a hollow victory if two-thirds of the world continued to be racked by deprivation and unrest."

As the American crisis at home moved increasingly into the crowded urban centers, the emphasis of the foundations' actions also shifted from that of curriculum reforms and from general grants to support of the fiscal structure of higher education to educational emergency action to halt the decay of the big cities.

The Ford Foundation gave official recognition to the new need when it launched its Great Cities Program, also known as the Grey Areas project. Aimed at improving social conditions in the urban centers, especially within the Negro ghettoes, through special, often compensatory education efforts, the program might be considered the forerunner of the governmental antipoverty and community action programs. It was a call to action—an attempt to wake up local community and school leaders and make them aware of education's responsibility.

The bible of much of this crucial work was Dr. Conant's *Slums and Suburbs,* the Carnegie-sponsored slim volume which coined a key slogan when it called the slums' out-of-school and out-of-work youth the "social dynamite" of contemporary America. It was the dynamite that so soon and so tragically was to explode in the urban riots—in Harlem, in Philadelphia, in Los Angeles, in Chicago, and a dozen other trouble spots across the map. At first, the big city school authorities were slow to respond. The kind of socio-educational preventive action they were asked to evolve had not been part of their thinking and their training. Nor had their limited budgets and spotty community support in the past given them much of a mandate to help reform urban society.

Foundation grants came as an urgent challenge and indispensable catalyst. Out of them emerged such programs as Pittsburgh's cooperation between the public schools and half a dozen universities and colleges. Out of them came, too, school teaching teams newly adapted to the need of the slum neighborhood. Parents were increasingly drawn into the school program; slum mothers were employed as members of the classroom teaching teams. Slowly, too, the search for talent, often submerged in the chaotic poverty of the slums, began. Special programs, such as New York's "Higher Horizons," tried to help youngsters catch up with the benefits of a child-centered middle-class society. Summer studies groomed disadvantaged youths for college. Tutoring projects were set up to provide equality of educational opportunities amid the squalid inequalities of the de facto segregated neighborhoods.

While the foundations' efforts to anticipate the War on Poverty were not confined to one race, it became quickly evident that the major effort had to concentrate on the long-delayed catching-up process for Negro youths and Negro institutions.

The problem was not all urban. Perhaps the most heartbreaking dilemma was that of some seventeen hundred Negro children in rural Prince Edward County, Virginia, who had been virtually withdrawn from formal schooling when, in a move of vicious spite against the Supreme Court's desegregation ruling, the white authorities closed down the public schools and established private education for all white children. With substantial aid from the foundations, the liberal leadership eventually—after too much delay, to be sure—developed a special education system for the excluded Negro children. The Ford Foundation offered $250,000 for the new program. Danforth, the Mary Reynolds Babcock Foundation, and the Alfred P. Sloan Foundation as well as the Rockefeller Brothers Fund pooled smaller amounts, and a host of small foundations departed from their more traditional plans to join in this dramatic lifesaving venture.

It was a symbolic effort. Foundations had been involved in upgrading Southern Negro education in the past, especially in the years after the Civil War. The George F. Peabody Fund, the philanthropy of a Baltimore banker, became deeply involved in such work in the late 1860's. The General Education Board, between 1902 and 1960, channeled over $40 million into the Negro colleges. Following Andrew Carnegie's personal campaign to provide libraries for Negroes in Southern communities, the Carnegie Foundation for the Advancement of Teaching made the support of the Negro colleges one of its priority enterprises. The Phelps-Stokes Fund and the Julius Rosenwald Fund made Negro education their special domain, with the latter foundation contributing $22 million to the improvement of Negro schools before it closed its books in 1948.

A host of other foundations joined in this earlier work. But it was not until the civil rights issue and the urban crisis became acute that the major foundations—Ford, Alfred P. Sloan, Danforth, Rockefeller, Carnegie—and an array of smaller ones—among them Taconic Foundation, New World Foundation, Stern Family Fund, Twentieth Century Fund—began to look for dramatic new departures. It had become evident that mere support of Negro institutions, important as such support still remains, could not avert the gathering storm. The issues to be faced were that only 180,000 Negroes are currently enrolled in higher education, compared with well over 4 million white students, while the unemployment rate for Negro youths was about twice that of their white contemporaries.

A variety of foundation-sponsored programs were initiated. The Ford Foundation, for example, gave $7 million to the National Merit Scholarship Corporation to help talented Negroes finance their college education. Since 1951, the Fund for the Advancement of Education has spent over $33 million for Negro higher education. A $13 million grant to the Atlanta University Center and eight predominantly Negro colleges in its area was intended to help these important institutions toward academic excellence. The Rockefeller Foundation has funded special summer sessions at Princeton University, Oberlin and Dartmouth Colleges to help promising Negro high school students to be groomed for college admission, and another grant to the Woodrow Wilson National Fellowship Foundation was earmarked to provide the money to send fellows to some forty Southern Negro colleges as teachers. It also gave $150,000 to ESI (see above) to conduct special summer institutes for promising Negro students.

The Carnegie Corporation has put most of its efforts into the promotion of direct, two-way cooperation between a Negro college and a predominantly white "prestige" institution, such as the link between Brown University and Tougaloo Southern Christian College, the University of Michigan and Tuskegee Institute, or Cornell and Yale with Hampton Institute. In these foundation-sponsored arrangements, faculty members, students, and ideas are exchanged and the Negro institution is steadily strengthened—always of course with the ultimate goal of dropping the label "Negro" entirely and simply creating another academically strong, integrated institution.

While the Carnegie Corporation has given the United Negro College Fund $1,500,000 to foster these "adoption" schemes, the Field Foundation has underwritten direct exchanges between students from Southern Negro colleges and others from Northern institutions. In addition, the National Scholarship Service and Fund for Negro Students has been given support by a number of foundations to provide scholarships which enable Negro students to attend integrated Northern and Western colleges. The Foundation Library Center estimates that the scholarship service has helped to place some 7,000 Negro students in 350 colleges.On the higher professional level, the Alfred P. Sloan Foundation and the New York Foundation have contributed to the support of Negro physicians who can benefit from postgraduate training.

But the combination of the civil rights struggle and the urban crisis has made it abundantly clear that it is not enough to open up the college gates to disadvantaged Negro youth. The real battle begins much earlier—in school and increasingly before school starts. It is on those levels that much of the pioneering foundation work was set in motion in the early 1960's. Thus, the foundation-created Educational Services Incorporated has diverted some of its curriculum-reform efforts and channeled them into special training for remedial reading instruction and unconventional teaching approaches to children from slum homes. The Field Foundation has supported Bank Street College in establishing an Educational Resources Center in Harlem. Ford and a number of other foundations have contributed to the pioneering experiments by Dr. Martin Deutsch at the Institute for Developmental Studies of New York

Medical College with the preschool education of three- and four-year-old children from slum homes.

Not all foundation efforts have been—or should be expected to be—successful. In some areas, notably in adult education, projects start with insufficiently sharp focus, drift along, and have little impact, like rivulets disappearing into the dry ground. In education as elsewhere, the ideal foundation-sponsored enterprise is one that blazes a new trail, thrives for a while on sponsored dollars, gathers momentum, and is quickly taken over as a permanent program by the local school board, the state education authority, or a university's own budget.

Much depends, of course, on the creativity and daring of the foundation executives and staff. While politicians have occasionally criticized foundation-sponsored education projects as too radical, the academic world is more likely to complain that the foundations, partly as a result of political pressures, have been too cautious. Burton Raffel, a former editor of *Foundation News* and now an assistant professor of English at the State University of New York at Stony Brook, wrote: "My main concern is that foundations are not living up to their potential, that their role as an impetus toward innovation is not being fulfilled as it could and should be. Despite all the talk of 'seed money,' it tends to be the safe bet on which foundations have been relying, of late. . . . The theory is noble; the practice is tending to be conservative, cautious, and distinctly non-innovational."

While the criticism is harsh, it has strong elements of truth. Like all other institutions, foundations are conscious of the pressures of organized society. Having been subjected to harassment, foundations and their staffs may become more careful not to offend. Fortunately, it is the current crisis of the cities, the undereducated Negro minority, and the civil rights issue itself which have synchronized the goals of the innovators and the purposes of the political establishment. It is in these critical areas therefore that the foundations are able to return to bold thinking and unconventional action. The civil rights movement has given educational foundation thinking a new infusion of daring and inventiveness.

In a most dramatic sense, the 1960's find the foundations in a new position. It is not only that the demands on education are changing. They are changing, and rapidly, and the foundations are responding—as when the Alfred P. Sloan Foundation gave the Massachusetts Institute of Technology a major grant for the continuous retraining of engineers and scientists on the highest level of professional success and activity. But even more fundamental will be the changes brought about by the new involvement of the federal government in educational purpose, planning, and financing.

With Washington's entry into education as the key priority in modern society, the forces of innovation are, to some extent, shifting. The small-scale foundation experiment is more likely to turn rapidly into a federally financed national project or even into a routine operation. This poses a new and exciting challenge. It would be wasteful for the foundations to turn themselves into a parallel force, doing simultaneously on a smaller scale what the federal government stands ready to support in far more massive proportions. The challenge for the foundations ought instead to be twofold: To sharpen the independent instruments of appraisal and criticism—in the Flexner-Conant tradition—so that novelty will not be mistaken for success and massive financing will not overshadow sound planning and wise leadership; and to turn the foundation dollar into an even more future-oriented instrument —in the vanguard of educational thought and action.

The nature of the new trend was underlined by the appointment of Mr. Gardner, the innovation-minded president of the Carnegie Corporation, as Secretary of Health, Education, and Welfare. It was Mr. Gardner's appeal to the established institutions that gave urgency to the need for a new combination of a striving for excellence and a restless sense of societal self-renewal.

The Gardner theory on institutions runs like this: "Experienced managers know that some organizations can be renewed through new leadership and new ideas. Others need a more massive infusion of new blood or far-reaching organizational changes. Still others can only be renewed by taking them apart and putting them together again. And some cannot be renewed at all."

This new tough line on the renewal and renovation of society summarizes the task of the foundations in education as they enter the next chapter of philanthropy. The challenge is to remain in the vanguard of inventive, innovative thinking, testing, experimenting, and to retain the independence of honest and even unpopular appraisal and criticism, in spite of the inhibiting pressures in a society of big, established, and conservative institutions.

CHAPTER 32

Philanthropic Foundations
and the Problem of Race

FLORA M. RHIND *and*
BARRY BINGHAM

Although much ambiguity attaches to the word *race,* for our purpose we shall take one of the broad definitions provided by Webster—"a class or kind of individuals with common characteristics, interests, appearance, or habits as if derived from a common ancestor." Since the study of which this paper is a part will examine the impact of the activities of philanthropic foundations on the development of various fields of knowledge and their contribution to the solution of certain worldwide problems, the problem of race in this context is the problem of the tensions and conflicts that result from discriminatory practices against any ethnic group. Few places in the world are totally free of such practices. In many areas they have been embedded in the culture for so long that they are rarely challenged and the misery that they cause is seldom recognized; in others they smolder and erupt periodically into bloody violence.

The twentieth century has seen these tensions take new forms. Out of two world wars have come a tremendous upsurge of nationalism and an insistent demand on the part of oppressed groups that their rights to human dignity and opportunity be honored. With great advances in all kinds of communication the struggle has become both more audible and more visible, and in the midst of rapidly shifting political and social structures men are more than ever aware of the dangers of racial and cultural conflicts.

But, despite the worldwide nature and urgency of the problem, philanthropic foundations have made few attempts to deal with it directly. While there have been many efforts to throw light on it through support of research in cultural and physical anthropology, sociology, linguistics, and political, social, and legal history, these efforts occupy a relatively small place in the broad picture of worldwide philanthropy. Furthermore, we have no means of evaluating the results of such efforts, although the increase in knowledge about race and culture in the last thirty or forty years has undoubtedly been substantial.

On the other hand, we can be fairly certain that there have been a great many indirect contributions by philanthropic foundations to improvement of intercultural relations. Insofar as these organizations have demonstrated a deep and abiding concern, without distinction of race or creed or color, for the welfare of men and women all over the world, and insofar as their programs have encouraged the cooperative efforts of persons of many different ethnic groups, they have helped to lessen racial tensions and to advance the cause of human dignity.

The African doctor working side by side with a white professor in a clinic of a medical school in Nigeria, the Mexican testing crops in the field with an American agriculturist, the Japanese geneticist studying at a Swedish laboratory, the Buddhist visiting an American theological center, the participants from many lands in a conference on national health problems meeting in Senegal —these and countless numbers like them will surely emerge from such experiences with broadened understanding and tolerance of cultural differences. The individual impact in some cases may be small, but as the programs stretch out to all corners of the earth and involve thousands of people in positions of leadership, the effect is cumulative.

The number of philanthropic foundations whose charters permit them to operate on a worldwide basis is relatively small. The Rockefeller Foundation was the first of the great American foundations to spend large sums abroad for the purpose of advancing knowledge and its application to human needs. Its notable achievements in the fields of public health, medical and nursing education, and agriculture, as well as its support of research over a broad spectrum, have involved grants to public and private institutions of higher learning in many lands, cooperative programs with governments in Europe, the Near East, Asia, Latin America, and Africa, and training programs for students from about one hundred different countries. Recently, in view of the enormous needs of the less-developed nations, the Rockefeller Foundation's program has expanded substantially in Africa, Asia, and Latin America. A large share of these activities have involved cross-cultural participation; all of them have given consideration to human needs without respect to creed, race, or color.

This also has been true of the work of the more recently organized Ford Foundation, whose enormous resources are being spent to attack fundamental problems of mankind on an interracial as well as international scale. A number of other foundations, such as the Carnegie Corporation, the Kellogg Foundation, and the International Education Board, have used their funds to support programs that brought students from many lands to this country and elsewhere for extended periods of research and study, thus giving them an opportunity to know and work in another culture under friendly circumstances.

As for the more direct contributions, as far back as 1926 we find the Laura Spelman Rockefeller Memorial giving consideration to the need for more knowledge about the cultures, traditions, and languages of Africa, and with an initial grant of $25,000 making possible the creation of the International Institute of African Languages and Cultures, with headquarters in London. General support of this organization (now known as the International African Institute) was continued by the Memorial and the Rockefeller Foundation over a period of more than thirteen years, making possible the collaboration of many notable scholars and scientists, in studies that have yielded valuable basic information about the emerging African nations. Similarly, encouragement and support were given to such organizations as the Institute for Comparative Research in Human Cultures in Oslo, Norway (Laura Spelman Rockefeller Memorial), the South African Institute of Race Relations in Johannesburg (Ford Foundation), the Institute of Race Relations in London (Ford Foundation), the London School of Oriental and African Studies and the Royal Anthropological Institute in London (Rockefeller Foundation), and the Bishop Museum in Hawaii (Rockefeller Foundation). Through research and training programs all have contributed to the advancement of knowledge in fields related to racial problems.

Support provided by a number of foundations, chiefly Rockefeller, Carnegie, and Ford, for the development of strong programs of "area studies" at various university centers has also been an important means of developing in-depth cross-cultural and inter-racial understanding. Another paper in this series treats this subject at some length and describes notable programs in our own country and abroad. Here we need note only that the basic concept of these area studies is the application of the social science and humanistic disciplines, and sometimes also the natural science disciplines, toward a better understanding of a single region, well defined in both geography and time, preferably through attention to specific problems. Thus a number of universities in the United States and in several centers in other parts of the world have built up rich resources relating to the histories, languages, and cultures of peoples in one or more areas other than their own. These centers provide broad training for persons who will eventually work in the selected areas in agencies of government, education, and business, and bring to the community in which they are located an awareness and appreciation of values and cultures other than their own.

In this paper, however, we shall not attempt to examine philanthropic programs which are so diverse in purpose and whose results in the field of race relations, while real, must for the most part be considered by-products hardly subject to measurement. In our own country the situation is somewhat different. Here many of the foundations have clearly recognized their responsibility to do something about racial tensions and, although they have in most cases approached the problem indirectly, nevertheless it is possible to trace the impact of their efforts.

In the United States the race problem means the Negro prob-

lem. Born in the bitterness of slavery and molded by the tragic
circumstances of civil war and the passions and violence of the
Reconstruction period, it has been an ever-present dilemma in a
country whose official political creed denounces, in general but
vigorous terms, all forms of oppression and discrimination, and
affirms equality of opportunity.

The Indian, the Mexican, and other minority groups have borne
and continue to bear a burden of discrimination, but in no way
have the problems emerging from their inferior position approached in complexity those of the Negro. Now constituting about
one-tenth of our population, and almost always readily recognizable by the color of his skin, he emerged from slavery only to
live under the dark shadows of ignorance, poor health, bad housing,
limited employment opportunities, and denial of his civil rights.

As the great foundations developed in the beginning of this
century, the problem of the Negro was to receive a considerable
share of their attention. While the climate of opinion in the South
was such that any direct attack on the problem on the part of
Northerners met with considerable hostility and threatened to
harm rather than advance the cause, nevertheless several foundations gave support to action programs designed to improve race
relations. Among these were the Laura Spelman Rockefeller
Memorial established by John D. Rockefeller in 1917, and the
Julius Rosenwald Fund, whose founder was deeply concerned
with racial and religious discrimination. Both aided in the establishment in 1919 and subsequent support of the Commission on
Interracial Cooperation, which had as its purpose "To quench, if
possible, the fires of racial antagonism which were flaming [after
the first World War] with such deadly menace in all sections of
the country." The commission had a long and difficult history and
went through many reorganizations, eventually becoming the
Southern Regional Council, now devoting a large share of its
activities to Negro voter registration. In reviewing the work of
the predecessor commission in 1944 the Swedish economist Gunnar Myrdal said:

> The Commission has a large share in the achievement of the
> dramatic decrease in lynching, and generally, in the greater enforce-
> ment of law in the South during the last two decades. The Com-

mission was able largely to nullify the influence of the fascistic Black Shirt movement that grew up during the 1930's to eliminate Negroes from all jobs while there was any unemployment of whites. Few other organizations could have made the effective appeal to Southern whites which the situation called for. The Commission's surveys—for instance, of the tenancy problem—have been of great importance in the national discussion and for national policy. The work of the Farm Security Administration, which for a long period was headed by W. W. Alexander, the Director of the Commission, is much in line with the efforts of the Commission and has set in effect many plans propagated and partly prepared by the Commission. The Commission has had its important part in the development of a friendlier attitude toward the Negro on the part of the white press in the South. The local interracial committees have also gotten much for the Negroes. . . .[1]

Myrdal's own comprehensive study of the Negro problem in democracy (*An American Dilemma*), was supported by the Carnegie Corporation, and is another instance of a direct attempt by a large foundation to awaken Americans to the evils of discrimination. There were others. Action groups such as the National Association for the Advancement of Colored People and the National Urban League received encouragement and support in their early days from foundations. As their membership has grown and provided a general base of support, foundation assistance for the most part has taken the form of aid for special projects, such as the League's Leadership Development Program and the NAACP Civil Rights Law Institutes. The Southern Reporting Service, established and supported by the Ford Foundation, another type of activity, is focused on the collection and regular reporting of unbiased factual information on matters affecting race relations in the South.

There has also been scattered support of research in the hope that increased understanding of racial problems would lead to their solution. Thus we find the National Industrial Conference Board undertaking a study of management opportunities relating to the employment of Negroes, and the University of North Carolina's Institute for Research in Social Science engaging in studies of the changing position of the Negro in American society, the University of Chicago making a study of the Chicago labor market,

434 / U.S. Philanthropic Foundations

and the Association of the Bar of the City of New York investigating procedural impediments to the federal protection of civil rights—all of these projects supported by grants from philanthropic foundations.

At the University of Louisville a conference of Southern police chiefs on the challenge of racial tension to law enforcement is a logical outgrowth of the Southern Police Institute, supported for many years by the General Education Board. Numerous other biracial conferences have received foundation support, and recently grants from such organizations have made available continuing conference facilities for interracial meetings through the purchase and remodeling of the Robert R. Moton home at Holly Knoll, Capahosic, Virginia.

While efforts such as these are important and have doubtless contributed in a positive way to the solution of America's Negro problem, the investment in them has been small compared to what the foundations have contributed to the advancement of Negro education.

Before the Civil War the education of slaves in many states had been illegal. In the chaos that followed Emancipation, the Freedmen's Bureau, missionary organizations, and interested philanthropists from the North began the slow and arduous task of providing essential educational facilities that would prepare the Negro for the responsibilities and opportunities of freedom. But in an impoverished and embittered South, which had not as yet recognized the necessity of free public schools even for white children, public education for the Negro came slowly, and when it came the pattern was one of sharp segregation. Provision for Negro schools was pathetically meager. The big cities occasionally provided an elementary school or two, but in most of the counties there were no public schools for colored children. The following description from the diary of a General Education Board staff member shows a situation typical at the turn of the century:

> We spent some hours [at Auburn, Alabama] looking into the affairs of the Negro school. . . . As a matter of fact, they have done next to nothing for the Negroes, simply giving them $450 with which to erect a building and then leaving the whole project to the execution of a group of untutored and inexperienced Negroes. Result, a

building that is worse than no building at all, and a school equipment that for inadequacy beggars description. . . .[2]

When the above was written, the South had no public high schools for Negro children and the training of Negro teachers, such as it was, was left to private academies and colleges supported chiefly by missionary groups and Northern philanthropy. It was this philanthropy which was to make the crucial difference in the development of Negro leadership, paving the way for the Supreme Court decisions of 1938[3] and 1954,[4] and the Civil Rights Act of 1964. While many social and economic factors, including the growing industrialization of the South and two World Wars, were at work during the years that led to these momentous decisions, it is clear that without education and the leadership it developed the Negro would never have been able to move forward as he has done in the last two decades.

In writing of the Reconstruction period following the Civil War, the great Negro scholar W. E. Burghardt Du Bois states that "Had it not been for the Negro school and college, the Negro would, to all intents and purposes, have been drawn back to slavery."[5] And in commenting on this Gunnar Myrdal in *An American Dilemma,* says, "The great wonder is that the principle of the Negroes' right to public education was not renounced altogether. But it did not happen. The explanation is the persistence and magnanimity of northern philanthropy."[6]

In the struggle to establish and support schools for Negroes during the period following the Civil War, missionary and church reform groups in the North contributed not only by sending down teachers but also by giving money for buildings and the support of students. Indeed, most of the Negroes who received education in the South between 1865 and 1880 were schooled in institutions supported largely by Northern churches, although the Negro communities themselves collected considerable money for their schools, particularly at the elementary school level. Fisk, Atlanta, Howard, and Hampton were founded in these years and Tuskegee followed soon after in 1881.

It was not until the turn of the century, however, that substantial foundation funds began to flow into Negro education, and then it began to gain real strength. The first of the philanthropic foundations to turn its attention to Negro education was the Peabody Education Fund, which, beginning in 1867, gave money to both white and Negro schools in the South. The John F. Slater Fund and the Jeanes Fund, both specifically devoted to Negro education, came shortly thereafter. All three of these were relatively small foundations and were later to be combined, along with the Virginia Randolph Fund, into a single organization to be known as the Southern Education Foundation, dedicated to advancing Negro education. In the 1900's Northern philanthropy stepped into the picture on a large scale, giving massive support not only to public education for Negroes at the elementary and secondary levels, but to the development of both public and private higher education.

Among the largest and most active foundations in this field were the General Education Board and the Julius Rosenwald Fund. These two organizations, working through dedicated and tireless staffs, were to spend many millions of dollars in a struggle to get the South to recognize its responsibility to establish tax-supported schools for colored people, to provide the means of training teachers for them, and to encourage the development of supervisory services that would maintain standards in Negro public schools of the South. Many millions were spent for strengthening the Negro colleges through grants for endowments, libraries, laboratories, teacher salaries, professional education including medicine, and fellowships for faculty members. The impact of their efforts goes far beyond the dollar spent, but it is interesting to note that these two foundations alone, both of which have now expended their funds and terminated their activities, spent close to $75 million[7] for the advancement of education for Negroes.

Many other foundations contributed funds for this purpose. Among them should be noted the Carnegie Corporation, which gave significant sums to Negro colleges and libraries, and the Duke, Field, Whitney, and Phelps-Stokes funds. More recently, assistance totaling more than $37 million has been provided by the Ford Foundation in the form of grants to specific institutions and for projects relating to Negro higher education, as well as some $8 million for preschool and elementary and secondary education.

The quality of segregated education thus supported varied widely, and in all but a few instances was inferior to that made available to white persons. From the beginning, the Negro schools were handicapped, not only by the poverty of their students and the limitations of their cultural environment, but by the widespread conviction that the Negro was not educable, or that, if he was, the only form of education appropriate to his status was industrial or vocational education. Foundation funds, generous as they were, were inadequate to remedy this situation. They did, however, effectively take the initiative in setting standards that would be steadily pushed upward, and they buttressed their support of Southern Negro education with large numbers of fellowships that made it possible for hundreds of able Negroes to do advanced study at first-rate Northern institutions, thereby providing the leadership that was to mean so much in the battle for civil rights.

In later years there has been some criticism of the foundations for having done less for the education of the Negro than was done for the education of whites, and they have been charged with perpetuating a system of segregation through their support of separate Negro schools and colleges. When the foundations began their work in the South the climate of opinion was a hostile one, and they were compelled to move with caution. The educational needs of the Southern region were enormous and it was necessary to strengthen education as a whole in order to achieve some recognition of the rights and needs of the Negro. As Mr. Fosdick has said in his *Adventure in Giving*:

> We cannot go back and rearrange the ideas of an earlier genera-
> tion to make them square with our conceptions today. The most we
> can do is to try to understand the framework within which the
> pioneers of that era carried on their tasks. . . . [They] lived in the
> belief that there was time and that there would always be time for
> intelligence to take hold. They never heard the trumpets of revolu-
> tion and immediacy calling around the world. They accepted the
> Southern pattern of school segregation because at the moment there
> was nothing else to do if education for the Negroes was to be
> developed. Their strategy was strongly pragmatic. To raise the level
> of education in the South involved raising the level of both races,
> and to do this it was necessary to work through the race in power.
> Sixty years ago there was no alternative to this approach; there
> was no public opinion to support any other course. For those who

were concerned with the development of Negro leadership through education, this was the only route to follow. . . .

. . . What can be said with truth and conviction is that at a time when education for colored people in the South was at its lowest depths, the General Education Board threw the weight of its enormous support behind the effort to bring it up to creditable levels, and that out of this effort has come the leadership which sparks the new thinking of today. . . .[8]

There can be no doubt that the development of an educated elite and of a lively sense of group identification among Negroes has been a significant factor in changing American race relations in a more equalitarian direction since the turn of the century. And it can truthfully be said that without the support and encouragement of the philanthropic foundations this educated elite might not have emerged at a time when it was desperately needed.

In this new atmosphere the philanthropic foundations are now playing a somewhat different but very important role. In the past decade increasing numbers of these organizations have started to help the Negro take advantage of recent liberalizing legislation and find his way into the mainstream of American society. In the words of Henry T. Heald, president of the Ford Foundation, there is "an air of urgency about these new programs." Thus, an important segment of the Rockefeller Foundation's program is now concerned with "the advancement of equal opportunity for all"; the Ford Foundation is devoting a considerable share of its grants to educational and action programs concerned with disadvantaged youth; the Carnegie, Sloan, Danforth, Rockefeller Brothers, Old Dominion, Taconic, New World, Field, Reynolds, Babcock and Stern funds, and the Southern Education Foundation—to mention only a few of the many participating organizations—are supporting educational institutions, experimental projects, action programs, and research designed to remedy existing inequalities in our treatment of minority groups; and, with the aid of a wide variety of scholarships and fellowships made available by Ford, Rockefeller, Sloan, Whitney, and numerous other foundations, a steadily growing number of well-trained Negroes are being developed for leadership in government, business, industry, and the professions.

The task ahead is a difficult one and much more than education is involved. Problems in the fields of employment, vocational training, housing, health, recreation, delinquency, and government must be attacked simultaneously with courage and all deliberate speed if we are ". . . to give to every man his chance—to every man regardless of his birth, his shining, golden opportunity—to every man the right to live, to work, to be himself, and to become whatever thing his manhood and his vision can combine to make him. . . ."[9]

While we know that the philanthropic foundations of America are giving generously to these new programs, the contributions of government and support by many private individuals through gifts or services make it difficult to estimate the extent and importance of foundation involvement. We do know that their contributions are large and that an increasing number of foundations are putting a substantial share of their funds into what is usually headed in their reports as "Race Relations," "Intercultural Relations," or "Equal Opportunity."

As the foundations move ahead in an effort to make this country truly a land of equal opportunity, there has also been a major push on the part of foundations with worldwide charters to help meet some of the basic problems created by the emergence of new nations with a whole wide range of problems in health, nutrition, and education. Working with many different nationalities and races, the philanthropic foundations are demonstrating anew that discriminations arising from considerations of race and creed have no place in a world which can survive only if it finds ways for many different cultures to live in harmony and in peace.

Concluding Remarks to Part II:
The Consensus

WARREN WEAVER

I suppose it inevitable that some readers will have skipped some of the preceding eighteen chapters, thinking that they were not specially interested in, say, the dance or law or biochemistry. Having written none of these chapters myself, I can observe without immodesty that any such omission was a mistake. But a person who has read even a sample of these statements will, I think, come to certain firm conclusions.

These chapters—necessarily subjective in character but based on observation and experience—cover a wide range of the recognized fields of knowledge, include representative aspects of the humanities and the creative arts, and reach out to a number of broad problems that significantly affect the well-being of all present and future persons. Although many fields and topics are not included, the evidence is broadly enough based to be impressive.

It is interesting to note the frequency of favorable reference to certain of the large foundations, as the collaborators reviewed what they considered to be significant advances; and equally impressive to note the large number of medium-size and smaller foundations which also came in for favorable mention. No sensible person would think of rating the foundations on the basis of the number of times the names turn up in favorable context; but it is nevertheless interesting to observe that the Rockefeller Foundation is mentioned well over 150 times, and the much younger Ford

Foundation over 100 times. The Carnegie Corporation, the Sloan Foundation, the Kellogg Foundation, and the Rockefeller Brothers Fund (to mention four more in the "big ten") also are cited frequently.

Certain older foundations, no longer active, are referred to a number of times. The General Education Board, the International Education Board, and the Laura Spelman Rockefeller Memorial (three earlier Rockefeller boards) lead that list, with the Peabody Fund and the Rosenwald Fund coming in for honorable mention. Something over a dozen well-known foundations of moderate size —such as the John Simon Guggenheim Memorial Foundation, the Commonwealth, the Danforth, the Macy, the Milbank, the Markle, the Research Corporation, and the Twentieth Century Fund—are mentioned several times each.

In addition, and as impressive evidence of the wide variety of foundation activity, the contributed chapters contain reference to three community trusts, to five company-sponsored foundations, to ten foreign foundations, to about thirty special purpose foundations, and to nearly sixty family foundations.

The contributed chapters inform us that foundations, apart from some activities in the humanities and creative arts, have largely worked through universities and colleges, research institutes, professional institutions, and learned societies. This is wholly understandable, for in such places are located the great majority of individuals who have the training, the capacity and the determination to accomplish the purpose that so generally preoccupies foundations, namely, the extension of the frontiers of knowledge. Individuals, groups, nations—the whole of human society —get into trouble when handicapped by ignorance and are helped to find their way out of difficulties and toward a better life when the relevant knowledge is available. This is partly a conclusion based on experience and partly a statement of faith. It is a faith that is central to our whole educational system; indeed, it is a faith which heavily influences our personal lives. It is the faith that underlies practically all the activities of the great general purpose foundations. A critic who is not prepared to recognize, credit, and share this faith is bound to misunderstand and underestimate many of the activities of philanthropic foundations.

Foundations are concerned with institutions not for their own sake, but because these institutions contain *individual persons* of imagination and capacity, and furnish these individuals with an environment which makes them effective. The reports in Part II frequently mention and highly value the great concern that has led foundations to seek out and assist worthy and creative individual persons. The heavy emphasis on scholarships and fellowships in the Rockefeller, Sloan, Guggenheim, and many other foundations is particularly noted and approved. The federal government is now taking over the mass aspect of this problem. But the pioneering demonstration was made by the foundations, and the flexible treatment of important exceptional cases will continue to be handled best by them.

The role of the foundations in helping create new types of institutions and agencies is recognized in these essays, as well as the role in helping create new types of activity—psychiatry in medical schools, foreign area studies, molecular biology, methods of effective population control, novel collaborations of scientists and educators in improving curricula and teaching tools, new schools for training business executives, and many more.

These reports make it clear that philanthropic foundations have, over the past half century, been a major force in establishing this country's present level of basic research in the physical, biological, and medical sciences. There has been massive assistance for many aspects of the social sciences. Aid to the humanities is, fortunately, growing. Philanthropic involvement in the creative and performing arts is relatively recent; and the reports, while very enthusiastic about what has been done, are properly hopeful that more foundation activity may develop in these areas. The recent large gifts for symphonic music are extremely encouraging.

Although the opinions of the collaborators are in very large measure laudatory of foundation activities, there are, quite naturally and quite inevitably and desirably, some notes of reservation or disapproval. In part, this results from the fact that certain disciplines—such as the social sciences, for example—are still in a stage of development that necessarily involves a considerable element of dissent. The fact that financial assistance, furthermore, does not always or automatically result in admiration or approval is something that our country has learned in connection with its aid programs. And, if the behavior of foundations had been so universally bland that no one could object to any aspect, this would certainly not have been a good thing. Any record which is vigorous and imaginative enough to deserve a high proportion of praise will also receive a small proportion of complaint. Dissent and criticism are clearly desirable. The collaborators all wrote precisely what they themselves wanted to say.

Ten of the contributors did not see fit to include any negative criticisms. The four who wrote concerning literature, the pictorial arts, music, and the dance all expressed regret at the "minuscule consideration" given to their fields by philanthropic foundations, although appreciation was expressed that the tide seems to be turning. Two of these men spoke of the fact that their areas receive only about one percent of the total of foundation grants. One can sympathize with their statements at the same time that one recognizes the arithmetical dilemma inherent in the fact that very substantially more than one hundred fields each consider one percent to be a meager allotment.

It is inevitable that dedicated specialists consider their specialty to be undersupported, but their comments deserve attention, for imbalance may exist. Beckman, for example, states that expansion of Latin American area studies is long overdue. As another example of possible imbalance, Griswold argues that legal education requires general strengthening, and that great capital funds for construction, equipment, and endowment should be made available to law schools. As an example of underemphasis which affects all fields, Beadle pleads for more favorable consideration for "bricks and mortar" requests.

A pungent criticism from the creative artists is their feeling that foundations have not made use, either as staff members or advisers, of persons who have outstanding professional competence in the arts, and the charge that most philanthropic foundations have "not broadened their outlook to consider ministering to the spirit through the arts."

A criticism of general significance, made by two of the contributors, is that foundations sometimes start with too little and tend to stop too soon. Beckmann makes this point with respect to area studies, and Hechinger, speaking of projects in adult education, says that they often "drift along and leave little impact."

Stigler has a number of criticisms: that small foundations sometimes foster their own particular viewpoints with "repellent rigidity"; that they tend to implement the interests of the donors; that area institutes (which have often been foundation assisted) have made no significant contribution to economics theory or to research methodology and that these institutes have not "attracted or trained two economists of first rank"; that foundations reinforce the homogeneity of research; that the work of no one of the big names in economics has been significantly aided in his theoretical researches by foundations; and that foundations tend to favor the innovators over the conservators of the scientific traditions. Whether the reservations expressed by Stigler reflect a certain amount of inadequate and incompetent attention by foundations to the field of economics or whether these difficulties are inherent in the nature and stage of advancement of the subject, this author is incompetent to judge.

To turn to the more favorable opinions—which are overwhelmingly in the majority—in the comments that are expressed in practically all of the contributed papers there is gratifying emphasis that philanthropic foundation aid has in many instances been forthcoming at an early moment in the pioneering stages of some development, so that the timing of the support was critically important. The matter of promptness of decision is often also particularly important. It is not reasonable to expect huge grants to be decided on overnight; this, in fact, should not occur and does not. But foundations can, generally speaking, move with decent speed. And practically all sizable foundations have especially nimble procedures that can be invoked for sums of modest size—say, up to $10,000 or even $25,000. In this respect they have a great advantage over federal agencies, which necessarily and properly have to "move through channels." For reasons that are partly good, partly bad, and partly just inevitable, movement through channels occurs at a very low velocity.

For example, in the early days of Rockefeller Foundation agricultural activity in Colombia, the federal government sent some experts in farm machinery to the college at Medellin. When the men arrived they were stymied because they found they did not have available there the ordinary hand tools—wrenches, hammers, etc.—necessary to repair and service the machinery with which they were to work. A telephone call, an airmail list, and an air freight shipment made the necessary tools available in less than a week. This was done by the Rockefeller Foundation, which helped out because the federal government simply could not do it on that sort of schedule.

Sometimes it is essential to hurry, and sometimes it is disastrous to hurry. Foundations must have enough sense and knowledge to decide whether to hurry or not. In significant instances foundations have the important power to do either.

Speed of action and action at a critical juncture are closely allied to, but not the same thing as, venturesome action at a time when confidence and hope exist, but when conservative proof of feasibility does not exist. The question of "how much chance do we take" is an important and difficult one for a foundation to answer. We have considered this problem more generally in the portion of this book devoted to criticisms of foundations; but at the moment we note the evidence, stated at several places in the contributed chapters, that foundations have often and with good results been venturesome.

One of the aspects of foundation aid almost universally praised in the contributed chapters is its flexibility. Most experienced foundations try to be as meticulous and precise as possible in the gathering of evidence as to whether a grant should be made. But, once the affirmative decision has been made, the good foundations try to impose a minimum of formality and restraint. Budgets as originally submitted are very helpful in indicating the scholar's expectation and intent, but subsequent modifications are considered with professional understanding. Foundations must of course carry out their financial transactions in a responsible way, and they do have treasurers and controllers, but the good financial officers, when faced with a problem, say, "Let's figure out how we can properly do this."

In many instances budgets are considered from the outset as approximate, and freedom for reasonable modification is assumed. On dozens and dozens of occasions, in the personal experience of this author, scientists who had grants from the

Rockefeller Foundation wrote and asked for advice, permission, or instructions relative to the management of their grant. There were, of course, cases in which instruction was necessary—one inflexible rule, for example, was that the money had to be used for the general purpose or purposes set forth by the applicant in his request. Such a restriction is a legal necessity. But in the vast majority of requests involving modifications within the framework of the original plan the answer was, in effect, that the grant had been made because of trust in the judgment of the recipient, and that he therefore should make the decision himself.

One minor aspect, cumulatively not unimportant, of this desirable flexibility has to do with the submitting of requests and the filing of papers. It is simply criminal to overburden scholars and scientists with unnecessary formal paperwork. It is a great delight to a foundation officer when someone writes in and asks for "blanks," how requests must be made, and how many copies he must submit, to be able to tell him that there are no blanks, and that the foundation can be approached by a letter, phone call, or in person. This approach is, after all, only the first step. And, in all cases of significant size, the meaningful information comes not from this initial approach, but from visits by a foundation officer to the laboratory of the scientist, to see at first hand his setup, to meet his assistants, and to discuss informally the scientific issues involved. All the Rockefeller Foundation officers, for example, have always traveled widely and frequently, and recorded all their discussions in extensive diaries which were available to their fellow officers but were otherwise completely confidential. We did not need blanks, or even, except in unusual circumstances, written recommendations. We characteristically proceeded on the basis of first-hand, not second- or third-hand information. It is my impression that even the largest philanthropic foundations continue to operate in this direct and informal way.

As to reports, at the Rockefeller Foundation the scientists were told that we would continue, after the grant was made, to be vitally interested in them and in their work but that there were no fixed formal requirements for scientific reports. (The legalities made necessary a formal financial report.) We made it clear that we hoped to be kept informed simply because we were interested, but this could be done by letters or phone calls or visits, on any schedule that proved convenient.

With the present large programs of support, and with the clear necessity that a foundation constantly restudy and revalue its own procedures, some reasonable requirements that grantees report are doubtless necessary in certain cases. Regular financial reports are certainly essential. But too frequent and too lengthy reports in multiple copies are certainly unnecessary. If a foundation says to a scholar or scientist who receives a grant, "we are a minor partner in this enterprise, we are deeply interested, and we hope that you will keep us informed about how things are progressing" —then, in the large majority of cases, the foundation will receive, in one way or another, all it wishes or needs to know.

Many of the comments of the preceding chapters recognize that one value of foundation assistance arises because of the way in which this aid enhances the chance to get additional money from other sources. This aid occurs on an explicit basis when a "conditional" or "matching" grant is made: it occurs also because of the widely recognized prestige value of a grant made by one of the foundations that has established a reputation for careful and sound judgment in choosing its recipients.

There are some activities of philanthropic foundations that have concrete, measurable, and indisputable value. In the twenty years following 1943, when the Rockefeller Foundation effectively began its agricultural program in Mexico, the population of that country increased by 75 percent; but the production of their basic foods increased by 300 percent. This kind of accomplishment is easy to measure and to appreciate. There are many other foundation activities that are less easy to assess, and there are activities that are really impossible to assess in any provable way. When dealing with this last category, one simply has to have faith in the ultimate value of sincere, honest, dedicated, well-intentioned and ably-manned attempts. However difficult assessment is, the fact remains that competent persons, expert and experienced in a wide variety of fields, have in these preceding contributed chapters borne clear witness to their own convictions that foundations are serving society well.

In fact and in summary, what is the over-all evidence furnished by the authors of the preceding eighteen chapters? It is that foundations have freed large parts of the world from the curse of diseases such as malaria and yellow fever; have brought enjoyment of the arts to millions of people; have created and helped support universities and research institutes; have clarified and otherwise served the law; have in many practical ways promoted international understanding and have encouraged the cause of peace; have shown how population can be controlled and people fed; have helped develop broadly trained leadership for business and government; have significanty aided the emerging nations; have importantly contributed to our growing knowledge of physical and living nature; have been alert in aiding new fields of activity; have helped to clarify the goals of present-day humanistic scholarship; have made possible the development of important new scientific instruments for studying the atom, the cell, and the star; have, in language and area studies, anticipated and provided for some of the pressing needs of our country in its new worldwide responsibility; have created multi-million-dollar free funds for basic research; have recently developed and supported several projects to extend the opportunities of higher education to qualified Negroes; and have liberated thousands of gifted individuals from the limitations of inadequate education, thus freeing them for greater service to society.

Biographical Notes on Contributors

GEORGE W. BEADLE

After preliminary training at the University of Nebraska, George W. Beadle took his doctor's degree at Cornell University and began his scientific career there. He went on to the California Institute of Technology as a National Research Fellow, and, after a year at the Institut de Biologie in Paris, spent successive periods at Harvard and Stanford before returning to the California Institute of Technology. There he was made chairman of the Division of Biology. In 1961 he became president of The University of Chicago. He holds numerous honorary degrees and has received a number of distinguished prizes, including the Nobel Prize in 1958 for research in genetics.

His essay on biology is somewhat longer than several of the other papers. This is appropriate because of the fact that biology has been experiencing an unprecedented period of activity, with specially noteworthy advances in those basic studies, including genetics at a molecular level, in which Dr. Beadle has himself been a leader. In preparing his paper, Dr. Beadle consulted a number of scientists, including Boris Ephrussi, A. D. Hershey, Arthur Kornberg, H. J. Muller, Severo Ochoa, Ray D. Owen, Max F. Perutz, Tracy M. Sonneborn, E. C. Stakman, Wendell M. Stanley, A. H. Sturtevant, E. L. Tatum, J. Herbert Taylor, Victor C. Twitty, and James D. Watson.

ARNE TISELIUS

Professor Arne Tiselius is professor of biochemistry at the University of Uppsala, Sweden. The importance of his own research in biochemistry was recognized by the award to him in 1948 of the Nobel Prize in chemistry: and by honorary degrees from Paris, Cambridge, Bologna, Glasgow, Madrid, Oxford, Lyon, Berkeley, etc. He has for years been one of the top scientists of Sweden, and his influential role in the organization and development of science in his country is attested by his past chairmanship of the Science Research Council, his membership in the Swedish Government's Science Advisory Council, his past presidency of the Nobel Foundation, and his chairmanship of the Nobel Committee for Chemistry.

Professor Tiselius has been in the United States on many occasions, and is well informed concerning the research situation in our country, as well, of course, as the research personnel, facilities, and activities in Europe.

LEE A. DUBRIDGE

Lee A. DuBridge, the president of the California Institute of Technology, is a physicist. A graduate of Cornell College (Iowa), Dr. DuBridge earned advanced degrees at the University of Wisconsin, where he began his career as a physics teacher. A National Research Council fellowship at the California Institute of Technology in 1926-28 was followed by professional appointments at Washington University, and then as professor of physics at the University of Rochester. At the latter institution he was dean of the Faculty of Arts and Sciences from 1938 to 1941.

During World War II he played an important role as director of the so-called Radiation Laboratory at the Massachusetts Institute of Technology, the major academic center for research and development of radar.

His memberships in government councils in the years following World War II include the General Advisory Committee of the Atomic Energy Commission, Naval Research Advisory Committee, Air Force Science Advisory Board, President's Communications Policy Board, and the National Science Board. Dr. DuBridge is a trustee for the Mellon Institute, the Rockefeller Foundation, and the National Merit Scholarship Corporation; he is widely recognized for scientific ability, academic leadership, and the wisdom and energy which he devotes to national affairs.

JOSEPH C. HINSEY

Joseph C. Hinsey, director of New York Hospital–Cornell Medical Center since 1953 and professor of neuroanatomy since 1956, had been in prior years professor of physiology, professor of anatomy, chairman of both these departments, and from 1942 to 1953 dean of Cornell's Medical School. Dr. Hinsey taught at Northwestern, Washington

University, Western Reserve, and Stanford before coming to Cornell.

Few medical educators are as widely acquainted and as intimately informed as is Dr. Hinsey. For years his counsel has been sought in connection with problems at numerous medical schools all over the country, a record of national service only very partially reflected in the long list of appointments and honors which are listed in his formal record.

GEORGE J. STIGLER

Economist and educator, George J. Stigler has since 1958 been Charles Walgreen Distinguished Service Professor of American Institutions at the University of Chicago. His B.B.A. is from the University of Washington, of which state he is a native, M.B.A. from Northwestern University, and Ph.D. from the University of Chicago. Dr. Stigler has taught economics at Iowa State College, the University of Minnesota, and at Brown and Columbia universities. A Guggenheim fellow in 1955, he spent 1957-58 as a fellow at the Center for Advanced Study in Behavioral Sciences. Dr. Stigler's stature in his discipline is evident from his membership on the research staff of the National Bureau of Economic Research and the Attorney General's Committee for Study of Anti-Trust Laws, his recent presidency of the American Economic Association, his lectureship at the London School of Economics, and his authorship of technical treatises.

ERWIN N. GRISWOLD

Erwin N. Griswold has been dean of Harvard University Law School since 1946, and the Langdell Professor of Law since 1950. Dr. Griswold was admitted to the Ohio bar in 1929 and served in the office of the Solicitor General, and as special assistant to the Attorney General in Washington, before returning to Cambridge in 1934. He became professor of law the following year and held the Charles Stebbins Fairchild professorship from 1946 to 1950. He is the author of several treatises on law, and is the general editor of the American Case Book Series. President of the Association of American Law Schools in 1957-58, Dean Griswold was appointed by President Kennedy in 1961 a member of the United States Civil Rights Commission, and he is on the board of directors of the American Council of Learned Societies. Dr. Griswold's eminence in his profession has been recognized by a large number of honorary degrees from universities in this country and elsewhere.

WHITNEY J. OATES

Whitney J. Oates, Avalon Professor of Humanities, Princeton University, is chairman of the Council of the Humanities at that university. Dr. Oates earned A.B., A.M., and Ph.D degrees at Princeton and commenced his teaching career there in 1927. After a Rockefeller postwar fellowship in 1948, he was named Andrew Fleming West Professor of Classics, and remained in this capacity until 1962, at which time he moved into his present chair. He holds the honorary degree of L.H.D. from Brown University and Rockford College, and the degree of Litt.D. from Middlebury College. He is a trustee of the National Woodrow Wilson Fellowship Foundation and of the Princeton University Press; senator and currently president of the United Chapters of Phi Beta Kappa; senior fellow of the Center for Hellenic Studies of Harvard University in Washington, D.C.; and a member of the Commission on the Humanities sponsored by the American Council of Learned Societies, the Council of Graduate Schools in the United States, and the United Chapters of Phi Beta Kappa. His most recent book, *Aristotle and the Problem of Value,* was published in 1963 by the Princeton University Press.

BROOKS ATKINSON

Brooks Atkinson, 1947 Pulitzer Prize journalist, retired from the *New York Times* as critic at large on May 1, 1965. He was the *Times*'s widely read drama critic for most of his career on that newspaper. Upon his graduation from Harvard in 1917 Mr. Atkinson spent one year as an instructor of English at Dartmouth, but he had already had a brief experience as a reporter on the Springfield *Daily News,* and he promptly became assistant to the drama critic of the Boston *Evening Transcript.* He joined the *New York Times* in 1922. He was editor of the *Book Review* (1922 to 1925), drama critic (1925 to 1942 and 1946 to 1960), war correspondent in China (1942 to 1944) and news correspondent in Moscow (1945 to 1946). Mr. Atkinson is the author of several books and has edited one-volume editions of the writings of Henry David Thoreau and Ralph Waldo Emerson.

ANATOLE CHUJOY

Anatole Chujoy, born in Latvia and educated in law in Petrograd, has been a United States citizen since 1930. From 1933 on he held editorial positions on various magazines devoted to the dance, and since 1942 he has been the editor and publisher of *Dance News*. He is the author of numerous articles on the dance; and his books include *Ballet* (1936), *Symphonic Ballet* (1937), *The Dance Encyclopedia* (1949), and *The New York City Ballet*, a history of the company (1953). He was the translator and editor of *Fundamentals of the Classic Dance* by the great Russian teacher Agrippina Vaganova (1946), which has become a standard textbook on ballet in the United States and the United Kingdom, and the editor of *Foline, Memoirs of a Ballet Master* (1961).

In 1950, Mr. Chujoy was awarded a diploma for meritorious research and fruitful activities in the realm of the dance by the Archives Internationales de la Danse, Paris.

DONALD L. ENGLE

Donald L. Engle received the degrees Bachelor of Music and Bachelor of Science from Kansas State University, and, after a year on the music faculty there, completed a Master of Arts degree at the Eastman School of Music. Before entering military service he was employed briefly by the National Broadcasting Company in New York and the Radio Corporation of America in Camden, New Jersey. During World War II and the Korean War he was an officer in the U.S. Army Signal Corps.

Mr. Engle has been a member of the Music Division of the Library of Congress, and music director of radio stations in Washington and Philadelphia. For eleven years he was on the staff of the Philadelphia Orchestra as press representative and program annotator, assistant manager, and manager. In 1959 he was appointed director of the Martha Baird Rockefeller Aid to Music Program, a personal philanthropy of Mrs. John D. Rockefeller, Jr., which in 1962 became the Martha Baird Rockefeller Fund for Music, Inc. He has been organist and choir director in a number of churches, and is at present a member of music advisory committees for the Institute of International Education and the New York State Council for the Arts.

RICHARD MCLANATHAN

Richard McLanathan is a museum and art consultant with two decades of experience as a museum curator and director. A graduate of Harvard, he taught in New York from 1938 to 1942, and in 1946 began an association with the Museum of Fine Arts, Boston. In 1948 he received a Prix de Rome in the history of art, and in 1951 earned a Ph.D. from Harvard, where he was a member of the Society of

Fellows. Dr. McLanathan served the Boston Museum as secretary and editor of Publications, as well as being Curator of Decorative Arts. In 1957 he became director of the Munson-Williams-Proctor Institute in Utica, New York, and two years later acted as curator of the American Art Exhibit at the Moscow Fair for the USIA. He was appointed by Governor Rockefeller as an original member of the New York State Council on the Arts. Since 1961 Dr. McLanathan has lived in New York City, where he writes and lectures on art.

BROCK CHISHOLM

Brock Chisholm is a physician of Ontario, Canada, who has had distinguished and authoritative association with world health problems, having been from 1948 to 1953 the director-general of the World Health Organization, one of the special agencies of the United Nations.

Dr. Chisholm was originally trained at the University of Toronto, did postgraduate work in London hospitals, and served in the Canadian army in both world wars, advancing to the grade of major general. He was Deputy Minister of Health of Canada from 1944-46, and has been president of the World Federation for Mental Health. He holds numerous degrees and other honors, in tribute to his outstanding contributions, on a worldwide scale, to problems of health, mental hygiene, psychosomatic medicine, world federation, and humanism.

JOHN BOYD-ORR

John Boyd-Orr, since 1946 chancellor of Glasgow University and since 1961 president of the World Academy of Science and Art, is a British physiologist whose work in the science of nutrition led to his appointment as director general of the Food and Agricultural Organization, an office he held from 1945 to 1948. Born in 1880, Lord Boyd-Orr (1st Baron, created 1949), studied at Glasgow University, served in the Royal Army Medical Corps during World War I, and directed Rowett Research Institution on Animal Nutrition for more than twenty-five years thereafter. In 1949 he was awarded the Nobel Peace Prize.

FREDERICK OSBORN

Frederick Osborn, a New York corporation executive with a long record of distinguished public service, graduated from Princeton in

1910 and continued his studies at Trinity College, Cambridge. Leaving an active business career in 1929, he became a research associate at the American Museum of Natural History. During World War II he was director of the U.S. Army and Air Force's Information and Education Division, and he subsequently served for several years as Deputy U.S. representative on the UN Atomic Energy Commission.

Mr. Osborn's long-time interest in the population problem eventually brought him to the presidency of The Population Council, in which office he served from 1952 to 1959. He is still a trustee, as he also is of the Frick Collection and Princeton University. At present Mr. Osborn is secretary-treasurer of American Eugenics Society.

PHILIP E. MOSELY

Philip E. Mosely, director of the European Institute and professor of international relations, Columbia University, is also associate dean of the university's Faculty of International Affairs. A graduate of Harvard in 1926, Dr. Mosely earned his Ph.D. there after several years of historical research in Moscow. Teaching assignments at Princeton, Union College, and Cornell, and sociological research in the Balkans were followed by service with the Department of State. Throughout World War II he was assistant chief, Division of Political Studies, and chief, Division of Territorial Studies. Dr. Mosely advised the U.S. delegation at the Moscow and Potsdam conferences, and served the Secretary of State in a similar capacity at the London and Paris meetings of the Council of Foreign Ministers in 1945 and 1946. In 1944 and 1945 he was political advisor and a principal negotiator in the U.S. delegation to the European Advisory Commission in London, which worked out the initial postwar arrangements for Germany, Austria, and Bulgaria. Dr. Mosely directed the Russian Institute at Columbia from 1951 to 1955 and then for eight years served the Council of Foreign Relations as director of studies.

GEORGE M. BECKMANN

George M. Beckmann, professor of history and director of the East Asian Studies Program, Claremont Graduate School and University Center, was formerly professor of history at the University of Kansas, associate dean of faculties and chairman of The Council on International Programs. His undergraduate study at Harvard University (in Far Eastern Languages) was interrupted by service in the U.S. Navy during World War II. His assignments included study of Japanese at the Navy's Language School, and duty in the Philippines, Japan, and Korea. Professor Beckmann's Ph.D. (in history) was received from Stanford University in 1951. He was a Fulbright Research Scholar and Ford Foundation Area Fellow in Japan the following two years, and similar grants took him there in 1956 and 1960-61.

Dr. Beckmann's first faculty post was as instructor at the University of Kansas in 1951. Four years were spent as an assistant professor and four more as an associate, with full professorship in 1960. A program associate in the Ford Foundation's International Training and Research Program from 1961 to 1964, Dr. Beckmann serves them currently as a consultant. He has written extensively, both books and articles, on the Far East.

FRED M. HECHINGER

Education editor of the *New York Times,* Fred M. Hechinger was born in Germany and came to the United States in 1937. A Phi Beta Kappa graduate of the City College of New York, he has also studied at the University of London, in which city he was connected with both American and British wartime government offices from 1944 to 1946. Mr. Hechinger's newspaper career began with writing for the Educational Supplement of the *Times* of London. After returning to the United States he wrote and edited education news for the Bridgeport (Conn.) *Herald,* the Washington *Post* and the New York *Herald Tribune.* In 1959, after a three-year interval as associate publisher and executive editor of the Bridgeport *Sunday Herald,* Mr. Hechinger was appointed to his present post on the *New York Times.*

FLORA M. RHIND

Flora M. Rhind, now special assistant to the president of the Rockefeller Foundation, began her association with the organization in 1933 in the capacity of assistant to the Director for Social Sciences. In 1964 when she "retired" (at least formally) the record evidenced her roles at different times as secretary for General Education; assistant director, vice president, acting president, and, since 1960, trustee of the General Education Board; and in the Rockefeller Foundation she held the office of secretary from 1948 to her retirement. During her long period of distinguished service in the Rockefeller boards she has taken a special interest in the educational problems of the South, concerning which she has extensive and direct knowledge.

BARRY BINGHAM

Barry Bingham, editor-in-chief and publisher of the *Courier-Journal* and the Louisville *Times*, was a *magna cum laude* graduate of Harvard in 1928. He began as a reporter with the newspapers in 1930 and moved upward in management positions to the presidency in 1945. He served with the U.S. Navy in European and Pacific theatres, as commander, U.S.N.R. in 1945. Mr. Bingham is a trustee of the Rockefeller Foundation, a director of the American Press Institute, the American Society of Newspaper Editors, and a member of the Advisory Board for the Pulitzer Prizes.

Notes

CHAPTER 1: PRE-CHRISTIAN PHILANTHROPY

1. Hans Kalmus, "The Evolution of Altruism," *New Scientist*, London, November 28, 1963, p. 550.
2. Gordon Riley of Yale University: News release 64-145 by National Science Foundation, October 5, 1964.
3. "The Compassionate Creatures," *The Sciences*, New York Academy of Sciences, Vol. 4, No. 9, February, 1965, p. 5.
4. V. Stefansson, *Adventures in Error*, Robert M. McBride & Co., New York, 1936.
5. Lois Crisler, *Arctic Wild*, Harper & Brothers, 1958.
6. Sir Arthur Keith, *New Theory of Human Evolution*, Watts & Co., London, 1949, p. 451.
7. Ernest Victor Hollis, "Evolution of the Philanthropic Foundation," *Educational Record*, American Council on Education, Washington, D.C., October, 1939, p. 576.
8. F. Emerson Anndrews, *Philanthropic Giving*, Russell Sage Foundation, New York, 1950, pp. 31-35.
9. Bertrand Russell, *A History of Western Philanthropy*, Simon and Schuster, New York, 1945, p. 183.
10. Hollis, *op. cit.*, p. 577.

CHAPTER 2: A THOUSAND YEARS OF ECCLESIASTICAL FOUNDATIONS

1. F. Emerson Andrews, *Philanthropic Giving*, Russell Sage Foundation, New York, 1950, p. 34.
2. The Supreme Court has shown that the *cy pres* notion does not depend on Christianity but was applied by the Romans before Christianity became the official religion of the Roman Empire (12 Late Corporation of the Church of Jesus Christ of Latter Day

Saints vs. U.S. 1890 10 Supreme Court 792 136 U.S. 1, 52, 34 Lawyers Edition 478, 481). It is interesting to see how far back the principle is recognized. In the Pandects of Justinian are cases to the same effect as those referred to antedating the adoption of Christianity as the religion of the Empire.

3. George Gleason Bogert, *The Law of Trusts and Trustees,* West Publishing Co., St. Paul, 1935, Vol. 2A, section 431.

4. Sir Arthur Hobhouse, *The Dead Hand,* Chatto and Windus, Piccadilly, London, 1880, p. 223.

5. Julius Rosenwald, "Principles of Public Giving," *The Atlantic Monthly,* May, 1929, p. 601.

6. These and several other similar examples will be found in Appendix F of "Community Foundations in the United States and Canada, 1914-1961," prepared by Wilmer Shields Rich, National Council on Community Foundations (now National Council on Foundations), Inc., New York, 1961; and in the *Cy Pres Doctrine in the United States,* by Edith L. Fisch, Matthew Bender & Company, Albany, New York, 1950, pp. 141-42.

7. Though Plato's Academy produced only one later philosopher of the first order, it continued to exist as a corporate body down to A.D. 529, when the Emperor Justinian, in his zeal for Christian orthodoxy, closed the schools of Athens and appropriated their emoluments. (*Encyclopaedia Britannica,* 1947, Vol. 18, pp. 62-63.)

8. Henry Allen Moe, "Notes on the Origin of Philanthropy in Christendom," *Proceedings of the American Philosophical Society,* Vol. 105, No. 2, April, 1961, p. 142.

CHAPTER 3: THE SHIFT TO SECULAR CONTROL

1. The 1965 edition of *Statistical Abstract of the United States* (Bureau of the Census, Department of Commerce, Table 486) states the total national wealth as $1,682.9 billion as of 1958, whereas the total of the endowments of all U.S. foundations, as stated in a release of the Foundation Library Center dated January 4, 1964, was roughly $14.5 billion. The more recent increases in both figures have presumably not materially affected the ratio of the two.

2. W. K. Jordan, *Philanthropy in England, 1480-1660,* Russell Sage Foundation, New York, 1959, pp. 357-58.

3. *Ibid.,* p. 161.

4. F. Emerson Andrews, *Philanthropic Giving,* Russell Sage Foundation, New York, 1950, p. 37.

5. Ernest Victor Hollis, "Evolution of the Philanthropic Foundation," *Educational Record,* October, 1939, p. 582.
6. Ernest Victor Hollis, *Philanthropic Foundations and Higher Education,* Columbia University Press, New York, 1938, p. 16.
7. Henry Allen Moe, " 'The Vision of Piers the Plowman' and the Law of Foundations," *Proceedings of The American Philosophical Society,* Philadelphia, Pa., Vol. 102, No. 4, August, 1958, p. 373.
8. Hollis, "Evolution of the Philanthropic Foundation," pp. 583-84.
9. J. Bronowski, *Introduction to Darwinism and the Study of Society,* Michael Banton, Editor, Tavistock Publications, London; Chicago, Quadrangle Books, 1961, p. xi.

CHAPTER 4: EARLY AMERICAN PHILANTHROPIC
ORGANIZATIONS

1. All of the dates are here stated in acordance with our present calendars, rather than in accordance with the calendar used by the Pilgrims, which assigned dates ten days earlier. The main shift from the Julian to the present calendar was originally made in 1582, but was not adopted in England until 1752.
2. William Bradford's journal, *Of Plymouth Plantation, 1620-1647* (new edition published by Alfred A. Knopf, New York, 1952) recorded that they "tacked about and resolved to stand for the southward (the wind and weather being fair) to find some place about Hudson's River for their habitation." But they encountered "dangerous shoals and roaring breakers," presumably on Pollock Rip, so that they turned back.
3. Presumably, according to Warren Sears Nickerson in *Land ho!— 1620* (Houghton Mifflin Co., Boston, 1931) about one-eighth mile inside Long Point.
4. George Ernest Bowman, *The Mayflower Compact and Its Signers,* Massachusetts Society of Mayflower Descendants, Boston, 1920, p. 9.
5. Henry Allen Moe, "Notes on the Origin of Philanthropy in Christendom," *Proceedings of The American Philosophical Society,* Vol. 105, No. 2, April, 1961, p. 141.
6. Luke 6:24, 38.
7. John Winthrop, "A modell of Christian charity, Winthrop Papers," *Massachusetts Historical Society Proceedings,* 1931, p. 282-95.
8. Robert H. Bremner, *American Philanthropy,* The University of Chicago Press, Chicago, 1960, p. 7.

9. Merle Curti, "Tradition and Innovation in American Philanthropy," *Proceedings of The American Philosophical Society*, Vol. 105, No. 2, April, 1961, p. 146.

10. Penn himself proposed the name "Sylvania," but Charles II added the "Penn" in honor of William Penn's father.

11. Ann D. Walton and Marianna O. Lewis (eds.), *The Foundation Directory, Edition 2*, prepared by the Foundation Library Center, Russell Sage Foundation, New York, 1964.

12. F. Emerson Andrews, "Growth and Present Status of American Foundation," *Proceedings of The American Philosophical Society*, Vol. 105, Number 2, April, 1961, p. 157.

13. Walton and Lewis (eds.), *The Foundation Directory*, p. 498.

14. Robert S. Morison, "Foundations and Universities," *Daedalus*, Fall, 1964, p. 1111.

15. Burton J. Hendrick, *The Life of Andrew Carnegie*, 2 vols., Doubleday, Doran & Co., New York, 1932, Vol. II, p. 139.

16. *Ibid.*, p. 387.

17. The phrase was not Carnegie's but he recognized its aptness and appeal and adopted it immediately. This original article first appeared under the title "Wealth" in the *North American Review*, CXLVIII, June, 1889, pp. 653-64. Gladstone asked to have it reprinted in England. It then appeared in several publications there, but in the *Pall Mall Gazette*'s version the editor, William T. Stead, supplied a new title, "Gospel of Wealth." Thus when Carnegie came to write the second installment of his piece (subtitled "The Best Fields for Philanthropy") for the December, 1889, issue of the *North American Review*, he referred to the earlier segment as the "Gospel of Wealth," and since then the two writings together have been so titled. The name of one of two books containing Andrew Carnegie's collected articles, including the "Gospel" pieces, is also *The Gospel of Wealth and Other Timely Essays*, The Century Company, New York, 1900.

18. All of the quotations referring to Carnegie are taken from his "Gospel of Wealth," as printed in the *North American Review* in 1889.

19. Florence Anderson, *Library Program 1911-1961*, Carnegie Corporation of New York, 1963, p. 4.

20. Andrew Carnegie, *Autobiography of Andrew Carnegie*, Houghton Mifflin Co., Boston, 1920, pp. 256, 257.

21. Hendrick, *op. cit.*, p. 349.

22. Hendrick, *op. cit.*, pp. 350-51.

23 Andrews. "Growth and Present Status of American Foundations," p. 158.

24. Hendrick, *op. cit.*, pp. 352-53.

25. Carnegie, *The Gospel of Wealth*, p. 16.

26. Allan Nevins, *John D. Rockefeller, the Heroic Age of American Enterprise*, Vol. I, Charles Scribner's Sons, New York, 1940, p. 21.

27. Allan Nevins, *Study in Power, John D. Rockefeller, Industrialist and Philanthropist*, Vol. I, Charles Scribner's Sons, New York, 1953, pp. 5-6.

28. *Ibid.*, p. 9.

29. Nevins, *John D. Rockefeller*, p. 614.

30. Raymond B. Fosdick, *John D. Rockefeller, Jr.*, Harper & Brothers, New York, 1956, p. 96.

31. Merle Curti, Judith Green, and Roderick Nash, "Anatomy of Giving: Millionnaires in the Late 19th Century," *The American Quarterly*, Vol. 15, Fall, 1963, pp. 415-35.

32. *Ibid.*, p. 424.

33. Raymond B. Fosdick, *The Story of The Rockefeller Foundation*, Harper and Brothers, New York, 1952, p. 1.

34. *Ibid.*

CHAPTER 5: KINDS OF FOUNDATIONS

1. Thus the City of New York, through the Health Research Council, grants approximately $8 million annually for research in fields basic to health.

2. Its assets, at the time of their 1962 report to the U.S. Government, were $1,584,737.

3. At the time of its 1962 report to the U.S. Government, its assets were $341,239.

4. Sydney Shepherd Spivak, *Foundations and Accountability*, unpublished, 1953, p. 107. A master's thesis submitted to Columbia University.

5. F. Emerson Andrews, *Philanthropic Foundations*, Russell Sage Foundation, New York, 1956, p. 21.

6. Wilmer Shields Rich, *Community Foundations in the United States and Canada, 1914-1961*, Second edition, National Council on Community Foundations, 1961, p. 9.

7. Rockefeller Brothers Fund, 1964 Report, New York.

CHAPTER 6: THE ARITHMETIC, CHRONOLOGICAL, AND
GEOGRAPHIC FACTS ABOUT FOUNDATIONS

1. Ann D. Walton, and O. Marianna Lewis (eds.), *The Foundation Directory*, edition 2, prepared by the Foundation Library Center, Russell Sage Foundation, New York, 1964, p. 11.
2. The Foundation Library Center, *Annual Report 1965*, pp. 11, 14.
3. *The Foundation Directory*, Edition 2, p. 13.
4. More accurately, of foundations still in existence, having assets of *Directory*, Edition 2, size, on which founding data are available, and which were not established after 1959.
5. *The Foundation Directory*, Edition 2, p. 15.

CHAPTER 7: THE RESOURCES OF FOUNDATIONS AND
THEIR SHARE OF PHILANTHROPY

1. The Foundation Library Center, *Annual Report 1965*, New York, p. 14.
2. John Scarne, *Complete Guide to Gambling*, Simon and Schuster, 1961, p. 1.

CHAPTER 8: REASONS FOR ESTABLISHING FOUNDATIONS

1. Shelby M. Harrison and F. Emerson Andrews, *American Foundations for Social Welfare*, Russell Sage Foundation, New York, 1946, pp. 2-3.
2. Armand C. Marts, *Philanthropy's Role in Civilization*, Harper & Brothers, New York, 1953, p. 21.
3. *New York Times*, March 18, 1964, signed article by Allen Hughes, p. 48.
4. F. Emerson Andrews, *Philanthropic Foundations*, Russell Sage Foundation, New York, 1956, p. 41.
5. *Fortune*, February, 1966, Vol. LXXIII, No. 2, p. 76.
6. F. Emerson Andrews, *op. cit.*, p. 41.
7. See Robert S. Morison, M.D., "Some Illnesses of Mental Health," *The Journal of Medical Education*, Vol. 39, No. 11, November, 1964, p. 985.
8. E. G. Sherburne, Jr., "ETV Research in the Decade Ahead," *A. V. Communication Review*, Vol. 8, No. 4, July-August, 1960, p. 197.

CHAPTER 9: LEGAL AND FINANCIAL ASPECTS OF
FOUNDATIONS

1. *Income Tax Regulations as of August 3, 1965, Volume One,*
   Commerce Clearing House, Inc., Chicago, Illinois, Reg. 1.501(c)
   (3)(ii), pp. 33, 411.
2. *Internal Revenue Code, Income, Estate and Gift Tax Provisions,*
   Commerce Clearing House, Inc., Chicago, Illinois, 1954 Code—
   Subtitle A, Ch. 1 F, Part I, Sec. 501(c)(3), p. 4183.
3. *Ibid.,* Reg. 1.501(c)(3)—(a)(1), pp. 33, 409.
4. *Income Tax Regulations, op. cit.,* Reg. 1.501(c)(3)—1(d)(2),
   pp. 33, 411.
5. Albert M. Sacks, "The Role of Philanthropy: An Institutional
   View," *Virginia Law Review,* Vol. 46, No. 3, 1960, p. 517.
6. Armand C. Marts, *Philanthropy's Role in Civilization,* Harper &
   Brothers, New York, 1953, p. 3.
7. Marion Fremont-Smith, "Corporation versus Trust," *Foundation
   News,* Vol. VI, No. 2, March, 1965, p. 26.
8. Eleanor K. Taylor, *Public Accountability of Foundations and
   Charitable Trusts,* Russell Sage Foundation, New York, 1953, pp.
   150-78.
9. F. Emerson Andrews, *Philanthropic Foundations,* Russell Sage
   Foundation, New York, 1956, pp. 420-21.
10. *Indenture of James B. Duke Establishing The Duke Endowment,*
    1932, pp. 14 and 15.
11. Sir Arthur Hobhouse, *The Dead Hand,* Chatto & Windus, London,
    1880.
12. Edwin R. Embree and Julia Waxman, *Investment in People: The
    Story of the Julius Rosenwald Fund,* Harper & Brothers, New
    York, 1949, p. 31.
13. Andrews, *Philanthropic Foundations,* pp. 103-104.
14. Under the auspices of The Foundation Library Center, Dr. Ralph
    Nelson carried out a detailed study of investment policies of
    foundations. It is now scheduled for publication as *The Invest-
    ment Policies of Foundations* by the Russell Sage Foundation in
    1966.
15. *Treasury Department Report on Private Foundations,* Committee
    on Finance, United States Senate, U.S. Government Printing
    Office, Washington, D.C., February 2, 1965.

CHAPTER 10: THE STRUCTURE, STAFFING, AND PROCEDURES OF
FOUNDATIONS

1. Peter J. W. Debye, "An Interview," *Science,* Vol. 145, No. 3632, August 7, 1964, p. 558.
2. Frederick P. Keppel, *Report of the President and of the Treasurer,* Carnegie Corporation of New York, 1937, p. 39.
3. Frederick P. Keppel, "Opportunities and Dangers of Educational Foundations," *School and Society,* Vol. XXII, No. 574, December 26, 1925, p. 799.
4. Keppel, *Report of the President and of the Treasurer,* p. 39.
5. Edwin R. Embree, "Timid Billions—Are the Foundations Doing Their Job?" *Harper's Magazine,* March, 1949.
6. Eleanor K. Taylor, *Public Accountability of Foundations and Charitable Trusts,* Russell Sage Foundation, New York, 1953, p. 5.
7. F. Emerson Andrews, *Philanthropic Foundations,* Russell Sage Foundation, New York, 1956, p. 302.
8. J. Richard Taft, "Reporting Problems and Realities," *Foundation News,* Vol. VI, No. 5, September, 1965, p. 90.
9. Raymond B. Fosdick, *A Philosophy for a Foundation, on the Fiftieth Anniversary of the Rockefeller Foundation, 1913-1963,* Rockefeller Foundation, New York, 1963, pp. 20 and 21.
10. "Science at Amherst," *Amherst Reports,* Amherst College, September, 1962.

CHAPTER 11: FOUNDATIONS AND INDIVIDUALS

1. Burton Raffel, "A Critique of American Foundations," *Foundation News, Bulletin of the Foundation Library Center,* Vol. VI, No. 3, May, 1965, pp. 46-47.
2. Frederick L. Redefer, "A Magnet for Ideas," *Saturday Review,* August 8, 1964, p. 20.

CHAPTER 12: FOUNDATIONS AND UNIVERSITIES

1. W. Allen Wallis, "Centripetal and Centrifugal Forces in University Organization," *Daedalus,* Fall, 1964, Vol. 93, No. 4, p. 1078.
2. John C. Weaver, *Campus Review,* Ohio State University, January, 1965, p. 7.
3. R. S. Morison, "Foundation and Universities," *Daedalus,* Fall, 1964, Vol. 93, No. 4, 1109-40.

CHAPTER 13: FOUNDATIONS AND GOVERNMENT

1. F. Emerson Andrews (ed.), *Foundations—20 Viewpoints,* Russell Sage Foundation, New York, 1965, pp. 5 and 6.

2. Statement released by White House Press Secretary, *Statement of the President to the Cabinet on Strengthening the Academic Capability for Science throughout the Nation,* September 14, 1965.

3. Proceedings before the Committee on Science and Aeronautics, U.S. House of Representatives, Eighty-ninth Congress, Second Session [No. 3], January 25, 26, and 27, 1966, U.S. Government Printing Office, p. 50.

4. Information obtained from the Office of Program Planning and Evaluation, U.S. Office of Education, Department of Health, Education, and Welfare.

5. *New York Times,* Wednesday, April 6, 1966, p. 25.

6. *Industrial Relations:* Final Report and Testimony submitted to Congress by the Act of Congress of August 23, 1912, Vol. VIII, U.S. Government Printing Office, Washington, D.C., 1916.

7. John Lankford, *Congress and the Foundations in the Twentieth Century,* Wisconsin State University, River Falls, 1964, pp. 30-32.

8. *Hearings before the Select Committee to Investigate Tax-Exempt Foundations and Comparable Organizations,* U.S. House of Representatives, Eighty-Second Congress, Second Session, U.S. Government Printing Office, Washington, D.C., 1953, pp. 463-464.

9. Lankford, *op. cit.,* p. 38.

10. *Hearings before the Select Committee to Investigate Tax-Exempt Foundations . . . , op. cit.,* p. 1.

11. Lankford, *op. cit.,* p. 44.

12. *Congressional Record,* 83rd Congress, First Session, Vol. 99, Part 8, p. 10015.

13. Lankford, *op. cit.,* pp. 55 and 56.

14. Washington *Post,* August 2, 1953.

15. The quotation given comes from Sumner Slichter's article "Undermining the Foundations," *Atlantic Monthly,* September, 1954. This article preceded the Dodd Report, which was published December 16, 1954, and Slitchter's quotations are thus from the Dodd testimony, rather than from the Dodd Report.

16. *Ibid.,* p. 65.

17. *Ibid.,* p. 83.

18. Robert M. Hutchins, *Freedom, Education and the Fund: Essays and Addresses 1946-1956,* Meridian Books, New York, 1956, p. 201.

468 / *Notes*

19. Bernard DeVoto, "The Easy Chair: Guilt by Distinction," *Harper's Magazine*, April, 1955, p. 20.
20. *Ibid.*, p. 14.
21. *Tax-Exempt Foundations and Charitable Trusts: Their Impact on Our Economy.* Chairman's Report to the Select Committee on Small Business, House of Representatives, Eighty-seventh Congress, U.S. Government Printing Office, Washington, D.C., December 31, 1962.
22. John Walsh, "Foundations: Patman Plugs Away at Theme that Growth Operations of Tax-Exempts Call for Scrutiny," *Science*, Vol. 142, October 18, 1963, p. 370.
23. *Tax-Exempt Foundations*, Patman Report, p. v.
24. Roger K. Powell, "The Patman Report and the New Reporting Requirements," *New York University, Proceedings of the Twenty-second Annual Institute on Federal Taxation*, edited by Henry Sellin, Matthew Bender & Company, Inc., New York, 1964, p. 922.
25. *Tax-Exempt Foundations*, Patman Report, p. vi.
26. Powell, *op. cit.*, p. 924 .
27. *Tax-Exempt Foundations*, Patman Report, p. 1.
28. *Ibid.*, p. 3.
29. Lankford, *op. cit.*, p. 96.
30. *Tax-Exempt Foundations*, Patman Report, p. 18.
31. *Ibid.*, p. (v).
32. *Ibid.*, p. 1.
33. *Ibid.*, pp. 133-35.
34. *Tax-Exempt Foundations and Charitable Trusts: Their Impact on Our Economy (Second Installment)* Subcommittee Chairman's Report to Subcommittee No. 1, Select Committee on Small Business, House of Representatives, Eighty-eighth Congress, First Session, U.S. Government Printing Office, Washington, D.C., October 16, 1963.
35. *Ibid.*, p. iii.
36. *Tax-Exempt Foundations and Charitable Trusts: Their Impact on Our Economy (Third Installment)*, Subcommittee Chairman's Report to Subcommittee No. 1, Select Committee on Small Business, House of Representatives, Eighty-eighth Congress.
37. *New York Times*, September 5, 1964, p. 20.
38. *New York Times*, October 6, 1963.
39. Barry R. Peril, "Tax-Exempt Targets: The Patman Report and Private Charitable Foundations," *Taxes, The Tax Magazine*, Vol. 42, No. 2, February, 1964, p. 81.

40. John W. Gardner, "Private Initiative for the Public Good," *Annual Report,* Carnegie Corporation of New York, 1964, p. 9.
41. *The Rockefeller Foundation President's Review, 1964,* p. 3.
42. F. Emerson Andrews, "Report of the Director," *The Foundation Library Center Annual Report 1962,* pp. 12-13.
43. *New York Times* editorial, July 28, 1962. (Also *Ibid.,* p. 12).
44. *Treasury Department Report on Private Foundations,* printed for the Committee on Ways and Means, U.S. House of Representatives, and the Committee on Finance, U.S. Senate, U.S. Government Printing Office, Washington, D.C., February 2, 1965, 110 pp.
45. Carbery O'Shea, "Foundations for Individual and Corporate Purposes," *Proceedings of the Fourth Annual Tulane Tax Institute,* Matthew Bender & Company, Inc., Albany, New York, 1955, p. 262.
46. Dean Rusk, "Tax Exemption and the Public Purse," A portion of the remarks of Mr. Rusk before the Junior Chamber of Commerce, Cincinnati, Ohio, January 25, 1956, Rockefeller Foundation, New York, 1956, 16 pp.
47. *Ibid.*
48. The statements on taxes are taken in part from John Pearson, "Death and Taxes," *Atlantic Monthly,* May, 1949, p. 45.
49. Chauncey Belknap and Philip Mandel, *The Federal Income Tax Exemption of Charitable Organizations: Its History and Underlying Policy,* Patterson, Belknap and Webb, New York, 1954, pp. 28, 29.
50. Dean Rusk, "Philanthropy in a Free Society," *The Role of the Foundation in American Life,* Claremont University College, 1961, pp. 15 and 29.
51. Albert M. Sacks, "The Role of Philanthropy: An Institutional View," *Virginia Law Review,* Vol. 46, No. 3, 1960, p. 524.

CHAPTER 14: FOUNDATIONS AND SOCIETY

1. Albert M. Sacks, "The Role of Philanthropy: An Institutional View," *Virginia Law Review,* Vol. 46, No. 3, 1960, p. 529.
2. *Treasury Department Report on Private Foundations,* U.S. Government Printing Office, February 2, 1965, p. 5.
3. Merle Curti, "Subsidizing Radicalism: The American Fund for Public Service, 1921-41," *The Social Science Review,* Vol. XXXIII, No. 3, University of Chicago, September, 1959, p. 274.
4. *Ibid.,* p. 275.

5. *Ibid.*, p. 277.
6. *Ibid.*, p. 295.
7. "Right Wing Faces U.S. Tax Scrutiny," *New York Times*, December 20, 1964.
8. *Ibid.*
9. Philip M. Stern, "An Open Letter to the Ford Foundation," *Harper's Magazine,* January, 1966, p. 83.
10. *New York University Proceedings of the Seventh Biennial Conference on Foundations,* edited by Henry Sellin, Matthew Bender & Company, Inc., Albany, New York, 1965, p. 240.
11. *Ibid.*, pp. 265, 267.
12. *Ibid.*, p. 253.
13. *Ibid.*
14. Matthew 7:21.
15. John Walsh, "Foundations: Patman Plugs Away at Theme That Growth Operations of Tax Exempts Call for Scrutiny," *Science,* Vol. 142, October 18, 1963, p. 370.
16. Mortimer M. Caplin, text of remarks before the National Council on Community Foundations, Inc., Cleveland, Ohio, May 16, 1963, 15 pages multilithed.
17. Berien C. Eaton, Jr., "Charitable Foundations and Related Matters under the 1950 Revenue Act (Part I)," *Virginia Law Review,* Vol. 37, No. 1, January, 1951, p. 1.
18. William R. Huey, Jr., "Charitable Giving through Private Foundations," *The Journal of the American Society of Chartered Underwriters,* Vol. XV, No. 3, Summer, 1961, p. 222.
19. The quotes given come from various of the Patman Reports, and are commented upon by Barry R. Peril, "Tax-Exempt Targets: The Patman Report and Private Charitable Foundations," *Taxes, The Tax Magazine,* Vol. 42, No. 2, February, 1964.
20. *Tax-Exempt Foundations: Their Impact on Small Business,* Hearings before Subcommittee No. 1 on Foundations, Select Committee on Small Business, House of Representatives, Eighty-eighth Congress, Second Session, U.S. Government Printing Office, Washington, D.C., 1964, p. 65.
21. *Treasury Department Report on Private Foundations,* U.S. Government Printing Office, February 2, 1965, p. 18.
22. *Foundation News,* Vol. VII, No. 1, January, 1966, p. 3.
23. *Treasury Department Report on Private Foundations,* U.S. Government Printing Office, February 2, 1965, p. 5.
24. *Ibid.*, p. 2.

CHAPTER 18: THE ROLE OF PRIVATE FOUNDATIONS IN THE
DEVELOPMENT OF MODERN MEDICINE

1. "Foundation Expenditures for Medical and Health-Related Research and Education, 1960," *Resources for Medical Research,* Resources Analysis Branch, Office of Program Planning, National Institutes of Health, November, 1962.
2. Robert Shaplen, *Toward the Well-Being of Mankind—Fifty Years of The Rockefeller Foundation,* Doubleday & Co., Garden City, 1964.
3. *Annual Report for 1962,* W. K. Kellogg Foundation, Battle Creek.
4. *The Commonwealth Fund—Historical Sketch 1918-1962,* Harkness House, New York, 1962.
5. *Report for 1963-64,* Alfred P. Sloan Foundation, New York.
6. Abraham Flexner, *An Autobiography,* Simon and Schuster, New York, 1960.
7. Abraham Flexner, *Medical Education in the United States and Canada,* Bulletin Number Four, The Carnegie Foundation for the Advancement of Teaching, New York, 1910.
8. John E. Dietrick and Robert C. Berson, *Medical Schools in the United States at Mid-Century,* McGraw-Hill Book Co., Inc., New York, 1953.
9. George W. Corner, *A History of the Rockefeller Institute, 1901-1953—Origins and Growth,* The Rockefeller Institute Press, New York, 1964.
10. Raymond B. Fosdick, *The Story of The Rockefeller Foundation,* Harper & Brothers, New York, 1952.
11. G. Canby Robinson, *Adventures in Medical Education,* published for the Commonwealth Fund by the Harvard University Press, Cambridge, 1957.
12. Willard C. Rappleye, *The Current Era of the Faculty of Medicine, Columbia University, 1910-1958,* Columbia University, New York, 1958.
13. George H. Whipple, and others, *The Quarter Century, A Review of the First Twenty-Five Years, 1925-50,* The University of Rochester, Rochester, 1950.
14. *1963-64 Annual Report,* The John and Mary R. Markle Foundation, New York, 1965.
15. Lowell T. Coggeshall, *Planning for Medical Progress through Education,* Association of American Medical Colleges, Evanston, 1965.

16. Robert S. Morison, "Some Illnesses of Mental Health," *Journal of Medical Education,* 39, 985-99, 1964.

17. Howard C. Taylor, and others. *The Recruitment of Talent for a Medical Specialty,* The C. V. Mosby Co., St. Louis, 1961.

18. Willard C. Rappleye, "Partnership of Government and Voluntary Agencies in Strengthening the Organization of Health Services," *Bulletin No. 41,* New York Academy of Medicine (quoted from a pre-publication reprint), 1965.

CHAPTER 27: THE PROBLEM OF THE WORLD'S FOOD SUPPLY AND THE ROLE OF PHILANTHROPY

1. J. H. Efferson, *The Production and Marketing of Rice,* The Rice Journal, New Orleans, 1952, p. 2.

CHAPTER 29: INTERNATIONAL AFFAIRS

1. For a broad view of the development of political science, David B. Truman, "Disillusion and Regeneration: The Quest for a Discipline," *American Political Science Review,* Vol. LIX, no. 4, December, 1965, pp. 865-73.

2. Merle E. Curti, *American Peace Crusade, 1815-1860,* Octagon, 1929, 1965.

3. I am indebted to Oliver J. Lissitzyn, professor of international law, Columbia University, for several very enlightening discussions of the development of the study of international law; he is not responsible for this highly condensed summary.

4. For a somewhat different impression of the 1930's, see Quincy Wright, *The Study of International Relations,* Appleton-Century-Crofts, New York, 1955, p. 70.

5. See Chapter XXX of this book by Dean George M. Beckmann. See also *The University and World Affairs,* The Ford Foundation, 1961, 84 pages. For the impact of the war on the development of Russian studies, see Philip E. Mosely, "The Growth of Russian Studies," *American Research on Russia,* edited by Harold Fisher, Indiana University Press, 1959, pp. 1-22.

6. Bruce L. R. Smith, *The RAND Corporation; Case Study of a Non-Profit Advisory Corporation,* Cambridge, Mass., Harvard University Press, 1966, pp. xiii, 332.

7. Compare David B. Truman, *op. cit.*

CHAPTER 30: THE ROLE OF THE FOUNDATIONS IN
NON-WESTERN STUDIES

1. *The University and World Affairs,* Ford Foundation, New York, 1960; *The College and World Affairs,* Education and World Affairs, New York, 1964.
2. *Report of The Commission on the Humanities,* American Council of Learned Societies, New York, 1964, p. 86.

CHAPTER 31: PHILANTHROPIC FOUNDATIONS AND
THE PROBLEM OF RACE

1. Gunnar Myrdal, *An American Dilemma,* Revised Edition, Harper, New York, 1962, p. 846.
2. General Education Board, *Reports on Visits to Institutions,* 1902-1903, GEB Files.
3. 163 U.S. 537 (Gaines Case).
4. 305 U.S. 337 (School Segregation Cases).
5. W. E. Burghardt Du Bois, *Black Reconstruction in America,* Russell G. Russell, Inc., New York, p. 667.
6. Myrdal, *op. cit.,* p. 888.
7. Edwin R. Embree, *Investment in People,* Appendix D: $11,-330,704. General Education Board, *Final Report,* 1964: $62,-675,362.
8. Raymond B. Fosdick, *Adventure in Giving,* p. 323.
9. Thomas Wolfe, *You Can't Go Home Again,* Harper, New York, 1940.

490 / *Index*